Beginning postcoloni

Manchester University Press

Beginnings
Series editors: Peter Barry and Helen Carr

'**Beginnings**' is a series of books designed to give practical help to students beginning to tackle recent developments in English, Literary Studies and Cultural Studies. The books in the series

- demonstrate and encourage a questioning engagement with the new;
- give essential information about the context and history of each topic covered;
- show how to develop a practice which is up-to-date and informed by theory.

Each book focuses uncompromisingly upon the needs of its readers, who have the right to expect lucidity and clarity to be the distinctive feature of a book which includes the word 'beginning' in its title.

Each aims to lay a firm foundation of well understood initial principles as a basis for further study and is committed to explaining new aspects of the discipline without over-simplification, but in a manner appropriate to the needs of beginners.

Each book, finally, aims to be both an introduction and a contribution to the topic area it discusses.

Also in the series

Beginning theory (2nd edition)
Peter Barry

Beginning film studies
Andrew Dix

Beginning realism
Steven Earnshaw

Beginning ethnic American literatures
*Helena Grice, Candida Hepworth,
Maria Lauret and Martin Padget*

Beginning Shakespeare
Lisa Hopkins

Beginning postmodernism
Tim Woods

Beginning postcolonialism

Second edition

John McLeod

Manchester University Press

Manchester and New York

distributed in the United States exclusively
by Palgrave Macmillan

The right of John McLeod to be identified as the author of this work has been asserted by him in accordance with the Copyright, Designs and Patents Act 1988.

First edition published 2000 by Manchester University Press

This edition published 2010 by Manchester University Press
Oxford Road, Manchester M13 9NR, UK
and Room 400, 175 Fifth Avenue, New York, NY 10010, USA
www.manchesteruniversitypress.co.uk

Distributed in the United States exclusively by
Palgrave Macmillan, 175 Fifth Avenue, New York,
NY 10010, USA

Distributed in Canada exclusively by
UBC Press, University of British Columbia, 2029 West Mall,
Vancouver, BC, Canada V6T 1Z2

British Library Cataloguing-in-Publication Data
A catalogue record for this book is available from the British Library

Library of Congress Cataloging-in-Publication Data applied for

ISBN 978 0 7190 7858 3 paperback

This edition first published 2010

Reprinted 2012

The publisher has no responsibility for the persistence or accuracy of URLs for any external or third-party internet websites referred to in this book, and does not guarantee that any content on such websites is, or will remain, accurate or appropriate.

Typeset in Ehrhardt
by Action Publishing Technology Ltd, Gloucester
Printed in Great Britain
by Bell & Bain Ltd, Glasgow

For my parents,
Veronica and James McLeod

Contents

Acknowledgements

Since the first edition of *Beginning Postcolonialism* appeared in 2000 I have been fortunate to meet many students and scholars who have kindly offered me their views on its strengths and weaknesses. I have endeavoured to use their advice in preparing this second edition, and I am very grateful to them for their generosity and candour. My own thinking as regards postcolonialism remains indebted to the friendship and conviviality of many postcolonial scholars and writers whom I'd like to thank for sharing with me their expertise and wisdom: Elleke Boehmer, Sarah Brouillette, Maurizio Calbi, Isabel Carrera Suárez, Claire Chambers, Shirley Chew, Laura Chrisman, Stef Craps, Sandra Courtman, Pilar Cuder, Nic Dunlop, Sam Durrant, Bernardine Evaristo, Luz Mar González Arias, David Farrier, Francesca Giommi, Dave Gunning, Caroline Herbert, Graham Huggan, Ananya Jahanara Kabir, Tsunehiko Kato, Michelle Keown, Joel Kourtti, Bénédicte Ledent, Gail Low, Belén Martín-Lucas, Judith Misrahi-Barak, Anshuman Mondal, Bart Moore-Gilbert, Peter Morey, Stephen Morton, David Murphy, Stuart Murray, Susheila Nasta, Brendon Nicholls, Jopi Nyman, Melanie Otto, Caryl Phillips, Sandra Ponzanesi, James Procter, Ato Quayson, Alan Rice, David Richards, Gemma Robinson, Mark Shackleton, Neelam Srivastava, Mark Stein, John Thieme, Sara Upstone, Rashmi Varma, Abigail Ward, Andrew Warnes, Janet Wilson and Bruce Woodcock. A special thank you is due to Peter Barry for involving me in the *Beginnings* series, and also to Manchester University Press's Matthew Frost for entrusting me with the responsibility of writing this book and for his unique support over many years (especially on Friday 25 August, 2000, Helsinki, Finland).

Friends, colleagues and my family have endured my life-long passion for postcolonialism with patience and good cheer. Thanks in particular to Richard Brown, Lucy Evans, Alberto Fernández Carbajal, Tracy Hargreaves, Rick Jones, Katy Mullin, Alex Nield, Francis O'Gorman, Matthew Pateman, Martin Rushworth, Alistair Stead, Mark Taylor-Batty, Ceri Thomas and Agnes Woolley. I am especially grateful to Colin and Margaret Adams for their enthusiasm, encouragement, and the gift of Burnham Market, while the aptly named Joys are a constant source of support: Linda, Brian, Caitlin, Lydia and Madeleine. My parents, Veronica and James McLeod, remain the people whom I admire the most. This book is for them, with love.

Finally, I must thank Julie Adams for playing a major role in the preparation of this second edition.

John McLeod
University of Leeds

Preface to the second edition

It is a rare privilege to publish any book, but especially one which is intended to welcome new readers to a field of study that has fascinated and inspired me over many years. It is rarer still to be given the opportunity to revise a book for a second edition, and I have both enjoyed and been daunted by the exciting challenge of revisiting and refreshing *Beginning Postcolonialism*. In the ten years that have passed since I finished the first edition, postcolonialism has cemented its place within a wide range of academic disciplines, while the creative endeavours of postcolonial writers, artists and thinkers have become increasingly familiar beyond a strictly academic context and today sit firmly in the vanguard of contemporary literature, music, film and many other spheres besides. But this has not necessarily meant an increase in the acceptance, or the understanding, of postcolonial cultures and their critique, and there remains more than a degree of resistance to the insights and vocabularies of the postcolonial. When a critic as astute as Bruce King writes that 'postcolonialism became fashionable in the academy as part of the culture wars that followed the battle over Vietnam' and has subsequently 'lost touch with the basis of the great migration of the world's people' (*The Oxford English Literary History, Volume 13, 1948–2000: The Internationalization of English Literature*, Oxford University Press, 2004, p. 5), one is made mindful perhaps of the continued need for books which open up postcolonialism for newcomers responsibly, and with accuracy and patience. Beginning postcolonialism today is both easier and harder than it was a decade ago – easier because of its relative visibility and

due to the greater number of useful books available which engage
with it, but harder because of the misunderstandings and hostility
regarding its significance which circulate and which are partly due
to the ways in which postcolonialism continues to take issue with
several central ideas beloved of certain critics.

In preparing this second edition I have tried to give a sense of the
continuing debates about postcolonialism while seeking to anchor
some of its key themes and vocabularies securely for its readers. But
I have also tried not to change too much, partly because most
readers of the first edition I have met have tended to speak positively
of the book's organisation, content and approach, but also because
the impact of much of the late-twentieth-century discussions of
postcolonialism are no less important today and still require our
cognisance as we make our beginnings in the field. That said, in each
chapter I have incorporated new materials where appropriate,
mostly in the spirit of updating, finessing and extending the ways in
which key ideas might be articulated. I have also taken the chance to
correct some errors of fact and spelling which appeared in the first
edition (I don't think I shall ever live down spelling Tasmania with a
'z'), and I have also attempted to engage with some central
postcolonial ideas with greater sharpness, fluency and accuracy – I
was never very happy with the account of the ideas of mimicry and
ambivalence in colonial discourses that I gave the first time around,
and also I wanted to capture better Fanon's sense of national culture
and national consciousness this time around. These and certain
other passages in the book have, I hope, been tightened up, to the
benefit of the book as a whole. Readers familiar with the first edition
of *Beginning Postcolonialism* will notice in particular a new sub-
section in Chapter 1 called 'Into the twenty-first century', while
Chapter 8 – which was previously titled 'Postcolonialism and the
Critics' – has been substantially rewritten as 'The Limits of Postcolonialism?' in order to give an expanded sense of some of the key
critiques of the field as well as engage with emergent matters that
have appeared on the horizon, such as the issue of globalisation and
the advocacy of 'tricontinentalism'.

It was never my intention to aim for coverage in the first edition
of *Beginning Postcolonialism*; rather, my strategy was to ground
selected key themes and ideas for new readers very much in the

spirit of opening doorways into a wider and more complex field. I always wanted this book to be a first port of call for those dealing with postcolonialism rather than be thought of as the last word or as a potted account of the field in its neat totality. I've stuck to my guns in this second edition and continued to prioritise certain issues and texts, rather than (to speak proverbially for a moment) trying to touch every pebble on the beach. No single book can encompass everything, especially not in a field of such range and in a book of this nature. But I hope that in opening this rewritten and refreshed second edition of *Beginning Postcolonialism*, you have in your hands a more useful and productive text than before, one that will help shape your initial studies and encourage your enthusiasm for all things postcolonial.

Introduction

Beginning

Any new beginning poses several important questions. Exactly what am I beginning, and what am I about to encounter? How shall I best proceed? Where might be the most appropriate position to start from? What do I need to know first? Beginnings are exciting things, inviting us to explore that which we may not have previously visited; but they also expose us to the unfamiliarity and inevitable disorientation of doing something new.

Beginning Postcolonialism is my attempt to help you make your own beginnings in one of the most exciting and challenging fields of study that has established itself in recent years. It takes as its primary focus the various reading practices which distinguish and characterise much of the field – practices which for the purpose of this book attend chiefly to literary texts, but which can be applied beyond a strictly literary context to other cultural phenomena. In the following chapters this book will introduce you to the various ways we can approach, perhaps for the first time, the creative endeavours of those who either come from, or have an ancestral purchase upon, countries with a history of colonialism. In addition, we will reconsider our approaches to older, more familiar or canonical works that seem to have little to do with the fortunes of Empire. By the end of this book you will have encountered many new concepts which will help you build and develop your readings of the range of texts which preoccupy postcolonialism. Along the way, you will be continually invited to think critically about the key concepts in the field, and measure your own satisfaction with the different strands of thought which inhabit and shape postcolonial studies. If *Beginning Postcolonialism* is designed to help you explore postcolonial ways of reading and thinking, it is also intended to encourage you from the beginning to think for yourself about many of the key issues pursued in the field.

That said, we should also be clear about what this book is *not*. It will not be attempting to offer a full history of the various literatures often considered as postcolonial. There already exists some excellent work which narrates the emergence and fortunes of postcolonial literatures throughout the twentieth and into the twenty-first centuries. Neither should we presume that the texts we consider in this book are typical of, or adequately represent, the wide-ranging field of postcolonial cultural production. The choice of texts in the chapters that follow is informed on the whole by my experience of teaching many of them to undergraduate students, and they inevitably reflect some of my own areas of interest. They have served well in seminars to stimulate successfully a discussion of the reading practices, issues and concepts with which this book is concerned. But they are not the only texts we might choose, and we should not treat them as paradigmatic of postcolonialism.

I hope that this book will assist in kindling your excitement and enthusiasm for the texts and the approaches we cover, and will stabilise to an extent some of the disorientation that is inevitable with any new departure. Yet, disorientation is also very much a productive and valuable sensation, and it is fair to say that many of the reading and writing practices often considered postcolonial achieve much of their effectiveness in derailing accustomed trains of thought. For many of us, perhaps, postcolonialism challenges us to think again and question some of the assumptions that underpin both *what* we read and *how* we read. So it is important, throughout this book, that some of this valuable disorientation will be maintained.

Postcolonialism?

It is fair to say that beginning postcolonialism is an especially challenging procedure because it is particularly difficult to answer those questions with which we started. Such is the variety of practices often called postcolonial that it is not very easy to find an appropriate point of departure. For example, the literatures of nations such as Canada, Australia, New Zealand, Nigeria, Kenya, India, Sri Lanka, Jamaica and Ireland have been declared postcolonial at one time or another. Are they all postcolonial in the same way? What is the best way to begin reading them? Could such a 'best way' ever exist, one that is appropriate to all these literatures (and should we be looking for it)? In addition, readings of postcolonial texts sometimes are resourced by concepts discovered across a range of intellectual disciplines and practices, such as anthropology, philosophy, feminism, Marxism, psychoanalysis, politics, poststructuralism, modern languages and linguistics. Such variety creates both discord and conflict within the field, to the extent that there seems no single critical procedure that we might identify as definitively postcolonial.

Due to the variety and wide range of our field, it is worth considering if we can ever really talk of a 'postcolonial*ism*', with all the coherency that this term implies. Rather than using an umbrella term that lets in so much, might it be better for us to begin by questioning postcolonialism as a meaningful concept – maybe even dispense with it altogether – and seek better ways to account for its prevailing, manifold subject matter and myriad critical approaches?

These have long been persisting questions for postcolonial thinkers, many of whom have struggled with the legitimacy of the term since it first emerged, and we shall be returning to such questions throughout this book. But it is important that we do not become transfixed by them as we try to make our beginnings, to the extent that we cannot proceed at all. For better or for worse, the term 'postcolonialism' does have a history. It has entered common parlance and is frequently used by critics, scholars, teachers and writers. It is important that we grasp the *variety* of what the term signifies if we want to begin to use it self-consciously and productively. The range of issues covered by the term is indeed large, and sometimes contradictory, as too is the array of critical engagements performed in its name. By using the term 'postcolonialism' in this book when describing such various activities, I by no means want to suggest that diverse and culturally specific writings, as well as critical theories of postcolonialism, can be readily homogenised. There is no one singular postcolonial*ism*. But one of the fundamental arguments of this book is that postcolonialism can be productively articulated in different ways as an enabling and critical concept, despite the difficulties we have to live with when we try to describe it. As we are about to see, 'postcolonialism' is not a word we can render precisely. But out of its very variety comes possibility, vitality, challenge. Post-colonialism, then, is a term we will use in this book to help us with our beginnings, a term we can begin with; but I hope that by the end of reading this book you will be using it with a healthy degree of self-consciousness and productive suspicion.

In order to bear witness to the enabling possibilities of postcolonialism, each chapter of this book concerns a specific issue – such as 'colonial discourses', 'the nation in question', 'diaspora identities'. They are designed to introduce some major areas of enquiry within postcolonialism, as well as offer concrete examples of various kinds of relevant reading and writing practices. But it is also the intention that we read *across* the chapters too. Many of the issues which are raised in each chapter can be relevant in other related areas, and I will endeavour to signal some useful points of connection and contrast as we proceed. It is always vital that we take into account the cultural and historical specificity of writers and thinkers when we consider their work, and understand the dynamic relationship between a writer and the culture(s) about which he or she writes. But it is also true that similar issues can and do preoccupy readers, writers and critics in different positions and at different moments, and the skills we collect from each chapter will offer productive ways of approaching many texts and contexts, not just the small selection we encounter in this book.

In order to enable us to think critically about the ideas and concepts raised in *Beginning Postcolonialism*, and in keeping with the format of the *Beginnings* series as a whole, I have at times inserted small sections called 'STOP and THINK'. In these sections we review the ideas which we have been exploring so far in the chapter and pose a series of questions about them. The responses to these questions will be, of course, your own. The 'STOP and THINK' sections are designed to assist you in making your particular judgements about the ideas raised within postcolonialism – and, ultimately, your overall sense of postcolonialism itself. In introducing several debates within the field throughout this book, my intention is to enable you to enter *actively* into these debates. I will not be providing definitive conclusions or answers to the questions we raise (although I cannot, and will not, pretend to remain neutral either). So, in order to help you begin your active participation in the field, the 'STOP and THINK' sections will identify focal points of debate for you to pursue critically; either with others with whom you may be studying postcolonialism, or in your own further reading. As regards this latter activity, each chapter concludes with a selected reading list which points you in the direction of some key and useful texts that concern that chapter's issues, as well as other texts in which the particular ideas we have been exploring have received more prolonged, sophisticated attention.

A note on terminology: or, on not using the hyphen

In Chapter 1 we will describe the terms 'colonialism' and 'postcolonialism' in some detail. But before we begin, we need to make some decisions about the form of the words 'postcolonial' and 'postcolonialism'. As we shall see, these terms have attracted much debate among scholars who often use them in contrary and confusing ways. Indeed, critics often cannot agree on how to spell postcolonialism: with the hyphen (as in 'post-colonialism') or without?

Let us be clear from the start: throughout *Beginning Postcolonialism* we will not use the hyphen but spell the term as a single word: 'postcolonialism'. There is a particular reason for this choice of spelling and it concerns the different meanings we might assign to 'post-colonial' and 'postcolonial'. The hyphenated term 'post-colonial' seems better suited to denote a particular *historical period or epoch*, like those suggested by phrases such as 'after colonialism', 'after independence' or 'after the end of Empire'. In its hyphenated form, 'post-colonial' functions rather like a noun: it names something which exists in the world. But for much of this book we will be thinking about postcolonialism not in terms of strict historical or empirical periodisation, but as referring to disparate forms of *representations, reading practices, attitudes* and *values*. These principally aesthetic phenomena can circulate *across* the historical border between colonial rule and national independence. To put this another way, we might say that postcolonialism does not refer to something which tangibly *is*, but rather it denotes something which one *does*: it can describe a way of thinking, a mode of perception, a line of enquiry, an aesthetic practice, a method of investigation. Therefore, 'postcolonialism' without the hyphen is best thought of as akin to an adjective, a word which describes the particular qualities of a thing or an action. Of course, it is not easy to keep apart these two realms, and in many ways the term 'postcolonialism' always exists somewhere in-between noun and adjective, between reality and its perception. So, in thinking about postcolonialism in this book primarily as signifying forms of representation, particular values, or modes of thought, we need to remember that the term is not simply contained by the tidy categories of historical periodisation – although it always remains firmly hinged to historical experiences.

To keep confusion to a minimum as we begin, let us use the phrases 'once-colonised countries' or 'countries with a history of colonialism' (rather than 'post-colonial countries') when dealing in strictly historical terms with those locations which were previously part of the European empires. When quoting from other critics we must, of course, preserve their own habits of spelling 'post-colonial'. But for the duration of *Beginning Postcolonialism*, 'postcolonial' and 'postcolonialism' will be used when talking about historically situated representations, reading practices, attitudes and values which range across past *and* present. How and why this is the case will be the subject of the first chapter.

1

From 'Commonwealth' to 'postcolonial'

Introduction

The purpose of this chapter is to approach a flexible but solid definition of the word 'postcolonialism'. In order to think about the range and variety of the term, we need to place it in two primary contexts. The first regards the historical experiences of decolonisation that have occurred chiefly in the twentieth century. The second concerns relevant intellectual developments in the latter part of the twentieth century, especially the shift from the study of 'Commonwealth literature' to 'postcolonialism'. After looking at each, we will be in a position at the end of this chapter to make some statements about how we might define 'postcolonialism'.

Colonialism and decolonisation

At the turn of the twentieth century, the British Empire covered a vast area of the earth that included parts of Africa, Asia, Australasia, Canada, the Caribbean and Ireland. At the beginning of the twenty-first century, although there remains a small handful of British Overseas Territories (see www.ukota.org), the vast bulk of the Empire has not survived. All over the world, the twentieth century witnessed the decolonisation of millions of people who were once subject to the authority of the British crown. For many, the phrase 'the British Empire' is most commonly used these days in the past tense, signifying a historical period and set of relationships which appear no longer current.

But if the political realities of Empire have been transformed with the coming of independent government to many once-colonised locations, the material and imaginative legacies of both colonialism and decolonisation remain fundamentally important constitutive elements in the contemporary world. These legacies continue to inflect contemporary geo-political realities and conflicts around the world and impact upon how different people (are forced to) live today. And they also remain in the arts, cultures, languages and intellectual disciplines to which we often turn to make sense of the world, in the past and the present: such as anthropology, economics, painting, politics, music, philosophy, the media and – as we shall be highlighting in this book – literature.

Colonialism has taken many different forms and has engendered diverse effects around the world, but we must be as precise as we can when defining its meaning. This can be gauged by thinking first about its relationship with two other terms: 'capitalism' and 'imperialism'. As Denis Judd argues in his book *Empire: The British Imperial Experience from 1765 to the Present* (HarperCollins, 1996), '[n]o one can doubt that the desire for profitable trade, plunder and enrichment was the primary force that led to the establishment of the imperial structure' (p. 3). Judd argues that colonialism was first and foremost a fundamental part of the commercial venture of Western nations such as Britain, France, Spain, the Netherlands and Portugal that developed from the late seventeenth and early eighteenth centuries. Some date its origins to the European 'voyages of discovery' in the fifteenth and sixteenth centuries, epitomised by those of Christopher Columbus who 'discovered' the Americas in trying to find a western sea route to the Indies. The seizing of 'foreign' lands for government and settlement was in part motivated by the desire to create and control opportunities to generate wealth and control international markets, frequently by securing the natural resources and labour power of different lands and peoples at the lowest possible cost to Europeans. As many colonial governments and entrepreneurs would come to realise, colonialism was big business and the profits to be made were hitherto unimaginable. The construction of the sugar industry in the Caribbean is one such example: the harvesting of sugar in the favourable environmental conditions by African slaves and, later, Indian indentured labourers meant that British businesses could produce a range of products at minimal cost which, when shipped to Europe, could be sold for extremely high profits. Colonialism was first and foremost a lucrative commercial operation, bringing wealth and riches to Western nations through the economic exploitation of others. It was pursued for economic profit, reward and riches. Hence, colonialism and capitalism share a mutually supportive relationship with each other. Indeed, the birth of European modernity was in many ways parented by this partnership of capitalism and colonialism, a fact which should remind us that colonialism is absolutely at the heart of Europe's modern history.

'Colonialism' is sometimes used interchangeably with 'imperialism', but in truth the terms mean different things. As Peter Childs and Patrick Williams argue, imperialism is an ideological project which upholds the legitimacy of the economic and military control of one nation by another. They define imperialism as 'the extension and expansion of trade and commerce under the protection of political, legal, and military controls' (*An Introduction to Post-Colonial Theory*, Harvester Wheatsheaf, 1997, p. 227). Colonialism, however, is only *one form of practice, one modality of control* which results from the ideology of imperialism, and it specifically concerns the *settlement* of people in a new location. Imperialism is not strictly concerned with the issue of settlement, and it does not demand the settlement of different places in order to function. In these terms, colonialism is one historically specific mechanism of imperialism which prioritises the act of settlement, and its manifestations can be varied; as Robert J. C. Young has written, 'colonialism involved an extraordinary range of different forms and practices carried out with respect to radically different cultures, over many different centuries' (*Postcolonialism: An Historical Introduction*, Blackwell, 2001, p. 17). It follows, then, that colonialism is not the only way of pursuing imperialist ideals. This is why some critics argue that while *colonialism* is virtually over today as a practice, *imperialism* continues apace as Western nations are still engaged in imperial acts, securing wealth and power through the continuing economic exploitation of other nations (we consider this in terms of globalisation in Chapter 8). Benita Parry spells things out helpfully for us when she describes colonialism as 'a specific, and the most spectacular, mode of the imperial project's many and mutable states, one which preceded the rule of international finance capitalism and in mutated forms has survived its formal ending' (*Postcolonial Studies: A Materialist Critique*, Routledge, 2004, p. 18.)

To recap: colonialism is a particular historical manifestation of imperialism, specific to certain places and times. Similarly, we can regard the British Empire as one form of an imperial economic and political structure among several which emerged in Europe. So we can endorse Elleke Boehmer's judicious definition of colonialism in her important book *Colonial and Postcolonial Literature* (second edition, Oxford University Press, 2005) as the 'settlement of territory, the exploitation or development of resources, and the attempt to govern the indigenous inhabitants of occupied lands, often by force' (p. 2). Note in this definition (a) the important emphasis on the *settlement* of land, (b) the *economic* aims at the heart of colonialism, and (c) *the unequal relations of power* which colonialism constructs between colonising and native peoples.

Boehmer's phrase 'the attempt to govern' points to the ways in which colonialism was never fully successful in securing its aims, despite its lucrative gains, and met with perpetual acts of resistance from the outset by indigenous inhabitants of colonised lands. In some cases too, members of the European communities who had settled overseas – in Canada and Australia, for example – in large numbers and who no longer wished to defer power and authority to the imperial 'motherland' came to agitate for forms of self-government. As regards the imperial venture of the British Empire, there are three distinct periods of *decolonisation* when the colonised nations won the right to govern their own affairs. The first was the loss of the American colonies and declaration of American independence in the late eighteenth century. The second period spans the end of the nineteenth century to the first decade of the twentieth century, and concerns the creation of the 'dominions'. This was the term used to describe the nations of Canada, Australia, New Zealand and South Africa. These nations (today referred to as 'settler' nations) consisted of large European populations that had settled overseas, often violently displacing or in some cases destroying the indigenous peoples of these lands – 'First Nations' peoples in Canada, Aboriginal communities in Australia, New

Zealand's Maori and the many different tribes in southern Africa. The 'settler' peoples of these nations campaigned for forms of self-government which they achieved as dominions of the British Empire. Yet, as a 'dominion' each still recognised and pledged allegiance to the ultimate authority of Britain as the 'mother country'. Canada was the first to achieve a form of political autonomy in 1867, Australia followed suit in 1901, New Zealand similarly in 1907, and South Africa in 1910. Slightly after this period, Ireland won self-rule in 1922, although the country was partitioned and six counties in the north east remained under British control as Northern Ireland. In 1931 the Statute of Westminster removed the obligation for the dominions to defer ultimate authority to the British crown and gave them full governmental control.

The third period of decolonisation occurred in the decades immediately following the end of the Second World War. Unlike the self-governing settler dominions, most colonised lands in South Asia, Africa and the Caribbean did not become sites of mass European migration, and tended to feature larger dispossessed indigenous populations settled and governed by small British colonial elites. The achievement of independence particularly in South Asia and Africa occurred often as a consequence of indigenous anti-colonial nationalism and military struggle. India and Pakistan gained independence in 1947, Ceylon (now Sri Lanka) in 1948. In 1957 Ghana became the first 'majority-rule' independent African country, followed by Nigeria in 1960. In 1962, Jamaica and Trinidad and Tobago in the Caribbean followed suit. The decades of the 1960s and 1970s saw busy decolonisation throughout the declining Empire. So, with the passing of Hong Kong from Britain to China on 1 July 1997, the numbers of those living under British rule fell below one million for the first time in centuries – a far cry from the days when British colonialism subjected millions around the globe.

There are, of course, as many reasons for decolonisation as there were once-colonised nations. One fundamental reason concerned the growth of many nationalist movements which mounted various challenges across the Empire – from passive resistance to armed struggle – to British colonial authority, and which very often took inspiration from each other in opposing colonial authority. Other reasons can be found too: one cause was the decline of Britain as a world power after 1945 and the ascendancy of the United States and the Soviet Union, while another reason concerns changes to technologies of production and international finance which enabled imperialist and capitalist ambitions to be pursued without the need for colonial settlement. Yet the dissident, often militant endeavours of colonised peoples and their sympathisers is a key preoccupation of postcolonial writers and thinkers, and in exploring the end of Empire it is important to many postcolonial scholars that such endeavours are sufficiently remembered and explored.

The emergence of 'Commonwealth literature'

Let us move from this very brief historical sketch of colonialism and decolonisation to the intellectual contexts and development of postcolonialism. In particular, we need to look at two areas of intellectual study that have come to influence its emergence as an academic pursuit – these are 'Commonwealth literature' and 'theories of colonial discourses' – on the way to acquiring a useful understanding of how postcolonialism has developed within and eventually beyond literary studies in recent years. Of course, I do not wish to imply that the narrative which follows is a full account or representative of all the work that has occurred in the field; far from it. But in pointing to a few key developments we can begin to understand the intellectual scope and focus of postcolonialism as it is now often understood today.

One important antecedent for postcolonialism was the growth of the study of Commonwealth literature. 'Commonwealth literature' was a term literary critics began to use from the 1950s to describe literatures in English emerging from a selection of countries with a history of colonialism. It incorporated the study of writers from the predominantly European settler communities, as well as writers belonging to those countries which were in the process of gaining independence from British rule, such as those from the African, Caribbean and South Asian nations. Literary critics began to distinguish a fast-growing body of literature written in English which included work by such figures as R. K. Narayan (India), V. S. Naipaul (Trinidad), Janet Frame (New Zealand) and Chinua

Achebe (Nigeria). The creation of the category of 'Commonwealth literature' as a special area of study was an attempt to identify and evaluate this vigorous literary activity, and to consider via a comparative approach the common concerns and attributes that these manifold literary voices might have. Significantly, neither American nor Irish literature were included in early formulations of the field, and so 'Commonwealth literature' was associated exclusively with selected countries with a history of colonialism.

The term 'Commonwealth literature' is important in the associations it beckons, and these associations have historical roots. One consequence of the decline of the British Empire in the twentieth century was the establishment of – to use its original title – the British Commonwealth of Nations. At first, this term was used to refer collectively to the special status of the dominions within the Empire and their continuing allegiance to Britain. However, as the relationship between Britain and the dominions changed in the first half of the century (with the term 'dominions' being gradually dropped) a different meaning of 'Commonwealth' emerged. In the early decades, Britain hosted frequent 'colonial conferences' which gathered together the Governors of the colonies and heads of the dominions. In 1907 these meetings were re-named 'imperial conferences' in recognition of the fact that the dominions were no longer strictly British colonies. After the Second World War, these meetings became 'Commonwealth conferences' and featured the Heads of State of the newly independent nations. The British monarch was recognised as the head of the Commonwealth *in symbolic terms only*; the British crown held no political authority over other Commonwealth nations, and the word 'British' was abandoned altogether. Thus, 'Commonwealth' became redefined after the war in more equitable terms, as meaning an association of sovereign nations without deference to a single authority. Today, the Commonwealth of Nations as a body exists in name only. It has no constitution nor any legal authority, and its membership – although based on the old map of Empire – is not compulsory for the independent nations. It aims to promote democracy, world peace, non-racialism, and consensus building within and across its 54 member states, as enshrined in its 1971 'Singapore Declaration of Commonwealth Principles' (see www.thecommonwealth.org). But it remains troubled by colonialism's legacies and violent contemporary conflicts. In the late 1990s, Nigeria was suspended from the Commonwealth after the execution in 1995 of the activist Ken Saro-Wiwa; Zimbabwe was suspended in 2002 and withdrew altogether the following year; and at the time of writing Fiji remains suspended after a military coup in 2006.

This shift from 'colonial' to 'Commonwealth' perhaps suggests a particular version of history in which the status of the colonised countries happily changes from subservience to filial equality. But we must avoid subscribing to this selective view, not least because the economic and political relations between Britain and the Commonwealth nations have remained far from equal. In many ways, the term 'Commonweath' proffers a sanitised vision of international fraternity which masks the exploitative and painful realities of British colonisation and its legacies. The identification and study of 'Commonwealth literature' certainly echoed the tenor of the specifically benign usage of 'Commonwealth', but it also had its own problems. In general the term welcomed a shared, valuable literary culture, freshly discerned within a disparate and variable collective of once-colonised nations. It distinctly promoted unity in diversity – revealingly, the plural term 'Commonwealth *literatures*' was rarely used. However, that common inheritance arguably served to reinforce the primacy of Britain among the Commonwealth nations. As A. Norman Jeffares declared in 1964, addressing the first conference of Commonwealth literature at the University of Leeds in the UK, 'one reads [Commonwealth writers] because they bring new ideas, new interpretations of life to us' (*Commonwealth Literature: Unity and Diversity in a Common Culture*, ed. John Press, Heinemann, 1965, p. xiv). It is not clear whether the 'us' in this sentence referred to the diverse audience at the conference comprising writers and academics from many Commonwealth nations, or specifically British (or, more widely, Western) readers in particular. 'Commonwealth literature' may well have been created in an attempt to bring together writings from around the world on an equal footing, yet the assumption remained that these texts were ultimately to be judged by a Western, English-speaking readership. Despite the egalitarian principles held by many such enthusiasts, the 'Commonwealth' in 'Commonwealth literature' was never fully free from the older, more imperious connotations of the term.

One of the fundamental assumptions held by the first Western critics of Commonwealth literature concerned the relationship between literature and the nation. In the introduction to a collection of essays *The Commonwealth Pen: An Introduction to the Literature of the British Commonwealth* (Cornell, 1961), the editor A. L. McLeod proposed that '[t]he genesis of a local literature in the Commonwealth countries has almost always been contemporaneous with the development of a truly nationalist sentiment: the larger British colonies such as Fiji, Hong Kong and Malta, where there are relatively large English-speaking populations, have produced no literature, even in the broadest sense of the term. The reason probably lies in the fact that they have, as yet, no sense of national identity, no cause to espouse, no common goal' (p. 8). Many agreed that the 'novel' ideas and new 'interpretations of life' in Commonwealth literature owed much to the ways that writers were forging their own sense of national and cultural identity. This was certainly one of the functions of the texts regarded as 'Commonwealth literature', and indeed the conjoining of such writing to issues of nation and nationalism has remained to this day (often to the frustration of many writers, we might add). We shall be examining closely the vexed relationship between literature and nationalist representations in Chapters 3 and 4.

Even so, the attention to the alleged nationalist purposes of much Commonwealth literature often played second fiddle to more abstract concerns which distracted attention away from specific national contexts. Many critics were primarily preoccupied with identifying a common goal shared among writers from many different nations that went beyond more 'local' affairs. Just as the idea of a Commonwealth of Nations suggested a diverse community with a common set of concerns, Commonwealth literature – whether produced in India, Australia or the Caribbean – was assumed to reach across national boundaries and deal with universal concerns. Commonwealth literature certainly dealt with national and cultural issues, but the best writing possessed the mysterious power to transcend them too.

Witness the editorial to the first edition of the *Journal of Commonwealth Literature* published in September 1965. The editorial saw the need to recognise the important national and cultural differences between writers from divergent locations. But it also revealed the ways in which literature from Commonwealth countries was unified through the category of Commonwealth literature:

> The name of the journal is simply a piece of convenient shorthand, which should on no account be construed as a perverse underwriting of any concept of a single, culturally homogeneous body of writings to be thought of as 'Commonwealth literature' ... Clearly, all writing ... takes its place within the body of English literature, and becomes subject to the *criteria of excellence by which literary works in English are judged*, but the *pressures* that act upon a Canadian writing in English differ significantly from those operating upon an Indian using a language not his mother tongue, just as both kinds differ from those that affect an Englishman. (*Journal of Commonwealth Literature*, 1 (1), 1965, p. v – my emphasis)

Such 'pressures' were presumably the historical and cultural influences upon each writer that differed across time and space. How, then, could one account for the *common* wealth of these writings? As the editorial claims, because the texts studied as Commonwealth literature were ostensibly in English, they were to be evaluated *in relation to* English literature, with the same criteria used to account for the literary value of the age-old English 'classics'. Commonwealth literature at its best was comparable with the English literary canon which functioned as the means of measuring its value. It was able to transcend its regional affiliations and produce work of *permanent* and *universal* relevance. As A. Norman Jeffares put it, a Commonwealth writer of value 'wants ultimately to be judged not because he [*sic*] gives us a picture of life in a particular place, in a particular situation, but by the universal, lasting quality of his writings, judged by neither local nor yet national standards. Good writing is something which transcends borders, whether local or national, whether of the mind or of the spirit' (*Commonwealth Literature*, p. vxiii).

Commonwealth literature, then, was really a sub-set of canonical English literature, evaluated in terms derived from the conventional study of English that stressed the values of timelessness and universality. For example, consider the following moment from

William Walsh's book *Commonwealth Literature* (Oxford University Press, 1973), when Walsh is discussing a novel by George Lamming. Lamming is from Barbados in the Caribbean and has African ancestry. This is what Walsh made of Lamming's novel *Season of Adventure* (1960):

> In this novel the African theme and connection become stronger and more positive, although it is never allowed to puff into a merely abstract existence. Indeed, Lamming's achievement is to make us hear the scream of the humiliated and persecuted and to make it simultaneously a metaphor for the damage *universal in mankind*. (p. 53 – my emphasis)

Walsh identifies 'African' elements in the novel that bear witness to the context of Lamming's position as a writer. But Africa and its legacies constitute only a 'theme' and are not allowed to be the *primary* focus of the work, which is the novel's attention to the 'damage universal in mankind'. Later in his book Walsh reads the Australian Patrick White's novel *Voss* (1957) in similar terms, as 'a powerful and humane work coloured with the light and soaked with the sweat and personality of Australia' (p. 134). So, for critics like Walsh, Commonwealth literature dealt fundamentally with the same preoccupations with the human condition as did the writing of Jane Austen or George Eliot. National differences were certainly important, adding the novelty of 'personality', 'light' and 'colour'; but ultimately these 'national' specifics were secondary to the fundamental universal meaning of the work.

Today this kind of critical approach that makes secondary the historical contexts that inform a work of literature is often described as 'liberal humanist' (for a discussion of this term, see Peter Barry, *Beginning Theory*, second edition, Manchester University Press, 2002, pp. 11–38). For liberal humanists the most 'literary' texts always transcend the provincial contexts of their initial production and deal with moral preoccupations deemed relevant to people of all times and places. In retrospect, many critics of Commonwealth literature appear very much like liberal humanists. Unlike later critics, they did not always think how the texts they read so enthusiastically might resist their reading practices and challenge the assumptions of universality and timelessness that legitimated the criteria of 'good writing'. Indeed, one of the fundamental differences that many postcolonial critics today have from their Commonwealth predecessors is their insistence that historical, geographical and cultural specifics are *vital* to both the writing and reading of a text, and cannot be so easily bracketed as secondary colouring or background. Such new kinds of writing require new, transformed modes of reading, according to several postcolonialists. But for many critics of Commonwealth literature, these texts conformed to a critical status quo. They were not considered especially radical or oppositional; nor were the seen to challenge the Western criteria of excellence used to read them. Their experimental elements, their novelty and local focus made them exciting to read and helped depict the nation with which they were concerned. But their potential differences were contained by the identification within them of universal themes that bound texts safely inside the aesthetic criteria of the West. For postcolonial critics the *different* preoccupations and contexts of texts were to become more important than their alleged *similar* abstract qualities.

However, it would be a travesty to condemn or dismiss the work of a previous generation of critics of Commonwealth literature, on the grounds that it does not fit the current critical climate. True, scholars like Jeffares and Walsh belong to an earlier phase of literary criticism that was soon to be radically challenged in the latter decades of the century. But they and others were instrumental in securing Commonwealth literature as an important category of artistic endeavour and as a viable area of academic study. We must not under-emphasise the significance of this investment in the value of Commonwealth writing. In isolating the liberal assumptions of these critics' reading practices it can be too easily forgotten that the attention they gave to Commonwealth literature, and the space they cleared for it on university English courses in the West, constituted a fundamentally important political act. Such scholars assisted in ensuring that these literatures were not a minor area of curiosity but a major field that merited serious attention on the same terms as the 'classics' of English literature. Sadly, this political element at the root of Commonwealth literary studies is often forgotten today. What might these days look like a liberal humanist enterprise was at the time an important political investment in these new literatures as significant, despite the limitations we have considered. The patient, detailed and enthusiastic readings of Commonwealth literature laid the foundations for the various postcolonial criticisms that were to follow, and to which much postcolonial critical activity remains indebted.

As Shirley Chew has explained, 'a paradox sits at the heart of the Commonwealth: described as a free association of equal and mutually cooperating nations, it is nevertheless drawn together by a shared history of colonial exploitation, dependence and interchange' ('The Commonwealth: Pedestal or Pyre?', *New Statesman and Society*, 21 July 1995, p. 32). If the study of Commonwealth litera-ture was pursued in the philanthropic spirit of the first side of this paradox, the critical activity of post-colonialism was to concentrate more on the other, darker side of exploitation and dependence. From the late 1970s and 1980s many critics endeavoured to discard the liberal humanist bias perceived in critics of Commonwealth literature and to read the literature in new ways, often inspired by developments in critical theory. In order to understand how and why this happened we need to look briefly at the second chief antecedent to postcolonialism: theories of 'colonial discourses'.

Theories of colonial discourses: Frantz Fanon and Edward Said

Theories of colonial discourses have been fundamental to the development of postcolonialism as an academic practice. In general, they explore the ways that *representations* and *modes of perception* are used as fundamental weapons of colonial power to keep colonised peoples subservient to colonial rule. Colonial discourses have been rigorously explored in recent years by critics working with developments in critical theory, and we shall be looking more closely at these ideas in Chapter 2.

A good introduction to the issues involved in the identification and study of colonial discourses can be made by considering the following statement by the Trinidadian writer Sam Selvon. At the beginning of his 1979 lecture, 'Three Into One Can't Go – East Indian, Trinidadian, West Indian', Selvon recalls an Indian fisherman who used to visit his street in San Fernando, Trinidad, when he was a child. The fisherman, Sammy, was partly paralysed and was often treated as a figure of ridicule by the children. One day Sammy brought a white assistant on his round with him, apparently an escaped convict. Selvon remembers his feelings of fury that were provoked by Sammy's employing of a white man as an assistant. This, it seemed to the young Selvon, was not the way life was organised: the white man should be the master, not Sammy. Selvon admits he felt sympathy and dismay for the white assistant, feelings he never had for the lame Sammy. He uses this anecdote to exemplify how as a child he had learned always to regard African- or Indian-descended people as inferior to white folks: the idea of a white assistant to the Indian Sammy was an affront to Selvon's childhood sense of order. This example of the *internalising* of certain expectations about human relationships speaks volumes about how colonialism operates discursively, as Selvon notes:

> When one talks of colonial indoctrination, it is usually about oppression or subjugation, or waving little Union Jacks on Empire Day and singing 'God Save the King'. But this gut feeling I had as a child, that the Indian was just a piece of cane trash while the white man was to be honoured and respected – where had it come from? I don't consciously remember being brainwashed to hold this view either at home or at school. (In *Foreday Morning: Selected Prose*, Longman, 1989, p. 211)

Where indeed? Much work has been done in recent years that could provide an answer to Selvon's question. Many writers and critics have striven to demonstrate how colonialism suggests certain ways of seeing, specific modes of understanding the world and one's place in it that assist in justifying the subservience of colonised peoples to the (oft-assumed) 'superior', civilised order of the colonisers. These ways of seeing, attitudes and values are at the root of the study of colonial discourses.

Colonialism is perpetuated in part by justifying to those in the colonising nation the idea that it is right and proper to rule over other peoples, and by getting colonised people to accept their lower ranking in the colonial order of things – a process we can call 'colonising the mind'. To put this frankly: colonialism establishes ways of thinking. It operates by persuading people to internalise its logic and speak its language; to perpetuate the values and assumptions of the colonisers as regards the ways they perceive and represent the world. Theories of colonial discourses call attention to the role which representation plays in getting people to succumb to particular ways of thinking that results in the kind of situation Selvon describes. Although the term is often used in the singular, it is more accurate to talk of colonial *discourses* rather than 'colonial discourse' due to its multifarious varieties and operations which differ in time and space. We shall use the plural term throughout this book to keep this fact firmly in mind.

Colonial discourses form the intersections where language and power meet. Language, let us remember, is more than simply a means of communication; it constitutes our world-view by cutting up and ordering reality into meaningful units. The meanings we attach to things tell us which values we consider are important, and how we learn or choose to differentiate between superior or inferior qualities. Listen to Kenyan novelist Ngugi wa Thiong'o on this point:

> Language carries culture, and culture carries, particularly through orature and literature, the entire body of values by which we come to perceive ourselves and our place in the world. How people perceive themselves affects how they look at their culture, at their politics and at the social production of wealth, at their entire relationship to nature and to other human beings. Language is thus inseparable from ourselves as a community of human beings with a specific form and character, a specific history, a specific relationship to the world.
> (*Decolonising the Mind: The Politics of Language in African Literature*, James Currey, 1986, p. 16)

As Ngugi stresses, language does not just passively reflect reality; it also goes a long way towards creating a person's understanding of their world, and it houses the values through which we live our lives. Under colonialism, a colonised people are made subservient to ways of regarding the world which reflect and support colonialist values. A particular value system is taught as the best, truest world-view. The cultural values of the colonised peoples are deemed as lacking in value, or even as being 'uncivilised', from which they must be rescued. To be blunt, Empire did not rule by military and physical force alone. It endured by getting *both colonising and colonised people* to see their world and themselves in a particular way, internalising the language of Empire as representing the natural, true order of life. Selvon's anecdote reveals just how far-reaching can be the invidious effects of internalising colonial assumptions about the 'inferiority' of certain peoples.

If the internalisation of colonial sets of values was to a degree, as Selvon's example shows, an effective way of disempowering people, it was also the source of trauma for colonised peoples who were made to look negatively upon their people, their culture and themselves. In the 1950s there emerged much important work that attempted to record the psychological damage suffered by colonised peoples who internalised these colonial discourses. Prominent was the psychiatrist Frantz Fanon, who wrote widely and passionately about the damage French colonialism had wreaked upon millions of people who suffered its power. Fanon is an important figure in the field of postcolonialism and we shall be meeting his work again later in this book. He was born in Martinique in 1925 and educated in Martinique and France. His experience of racism while being educated by and working for the French affected him deeply; in Algeria in 1956 he resigned his post as head of the Psychiatric Department in Blida-Joinville Hospital and joined with the Algerian rebels fighting against the French occupation of the country. Influenced by contemporary philosophers and poets such as Jean-Paul Sartre and Aimé Césaire, Fanon's publications include two polemical books – *Black Skin, White Masks* (trans. Charles Lam Markmann, Pluto [1952] 1986) and *The Wretched of the Earth* (trans. Constance Farrington, Penguin [1961] 1967) – that deal passionately with the mechanics of colonialism and its effects on those it ensnared. *Black Skin, White Masks* examined in the main the psychological effects of colonialism, drawing upon Fanon's clinical experience as a psychiatrist. In a narrative both inspiring and distressing, Fanon looked at the cost to the individual who lives in a world where due to the colour of his or her skin, he or she is rendered peculiar, an object of derision, an aberration. In the chapter 'The Fact of Blackness' he remembers how he felt in France when white strangers pointed out his blackness with derogatory phrases such as 'dirty nigger!' or 'look, a Negro!':

> On that day, completely dislocated, unable to be abroad with the other, the white man, who unmercifully imprisoned me, I took myself far off from my own presence, far indeed, and made myself an object.

What else could it be for me but an amputation, an excision, a
haemorrhage that spattered my whole body with black blood? But I
did not want this revision, this thematisation. All I wanted was to be a
man among other men. I wanted to come lithe and young into a world
that was ours and to help to build it together. (*Black Skin, White
Masks*, pp. 112–13)

In this scenario, Fanon's identity is defined in negative terms by
those in a position of power. He is forced to see himself not as a
human *subject*, with his own wants and needs as indicated at the end
of the quotation, but an *object*, a peculiarity at the mercy of a group
that identifies him as inferior and less than fully human, subservient
to their definitions and representations. The violence of this
'revision' of his identity is conveyed powerfully in the image of
amputation. Fanon feels abbreviated, violated, imprisoned by a way
of seeing him that denies him the right to define his own identity as
a subject. Identity is something that the French *make for him*, and in
so doing they commit a violence that splits his very sense of self.
The power of such description, of naming, and its internalisation is
not to be underestimated. The relationship between language and
power is far-reaching and fundamental.

Black Skin, White Masks explains the consequences of identity
formation for the colonised subject who is forced into the
internalisation of the self as an 'other'. The 'Negro' is deemed to
epitomise everything that the colonising French are not. The
colonisers are civilised, rational, intelligent: the 'Negro' remains
'other' to all these qualities against which colonising peoples derive
their sense of superiority and normality. Fanon's book explores the
consequences for the colonised who are doomed to hold a traumatic
belief in their own inferiority. One response to such trauma is to
strive to escape it by embracing the 'civilised' ideals of the French
'motherland'. But however hard the colonised try to accept the
education, values and language of France – to don the white mask of
civilisation that will cover up the 'uncivilised' nature indexed by
their black skins – they are never accepted on equal terms. 'The
white world', writes Fanon, 'the only honourable one, barred me
from all participation. A man was expected to behave like a man. I
was expected to behave like a black man' (*Black Skin, White Masks*,
p. 114). That imaginative distinction that differentiates between

'man' (self) with 'black man' (other) is an important, devastating part of the armoury of colonial domination, one that imprisons the mind as securely as chains imprison the body. For Fanon, the end of colonialism meant not just political and economic change, but psychological change too. Colonialism is destroyed only once its ways of thinking about matters such as identity (and lots of other things besides, of course) are successfully challenged.

In 1978 Edward W. Said's *Orientalism* was published. *Orientalism* is considered to be one of the most influential books of the late twentieth century, in which Said looked at the divisive relationship between the coloniser and the colonised and explored how colonialism institutionally created a wide-ranging body of knowledge which supported the divisive practices of colonial government and settlement. *Orientalism* draws upon developments in Marxist and poststructuralist theories of power, especially the political philosophy of the Italian intellectual Antonio Gramsci and France's Michel Foucault. We will be looking in detail at *Orientalism* in Chapter 2, and how it helps us read texts. Briefly for now, let us note that Said examined how the knowledge that Western imperial powers formed about their colonies helped continually to justify their subjugation. Western nations like France and Britain, he argued, spent an immense amount of time producing knowledge about the locations they dominated. Looking in particular at representations of Egypt and the Middle East in a variety of written materials, Said pointed out that rarely did Western travellers in these regions ever try to learn much about, or from, the native peoples they encountered. Instead, they recorded their observations based upon commonly held *assumptions* about 'the Orient' as a mythic place of exoticism, moral laxity, sexual degeneration and so forth. These observations (which were not really observations at all) were presented as scientific truths that, in their turn, functioned to justify the very propriety of colonial domination. Thus colonialism continuously perpetuated itself: colonial power was buttressed by the production of knowledge about colonised cultures which endlessly produced a degenerate image of the Orient for those in the West, or Occident. With the Orient perceived as inferior, its colonisation could be justified in benign or moral terms, as a way of spreading the benefits of Western civilisation and saving native peoples from their own perceived barbarism.

This is a cursory summary of Said's argument, and we will flesh it out in the next chapter. But at this stage we need to note that the work of Fanon and Said inspired a new generation of critics in the 1980s keen to apply their ideas to the reading and representation of once-colonised cultures. What critics learned from the work of people like Fanon and Said was the simultaneously candid and complex fact that Empires colonise imaginations. Fanon shows how this works at a psychological level for the oppressed, while Said demonstrates the legitimation of Empire for the oppressor. Overturning colonialism, then, is not just about handing land back to its dispossessed peoples, relinquishing power to those who were once ruled by Empire. It is also a process of overturning the dominant ways of seeing the world, and representing reality in ways which do *not* replicate colonialist values. If colonialism involves colonising the mind, then meaningful resistance to it requires, in Ngugi's phrase, 'decolonising the mind'. This is very much a challenge concerning language: the meanings it makes, the way it is used, the necessity of confronting the assumptions it carries. The Mumbai-born novelist Salman Rushdie puts it this way: 'The language, like so much else in the colonies, needs to be decolonised, to be remade in other images, if those of us who use it from positions outside Anglo-Saxon culture are to be more than artistic Uncle Toms' (*The Times*, 3 July 1982, p. 8).

So, freedom from colonialism comes not just from the signing of declarations of independence and the lowering and raising of flags. There must also be a change of minds, a disputing with the dominant ways of thinking. This is a challenge to those from both the *colonised* and the *colonising* nations. People on all sides need to refuse the dominant languages of power that have divided them into master and slave, the ruler and the ruled, if progressive and lasting change is to be achieved. As Fanon wrote, '[a] man who has a language consequently possesses the world expressed and implied by that language' (*Black Skin, White Masks*, p. 18). The ability to read and write *otherwise*, to rethink our understanding of the order of things, contributes to the possibility of change. Indeed, in order to challenge the colonial order of things, some of us may need to re-examine our received assumptions of what we have been taught as 'natural' or 'true'.

The turn to 'theory' in the 1980s

It would be grossly reductive to assert that Edward Said was the instigator of postcolonial thought, not least because this would ignore the important anti-colonial critiques prior to 1978 of Fanon, Ngugi and others who we will be meeting later in this book. However, it is perhaps reasonable to suggest that, institutionally, the particular success of *Orientalism* did much to encourage new kinds of study and the advent of the term 'postcolonialism' in critical circles. Sensitised by the work of Said and others to the operations of colonial discourses, a new generation of critics turned to more 'theoretical' materials in their thinking. This was probably the beginning of postcolonialism as the discipline which we understand today, and it marked a major departure from the earlier, humanist approaches which characterised criticism of Commonwealth literature. Emerging in the 1980s were dynamic, excitingly new forms of textual analysis notable for their eclecticism and interdisciplinarity, combining the insights of feminism, philosophy, psychology, politics, anthropology and literary theory in pro-vocative and energetic ways.

Three forms of textual analysis in particular became popular in the wake of *Orientalism*. One involved *re-reading canonical English literature* in order to examine if past representations perpetuated or questioned the latent assumptions of colonial discourses. This form of textual analysis proceeded along two avenues. In one direction, critics looked at writers who dealt manifestly with colonial themes and argued about whether their work was supportive or critical of colonial discourses. Nicholas Harrison has described this analysis as concerned with 'fleshing out and assessing [a text's] worldliness, which means, most obvi-ously, recovering those colonial and post-independence contexts and ideologies that the texts bring into play', while all the time remembering that 'literature can frame ideological and historical material in different ways' (*Postcolonial Criticism: History, Theory and the Work of Fiction*, Polity, 2003, pp. 147). One compelling example of such a text is Joseph Conrad's novel about colonial-ism in Africa, *Heart of Darkness* (1899). Critics have debated whether Conrad's novel perpetuated colonialist views of the alleged inferiority of other peoples, or if it questioned the entire colonial project, dissenting from colonial discourses. In another direction, texts that seemingly had little to do with colonialism, such as Jane Austen's *Mansfield Park* (1814) or Charlotte Brontë's *Jane Eyre* (1847), were also re-read provocatively in terms of colonial discourses, as we shall explore more fully in Chapter 5.

Second, a group of critics who worked in the main with the poststructuralist thought of Jacques Derrida, Michel Foucault and Jacques Lacan began to dwell in particular upon *the representation of colonised subjects* across a variety of colonial texts, and not just literary ones. If, as Said claimed, the West produced knowledge about other peoples in order to prove the 'truth' of their 'inferiority', was it possible to read these texts *against the grain* and discover in them moments when the colonised subject *resisted* being represented with recourse to colonial values? This issue was pursued in different ways during the 1980s by two of the leading and most controversial postcolonial theorists, Homi K. Bhabha and Gayatri Chakravorty Spivak, as well as the *Subaltern Studies* scholars based in India. In his work on 'mimicry', Bhabha explored the possibility of reading colonial discourses as endlessly ambivalent, split and unstable, never able to install securely the colonial values they seemed to support. In her influential essays 'Subaltern Studies: Deconstructing Historiography' (in *In Other Worlds: Essays in Cultural Politics*, Routledge, 1987) and 'Can the Subaltern Speak?' (in Patrick Williams and Laura Chrisman (eds), *Colonial Discourse and Post-Colonial Theory*, Harvester Wheatsheaf, 1993), Spivak explored the problem of whether or not it was possible to recover the voices of those who had been made subjects of colonial representations, particularly women, and read them as potentially disruptive and subversive. Since the 1980s, Said, Bhabha and Spivak have opened a wide variety of theoretical issues central to postcolonialism and we shall be exploring their ideas on several occasions in this book. They have also, for better or worse, been homogenised (in Robert J. C. Young's unfortunate phrase) as the 'Holy Trinity' of critics working in the field (*Colonial Desire*, Routledge, 1995, p. 163) and their predominance can sometimes be at the expense of other equally important voices. In recent years, the bracketing of these three critics together has thankfully receded as greater attention has been paid to their (at times major) differences of style and approach. Yet each remains identified as a key figure in the advent of what has come to be known as 'postcolonial theory'. As we shall presently consider, and especially in Chapter 8, in recent years the analogous ways of pursuing postcolonial critique opened up by Bhabha and Spivak (but to a lesser extent, Said) have become the target of fierce criticism from several postcolonial critics who are deeply worried about the consequences of their theoretically adventurous and predominantly discursive approaches to matters of colonialism and resistance.

The Empire 'writes back'

The third form of literary analysis engendered by the turn to theory brought together some of the insights gained by theories of colonial discourses with readings of the new literatures from countries with a history of colonialism. Using the work of Fanon and Said, and later Bhabha and Spivak, it became popular to argue that these literatures were primarily concerned with *writing back to the centre*, actively engaged in a process of questioning and travestying colonial discourses in their work. The nomenclature of 'Commonwealth' was dropped in preference for 'postcolonial' in describing these writers and their work, as if to signal a new generation of critics' repudiation of older attitudes in preference of the newer, more interdisciplinary approaches. In contrast to liberal humanist readings by critics of Commonwealth literature, the (newly named) 'postcolonial literatures' were at a stroke regarded as politically radical and locally situated, rather than universally relevant. They were deemed to pose direct challenges to the colonial centre from the colonised margins, negotiating new ways of seeing that both contested the dominant mode and gave voice and expression to colonised and once-colonised peoples. Postcolonial literatures were deemed actively engaged in the act of decolonising the mind, worldly rather than abstract, local and political rather than general and liberal.

This approach was crystallised in an important book that appeared at the end of the 1980s titled *The Empire Writes Back:*

Theory and Practice in Post-Colonial Literatures (Routledge, 1989), co-authored by three critics who were based in Australia: Bill Ashcroft, Gareth Griffiths and Helen Tiffin (a second edition appeared in 2002). Inspired by Rushdie's argument about the need to decolonise the English language, *The Empire Writes Back* orchestrated the issues we have been exploring into a coherent critical practice. It epitomised the increasingly popular view that literature from the once-colonised countries was fundamentally concerned with challenging the language of colonial power, un-learning its world-view, and producing new modes of representation. Its authors looked at the fortunes of the English language in countries with a history of colonialism, noting how writers were expressing their own sense of identity by refashioning English in order to enable it to accommodate their experiences. English was being displaced by 'different linguistic communities in the post-colonial world' (p. 8) who were remaking it as an attempt to challenge the colonial value-system it enshrined, and to bear witness to these communities' sense of cultural difference. In a tone often more prescriptive than descriptive, they expressed the belief that the 'crucial function of language as a medium of power demands that post-colonial writing define itself by seizing the language of the centre and replacing it in a discourse fully adapted to the colonised place' (p. 38).

This refashioning worked in several ways. Ashcroft, Griffiths and Tiffin claimed that writers were creating new 'englishes' (the lack of a capital 'E' is deliberate) through various strategies: inserting untranslatable words into their texts; by glossing seemingly obscure terms; by refusing to follow standard English syntax and using structures derived from other languages; of incorporating many different creolised versions of English into their texts. Each of these strategies was demonstrated as operating in a variety of postcolonial texts, and in each the emphasis was on the writer's attempt to subvert and refashion standard English into various new forms of 'english', as a way of jettisoning the colonialist values which standard English housed.

The Empire Writes Back asserted that postcolonial writing was always written out of 'the abrogation [i.e. discontinuing] of the received English which speaks from the centre, and the act of

appropriation [i.e. seizure] which brings it under the influence of a
vernacular tongue, the complex of speech habits which characterise
the local language' (p. 39). The new 'english' of the colonised place
was ultimately irredeemably different from the language at the
colonial centre, separated by an unbridgeable gap: 'This absence, or
gap, is not negative but positive in its effect. It presents the
difference through which an identity (created or recovered) can be
expressed' (p. 62). The new 'englishes' could not be converted into
standard English because they have surpassed its limits, broken its
rules. As a consequence of this irredeemable difference, new values,
identities and value-systems were expressed, and old colonial values
wholeheartedly rejected.

Widely influential in discussions of postcolonial literature in
university classrooms in the early 1990s, *The Empire Writes Back*
made a valuable contribution to literary studies in the field. It
seemed to shift the approach to literatures from the once-colonised
nations away from the abstract issue of a text's universal and
timeless value and towards a more politicised approach which
analysed texts primarily within historical and geographical contexts.
For Ashcroft, Griffiths and Tiffin, postcolonial texts challenged
generally held values rather than confirmed them. Their 'local'
concerns were fundamental to their meanings, not of secondary
importance; they were politically committed, not aloof from the
matter of history, engaged rather than detached from colonialism
and its legacies. Nonetheless, several criticisms have subsequently
been made of this important book, the chief one being that it is
remarkably totalising in its representation of how literatures from
many different areas function according to the same agenda. Its
account of postcolonial aesthetics is perhaps rather mechanical,
while its adherence to a centre–periphery model of metropolis–
colony potentially simplifies a far more complex and unsteady
cultural terrain. Throughout *Beginning Postcolonialism* we will
pause to consider the problems with postcolonialism as a term, and
in Chapter 8 we will think about some of the key debates which
continue to be waged about it. But it is useful to flag at this early
stage some of the potential problems with postcolonialism which we
can hold in our minds throughout this book. Three criticisms of *The
Empire Writes Back* are useful to list here because they can serve as

warnings to some of the problems within postcolonialism as a whole. It is important that we remain on our guard against some of the dangers with the term:

1. *Gender differences. The Empire Writes Back* neglects gender differences between writers. How does gender impact on these issues? As Anne McClintock argues in her famous essay 'The Angel of Progress: Pitfalls of the Term "Post-Colonialism"' (in *Colonial Discourse/Postcolonial Theory*, ed. Barker, Hulme and Iversen, Manchester University Press, 1994, pp. 253–66), and as we shall explore in Chapter 6, 'women and men do not live "post-coloniality" in the same way' (p. 261). Ashcroft, Griffiths and Tiffin offer us little way of accounting for gender differences in their theory of the uses of language in postcolonial texts. Exactly the same can be said for class differences. Important social facts of a writer's identity are passed over by the authors in an attempt to isolate an identifiable, common mode of postcolonial writing.

2. *Regional/national differences*. Similarly, there is little *sustained* attempt to differentiate within or between writings from divergent places. Did colonialism happen in the same manner in divergent locations? Can we assume that the writing from countries with such different historical and cultural relationships with the 'centre' functions in the same way? What status would we give to the writings of Maori peoples of New Zealand or First Nations peoples of North America, who might view white settler communities more as neo-colonial than postcolonial?

3. *Is 'writing back' really so prevalent?* Some critics have voiced their concern with the supposition that *all* writing from once-colonised locations is writing against colonial discourses. Arun P. Mukherjee makes the important point in an essay called 'Whose Post-Colonialism and Whose Postmodernism?' that this assumption 'leaves us only one modality, one discursive position. We are forever forced to interrogate European discourses, of only one particular kind, the ones that degrade and deny our humanity. I would like to respond that our cultural productions are created in response to our own needs' (*World*

Literature Written in English, 30 (2), 1990, p. 6). The issues surrounding colonialism and postcolonialism may be only *one* part of a wider set of concerns – albeit a fundamentally important part – that preoccupy those writers often regarded as 'postcolonial' due to their cultural or national position. It is vitally important to be clear at the beginning of our readings that we do not assume that all writing from countries with a history of colonialism is primarily concerned with colonial history, colonial discourses and 'decolonising the mind'.

Thus, for all its good intentions, *The Empire Writes Back* ultimately created as many problems as it solved. As Vijay Mishra and Bob Hodge argue convincingly in their essay 'What is Post(-)colonialism?' (in *Colonial Discourse and Post-Colonial Theory*, ed. Patrick Williams and Laura Chrisman, Harvester, 1993, pp. 276–90), Ashcroft, Griffiths and Tiffin collapse together a diverse and plural body of literatures from many places, neglecting to think carefully about the *differences* between the literatures they examine. The book creates a 'grand theory of post-colonialism' that ignores the historical and cultural differences between writers; thus 'particularities are homogenised ... into a more or less unproblematic theory of the Other' (p. 278). Diversity and variety are seemingly denied. So, we should be alert to the fact that theories of postcolonialism might not be so remote from the homogenising and generalising tendencies often asserted today as the central weakness of the field of 'Commonwealth literature'.

Into the twenty-first century

By the late 1990s, postcolonialism had become increasingly academically visible. During this decade, key thinkers in the field published several seminal works which have come to shape much contemporary postcolonial scholarship. These included Edward W. Said's *Culture and Imperialism* (Vintage, 1993), in which he extended the project of *Orientalism* in thinking about the ways in which European culture was indebted to imperialism, as well as exploring modes of resistance to Empire; Homi K. Bhabha's *The Location of Culture* (Routledge, 1994), which collected and revised a number of his key essays in one place and which furthered his discursive, poststructuralist envisioning of several salient issues including nation, identity and migration; and Gayatri Chakravorty Spivak's *A Critique of Postcolonial Reason: Toward a History of the Vanishing Present* (Harvard University Press, 1999), which also revised and orchestrated her thinking over several years via a characteristically dizzying, and at times confounding, written style. Indeed, by the end of the 1990s, this 'Holy Trinity' of postcolonial thinkers had become established at the vanguard of what had come to be known as 'postcolonial theory', which by now existed almost as a separate discipline in its own right.

A number of critical works subsequently appeared which attempted to guide readers through the fast-developing, and often abstruse, concepts and new vocabularies of postcolonialism that had been very much influenced by the terminologies used by Said, Bhabha and Spivak. These included Peter Childs and Patrick Williams, *An Introduction to Post-Colonial Theory* (Harvester Wheatsheaf, 1997), Leela Gandhi, *Postcolonial Theory* (Edinburgh University Press, 1998), Bill Ashcroft, Gareth Griffiths and Helen Tiffin, *Key Concepts in Post-Colonial Studies* (Routledge, 1998; revised in 2008), Ania Loomba, *Colonialism/Postcolonialism* (Routledge, 1998; second edition, 2005) the first edition of *Beginning Postcolonialism* (Manchester University Press, 2000), John Thieme, *Post-Colonial Studies: The Essential Glossary* (Arnold, 2003), Neil Lazarus (ed.), *The Cambridge Companion to Postcolonial Literary Studies* (Cambridge University Press, 2004), and John McLeod (ed.), *The Routledge Companion to Postcolonial Studies* (Routledge, 2007). The appearance of these texts and others bears witness to the ways in which postcolonialism today has become cemented as an academic discipline in a relatively short space of time, as well as suggesting how rapidly have evolved the understanding of, and debates about, the postcolonial.

One particularly important development in the field in recent years is the consolidation of a distinct strand of postcolonial scholarship which is extremely concerned about postcolonialism's shortcomings, especially as regards the ways it engages with the material realities of the colonised and once-colonised world. A significant amount of this critical work (often called 'materialist' or

Marxist) asks very searching questions about postcolonial theory's
seeming contempt for historical certainty. One early example was
Aijaz Ahmad's highly sceptical book *In Theory: Nations, Classes,
Literatures* (Verso, 1992), voiced from a stringently Marxist position
and replete with its coruscating critique of Said's *Orientalism*, that
pointed to a fast-developing critique of postcolonialism as a
dangerous, even bogus critical practice. Less militantly, there has
emerged a voluble materialist critique of many aspects of
postcolonial theory by Marxist critics who have become deeply
unhappy with postcolonialism's most popular assumptions,
concepts and critical positions, especially the alleged primacy of the
cultural and the discursive in the work of Said, Bhabha and Spivak.
These critics attempt to offer a reorientation of postcolonialism that
disconnects it from its theoretical antecedents and instead grounds
it in the revolutionary thought and resistance politics of anti-
colonial nationalist revolutionaries and Marxist thinkers. The most
significant such publication is Robert J. C. Young's *Postcolonialism:
An Historical Introduction* (Blackwell, 2001). Young foregrounds the
growth of colonised resistance movements that took their
inspiration from the thought of Karl Marx and Friedrich Engels,
and considers the various freedom struggles which where waged in
the nineteenth and twentieth centuries across what is termed the
'tricontinent': the lands of Asia, Africa and Latin America. Such
struggles, he argues, were part of a wider, international contestation
of capitalism that incorporated the socialist and communist
revolutions in Russia and China, and contributed to militant
thinking across the world. As he argues, postcolonialism as we have
come to know it today is actually profoundly indebted to, and made
possible by, a much longer history of political resistance inspired by
Marxist thinking which has impacted upon not only the political
realities of lives around the world but also the ways in which major
philosophers and theorists have come to reappraise the ways we
make knowledge about the world. However, this history of socialist
and communist anti-colonial dissidence had not been sufficiently
acknowledged in postcolonial studies by the end of the twentieth
century, especially in the work of those who can be perceived
(sometimes unfairly, it must be said) to focus upon colonial
discourses and cultures allegedly without proper consideration for

the material, lived realities and political movements within which they functioned.

In offering a revised account of postcolonialism, Young attempts to retrieve this forgotten history of postcolonial resistance and challenge the view that postcolonialism is primarily a matter of high-powered critical theory. In Chapter 8 we shall be returning to Young's book and thinking about some of its strengths and weaknesses; for now, we should note that a significant element of current critical debate in postcolonialism centres around the challenge to theoretical or culturally preoccupied models of post-colonialism voiced from those keen to (re)connect postcolonialism to its Marxist and materialist history of resistance. For such critics, the privileging in postcolonial theory of culture and the discursive above society and the material is fatally problematic.

Elsewhere, the pursuit of postcolonialism primarily through the study of culture – representations, discourses, signs and images – continues to flourish today. Indeed, these pursuits have helped maintain a sense of postcolonialism as fundamentally trans-figurative rather than fatally ineffective, incisively critical rather than inevitably compromised. Mindful perhaps of the adage that if we want to change the world then we have to change how we think about the world, many postcolonial scholars have committed themselves to understanding how postcolonial representations and culture can significantly and valuably affect the concrete and imaginative transformation of colonial conditions and legacies. These critics often (but not always) work abrasively with and extend the insights of Bhabha, Said, Spivak and other postcolonial theorists, either by specifically using their vocabularies or within the general spirit of their approach. A good example of this kind of work – sometimes called 'culturalist', but usually by its opponents – is Bill Ashcroft's book *Post-Colonial Transformation* (Routledge, 2001), where he conceptualises the ways in which postcolonial writing and thought have been closely involved in the contestation and transformation of colonial discourses as part of a wider opposition to colonialism and its legacies. Ashcroft explores a range of cultural examples where colonialism and its imaginative and material legacies find themselves contested and possibly transformed in the cultural sphere. For example, when exploring

the postcolonial critique of received models of history as particularly imperious modes of seeing brokered by colonial cultures,
Ashcroft suggests that the novel *Foe* (1986) by the South African
writer J. M. Coetzee actively disrupts the discursive features of
Western historical representation and lays bare its limits. The novel
makes a transformative intervention in the production of knowledge
of the world because it invites us to consider how received forms of
thought – of which history is one – might actually be complicit in
the perpetuation of colonialist values and discourses. There is 'a
process of historical revisioning at work', Ashcroft claims, one 'that
has a far more profound effect than "setting the story straight",
tidying up the margins of European history, of simply adding one
more voice to a Eurocentred pluralism of narratives' (p. 102). In
thinking about history from a postcolonial position, we might need
to transform our sense of what constitutes both the very form and
the content of historical representation. It is in this kind of
transformative process that *Foe* is involved.

As Ashcroft would have it, postcolonial culture is vitally transformative as it can intervene in contemporary conditions and effect
change. Transformative agency is not solely to be discovered in
political resistance or military struggle. Indeed, even the seemingly
innocuous cultural practices of everyday life can gather transformative potential. Ashcroft writes about the inhabitants of a
Ugandan town, Mbarara, for whom the advent of a BP petrol station
has made possible new forms of convivial encounter between local
people who meet there regularly for purposes not solely connected
to the buying of fuel: 'Groups of people can be seen sitting around
talking at all times of day' (p. 157). These people inhabit the petrol
station tactically on their own terms and give it 'a different *meaning*
... from the meaning it might have in the West'; hence their
habitation is 'a way of being which itself defines and transforms
place' (p. 157). Although Ashcroft's example raises all kinds of
challenging questions – not least about the extent to which such
local redefinitions of place can impact significantly and strategically
upon the ruthless operations of global interests such as the
petroleum industry – his investment in the transformation of
meaning as the marrow of the postcolonial is instructive. From this
standpoint, postcolonialism involves a contestation and reshaping

of meaning that is considered fundamental to significant change.

As Ashcroft's example of the BP petrol station suggests, recent work on postcolonial representations and discourses has extended beyond the predominantly literary focus of postcolonialism, which characterised late-twentieth-century scholarship, to other cultural realms that also include the seemingly innocuous practices of everyday life. There is today an emerging field of postcolonial cultural studies in which literature is only one part of a constellation of cultural phenomena that includes film, food, sport, dance, music and other such endeavours. Graham Huggan has written of 'the "first wave" of postcolonial criticism (the period between, roughly, the mid-1980s and the mid-1990s), [in which] literary modes of analysis were central, and most of the key figures to emerge from this period were trained literary critics' (*Interdisciplinary Measures: Literature and the Future of Postcolonial Studies*, Liverpool University Press, 2008, p. 10). Since then, he suggests, 'it would probably be true to say that the status of literature and the literary has shifted with the move to a more culturally oriented analysis' (p. 12), although '[l]iterature continues to play an important role' (p. 11). In such work we may detect the dual influence of materialist and theoretical or culturalist models of postcolonialism, as critics ask questions about cultural endeavours often in relation to distinct public social contexts. Postcolonial cultural studies continues to open up new avenues and fields of study in this latest round of critical endeavour.

One such example of this 'second wave' of postcolonial critique might be Simon Featherstone's book *Postcolonial Cultures* (Edinburgh University Press, 2005), in which Featherstone considers the impact and significance of a wealth of postcolonial cultural activities that include world music, dance, cricket, football, film, the novel, museums, carnival, and popular representations of the beach. Featherstone's perpetually impressive exploration of such cultural case studies is motivated by his sense of 'postcolonial studies' relative inattention to popular culture' (p. 8) and the myriad dissident endeavours of so-called ordinary people. In assessing their endeavours, he often weighs carefully the tensions between the creative, performative achievements found in such popular cultural activities on the one hand, and on the other their appropriation and marketing on a global scale as exotic commodities (we shall return to these tensions in more depth when we consider Huggan's concept of the 'postcolonial exotic' in Chapter 8). Featherstone chooses neither to applaud cultural innovation as automatically trans-formative nor to dismiss its popularity as evidence of global commodification that drains it of its transformative agency. The lesson of his book – that we must regard postcolonial represent-ations as both effecting change but susceptible to containment – is an extremely useful one which we might take forward as we make our beginnings in postcolonialism.

'Postcolonialism': definitions and dangers

Having looked at the historical and intellectual contexts for postcolonialism as well some of its recent developments, we are now in a position to make some working definitions.

First and foremost, we need to remember to be precise when we understand the relationship between 'colonialism' and 'post-colonialism'. As theories of colonial discourses argue, colonialism fundamentally affects modes of *representation*. Language carries with it a set of assumptions about the 'proper order of things' that is taught as 'truth' or 'reality'. Recalling the example I used from Sam Selvon's essay, it is by no means safe to assume that colonialism conveniently stops when a colony formally achieves its independ-ence. The symbolic hoisting of a newly independent colony's flag might promise a crucial moment when governmental power shifts to those in the newly independent nation, yet it is crucial to realise that colonial values do not simply evaporate on the first day of independence. As Stuart Hall argues in his essay 'When was "the Post-Colonial"? Thinking at the Limit' (in *The Post-Colonial Question: Common Skies, Divided Horizons*, ed. Iain Chambers and Lidia Curti, Routledge, 1996, pp. 242–60), life *after* independence in many ways 'is characterised by the persistence of many of the effects of colonisation' (p. 248). Colonialism's *representations*, *reading practices*, *attitudes* and *values* are not so easily dislodged. Is it possible to speak about a 'postcolonial' era if colonialism's various assumptions, opinions and knowledges remain unchallenged?

Postcolonialism, as we have seen, in part involves the *challenge* to colonial ways of knowing, 'writing back' in opposition to such views. But colonial ways of knowing still circulate and have agency in the present; unfortunately, they have not magically disappeared as the Empire has declined. Thus, one of Carole Boyce Davies's reservations about 'postcolonialism' is the impression it may give that colonial relationships no longer exist. In her book *Black Women, Writing and Identity* (Routledge, 1994) she argues that we must remember the 'numerous peoples that are still existing in a colonial relationship' around the world, as well as those 'people within certain nations who have been colonised with the former/ colonies (Native Americans, African-Americans, South Africans, Palestinians, Aboriginal Australians)' (p. 83). This comment raises the issue of *internal colonialism* which persists in many once-colonised countries; for such peoples, colonial oppression is far from over. This is why we should beware using 'postcolonialism' strictly as marking an historical moment or period, as I argued in the Intro-duction, and use it instead as a term which identifies an historically grounded and transformative approach, position, standpoint or way of thinking.

So, the term 'postcolonialism' is *not* the same as 'after colonialism', as if colonial values are no longer to be reckoned with. It does *not* define a radically new historical era. Nor does it herald a brave new world where all the ills of the colonial past have been cured. Rather, 'postcolonialism' recognises both historical *continuity* and *change*. On the one hand, it acknowledges that the material realities and discursive modes of representation established through colonialism are still very much with us today, even if the political map of the world has altered through decolonisation. But on the other hand, it prizes the promise, the possibility and the continuing necessity of change, while recognising that important challenges and changes have already been achieved. James Clifford helpfully sums up this way of thinking when he argues that the postcolonial points to 'real, *if incomplete*, ruptures with past structures of domination, sites of current struggle and imagined futures' ('Diasporas', *Cultural Anthropology*, 9 (3), 1994, p. 328 – emphasis added). As a committed critical practice dedicated to transformation, postcolonialism maintains a stake in the past, the present and the future.

So, with these points firmly in place, we can proceed to make some decisions about what is gathered under our umbrella-term 'postcolonialism'. Keeping in mind the disquiet with the range that the term often covers, we can identify at least three salient areas that fall within its remit. Very basically, postcolonialism involves one or more of the following:

- Reading the cultural endeavours produced by people from countries with a history of colonialism, primarily those concerned with the workings and legacy of colonialism, and resistance to it, in either the past or the present.
- Reading cultural texts produced by those that have migrated from countries with a history of colonialism, or those descended from migrant families, which deal in the main with diaspora experience and its many consequences.
- In the light of theories of colonial discourses, re-reading texts produced during the colonial period often by members of the colonising nations; both those that directly address the experiences of Empire, and those that seem not to.

A central term in each is 'reading', by which I mean not only the analysis of written materials (poetry, fiction, letters, reports) but also the wider sense of signifying the critical scrutiny of many creative endeavours (visual arts, film, music, etc.). The act of reading in postcolonial contexts is by no means a neutral activity. *How* we read is just as important as *what* we read. As we shall see throughout this book, the ideas we encounter within post-colonialism and the issues they raise demand that conventional reading methods and models of interpretation may need to be rethought if our reading practices are to contribute to the contestation of colonial discourses to which postcolonialism aspires. Rethinking conventional modes of reading and thinking, I believe, is fundamental to postcolonialism.

Of course, making distinctions like the ones above always involves a certain degree of generalisation. It would be impossible, as well as wrong, to unify these areas into a single coherent 'postcolonialism' with a common manifesto. Postcolonialism refers us to a debate, not to a happy consensus. Single-sentence definitions are impossible and unwise. In addition, we must be aware that each area *is itself* diverse and heterogeneous. For example, like colonialism, colonial discourses can function in particular ways for different peoples at different times. We should not presume consensus and totality where there is instead heterogeneity. A sense of the variable nature of the field will be reinforced, I hope, as you read through this book.

One last word of warning. Remember that postcolonialism may well *aim* to oppose colonialist representations and values, but whether it *fulfils* these aims remains a hotly debated issue in the field as we have briefly considered. Postcolonialism may bring new possibilities, but, as we shall see, it is not free from problems of its own. So, in beginning postcolonialism, it is important that we maintain a critical attitude towards it throughout our studies.

Selected reading

Ahmad, Aijaz, 'The Politics of Literary Postcoloniality' in Padmini Mongia (ed.), *Contemporary Postcolonial Theory: A Reader* (Edward Arnold, 1996), pp. 274–93.
    An essay highly critical of the ways in which postcolonialism has been enthusiastically discoursed upon in literary studies.
Ashcroft, Bill, *Postcolonial Transformation* (Routledge, 2001).
    An extremely insightful book which defines and explores the critical and transformative possibilities of postcolonial thought and culture.
Ashcroft, Bill, Gareth Griffiths and Helen Tiffin, *The Empire Writes Back: Theory and Practice in Post-Colonial Literatures*, second edition (Routledge, 2002).
    Recently revised, this book remains influential in the field today despite the several critiques of it which have been mounted since the date of its first publication in 1989.
Boehmer, Elleke, *Colonial and Postcolonial Literature*, second edition (Oxford University Press, 2005).
    A definitive and wide-ranging comparative account of the literary activity in countries with a history of colonialism, which begins with some very useful definitions.
Childs, Peter and Patrick Williams, *An Introduction to Post-Colonial Theory* (Harvester Wheatsheaf, 1997).
    The introduction, 'Points of Departure', offers an excellent and highly recommended account of the different ways of thinking about

postcolonialism which emerge from debates within literary theory.

Featherstone, Simon, *Postcolonial Cultures* (Edinburgh University Press, 2005).

As well as offering a focused and thought-provoking exploration of a number of different kinds of postcolonial cultural activities, the opening chapter ('The Nervous Conditions of Postcolonial Studies') is succinct and extremely useful. Make sure you read this.

Hall, Stuart, 'When Was "the Post-Colonial"? Thinking at the Limit' in Iain Chambers and Lidia Curti (eds), *The Post-Colonial Question: Common Skies, Divided Horizons* (Routledge, 1996), pp. 242–60.

This is a complex but enormously rich and rewarding discussion of 'the postcolonial' that raises a number of salient issues. An excellent place to continue your deliberations concerning the usefulness of this and related terms, but work through it slowly.

Lazarus, Neil (ed.), *The Cambridge Companion to Postcolonial Literary Studies* (Cambridge University Press, 2004).

Often voiced from a materialist standpoint, the essays in this volume cover a number of salient issues: national liberation, globalisation, feminism, migrancy and many others. The introduction is especially recommended to help you think about the pros and cons of postcolonialism.

Loomba, Ania, *Colonialism/Postcolonialism*, second edition (Routledge, 2005).

A long and detailed introduction to the field, particularly strong on colonial discourses and their critique.

McLeod, John (ed.), *The Routledge Companion to Postcolonial Studies* (Routledge, 2007).

This collection maps the major European Empires, key postcolonial locations, major formulations of postcolonial theory and key writers and thinkers beyond a strictly Anglophone bracket. The introduction raises a number of ways of thinking about the purposefulness of the term 'postcolonial'.

Mishra, Vijay and Bob Hodge, 'What is Post(-)colonialism?' in Patrick Williams and Laura Chrisman (eds), *Colonial Discourse and Post-Colonial Theory* (Harvester Wheatsheaf, 1993), pp. 276–90.

An excellent critique of *The Empire Writes Back* which also raises several of the problems and possibilities of postcolonialism.

Moore-Gilbert, Bart, *Postcolonial Theory: Contexts, Practices, Politics* (Verso, 1997).

One of the most detailed explorations available of the work of Bhabha, Said and Spivak. Its opening chapter, 'Postcolonial Criticism and Postcolonial Theory?', offers an extremely useful account of the emergence of postcolonial studies from Commonwealth literary studies and other antecedents.

Parry, Benita, *Postcolonial Studies: A Materialist Critique* (Routledge, 2004). One of the key materialist interventions in the field of postcolonialism, and necessary reading. The opening two chapters ('Beginnings, Affiliations, Disavowals' and 'Problems in Current Theories of Colonial Discourse') are essential reading. Although sometimes challenging for a beginner, this book is rewarding and important.

Poddar, Prem and David Johnson (eds), *A Historical Companion to Postcolonial Literatures in English* (Edinburgh University Press, 2005). An excellent resource which gives clear, intelligent and informative detail on the key locations, critical terms, major ideas, significant personages and historical circumstances which fall within the remit of postcolonial studies.

Thieme, John, *Post-Colonial Studies: The Essential Glossary* (Arnold, 2003). Arranged in an A-Z format, this book offers some very useful definitions of key terms, explanations of historical phenomena and introductions to key writers and thinkers in postcolonial studies.

Walder, Dennis, *Post-Colonial Literatures in English* (Blackwell, 1998). A clear and illuminating discussion of key issues and texts in the field. Very readable.

Walsh, William, *Commonwealth Literature* (Oxford University Press, 1973). A typical example of the older, 'liberal humanist' criticism of Commonwealth literature which surveys the field region by region.

Young, Robert J. C., *Postcolonialism: An Historical Introduction* (Blackwell, 2001). A major intervention in the field which contextualises postcolonialism firmly within a Marxist and militant history. The early chapters which define colonialism, imperialism, neo-colonialism and postcolonialism are highly recommended. Read slowly and with patience.

2

Reading colonial discourses

Ideology, interpellation, discourse

In Chapter 1 we touched briefly upon some of the issues raised by the study of 'colonial discourses'. Colonialism was often dependent upon the use of military force and physical coercion, but it could not function without the existence of a set of beliefs that are held to justify the (dis)possession and continuing occupation of other peoples' lands. These beliefs are encoded in the language which the colonisers speak and to which the colonised peoples are subjected. This results in the circulation of a variety of popularly held assumptions about the relative differences between peoples of allegedly dissimilar cultures. As Chris Tiffin and Alan Lawson explain, '[c]olonialism (like its counterpart, racism), then, is an operation of discourse, and as an operation of discourse it interpellates colonial subjects by incorporating them in a system of representation' (*De-Scribing Empire*, Routledge, 1994, p. 3). Their use of the term 'interpellates' is derived from Louis Althusser's work on the important role of interpellation in the functioning of ideology. As Ania Loomba explains, 'Althusser opened up certain important and new areas of enquiry such as how ideologies are internalised, how human beings make dominant ideas "their own", how they express socially determined views "spontaneously"' (*Colonialism/Postcolonialism*, second edition, Routledge, 2005, p. 32). Very basically, 'interpellation' describes a process by which individual subjects come to internalise the dominant values of society and think of their place in society in a particular way. In the previous chapter we looked at Fanon's memory of being called a 'dirty nigger' while in France, and the damaging impact this had on his sense of self and identity. Fanon is described pejoratively by others, and this means that he has to consider himself in terms of the racist ideology which informs how others see him. Ideology assigns him a role and an identity which he is meant to internalise as proper and true, and he is made subject to its iniquitous and disempowering effects, both psychologically and socially.

Theories of colonial discourses are certainly influenced by notions of ideology indebted to Althusser, as Tiffin and Lawson's comment reveals, but their most significant intellectual motivation comes from the work of the French poststructuralist philosopher Michel Foucault, especially his concept of discourse as a productive site where power and knowledge become intertwined. (The twinning of ideology and discourse in postcolonial criticism has frustrated some critics, who believe that they should be better distinguished.) Although the example of Fanon soberly highlights the *pain* of being represented pejoratively by other people, Foucault argues that power also worked through *gratification*. Power is not simply punitive; if it was, it could not function so successfully, gain so much day-to-day support nor ultimately maintain its authority. As Foucault proposed, '[p]leasure and power do not cancel or turn back against each other; they seek out, overlap, and reinforce one another' (*The History of Sexuality Volume 1*, Penguin, 1990, p. 48). Some would argue that it is easier to make a person act according to your wishes by helping them feel valuable, special and amply rewarded, rather than bereft or contemptuous, as this often fulfils an individual's sense of worthiness and makes them happy with the identity and role which have been fashioned for them. Indeed, we might consider that colonial discourses have been successful because they are so productive: they enable some colonisers to feel important, superior, noble and benign, as well as gaining the complicity of the colonised by enabling some people to derive a sense of self-worth and material benefit through their participation in the business of Empire. Such discursive operations supplement, and indeed may mask, the more pecuniary activities of military occupation and coercive rule.

Theories of colonial discourses, then, are interested in the ways in which *material reality* and *cultural representations* – the conditions of the world and the knowledge we make about the world – are always intertwined and mutually supportive. The realm of knowledge is inseparable from the influence and operation of power. The notion of discourse, derived from Foucault, turns upon this conjoining of knowledge and power, and points up the complicity of knowledge, representation and culture in the operation of power at any given moment and in any specific location. Discourses do not reflect a pre-given reality: they *constitute* and *produce* our sense of reality and objects of knowledge in the first place. Discourses make and shape the world. They are not modes of reflection, but agents of creation; and their operations are absolutely bound up with the interests and at the service of power.

Reading cultural texts in the context, or even as examples, of colonial discourses serves several purposes. First, this reading approach, sometimes called 'colonial discourse analysis', refuses the humanist assumption that literary texts exist above and beyond their historical contexts. It situates texts in history by exposing how their ideological and historical contexts influence the production of meaning within literary texts, and how literary representations themselves have the power to influence their historical moment. Second, and more specifically, the analysis of colonial discourses dares to point out the extent to which the (presumed) 'very best' of Western high culture – be it opera, art, literature, classical music – is caught up in the sordid history of colonial exploitation and dispossession. Third, the attention to the machinery of colonial discourses in the past can act as a means of resourcing resistance to the continuation of colonial representations and realities which remain after formal colonisation has come to an end: a condition we might term 'neo-colonialism'. In understanding how colonial discourses have functioned historically we are in a better position to refuse their prevailing assumptions and participate in the vital process of 'decolonising the mind'. So at the local level of (in this chapter, for example) literary study, our reading practices can constitute a political act. Reading practices are never politically neutral; how we come to read a text will always tell us something about the values we hold, or oppose.

In this chapter we will look first at Edward W. Said's most influential book *Orientalism* (Penguin, 1978). Although Said was not the first intellectual interested in what came to be called colonial discourses, his definition of Orientalism was important in theorising them and shaping postcolonial studies as we have seen, and his book remains highly influential (and, for some, controversial) today. Next, we shall survey some of the important criticisms of this book in order to gain a sense of how the study of colonial discourses has developed. The chapter concludes with a critical exploration of a poem from the colonial period that directly addresses colonial life, as we consider Rudyard Kipling's 'The Overland Mail' in the light of the reading strategies we have explored.

Reading *Orientalism*

Although our doorway into colonial discourses is through Said's concept of Orientalism, let us be clear from the outset that Orientalism and colonial discourses do *not* amount to the same thing. They are not interchangeable terms. As we shall see, colonial discourses can be more complex and varied than Said's specific model of Orientalism. Orientalism is one particular theorisation and manifestation of how colonial discourses might operate, specific to particular historical and colonial contexts. That said, many critics have found Said's notion of Orientalism fruitful in helping them understand the operations of colonial discourses across cultures and contexts.

As Bill Ashcroft and Pal Ahluwalia underline, *Orientalism* 'pivots on a demonstration of the link between knowledge and power, for the discourse of Orientalism constructs and dominates Orientals in the process of "knowing" them' (*Edward Said*, Routledge, 2001, p. 54). Said's book is an eclectic study of how the Western colonial powers of Britain and France represented and ruled North African and Middle Eastern lands from the eighteenth century. 'The Orient' is the collective noun which has been used to homogenise and refer to these places (although it is sometimes used by others when discussing the Far East, especially in the United States). 'Orientalism' refers to the sum of the *West*'s representations of the Orient, and it is with the powerful effects of these which concern Said for the most part. In the book's later chapters, Said looks at how Orientalism persisted into the late twentieth century in Western media reports of Eastern, especially Arab, lands, despite formal decolonisation for many countries. The persistence of Orientalist representations reinforces the point that the imaginative machinery of colonialism does not quickly disappear as soon as once-colonised lands achieve independence and can indeed endure in refreshed forms. Indeed, since the terrorist attacks on New York and Washington on 11 September 2001, it might be argued that Orientalism's homogenising representations have been once again recycled and supplemented as part of the US-led 'war on terror'.

One of *Orientalism*'s many commendable qualities is its readability. Indeed, Said's lucid, sophisticated yet plain written style distinguishes it from the writing of Homi K. Bhabha and Gayatri Chakravorty Spivak, with whom he is often discussed. A lengthy but approachable academic work that draws upon and adventurously juggles some complex critical ideas, Said's book raises many challenging notions and issues, and you may well profit by looking closely in the first instance at an extract or two, rather than initially attempting the book in its entirety. Several readers in post-colonialism include useful excerpts where you might experience the tenor and substance of *Orientalism* – such as Patrick Williams and Laura Chrisman (eds), *Colonial Discourse and Post-Colonial Theory* (Harvester Wheatsheaf, 1993, pp. 132–49) or Bill Ashcroft, Gareth Griffiths and Helen Tiffin (eds), *The Post-Colonial Studies Reader*, second edition (Routledge, 2006, pp. 24–67). Alternatively, the introductory chapter to *Orientalism* contains many of the ideas which Said elaborates in his book, and is worth getting to grips with before proceeding to the body of the text.

Let us now look at a brief outline of Said's definition of Orientalism that should help us begin. To support your study, choose one of these suggested excerpts and spend some time working through the ideas it contains in the light of my outline, allowing your understanding of Orientalism to build gradually to a suitable and productive level of sophistication. I have divided the outline into two sections: the first highlights the general *shape* of the discourse of Orientalism and its manifold manifestations as defined by Said, while the second looks in a little more detail at the set-piece and *stereotypical* assumptions about cultural difference which it fashions and asserts as truth. The salient points are summarised under a series of sub-headings. These do not exhaust the scope of the concept of Orientalism but rather create some useful doorways into Said's work.

The shape of Orientalism

1. Orientalism constructs binary oppositions

Fundamental to the view of the world fashioned by Orientalism is the binary division it makes between the Orient and the Occident (the West). The Orient is conceived as being everything that the West is *not*, its 'alter ego'. Each is assumed to exist in opposition to the other, with the Orient always coming off the worse from any comparison. The Orient is frequently described in negative terms that serve to buttress a sense of the West's superiority and strength. If the West is assumed as the global seat of knowledge and learning, then it will follow that the Orient is a place of ignorance and stupidity. Thus in Orientalism, East and West are positioned through the construction of an *unequal* dichotomy. The West occupies a superior rank while the Orient is its 'other', fixed eternally in a subservient position. This makes the relations between them asymmetrical.

It is important to grasp quickly that Orientalism in part provides the West with the means of fashioning an image of itself, by setting up a supposedly degenerate and brutish part of the world against which it can be beneficially compared. As David Richards points out in *Masks of Difference: Cultural Representations in Literature, Anthropology and Art* (Cambridge University Press, 1994), '[t]he representation of other cultures invariably entails the presentation of self-portraits, in that those people who are observed are overshadowed or eclipsed by the observer' (p. 289). Said stresses in the introduction to *Orientalism* that the Orient has been funda-mental in defining the West 'as its contrasting image, idea, personality, experience (p. 2). The West makes knowledge about itself *by proclaiming via Orientalism everything it believes it is not*. Consequently, Said claims that 'European culture gained in strength and identity by setting itself off against the Orient as a sort of surrogate and even underground self' (p. 3).

2. Orientalism is a Western fantasy

Following on from the previous point, it is important to grasp Said's fundamental argument that Western views of the Orient are not based on what may actually exist in Oriental lands, but result from the West's dreams, fantasies and assumptions about what this apparently radically different, contrasting place contains. Such things corrupt and shape the lenses through which the Orient is observed by those from the Occident. Orientalism is first and foremost a *fabricated* thing, a series of images, ways of seeing and thinking that come to stand (in) as the Orient's 'reality' for those in the West. Orientalism constitutes a vision of the Orient; it does not mirror what is there. Its contrived idea of 'reality' *in no meaningful way reflects* what may or may not actually happen in Oriental lands. It does not convey 'an inert fact of nature' (p. 4) but is instead 'man-made' (p. 5), a creation fashioned by those who presume to rule. So, Orientalism imposes upon the Orient specifically Western visions of its 'reality'. But crucially, its creation from the stuff of fantasy and make-believe does not make it any less remote from the social and political fortunes of the world; rather, it resources them. Orientalism may be fundamentally *imaginative*, but *material effects* result from its advent. Knowledge and power always work together.

3. Orientalism is institutional

The imaginative assumptions of Orientalism are often taken as hard facts. They find their way into, constitute and make possible a whole academic and institutional infrastructure where opinions, views and theses about the Orient circulate as legitimate knowledges, wholly acceptable truths, with tangible material effects. As Rana Kabbani argues in *Imperial Fictions: Europe's Myths of Orient* (Pandora, rev. 1994), 'the ideology of Empire was hardly ever a brute jingoism; rather, it made subtle use of reason, and recruited science and history to serve its ends' (p. 6). The Orient, writes Said, became something 'suitable for study in the academy, for display in the museum, for reconstruction in the colonial office, for theoretical illustration in anthropological, biological, linguistic, racial and historical theses about mankind and the universe, for instances of economic and sociological theories of development, revolution, cultural personality, national or religious character' (*Orientalism*, pp. 7–8). Such a dizzying, exhausting list underlines just how far-reaching Orientalism was, the large part it played in helping those in the West formulate their own knowledge of the world, and their (superior) place therein, across a variety of disciplines and within a number of institutions.

4. Orientalism is literary and creative

If Orientalism suffuses a vast academic and institutional network, it overlaps significantly with the multitude of creative arts. We can discern this overlapping when Said identifies as Orientalist the production of 'philology [the study of the history of languages], lexicography [dictionary making], history, biology, political and economic theory, novel-writing and lyric poetry' (p. 15). Orientalism also made possible new forms of representation and genres of writing that enshrined and often celebrated Western experience abroad, such as the heroic male adventure story popular during the Victorian period (see Joseph Bristow, *Empire Boys: Adventures in a Man's World*, HarperCollins, 1991). A plethora of artistic endeavours are influenced by the structures, assumptions and stereotypes of Orientalism, underlining the point that Western culture is inextricably bound up with Western colonialism.

5. Orientalism is legitimating and self-perpetuating

All the points made above underline the important detail that Orientalism is not just productive but reproductive: it perpetuates itself. In so doing, it acts as a far-reaching system of representations firmly bound to an imperial structure of political domination. Orientalist representations function to justify the propriety of Western colonial rule in foreign lands. They are a vitally important part of the arsenal of Empire. They legitimate the domination of other peoples and lubricate the political and judicial structures which maintain colonial rule through physical coercion.

6. There is a distinction between 'latent' and 'manifest' Orientalism

In order to emphasise the connection between the imaginative assumptions of Orientalism and its specific examples and effects, Said borrows some terms from Sigmund Freud to distinguish between a *latent* Orientalism and a *manifest* Orientalism. Latent Orientalism describes the dreams and fantasies about the Orient that, in Said's view, remain relatively constant over time. Manifest Orientalism refers to the myriad examples of Orientalist knowledge produced at different historical junctures. Said proposes that while the manifestations of Orientalism will inevitably be different, due to reasons of historical specificity and individual styles and perspectives, their underlying or latent premises will tend to be the same. For example, a Victorian travel writer and an Edwardian journalist might produce texts about the Orient which appear distinct and different, but their underlying assumptions about the division between East and West and the character of the Orient (and Orientals) will share the same underlying root.

Latent Orientalism, then, is like a blueprint; manifest Orientalism is evidenced by the many different versions that can be built from the same overall design. When a writer or painter makes an Orientalist representation, they will be drawing upon a common set of assumptions regardless of the different styles or forms they choose.

Stereotypes of the Orient and Orientals

1. The Orient is timeless

If the West is considered the place of historical progress and scientific development, then the Orient is deemed remote from the enlightening process of historical change. 'Orientalism assumed an unchanging Orient' (p. 96), Said states. The Orient is considered to be essentially no different in the eighteenth century than it was in the twelfth, trapped in antiquity far behind the modern developments of the 'enlightened' West. Conceived in this way, the Orient was often regarded as 'primitive' or 'backwards'. A Westerner travelling to Oriental lands was not just moving in *space* from one location to the other, potentially they were also moving back in *time*, out of history, to an earlier, pre-modern world. Hence, in Orientalism, the Orient is presented as a timeless place, changeless and static, cut off from the progress of Western history.

2. The Orient is strange

Crucial to Orientalism is the stereotype of the Orient's peculiarity. The Orient is not just different; it is *oddly* different – unusual, fantastic, bizarre. Westerners can meet all kinds of spectacle there, wonders that will beggar belief and make them doubt their Western eyes. The Orient's perceived eccentricity often functioned as a source of mirth, marvel, mysticism and curiosity for Western writers and artists; but ultimately its radical oddness was considered evidence enough of the Orient's intriguing inferiority. If the Occident is rational, sensible and familiar, then the Orient is irrational, extraordinary, bizarre. Such perceived strangeness often fascinated and horrified those in the West in equal measure.

3. Orientalism makes assumptions about people

Oriental peoples often appeared in Western representations as examples of various invidious racial, ethnic, religious and national stereotypes. Assumptions were often made about the innate characteristics and behaviours of Oriental peoples, which mani-fested themselves across a series of derogatory stereotypes. Such assumptions about the *inherent* characteristics of such peoples might include the murderous and violent Arab, the lazy Indian, the sexually obsessed African, the inscrutable Chinese. The Oriental's alleged 'race', or nationality, or ethnicity, or religious identity, somehow sums up what kind of person he or she is likely to be, despite their individual qualities and failings. Terms like 'Arabian' or 'Indian' come to be defined within the general negative representational framework typical of Orientalism. Therefore, such peoples are glibly homogenised and robbed of their individuality as Orientalism mobilised a set of generalised types. So *all* Arabs are violent, *all* Chinese are inscrutable. The homogenising propensity of Orientalism is one of its key elements.

4. Orientalism makes assumptions about gender

Similarly, popular gendered stereotypes circulated which underwrote the Orient's radical oddness, its lack of propriety, such as the effeminate Oriental male or the sexually lascivious exotic Oriental female. The Oriental male was frequently deemed insuffi-ciently 'manly' and displayed a luxuriousness and foppishness that made him a grotesque parody of the (itself stereotyped) 'gentler' female sex. The exoticised Oriental female, often depicted nude or partially clothed in plenty of Western representations during the colonial period, could be presented as an immodest, immoral, active creature of sexual pleasure who held the key to mysterious erotic sexual delights. In both examples, the Oriental is deemed as failing to live up to received, proper gender codes: men, by Western colonialist standards, were meant to be active, courageous, strong; by the same token, women were meant to be passive, moral, chaste. But Oriental men and women do not comply with these gender roles; their gender identity is regarded as transgressive. Once again, an homogenising logic takes over: *all* Oriental men and women are pre-judged as defective in gendered terms. This adds to the general sense of oddness and irregularity, both repulsive and titillating for many Western travellers, ascribed to the Orient.

5. The Orient is feminine

In addition to the gendering and homogenising of individuals we have just thought about, Orientalism also subscribes to a more general gendering of the opposition between the Occident and the Orient as one between rigidly stereotypical versions of masculinity and femininity. In Orientalism, the East as a whole is 'feminised', deemed passive, submissive, exotic, luxurious, sexually mysterious and tempting; while the West is thought of in terms of the 'masculine' – that is, active, dominant, heroic, rational, self-controlled and ascetic. This gendering is evidenced by a specifically sexual vocabulary used by many Westerners when describing the Orient: the Orient is 'penetrated' by the traveller whose 'passions' it rouses, it is 'possessed', 'ravished', 'embraced' – and ultimately 'domesticated' by the muscular coloniser. According to Said, this is in part a result of the fact that Orientalism was 'an exclusively male province' (p. 207). So it responded to and buttressed the discourses of heroic, brawny masculinity at large in the Western nations (and, no doubt, attracted many men to colonialism's cause).

It is worth considering the extent to which this vocabulary of sexual possession common to Orientalism reveals the Orient as a site of perverse desire on the part of many male colonisers. Projected onto the Orient are the fantasies of the West concerning supposed moral degeneracy, confused and rampant sexualities. These fantasies did much to stimulate the domination and colonisation of the Orient, but also its continuing fascination for many in the West. It seemed deliciously to offer Western men the opportunity to sample an untrammelled life free from the prohibitions of society back home. Travellers to the Orient might think they were going to a place where moral codes of behaviour did not function, and where they could actually indulge in forms of sexual excess. If the Occident was associated with the mind – with thought, intelligence, learning – then the Orient was linked to the body: another dichotomous distinction which underwrote the unequal split between the two realms. The sexual fantasy of the Orient as a desirable repository of all that is constrained by Western civilisation often acted as a continual stimulus for those who studied it or travelled through Oriental lands. So, as we noted previously, in representing the Orient and Orientals, Western artists were actually depicting themselves, putting on the page or in their pictures their own desires, fantasies and fears.

6. The Oriental is degenerate

Compositely, then, Orientalist stereotypes fixed the Orientals' typical and definitive weaknesses as (among others) cowardliness, laziness, untrustworthiness, fickleness, laxity, violence and lust. Oriental peoples were often considered as possessing a tenuous moral sense and the readiness to indulge themselves in the more dubious and criminal aspects of human behaviour. In other words, Orientalism posited the notion that Oriental peoples needed to be made civilised and made to conform to the perceived higher moral standards upheld in the West. In perpetually creating these discursive stereotypes, Orientalism justified the propriety of colonialism ideologically by claiming that Oriental peoples needed saving from themselves.

Criticisms of *Orientalism*

As Ashcroft and Ahluwalia contend, the publication of *Orientalism* 'made such an impact on thinking about colonial discourse that ... it has continued to be the site of controversy, adulation and

criticism' (*Edward Said*, p. 49). Having now arrived at a rough sense
of what is involved in Said's theory of Orientalism, let us turn next
to look at some critiques of it. As well as entering into debates
specifically about *Orientalism*, we will gain in general a fuller
understanding of how colonial discourses are deemed to operate.
These criticisms do not invalidate Said's ground-breaking study,
and you must think carefully about how convinced you are by each
of them as you proceed; but they do invite us to think flexibly about
the operations of colonial discourses. For the purposes of brevity we
shall consider only four criticisms. (You can extend your
engagement with critiques of *Orientalism* by looking at pp. 69–83 of
Ashcroft and Ahluwalia's useful book *Edward Said*, cited
previously.)

1. *Orientalism* is ahistorical

One major criticism of *Orientalism*, from which several of the others
stem, concerns its capacity to make totalising assumptions about a
vast, varied expanse of representations over a very long period of
history. As Dennis Porter describes it in an early but still useful
essay first published in 1983, '*Orientalism* and its Problems' (in
Williams and Chrisman (eds), *Colonial Discourse and Post-Colonial
Theory*, pp. 150–61), Said posits the 'unified character of Western
discourse over some two millennia, a unity derived from a common
and continuing experience of fascination with and threat from the
East, of its irreducible otherness' (p. 152). Said's examples of
Orientalist writing range from the Italian poet Dante writing in the
early fourteenth century up to twentieth-century writers. Porter's
essay invites us to ask: can it be true that they *all* hold essentially the
same latent assumptions? Can such a massive archive of materials be
so readily homogenised? Has nothing really changed? Said's view
takes in a broad generalising sweep of history but perhaps attends
too little to the uniqueness of *individual* historical moments, their
anomalies and specifics. Robert J. C. Young sums up this critical
point of view when he remarks that for some people Said's 'claim for
a general "discourse on colonialism" is totalizing and simply does
not answer to the range of historical and geographical differences
that exist in the real world either in the past or in the present'
(*Postcolonialism: An Historical Introduction*, Blackwell, 2001,

p. 391). This point of view is exemplified by John MacKenzie, who points out in his book *Orientalism: History, Theory and the Arts* (Manchester University Press, 1995) that Said's history of Orientalism is perhaps 'in itself essentially ahistorical' because it glosses over the various factors that make historical moments distinctive, such as the 'contrasting economic and social circumstances of different territories' (p. 11).

Therefore, we might argue that, first, Said trusts too much in the existence and unchanging character of a transhistorical latent Orientalism; and, second, that he privileges latent Orientalism over manifest Orientalism by neglecting to think whether the representations of the Orient made by those in the West might modify or even come to challenge the enduring assumptions of Orientalism. MacKenzie argues that Western artists have approached the Orient at various moments with perfectly honour-able intentions and 'genuine respect' (p. 60) for other peoples, in order to learn from and value newly encountered cultures. Not everyone looked down upon the Orient so crudely. Well, this was no doubt true in some cases. However, in fairness to Said, MacKenzie is perhaps too trusting of the examples of 'benign' representations of the Orient he reproduces in his book and he fails to grasp the point that even the most gracious and respectful artist may *unwittingly* reproduce Orientalist assumptions. If Said's work maybe privileges the latent aspect of Orientalism, MacKenzie pays it too scant attention and forgets that the road to hell is often paved with good intentions. It does not necessarily follow that a sympathetic representation of the Orient or Orientals will automatically be free from the latent assumptions of Orientalism. That said, does Said's notion of a *latent* Orientalism stand up to serious historical scrutiny? Can it really be assumed to exist?

2. Said ignores resistance by the colonised

This is another major criticism of *Orientalism*. If Said is to be believed, Orientalism moves in one direction from the active West to the passive East. But he does not really stop to examine how Orientalist peoples may have *contested* colonial discourses, challenged its constitutive agency, or confronted it with alternative forms of knowledge that resource resistance. In what ways did

colonised peoples respond to Orientalist discourses? Did they
readily submit to the colonisers' views? How might they have
opposed Orientalism and brought it to crisis? The lack of attention to
the colonised's dissidence and resistance in *Orientalism* is for several
figures a major failing of the book. As Patrick Williams and Laura
Chrisman have argued in their introduction to *Colonial Discourse
and Post-Colonial Theory* (see p. 16), there is little notion of the
colonised subject as a *constitutive* agent with the capacity for
political resistance. In the words of Aijaz Ahmad, one of Said's
fiercest critics, Said never thinks about how Western representations 'might have been received, accepted, modified, challenged,
overthrown or reproduced by the intelligentsias of the colonised
countries' (*In Theory: Classes, Nations, Literatures*, Verso, 1992, p.
172). In these terms, Said stands accused of writing out the
dissident agency and the voices of colonised peoples from history as
he does not consider the challenges made to dominant discourses.
In so doing, his work is in danger of being just as 'Orientalist' as the
field he is describing by not considering alternative representations
made by those subject to colonialism.

3. Said ignores resistance within the West

According to Said, 'every European, in what he could say about the
Orient, was consequently a racist, an imperialist, and almost totally
ethnocentric' (*Orientalism*, p. 204). This is certainly a sweeping
statement. But what about those within the colonising nations who
opposed colonialism, were horrified by the treatment of colonised
peoples, and campaigned for the end of brutal forms of oppression
such as the Atlantic slave trade? As Dennis Porter argues,
Orientalism leaves no room to accommodate what he calls, following
Antonio Gramsci, 'counter-hegemonic thought' ('*Orientalism* and
its Problems', p. 152); that is, opinions contrary to the dominant
views within the West which contest the normative claims of
Orientalist discourses. This problem leads Bart Moore-Gilbert to
suggest that Said takes 'insufficient account of resistance or
contradiction within imperial culture itself' (*Postcolonial Theory*,
Verso, 1997, p. 50).

4. Said neglects the significance of gender

This might seem at first an odd objection to make, given that Said acknowledged the gendering at the heart of Orientalist discourses and the 'manly' pursuit of colonialism and Empire. Said maintains that in Orientalist writing 'women are usually the creatures of a male power-fantasy. They express unlimited sensuality, they are more or less stupid, and above all they are willing' (*Orientalism*, p. 207). But is this also 'usually' true in writing about the Orient by women? Did Western women write about the Orient using the same assumptions and stereotypes? As Sara Mills has argued in *Discourses of Difference: An Analysis of Women's Travel Writing and Colonialism* (Routledge, 1992), many women travelled to the colonies and made their own observations; yet Said rarely looks at women's writing in *Orientalism*.

Let's pursue this last point further, as it both opens up the issue of gender and colonial discourses and allows us to look ahead to some of the ideas we will probe in Chapter 6. On the point of Western women's writing about the Orient, it is not just a case of 'adding in' such writing to Said's theory in order to fill in an absence. Mills points out that the position of women in relation to Orientalism is often different to that of men because of the tensions between the discourses of colonialism and the discourses of gender. Looking at late Victorian and early-twentieth-century travel writing by women, Mills maintains that these women were, at one level, *empowered* by colonialism owing to the superior position they perceived themselves to hold in relation to colonised peoples. Yet, in an analogous way to colonised peoples, women were *disempowered* owing to the inferior position they were placed in relation to Western men. This might make available, if only fleetingly, a partial and problematic accord between the Western woman traveller and the colonised peoples she encountered. Her position in relation to the colonised is not necessarily the same as a Western male's. Hence, the intersection of colonial and patriarchal discourses often places Western women in a contradictory position. They occupy a dominant position due to colonialism, but a subordinate position in patriarchy. Women 'cannot be said to speak from outside colonial discourse, but their relation to [it] is problematic because of its conflict with the discourses of "femininity", which were operating on them in equal, and sometimes stronger, measure. Because of these discursive pressures, their work exhibits contradictory elements which may act as a critique of some of the components of other colonial writings' (*Discourses of Difference*, p. 63). Women's writing about the colonies may not be so readily explained with recourse to Said's theory of Orientalism, because of its particular contradictions borne out of the contrary positions that might be held by women.

As Sara Mills's argument exemplifies, many criticisms of Said's work turn upon the view that colonial discourses are multiple, precarious, contested and more ambivalent than Said conveys in *Orientalism*. They do not function with the smoothness or the perfect success that he seems to credit to the totalising concept of Orientalism. It is important to keep in mind that colonial discourses were in constant confrontation with resistance and contrary views as part of a wider struggle with, and for, power, in the colonies and in the West. Colonial discourses, then, are by no means homogeneous or unitary. Said is certainly right to identify the modes of representing the Orient which functioned as a part of colonial rule, its legitimation and administration. But Orientalist representations were not monolithic, static or uncontested.

The development of theories of colonial discourses since Said's book enables us to consider Said's notion of Orientalism as describing the operations of colonial discourses up to a point. The institutionalised system of asymmetrical, repetitive stereotypes is one part of the story of how colonial discourses function in the world. To be fair, Said responded positively to some of the key criticisms of *Orientalism*, especially the argument that he ignores insurgency, although he disagreed with certain of the charges made against him such as the accusation that his work is ultimately ahistorical (see Said's 'Afterword' to the 1995 Penguin edition of *Orientalism*). In his later work he looked more closely at the resistance to Orientalism, as well as its continuing presence in the colonial world. These are some of the major preoccupations of his later book *Culture and Imperialism* (Vintage, 1993). None the less, we should not underestimate the power which Orientalist representations clearly wielded when holding up Said's theory of

Orientalism for questioning. Just because these discourses were more volatile than Said perhaps implies, it does not mean they were (and are) without substantial power and influence in Westerners' views of, and conduct in relation to, other peoples. This, the central premise of *Orientalism*, must not be underestimated or too-readily dismissed.

'Ambivalence' and 'mimicry' in colonial discourses

Let us probe further into how colonial discourses are not always so sure of themselves as might be presumed. In '*Orientalism* and its Problems', Dennis Porter argues that even the most seemingly Orientalist text can contain moments when Orientalist assumptions come up against alternative views that throw their authority into question. Texts rarely embody one point of view, after all. They are often places of thought and debate rather than modes of unequivocal or consistent statements, and the presence of contrary attitudes can either be consciously or unwittingly communicated. Texts can bring into play several different ways of seeing without always firmly deciding which is the true or most appropriate one.

Porter's example is T. E. Lawrence's *The Seven Pillars of Wisdom* (1922). Sure, he admits, this text might seem a fairly robust example of Orientalism. But we can identify moments when Lawrence seems to depart from an Orientalist position and articulate *alternative* ways of thinking about the differences between East and West. Porter concludes with the important point that 'literary texts may in their play establish distance from the ideologies they seem to be producing' ('*Orientalism* and its Problems', p. 160). Even the most seemingly Orientalist text can articulate 'counter-hegemonic' views. As Porter usefully reminds us in his use of the helpful phrase 'in their play', most modes of cultural endeavour are mobile and often contradictory affairs, positing several perspectives rather than just one. Cross-currents of Orientalist and counter-Orientalist thinking might exist within a single text.

Such questions about the stability and conviction of colonial discourses have also preoccupied Homi K. Bhabha who, like Said, is considered to be one of the leading voices in postcolonialism today. Unlike Said's, Bhabha's writing is often very challenging to comprehend at a first reading because of his compact and complex written style. In his essay 'The Postcolonial Aura: Third World Criticism in the Age of Global Capitalism' (in *Critical Inquiry*, 20, 1994, pp. 328–56), Arif Dirlik argues that Bhabha is 'something of a master of political mystification and theoretical obfuscation' (p. 333) as part of his attack on Bhabha's perceived incomprehensibility. This is a familiar (almost clichéd) if not entirely fair critique of Bhabha's written style. To be sure, Bhabha can be difficult to read, and approaching his work can at times feel akin to tackling an experimental modernist novel. But his work rewards the effort it takes to get to grips with it, and in many ways Bhabha's writing dares to demand a new kind of intellectual writing and reading as part of his wider postcolonial challenge to received, orthodox (perhaps Orientalist?) ways of thinking. It is not always clear if Bhabha's detractors simply fail to understand his work or prefer not to try to understand his thinking; dismissing something simply because it is difficult is a peculiar response for an academic, perhaps. Bhabha's ideas can be some of the most thought-provoking within postcolonialism. But whereas Said draws upon forms of post-structualist theory with a markedly materialist slant (such as Foucault), Bhabha is indebted more to Freudian psychoanalysis, the Fanon of *Black Skin, White Masks*, and the poststructuralism of Jacques Lacan.

The first of Bhabha's essays we consider in this section is Chapter 3 of his book *The Location of Culture* (Routledge, 1994) and is called 'The Other Question: Stereotype, Discrimination and the Discourse of Colonialism'. The second essay, 'Of Mimicry and Man: The Ambivalence of Colonial Discourse', is Chapter 4 of the same book. I suggest that you read Bhabha's essays slowly in the light of the abridged and deliberately basic accounts you will meet below, which strategically sacrifice some of his ingeniousness for the sake of clarity. The accounts I give cannot really capture the theoretical innovation – as well as frustration – of his work, but it is hoped that they will prove useful doorways into Bhabha's thinking. The purpose of looking at Bhabha's thought in this chapter is to build a working knowledge of his concepts of 'ambivalence' and 'mimicry' in the operations of colonial discourses.

Let's take 'ambivalence' first. Like Said, Bhabha argues that colonial discourses are characterised by a series of assumptions which aim to legitimate the colonial settlement of other lands and peoples. 'The objective of colonial discourse', writes Bhabha, 'is to construe the colonised as a population of degenerate types on the basis of racial origin, in order to justify conquest and establish systems of administration and instruction' (*The Location of Culture*, p. 70); hence, as we have seen, the emergence of colonialist stereotypes that construct colonised peoples in various derogatory ways. However, in both a departure from and extension of Said's thinking in *Orientalism*, Bhabha argues that this important aim is *never fully met*. This is because the 'discourse of colonialism' (we'll have to use Bhabha's preferred singular term for now) does not function according to plan because it is always pulling in two contrary directions at once.

On the one hand, the discourse of colonialism would have it that the Oriental – or, in Bhabha's parlance, the 'colonised subject' – is a radically strange creature whose bizarre and eccentric nature is the cause of curiosity and concern. Conceived as such, the colonised are figured as the 'other' of the Westerner (or 'colonising subject'), essentially *beyond* Western comprehension, outside Western culture and civilisation. Yet, on the other hand, the discourse of colonialism attempts to domesticate the perceived radical difference of colonised subjects and lessen this radical 'otherness', bringing them *within* Western understanding through the Orientalist project of constructing knowledge about them and constituting them as an object of study. Crucially for Bhabha, the colonialist construction of 'otherness' is hence *split* by the contradictory positioning of the colonised as simultaneously inside and outside of Western knowledge and comprehension. Or as Bhabha puts it, 'colonial discourse produces the colonised as a social reality which is at once "other" and yet entirely knowable and visible" (pp. 70–1).

This contradiction, which exposes the splitting within colonial discourse, can be grasped through the function of the colonialist stereotype. On the one hand, stereotypes translate the unfamiliar into coherent terms by seeming to understand, fix and explain the alleged strangeness of other peoples: the Irish are inevitably unintelligent, the Chinese are always inscrutable, the Arabs are essentially violent. Securing the identity of the colonised in this way *lessens* the perceived distance between the colonisers and the colonised by bringing the colonised inside colonialist modes of representation. But at the same time, the stereotype functions in a contrary direction to *maintain* a sense of difference and distinction between the colonisers and the colonised. The colonisers cannot entertain the fact that other people might not be especially different after all, as this would undercut the polarising, binary thinking of colonial discourses which supports colonialism's propriety. Hence, the stereotype installs a degree of otherness which keeps the colonised at arm's length. The stereotype both *installs* and *disavows* difference: it ensures that the colonised are at the same time radically other yet capable of being understood. It is as a consequence of such contradictions and splittings that Bhabha claims colonial discourse to be fundamentally unstable and ambivalent.

Probing Said's argument that Western representations of the East are based primarily on fantasies, desires and imaginings, and drawing upon psychoanalytical theory, Bhabha pursues the fact that many representations of the colonial stereotype appear as horrors. The discourse of colonialism is frequently populated with '*terrifying* stereotypes of savagery, cannibalism, lust and anarchy' (p. 72 – my italics). Any attempt to subdue the radical otherness of the colonised is perpetually offset by the alarming fantasies projected onto them. Or to put this differently, the colonised are considered simultaneously capable of domestication and also as radically, frighteningly other. On the one hand, their very existence challenges the ability of Western reason to explain their being, while on the other hand their presence threatens to reveal the edges, limits and shortcomings of Western reason's confidence in being able to explain the matter of the world in its entirety. This is why the colonised are both fascinating and frightening to the colonisers: they are domesticated, explicable, knowable; but also *at the same time* wild, mysterious, harmful. As a discursive projection, their representation vacillates between Western reason and fantasy. Rather than being static objects caught securely within colonialist perception, colonised subjects, like the discourses used to represent them, are profoundly ambivalent.

Bhabha argues that within colonialist representations the colonised subject is always in motion, sliding ambivalently between the polarities of similarity and difference, rationality and fantasy.

He or she will simply not stand still. Hence the prevalence for stereotypes in colonialist discourses: stereotypes are an attempt to arrest this motion and fix the colonised once and for all. But the operation of such stereotypes will always fail to override the ambivalence of colonial discourses. Bhabha points out that stereotypes are *frequently repeated* in an anxious, imperfect attempt to secure the colonised subject within the discourses of colonialism. As he puts it, 'the *same old* stories of the Negro's animality, the Coolie's inscrutability or the stupidity of the Irish *must* be told (compulsively) again and afresh, and are differently gratifying and terrifying each time' (p. 77). The *repetition* of the colonial stereotype is an attempt to secure the colonised in a fixed position, but also an acknowledgement that this can never be achieved.

Thus, to sum up, Bhabha's 'discourse of colonialism' differs quite radically from Said's notion of Orientalism, not least because it is a much more slippery thing than Said had considered. For Bhabha, colonial discourses are characterised by both ambivalence and anxious repetition. In trying to do two things at once – construing the colonised as both *similar* to and the *other* of the colonisers – it ends up doing neither properly. Instead it is fated to be at war with itself, positing radical otherness between peoples while simultaneously trying to lesson the degree of otherness. Although the aim is to fix knowledge about other peoples once and for all, this goal is inevitably and endlessly deferred. The best it can do is set in motion the anxious repetition of the colonised subject's stereotypical attributes that attempt to fix it in a stable position. But the very fact that stereotypes must be *perpetually* repeated reveals that this fixity is never achieved. For these reasons, colonial discourses are characterised more by the ambivalence discovered in their function rather than the security and stability they aim for.

In his essay 'Of Mimicry and Man', Bhabha builds upon these ideas and explores how the ambivalence of colonial discourse and the colonised subject threatens the very authority which colonial discourses presume. Bhabha describes mimicry as 'one of the most elusive and effective strategies of colonial power and knowledge' (p. 85). He focuses on the fact that in colonised locations such as India, the British authorities required native peoples to work on their behalf and thus had to teach them the English language. An example is Macaulay's famous 1835 'Minute' on Indian education (in Bill Ashcroft, Gareth Griffiths and Helen Tiffin (eds), *The Post-Colonial Studies Reader*, second edition, Routledge, 2005, pp. 374–5), in which Macaulay argued that the British in India needed to create a class of Indians capable of taking on English opinions, morals and intellect (we will be taking another look at this 'Minute' in Chapter 5). These figures, comparable with Fanon's French-educated colonials depicted in *Black Skin, White Masks*, are described by Bhabha as 'mimic men' who learn to act English but who do not look English and are not accepted as such. They are Anglicised, rather than English. And as Bhabha states, 'to be Anglicised is emphatically *not* to be English' (*The Location of Culture*, p. 87).

Bhabha is interested in how such mimic men are far from the slavish, disempowered individuals required by the British in India. Indeed, their necessity and presence is unnerving, as is their ability as so-called 'others' to learn the ways and language of the colonisers. Bhabha argues that the presence of such Anglicised peoples – not exclusively native, not quite English, but something in-between – menaces the discourse of colonialism because they threaten to expose the ambivalence at its heart. Hearing their language coming through the mouths of the colonised, the colonisers are faced with the *worrying threat of resemblance* between coloniser and colonised. This threatens to collapse the Orientalist structure of knowledge in which such oppositional distinctions are made. If civilisation, learning, even (being) English can be learned by the colonised, then just how inherent and exclusive are these things to the colonisers? That emphatic distinction declared between being Anglicised and being English is another shrill attempt to keep fixed a significant distinction which is in danger of being breached. The ambivalent position of the colonised mimic men in relation to the colonisers – '*almost the same but not quite*' (p. 89) – is more evidence that the discourse of colonialism is internally split and teeming with anxieties. The economy of representation it seeks to install – chiefly that binary distinction between colonial self and civility on the one hand, and the colonised's otherness and barbarism on the other – never entirely happens, and indeed is threatened with collapse both as a consequence of its internal ambivalent dynamics and through its operation in the world.

This is a different assertion to Said's model of Orientalism, which does not consider how colonial discourses generate the possibilities of their own critique. It is also something of a controversial argument to make. Bhabha locates the possibility of the critique of colonial discourses not in the conscious activities of the colonised, in their acts of resistance or alternative knowledges, but *within the very substance of colonial discourses themselves*. Dissident agency is not considered to be the property of the colonised's radical conscious-ness or to be found in political resistance, but triggered within the very operations of discourse. It is this discursive privileging (or, remembering Chapter 1, this *culturalist* bent), which has most often been denounced by Bhabha's critics. Yet in seizing upon mimicry as a potentially menacing modality, Bhabha departs from a way of thinking about mimicry as describing the condition of the colonised's subservience, doomed forever to impersonate the civilised values and behaviour of the 'First World' – a way of thinking powerfully encapsulated by the Trinidadian-born novelist V. S. Naipaul's penetrating novel of colonial pain, *The Mimic Men* (1967). By revealing that the discourse of colonialism is forever embattled and split by ambivalence through the negotiation of stereotypes and the function of mimicry, Bhabha daringly invites us to think about the ways in which colonial discourses can always break down when attempting to secure their primary aims.

STOP and THINK

As his critical vocabulary might suggest, Bhabha deals with the (singular) discourse of colonialism at a very abstract level. Terms like 'colonising subject', 'the colonial stereotype', and 'colonial discourse' are rather transcendent and absolute. As the anthropologist Nicholas Thomas has argued, Bhabha's work is maybe weakened by its 'generalising strategy' (*Colonialism's Culture: Anthropology, Travel and Government*, Polity, 1994, p. 43). Is the discourse of colonialism the same in India as in Algeria? Also, to what extent do you think Bhabha makes an attempt to think about differences of gender or social class as complicating the discourse of colonialism? Think back to Sara Mills's points about women travellers: would the discourse of colonialism be the same for them? Some of the criticisms made against Said could also be applied to Bhabha, particularly those concerned with ahistoricity and gender. That said, might there be something positive to be said about such abstract theorisation too? Might the risks involved be worth it, if it enables us to understand much better how colonial discourses attempted to constitute their objects of knowledge in different ways around the world? Can't 'abstract' theorising be just as enriching, perhaps, as always historicising?

As we have acknowledged, Bhabha's writing is dazzling and inspiring in many respects, but also notoriously difficult because of its abstruse diction, cryptic manner and dense thinking – often it is hard to see the intellectual wood for the linguistic trees. This is not accidental, as I hinted previously: Bhabha insists upon representing his ideas in a certain manner. What is your attitude to Bhabha's style? Is it part of his overall critical strategy, or does it problematise it? What might he hope to achieve in writing in such a compact and challenging way? (You might want to compare Bhabha's writing to Said's and weigh up their strengths and weaknesses. What kinds of readership might each figure be aiming at, or able to engage with?)

Think further about ambivalence and mimicry. If Bhabha is correct in identifying how colonial discourses create the conditions for their own critique, then even the most fiercely argued or confident Orientalist tract will not be immune from splitting and ambivalence. This view avoids some of the pitfalls of Said's notion of Orientalism perhaps, especially the charge that Said's book offers no way of thinking or theorising a critique of colonial discourses. However, if colonial discourses are endlessly split, anxiously repetitive and menaced by mimicry, as Bhabha would have it, we might want to ask: how could colonialism survive for as long as it did? Do you think that Said's account of the institutionalisation and self-perpetuation of Orientalism is a better model for thinking about the *effects* of colonial discourses?

In the light of the ideas we have considered in this chapter thus far, we are now in a position to recap the key elements of colonial discourses that might also resource our reading practices. We have seen how colonial discourses are characterised in part by their attempts to constitute and perpetuate the many colonised peoples, lands and cultures as one subjugated and unequal part of an asymmetrical binary relationship of power – between East and West, Orient and Occident, colonised and coloniser. But these attempts are not straightforward and do not necessarily operate smoothly or without critique. According to Bhabha, the discourse of colonialism is buckled by its internal contradictions that make it a profoundly precarious and ambivalent affair. As others have claimed, rarely does it occur without meeting opposition or encountering challenging ways of seeing. Indeed, an array of different ways of regarding colonialism can appear within seemingly Orientalist writings.

Colonial discourses and Rudyard Kipling: reading 'The Overland Mail'

Let us turn to a literary example in order to put into practice some of the ideas we have gathered. In this concluding section we will look at a poem by Rudyard Kipling called 'The Overland Mail'. The poem is reproduced in the Appendix (pp. 315–316), and you should read it now a couple of times before continuing.

Why Kipling, and why this poem in particular? Kipling was born in India in 1865 and, although educated in England, spent much of his time as a young man in the country of his birth, which was also at the same time Britain's largest colony in the Empire. His life coincided with a period of history when the Empire was at its zenith in the late nineteenth and early twentieth centuries. In addition to India, Kipling lived in and travelled among many colonial locations, such as Canada, New Zealand and South Africa. His literary works speak often of the countries he witnessed, the people he met and witnessed, the colonial administrations and shipping lines that kept the wheel of Empire turning. He died in 1936.

As Benita Parry claims, 'Kipling is an exemplary artist of imperialism' (*Postcolonial Studies: A Materialist Critique*, Routledge, 2004, p. 130). This statement is not as straightforward as it might first appear. As Parry considers, the wealth of Kipling's work 'can be made to reveal both imperialism's grandiloquent self-presentation and those inadmissible desires, misgivings and perceptions concealed in its discourses' (p. 131). To make this point less elegantly, we might say that Kipling's writing can be approached on the one hand as demonstrating the attitudes and self-certainties of colonial discourses, but also on the other hand as betraying an array of other sensitivities which, in the play of the literary text, offer alternative and less certain vistas. This makes a reading of his work especially inviting in the context of our exploration of colonial discourses.

First published in 1886 in the second edition of his collection *Departmental Ditties*, 'The Overland Mail' concerns the transportation of letters to British exiles in India who are residing in the Indian hill stations. These were popular retreats for those who found the Indian climate intolerable through the summer months. The most popular, Simla, often grew to three times its population when the British beat their annual retreat from the heat. Kipling's poem looks in particular at the 'foot-service to the hills', the journeys undertaken by Indian runners employed to carry mail from the railway station to the exiles.

I have chosen this short poem for several reasons. First, it makes interesting remarks about the Indian landscape through which the Indian runner who carries the mail must move. Second, its subject is in part the Indian runner himself, the 'colonised subject' of colonial discourses. Third, as Peter Keating argues in his book *Kipling the Poet* (Secker and Warburg, 1994), 'The Overland Mail' is not 'simply a celebration of the postal service: it is also one of Kipling's most joyful endorsements of imperial endeavour, with the postal activity offered as a microcosm of the far-flung Empire' (p. 21), so it would seem ripe for reading as a manifestation of Orientalism. However, using Bhabha's ideas, I want to examine how even this 'joyful endorsement' of Empire is more anxious and ambivalent than Keating suggests, and think about (following Parry's argument) any troublesome desires, misgivings and perceptions it may also secrete.

Let us deal first with the depiction of the Indian landscape. The poem begins as dusk falls. The Indian runner has received the post from the railway and will be undertaking his journey by night, in darkness. In the first stanza there is created the sense that the landscape which lies ahead is not going to be hospitable. It is referred to bluntly as a 'Jungle' (l. 2), and the poet warns of 'robbers' and 'tigers' that must 'make way' for the mail to be delivered in the 'Name of the Empress of India', Britain's Queen Victoria. India is represented as containing formidable obstacles to the delivery of mail from the homeland to the exiles in the hills, which must be overcome if the messages are to get through safely.

But once the runner's journey gets underway, even more challenges appear to bar the passage of the mail. In the third stanza torrents of water threaten the runner's path, rainfall has the potential to destroy roads, and the possibility of tempests is also entertained. Nature is represented as dangerous and destructive, a malignant force, hazardous and unaccommodating. The higher the runner ventures, the more precarious his surroundings seem, as evidenced in the fourth stanza. From the less threatening locations that feature rose-oaks and fir trees, he journeys upwards to the more precarious rock-ridge and spur. A less menacing, arduous landscape is reached only in the last stanza, when the mail is delivered to the exiles in the hill station. Now 'the world is awake and the clouds are aglow' (l. 28), and the sun has come out to shine on the successful runner. Everything is calm again. The disconcerting tigers and Lords of the Jungle that mysteriously roam in the first stanza are, in the final one, substituted by the comparatively less sinister 'scuffle above in the monkey's abode' (l. 27). The journey has been completed successfully. The mail has arrived safe and sound.

Using the ideas of Said and others, there are at least three significant observations we can make about the landscape. First, it is remarkably empty. Where is everyone? As the novelist Salman Rushdie once remarked, it is virtually impossible to view any landscape in India, however 'remote' it might seem, that is devoid of people. But in the poem, apart from the roaming Lords of the Jungle and the odd tiger turning tail, the only human characters mentioned are the Empress of India (who appears as a symbolic invocation rather than in flesh and blood), a vague body of 'we exiles', barely glimpsed, the retreating robber and the runner himself. This is a depopulated landscape. The only figures who feature are those significant to the British in the Indian hills and who either maintain or threaten the smooth running of their postal service. In presenting this part of India as a wilderness of obstacles, an ominous, anonymous jungle, Kipling virtually empties it of indigenous Indians. This depiction of the landscape is clearly mediated by the limited perception of the British and shapes a particular and selective envisioning of space.

Second, and following on from the previous point, until we reach the calm of the British in the hills the following morning, India seems wild and out of control. It appears in the main as dark, menacing and dangerous; full of tempests and floods where even the roads are vulnerable. The association of the exiles in the hills with the break of day, and an untamed India with the dangerous night, is exactly the kind of opposition which Said suggests is common to Orientalism: where there is Western civilisation there is daylight, but a sinister darkness resides otherwise.

Third, as we might expect in a poem about a foot-service to the hills, the landscape progressively rises, taking the runner up higher and higher. Reading this figuratively, we could argue that the poem's movement up through the landscape rehearses in microcosm the conquest of India by the British. In the poem, India's various wild aspects stand in the way of an easy passage; yet, on the other side of the rivers, ravines and rock-ridges we find the exiles patiently waiting for their mail. The landscape may be troublesome, but ultimately it has not stopped the ascent of the British up the hills. They have already defeated these imposing surroundings, have met in the past the challenges presented by the landscape and overcome them, challenges that the Indian runner rehearses every time he delivers the mail. The exiles' residence in the hills seems all the more impressive when one realises what has been previously negotiated in order to establish it. Similarly, the geography of the poem seems to applaud the conquering British. If, like the runner, one moves 'up, up through the night' of a wild, dark undomesticated India, one comes to the civil daylight of British colonial rule. The hill station sits above the surrounding landscape like the Empress of India sits over her subjects, looking out across a landscape that may be wild, yet has been conquered and is under British command.

So, we can detect a pattern of asymmetrical oppositions underpinning the landscape's representation: night vs. day, wild vs. civilised, below vs. above. The first term is associated negatively with India, the second with the civilising presence of the British. These oppositions would seem to support Said's argument that Orientalism divides the world into two opposing sides, in which the colonial location comes off the worst.

Let us turn next to the characters of the poem. There are at least two important figures we can consider. The first, referred to fleetingly, is the 'robber' in line 5; the second is the Indian runner. Although he is mentioned just the once, the robber is not the marginal figure in this poem that he seems. At an immediate level, he appears as one of the various dangers of the wild landscape of India that the runner must avoid when delivering the mail to the exiles. If we presume that the robber is also an Indian (the poem does not explicitly state this, but the reference to the 'brawny, brown chest' suggests an Indian runner), here, then, are the split positions commonly available to the 'colonised subject' in colonial discourses. The colonised is either the dangerous, brigandly *other* of colonialism, challenging the order of Empire by stealing the mail; or he is the domesticated *obedient* servant of the Empire, like the runner who provides the foot-service to the hills. No other positions are recognised (hence, perhaps, the depopulated landscape).

At first glance, it might seem that the runner is represented in a sympathetic light. He lets nothing stop the delivery of his mail. He seems competent, reliable and trustworthy. Here perhaps is a sympathetic representation of a colonised subject which, as John MacKenzie argued, Said's *Orientalism* ignores. Indeed, there is a certain sense of camaraderie between the speaker of the poem and the Indian runner. But let us probe more closely the relationship between the speaker and his subject. The runner is given no name of his own, save that of the important baggage he delivers. He is significant only as the facilitator of the Overland Mail; he has no other purpose. Furthermore, notice how in the vocabulary of the poem the runner is made subservient to the compulsion of the exiles. In the third stanza, the speaker repeats 'must' on three occasions when describing the passage through the foreboding landscape. The runner 'must' ford the river, he 'must' climb the cliff, and he 'must bear without fail' the Overland Mail. Any fortitude on the part of the runner is seen not to be due to his own virtues, but as the product of the colonial service that commands him to perform his actions. Indeed, the speaker anticipates the runner to be a rather pusillanimous creature in his statement that 'the service admits not a "but" or an "if"' (l. 16), almost as if he is expecting the runner to complain about his task. The suggestion is, perhaps, that the true nature of the runner tends towards faint-heartedness; only his service to the Empire makes him an admirable, athletic fellow capable of performing laudable feats. Furthermore, this service is a life-sentence, as suggested by the sinister phrase: 'While the breath's in his mouth, he must bear without fail' (l. 17). The runner is compelled to undertake his duties, it seems, so long as he has life in his body.

At this point too, you might also like to think if the depiction of the runner's body might have a distinctly *erotic* element to it: what sort of appreciation is being nurtured for this brave, valiant runner with 'soft-sandalled feet' and 'brawny, brown chest' (l. 22), who heroically conquers torrents and tempests? To use a pun which the poem perhaps unwittingly intends, is the speaker attracted to this overland male whom is described in exquisite detail? The allegedly sympathetic representation of the runner maybe has been triggered by particular kinds of motives and desires which both sexualise as well as domesticate him as a servant who satisfies the needs of the colonisers.

In these terms, the poem enacts the disciplining power of colonialism by rehearsing the runner's subservience both to the will of the exiles and to the speaker's power of representation. This point is cemented by the poem's final line, when the runner hails the exiles with 'In the name of the Empress, the Overland Mail!' (l. 30). In declaring his arrival, the hail repeats in part the poem's opening line and thus underlines the extent to which he is perpetuating through his own mouth the language of the Empire by upholding the authority of the Empress of India. Read in this way, the runner has been thoroughly domesticated as the obedient servant of the Empire.

So far, in looking at the landscape and the Indian runner, we have read 'The Overland Mail' as exemplifying various Orientalist assumptions and strategies of representation. But as we remarked when holding Said's notion of Orientalism up to question, colonial discourses are often more ambivalent than resolute in their aims. Despite Keating's claims about it, we can perhaps identify certain anxieties in Kipling's poem that threaten to make its endorsement of Empire rather unsteady.

In order to make this reading, let us draw upon Bhabha's argument concerning the ambivalence in the discourse of colonialism which is linked to the simultaneous attempt to reduce *and* maintain the otherness of colonised subjects. In the poem, this double movement is indexed by the contrast between the runner and the robber which we glimpsed in the first stanza. As we noted, in the robber we have the colonised who exists as *other* to the West, threatening by his very occupation to disobey its rules, while the runner signifies the domesticated colonial subject. Significantly, the beginning of the poem attempts to banish the robber from the landscape by referring to him retreating into the anonymity of the 'Jungle'. Yet, we could argue that the threat of the robber is *never entirely banished*, but instead haunts the speaker's representation of the runner throughout the poem. The roles of runner and robber are not so easily kept apart, and they threaten to merge. The messages entrusted to the colonised need not get safely given back to the British. The speaker anxiously recognises that the colonised have the potential for subversion – a recognition which he attempts to disavow.

The day-to-day business of the Empire commands the obedience of the Indian subjects, requiring that they become trusted runners, not malevolent robbers. The mail could not get delivered without them and messages would not get through. In these terms, the speaker's repeated demand that the runner 'must' ford, 'must' climb and 'must bear without fail' the Overland Mail *so long as there is breath in his body* seems overstated to say the least. These repetitions reveal perhaps a half-hidden anxiety that the civilised, obedient runner has the potential to slip into another less civil role. Paradoxically, in stating that the service 'admits not a "but" or an "if"' to be uttered by the runner, the speaker actually acknowledges the very possibility of disobedience that threatens the exiles' survival abroad. This acknowledgement serves, on the one hand, to justify the runner's subservience to Empire, but on the other, it makes the unsavoury recognition that the runner has the potential to subvert order. Thus, he has to be *repeatedly* told what to do and how to behave. Hence, the repetition of the speaker's commands ('must' ... 'must' ... 'must') in the third stanza is an anxious, imperfect attempt to fix the obedience of the colonised subject and jettison these uncertainties – but one that unavoidably reveals the capacity for disobedience.

Note too that the runner's travails mimic the journey of the British into the hills, and his cry 'In the Name of the Empress, the Overland Mail!' (l. 30) also mimics the speaker's lines which conclude stanzas 1 and 3. There is, perhaps, something menacing in the runner's duplication of the colonisers' journey to the hills, exposing the resemblance of the Indian's endeavours with that of the British. Maybe his journey makes him not so different from the colonisers themselves? That final cry of 'the Overland Mail!' merges the runner's voice with the speaker's, and in so doing it conflicts with those aspects of the poem that attempt clearly to separate out one from the other through the disciplinary strategies we noted above. Exactly what kind of message is the runner delivering at the end of the poem? Is he endorsing the superiority of the British or revealing his similarity to them? Does he bring a menacing moment of Anglicised resemblance, one which is uneasily disavowed in the poem, appearing as the domesticated mimic man: almost the same, *but not quite*? Note that by the final stanza, the runner's body has almost been removed from the poem's vista. He has become a 'dot' or a 'speck', barely visible to the eye. Yet he exists both within and beyond representation: the jingle of his bells and his voice endure, perhaps to menace and mock the civility of the British in the hills who cannot receive their messages without his labour. Ultimately, *he* brings the name of the Empress of India to *them*, reversing and unnerving the power relations between the colonising British and the colonised runner, obeying yet escaping their representation and authority.

So, following Bhabha, we might argue that the runner is an ambivalent figure in the poem, both praised and commanded, congratulated yet disciplined, elided yet audible, trustworthy yet potentially inconstant. His presence is vital to the exiles' survival in the hills, but also creates anxieties because of the perceived threat he may pose to its smooth running. These anxieties emerge in the repetition of the speaker's commands which, in both acknowledging and disqualifying the runner's potential for disorder, ultimately split the authority and confidence of the speaking voice. The threat to authority epitomised by the robber is not as easily banished as the poem would prefer. Read in this way, Kipling's seeming celebration of the obedient colonised subject begins to seem begotten by anxieties that result from the recognition and disavowal of the colonised's capacity for *disobedience*. Although an 'Orientalist' reading of the poem might usefully expose its deployment of latent Orientalist views in the manifest matter of the writing, the latter points we have considered attend to those moments when colonial discourses seem to be splitting and sliding ambivalently between contrary vistas, perhaps even malfunctioning and short-circuiting.

Contesting the (continuing) agency of colonial discourses to constitute and define the world requires that we expose their assumptions, contradictions and shortcomings, and reveal how their seemingly 'factual' depictions of reality are a product of the combination of power and knowledge, not truth, and are often connected to half-hidden fears and fantasies. Remembering the point I made in the Introduction that postcolonialism is something which one *does*, we might conclude that our critical approach to and comments about 'The Overland Mail' constitute a specifically *postcolonial* reading practice.

Selected reading

Ahmad, Aijaz, *In Theory: Classes, Nations, Literatures* (Verso, 1992).
    Chapter 5, 'Orientalism and After', is an extended critique of Said from a
    staunchly Marxist position.
Ashcroft, Bill and Pal Ahluwalia, *Edward Said* (Routledge, 2001).
    An excellent introductory guide to Said's many scholarly works and
    ideas, which includes a highly recommended chapter on *Orientalism*.
Bhabha, Homi K., *The Location of Culture* (Routledge, 1994).
    Chapter 3, 'The Other Question: Stereotype, Discrimination and the
    Discourse of Colonialism', includes Bhabha's engagement with Said's

Orientalism and is one of his most influential pieces on the function of ambivalence; Chapter 4, 'Of Mimicry and Man', theorises the menacing propensities of mimicry. Proceed with patience.

Childs, Peter and Patrick Williams, *An Introduction to Post-Colonial Theory* (Harvester Wheatsheaf, 1997).

Features two clear chapters on the work of Said and Bhabha, and is a good place to continue with your beginnings.

Huddart, David, *Homi Bhabha* (Routledge, 2006).

A clear and very useful account of Bhabha's influential work that deals with his key concepts patiently and intelligently.

Huggan, Graham, *Interdisciplinary Measures: Literature and the Future of Postcolonial Studies* (Liverpool University Press, 2008).

Chapter 12, '(Not) Reading Orientalism', playfully and inventively looks across the critical response to *Orientalism* in postcolonial studies.

Kabbani, Rana, *Imperial Fictions: Europe's Myths of Orient* (Pandora, rev. 1994).

An excellent study of travel writing and painting which details the centrality of gender in Orientalist representations.

Loomba, Ania, *Colonialism/Postcolonialism*, second edition (Routledge, 2005).

Includes a long, patient section which covers colonial discourses.

McClintock, Anne, *Imperial Leather: Race, Gender and Sexuality in the Colonial Contest* (Routledge, 1995).

A fascinating and influential study which pursues the centrality of representations drawn from a wide cultural terrain to the workings of colonial authority.

MacKenzie, John M., *Orientalism: History, Theory and the Arts* (Manchester University Press, 1995).

A highly sceptical critique of *Orientalism* which argues that East/West encounters were not always part of the unequal power relations of colonialism. MacKenzie illustrates his argument with a wealth of different cultural endeavours ranging from art to theatre.

Mills, Sara, *Discourses of Difference: An Analysis of Women's Travel Writing and Colonialism* (Routledge, 1992).

Gives a useful theoretical critique of Said's *Orientalism* and offers close analyses of women's travel writing in relation to Orientalist representations.

Moore-Gilbert, Bart, *Postcolonial Theory: Contexts, Practices, Politics* (Verso, 1997).

Includes long, detailed chapters on the work of Said and Bhabha which is attentive to their shifting affiliations with different critical theorists. Highly recommended.

Parry, Benita, *Postcolonial Studies: A Materialist Critique* (Routledge, 2004).
Chapter 2, 'Problems in Current Theories of Colonial Discourse', was first published in 1987 and (having been revised) remains the most penetrating critique of the ideas we've raised in this chapter. There is also an excellent critique of Bhabha in Chapter 4, 'Signs of the Times', while Parry's judicious engagement with Kipling in Chapter 8 is both instructive and challenging.

Porter, Dennis, '*Orientalism* and its Problems' in Patrick Williams and Laura Chrisman (eds), *Colonial Discourse and Post-Colonial Theory* (Harvester Wheatsheaf, 1993), pp. 150–61.
An early but still very useful critique of *Orientalism* which is recommended as you continue making your beginnings in the study of colonial discourses.

Said, Edward W., *Orientalism*, second edition (Penguin, 1995).
The second edition of Said's 1978 book includes an important 'Afterword' in which he addresses many of the criticisms of his book and discusses the relationship between *Orientalism* and postcolonialism.

Said, Edward W., 'Orientalism Reconsidered' in *Reflections on Exile and Other Literary and Cultural Essays* (Granta, 2000) pp. 198–215.
An early response to the initial academic reception of *Orientalism*, collected with Said's other occasional writings.

Thomas, Nicholas, *Colonialism's Culture: Anthropology, Travel and Government* (Polity, 1994).
Chapter 2, 'Culture and Rule: Theories of Colonial Discourse', includes a far-reaching (if these days conventional) critique of Bhabha's thinking on the grounds of its lack of attention to specific historical and geographical contexts.

Young, Robert J. C., *White Mythologies: Writing History and the West* (Routledge, 1990).
Includes a helpful and clear critique of both Said and Bhabha in terms of their relation to Marxism and poststructuralism.

Young, Robert J. C., *Postcolonialism: An Historical Introduction* (Blackwell, 2001).
Chapter 26, 'Edward Said and Colonial Discourse', looks across the various critiques of Said's work and critically considers his appropriation of Foucault's model of discourse.

3

Nationalist representations

Introduction

In the previous chapter we examined colonial discourses in relation to writings from the colonial period. In this and several of the following chapters we will explore many of the different strategies with which the authority of colonialism and colonial discourses has been combated. This chapter and the next are concerned with representations related to anti-colonial nationalism and their impact upon political, social, cultural and literary contexts. Attitudes to nationalism in postcolonialism are wide-ranging and conflicting. As our immediate concern in these two chapters is to become sensitised to the possibilities and problems surrounding nationalist representations when reading postcolonial texts, we need to examine some of the different views which have emerged.

In this chapter we will approach various attitudes towards nationalist representations in literary and other writings during the busy period of decolonisation in the 1950s and 1960s. There were, of course, nationalist representations in previous periods, particularly in the settler colonies, such as those by the Australian writers Henry Lawson and A. B. 'Banjo' Paterson in the 1890s (see *Empire Writing: An Anthology of Colonial Literature, 1870–1918*, ed. Elleke Boehmer, Oxford World's Classics, 1998, which gathers together a variety of writing about Empire from several contrasting perspectives during the period of British 'high imperialism' in the late nineteenth and early twentieth centuries). However, we will confine ourselves mostly to later-twentieth-century discussions of nationalism because several of the most salient writings on nationalism from this period in particular have been of critical significance to postcolonial theory. In the following chapter, 'The Nation in Question', we shall examine some critical perspectives of nation and nationalist representations in the light of the mixed fortunes of anti-colonial nationalism in certain countries since the achievement of independence.

But first, we need to think about the nation in more general, abstract terms before examining its use as a profitable idea mobilised by many struggling to free themselves from colonial authority. This will allow us to explore at the end of this chapter Ngugi wa Thiong'o's novel *A Grain of Wheat* (1967) as one kind of postcolonial nationalist representation.

Imagining the nation: forging tradition and history

Nations are not like trees or plants: they are not naturally occurring phenomena. Yet the nation has become one of the most important modes of social and political organisation in the modern world and these days we perhaps assume that nations are simply 'just there'. Most commentators agree that the idea of the nation is Western in origin. It emerged with the growth of Western capitalism and industrialisation and was a fundamental component of imperialist expansion. It is almost second nature these days to map the world as a collective of different nations, each separated from the other by a border. But borders between nations do not happen by accident. They are constructed, crossed, defended and (in too many tragic cases) bloodily contested by warring groups of people. It is important that we come to think about nations fundamentally as fabrications. As Ernest Gellner argues in his book *Nations and Nationalism* (Blackwell, 1983), '[n]ations are not inscribed into the nature of things' (p. 49). Nations, like buildings, are designed by people and built upon particular foundations – which means that, like buildings, they can also rise and fall.

Instead, let's think about the nation first and foremost as an idea. It has become customary in postcolonial studies to talk about the 'myth of the nation' in recognition of this. In his influential book *Imagined Communities: Reflections on the Origins and Spread of*

Nationalism, second edition (Verso, 1991), Benedict Anderson defines the nation primarily as 'an imagined political community' (p. 6). This is because 'the members of even the smallest nation will never know most of their fellow-members, meet them, or even hear of them, yet in the minds of each lives an image of their communion' (p. 6). Individuals come to *think* they are part of a greater collective, that they share a 'deep, horizontal comradeship' (p. 7) with many others. In a similar vein Timothy Brennan points out in his essay 'The National Longing for Form' (in *Nation and Narration*, ed. Homi K. Bhabha, Routledge, 1990, pp. 44–70) that the nation refers 'both to the modern nation-state and to something more ancient and nebulous – the "natio" – a local community, domicile, family, condition of belonging' (p. 45). So, central to the idea of the nation and part of its imaginative foundations are notions of collectivity and belonging, a *mutual* sense of community that a group of individuals imagines it shares. These feelings of community are the emotive foundation for the organisation, administration and membership of the 'state', the political apparatus which enforces the social order of the nation.

It is often pointed out that a sense of mutual belonging is manufactured by the performance of various *traditions*, *narratives*, *rituals* and *symbols* which stimulate an individual's sense of being a member of a particular national collective. As Eric Hobsbawm has argued, the nation depends upon the invention of national traditions which are made manifest through the repetition of specific symbols or icons. The performance of national traditions helps secure in place an important sense of continuity between the nation's present and its past, and assists in concocting the unique yet ultimately fabricated sense of a *shared history* and *common origins* of its people. Nations homogenise: they fashion unity and togetherness. They often traffic in highly revered symbols that help forge a sense of its particular, idiosyncratic identity in which the nation's people come to emotionally invest. Reviewing the history of European nations since the eighteenth century, Hobsbawm notes that

> entirely new symbols and devices came into existence as part of national movements and states, such as the national anthem (of which the British in 1740 seems to be the earliest), the national flag (still

largely a variation on the French revolutionary tricolour, evolved
1790–4), or the personification of 'the nation' in symbol or image,
either official, as with Marianne and Germania, or unofficial, as in the
cartoon stereotypes of John Bull, the lean Yankee Uncle Sam or the
'German Michel'. (Eric Hobsbawm, 'Introduction: Inventing
Traditions' in *The Invention of Tradition*, ed. E. Hobsbawm and T.
Ranger, Cambridge University Press, 1983, p. 7)

The emergence of national symbols such as the flag or the national
anthem are part of the 'invention of tradition' in which all nations
participate: the repeated performance of rituals, events or symbols
that take on an emotive and semi-sacred character for the people. As
Arjun Appadurai explains, nations cohere imaginatively by using 'a
system of semiotic recognition and communication, composed of
such simple items as flags, stamps, and airlines' (*Fear of Small
Numbers: An Essay on the Geography of Anger*, Duke University
Press, 2006, p. 25). Think of how the burning of a nation's flag as a
form of protest is often a highly provocative act. Such idiosyncratic
symbols serve as focal points around which a large number of people
gather emotionally and imaginatively as a single, national body.

If the invention of tradition is central to the nation, then so is the
confection and narration of its *history*. Nations are often
underwritten by the positing of a common historical narrative that
enshrines the common past of a collective people. The nation has its
own historical account which posits and explains its origins, its
individual character and the victories won in its name. In reality,
there are as many potentially different versions of history as there
are narrators; but a national history legitimates *one* particular
version of the past as the only one that matters. In many national
histories, certain events are ritually celebrated as fundamental to the
nation's past fortunes and present identity, which directly connect
the narration of history with the repeated performance of those
symbols and icons mentioned a moment ago. Think about the
annual commemoration of events such as Independence Day (4
July) in the United States, Guy Fawkes Night (5 November) in
Britain, or Freedom Day (27 April) in South Africa. Each looks back
to an occasion that is considered a defining moment in the history of
the nation, the celebration of which helps cement the people's
relationship with their past as well as highlights their togetherness

in the present by gathering them round one emotive symbol, such as a flag or the burning of the Guy on the bonfire. Similarly, individual figures are often identified heroically as the chief agents of the story of the nation: great leaders, scientists, martyrs, writers, generals or admirals. The common currency of these perceived extraordinary public figures helps the nation's history assume a degree of intimacy and become like a 'story of the tribe', providing the people with a shared sense of a common past, a myth of origins and a collective identity in the present.

In talking about the nation as a concept, then, we are dealing with something which bridges material and emotional realms, political and psychological phenomena: keep in mind Brennan's remark about the nation as naming a political mechanism but also forging a 'condition of belonging', a way of feeling and identifying oneself. That heady combination of the spheres of authority and affect has contributed greatly to the remarkable impact of the nation during European modernity, anti-colonial resistance and postcolonial critique.

To get the measure of just how inordinately powerful are the feelings stimulated by evocative national symbols, and how they intertwine with far-reaching matters of power and authority, consider an example offered by the Jamaican writer Mervyn Morris in his essay 'Feeling, Affection, Respect' (in *Disappointed Guests: Essays by African, Asian and West Indian Students*, ed. H. Tajfel and J. L. Dawson, Oxford University Press, 1965, pp. 5–26). Morris's essay records his impressions on his first journey to England, by boat, in the 1960s:

> I learnt the fundamental lesson of nationalism ... half an hour away from England, approaching the cliffs of Dover. There was excitement among the English on board. I looked, but the cliffs seemed very ordinary to me. And then I realised that of course the cliffs are not cliffs: to the Englishmen they are a symbol of something greater, of the return from a land of strangers, of the return home. Nothing is more important in nationalism than the feeling of ownership. (pp. 25–6)

'A symbol of something greater': with this phrase, Morris exposes the cultural workings of the imagining of the nation and its emotional reach. The symbolic suggestiveness of the cliffs functions to bond the travelling coincidence of the English, who all respond similarly to what they see. The same emotive reaction occurs throughout a coincident body of people because it is customary for them to associate these 'ordinary' cliffs with something specific. The cliffs of Dover have long been an important symbolic location in the imagination of the English, and their symbolic importance was heightened during the Second World War in popular songs which afforded a new performance of an old myth. When viewing the cliffs in the 1960s, the English 'see' more than inert, blank chalk. United for a moment by the sight they share, they are in the presence of an important element of the national imaginary. Additionally, the cliffs also function as a border, a 'first sight' of England that marks the distinction between the world outside and within the nation. Because of his vantage point at one remove from the all the excitement as a Jamaican visiting a new country, Morris does not see at first sight what is so obviously 'there' for the English, and his recollection reminds us that the wonder of the cliffs is entirely mythic. As he reminds us, the cliffs of Dover are, after all, just ordinary cliffs. But it is what they have been *made to mean* which matters, as this example exposes.

Morris's remarks also point to the ways in which the symbolic freight of nationalist representations helps nurture a sense of *legitimate tenure*, a feeling of justifiable ownership which links the people to a landscape. As we will think about more in a moment, this issue poses particular problems for the act of colonial settlement. But to remain at a more abstract level for the moment, note how Morris is alert to how the symbolic associations of the cliffs of Dover stimulate a vital sense of *possession*: the English feel that they belong to the land and that the land belongs to them. Or, to use one of the most simple-sounding yet actually most complex of concepts, the ship-bound English feel that they are heading for *home*.

STOP and THINK

If you have any stamps, coins or banknotes in your pocket that have been issued by a national government, take them out and have a look at them. What 'great' figures, buildings, inventions, leaders, etc., do they depict, and what might this tell you about the image of the nations they help convey? How is national collectivity, history or tradition confected via such choice symbolic resources?

In a similar fashion, choose a nation different to the one(s) you identify with and try to list the key symbols you would associate with it. Where are they generally to be found? What do they relate to? Can you discover how they were first produced? How do the nation's people revere such symbols? Have any new ones appeared in recent years?

The point of asking these questions is to get us thinking about the myth of the nation, its imagining and its symbolic resources, all highly influential in postcolonial studies. But how taken are you with this way of conceiving of the nation in the first place?

Language, space, time

As Benedict Anderson argues in *Imagined Communities*, a defining feature of the nation is the standardisation of *one unitary language* that all members can understand and with which they communicate. Although people from different parts of the nation may use regional variations, and indeed in some cases different languages, in theory all of the nation's people have the means to use a standard language which enables them to deal with each other despite their individual differences. The issue of the nation's unitary or standard language is a notoriously difficult one, and some have noted that actually it is exceptional for a nation to have just one language – while the issue of language standardisation becomes even more complex in countries with a history of colonialism, as we shall see in Chapter 4. But for now, it is important that we begin to understand the relationship between nation, people and language: the combining of a common language with the idea of a *national* language remains a very powerful assumption, regardless of how possible it is to establish or observe in action. As Anderson would have it, the notion of a national language is a key mode of collectivity which services the unifying propensity of the nation.

Anderson's work on the imagined community of the nation also deals with the *style* in which the nation is narrated and represented, and this involves producing further assumptions about the *space* and *time* of the nation. He argues that the imagining of the nation displays specific features exemplified by two particularly modern forms of writing: the realist novel and the daily newspaper. Each 'provided the technical means for "re-presenting" the *kind* of imagined community that is the nation' (*Imagined Communities*, p. 25). Or, to put this differently, the assumptions made about space and time in these two modes of writing are duplicated in the ways nations are imagined. How so?

Nations tend to gather a variety of people into one collective body, but it is highly unlikely that one person will ever meet all of his or her fellow nationals. Similarly, in most novels rarely will every single character meet everybody else. Anderson notes that in realist novels the multitude of characters are none the less bounded by *space* and *time*. They are connected by the same encircled, fixed landscape within which they all simultaneously exist. Also, the diverse activities of characters take place according to the same temporal scheme: the steady, onward movement of calendrical time epitomised by the ticking of the second hand on the clock. (It does not matter if the novel's temporal passage seems to speed up or slow down: it is the *authority* of linear time that matters, not necessarily its rate.) In reading novels we sometimes notice different characters, unaware of each other's existence, performing separate activities at the same time. Here's the opening of Chapter 9 of George Eliot's novel *Middlemarch* (1874): 'When George the Fourth was still reigning over the privacies of Windsor, when the Duke of Wellington was Prime Minister, and Mr Vincy was mayor of the old corporation in Middlemarch, Mrs Casaubon, born Dorothea Brooke, had taken her wedding journey to Rome'. Although these figures never all meet up in the novel, their activities are taking place 'meanwhile', at the same time, along the same temporal plane, so that we are able to imagine a diverse and multifarious cross-section of English life bounded by its *simultaneity.*

These simultaneities of space and time are also at work in the form of the daily newspaper. Newspapers create communities from coincidence. They provide news of manifold events that have often inadvertently occurred at roughly the same time, within the cycle of twenty-four hours. These events are further bounded by their occurrence in a location presumed to be of common and primary interest to readers: it will usually be assumed that, say, an Irish reader of an Irish newspaper in Cork will be more immediately concerned with a fatal traffic accident in Dublin than a light aircraft collision in Colombo. The division of many national newspapers' contents into a home section and then an overseas or world section (with the former usually coming first and getting more coverage) helps install a sense of national circumscription and collectivity. As Anderson further explains, the *act of reading* the newspaper is also something of a ritual which endorses the imagining of the nation's community. When we read the paper at breakfast, or on the way home from college or work, we are tacitly aware that possibly thousands of fellow nationals are doing exactly as we are, at precisely the same time. We perform a collective custom.

The simultaneities of space and time exemplified in the formal properties of the novel and the newspaper are at the heart of the ways by which national subjects consider themselves part of a national community, and build an identity informed by the national imaginary. As Anderson's work boldly underlines, like novels and newspapers, nations are narrations through which individuals come to consider themselves as belonging to

> a solid community moving steadily down (or up) history. An American will never meet, or even know the names of more than a handful of his ... fellow-Americans. He has no idea what they are up to at any one time. But he has complete confidence in their steady, anonymous, simultaneous activity. (p. 26)

Steady, anonymous, simultaneous – Anderson's vocabulary reflects the robust and orderly foundations upon which the myth of the nation rests. It promises structure, shelter and sequence for individuals, cementing a 'deep, horizontal comradeship' which unites the many into one imagined community through the function of *specific styles of narrative*.

There is one further important element that is often fundamental to nationalist representations: constructions of otherness. We thought in the previous chapter about the creation of 'others' when considering the construction of differences between the allegedly civilised Occident and savage Orient. Every definition of identity is always made *in relation* to something else, a perceived other. The drawing of imaginative borders between nations – borders which then become real in their policing and patrolling – is fundamental to the legitimacy of the nation, and borders formulate the distinction between the nation's people and those others outside and beyond. But as we shall see in the next chapter, the imaginative construction of the nation's borders is a process fraught with difficulties; and this, along with its propensity to construct others, has all too often been its undoing.

Let us review these ways of thinking about the nation as a 'myth':

- Nations are imagined communities.
- Nations gather together many individuals who come to imagine their simultaneity with others. This unified collective is the nation's 'people'.
- Nations depend for their survival upon the invention and performance of histories, traditions and symbols which sustain the people's specific identity continuously across past and present.
- Nations can evoke powerful feelings of identity, belonging, home and community for the people.
- Nations stimulate the people's sense that they are the rightful occupants and owners of a specific landscape.
- Nations mobilise a unitary language theoretically accessible to all the people.
- Nations rely on a style of narration that promotes the unities of space and time.
- Nations draw up borders that separate the people 'within' from other peoples outside.

National liberation vs. imperialist domination

So far we have begun to grasp how, in Paul Gilroy's words, nations are created 'through elaborate cultural, ideological and political processes which culminate in [the individual's] feeling of connectedness to other national subjects and in the idea of a national interest that transcends the supposedly petty divisions of class, region, dialect or caste' (*Small Acts: Thoughts on the Politics of Black Cultures*, Serpent's Tail, 1993, p. 49). These feelings of con-nectedness have proved a valuable resource to many anti-colonial movements, which have turned to the nation and nationalism as primary resources in contesting European colonial settlement.

Tamara Sivanandan has pointed out that anti-colonial nationalism historically functioned 'as an instrument of cultural resistance against a racist colonial discourse which had long denied all cultural value to its subject peoples, claiming them culturally incapable, therefore, of ruling themselves in the modern world' ('Anticolonialism, National Liberation, and Postcolonial Nation Formation' in *The Cambridge Companion to Postcolonial Literary Studies*, ed. Neil Lazarus, Cambridge University Press, 2004, p. 49). John Thieme also attends to the 'positive force' of anti-colonial nationalism in reminding us that its various versions across the colonised world 'assert[ed] people's rights to self-determination and freedom from oppression' (*Post-Colonial Studies: The Essential Glossary*, Arnold, 2003, p. 182).

Historically, the myth of the nation has proved highly potent and productive in forging effective resistance to colonialism. It was popular with a variety of independence movements because it served many of their intellectuals and leaders as a valuable ideal behind which anti-colonial endeavours could collect and unite. Speaking in 1970, Amilcar Cabral, a leading figure in the independence movement in Guinea-Bissau, described the contemporary conflict within several African colonies (as, indeed, it was in many other colonies throughout the world previously) as one of 'national liberation in opposition to imperialist domination' (see Amilcar Cabral, 'National Liberation and Culture' in *Colonial Discourse and Post-Colonial Theory*, ed. Patrick Williams and Laura Chrisman, Harvester Wheatsheaf, 1993, pp. 54–5). If colonialism had condemned millions to a life of subservience and dispossession, then anti-colonial nationalisms promised a new dawn of independence, suffrage and political self-determination for colonised peoples. Many colonies were represented in this period as nations-in-chains, shackled by the forces of colonialism, whose peoples had been alienated from the land which was their rightful possession and which would be returned to them once independence dawned.

Two important observations need to be made next. First of all, it is imperative to realise that the various anti-colonial nationalisms across the colonised world – in Africa, South Asia and the Americas, for example – were not necessarily identical. As the editors of *Nationalisms and Sexualities* (ed. Andrew Parker, Mary Russo, Doris Sommer and Patricia Yaeger, Routledge, 1992) explain, 'there is no privileged narrative of the nation, no "nationalism in general" such that any single model could prove adequate to its myriad and contradictory historical forms' (p. 3). While many anti-colonial nationalist movements drew inspiration from each other, the cultural and historical specifics of each struggle meant that the 'derivative discourse' of nationalism was rendered different in each case (we shall explore this phrase in Chapter 4). Second, anti-colonial nationalist movements often accepted and worked with the national territorial borders that *had not necessarily existed* prior to the advent of European colonialism and were often invented by the colonising nations. For example, at the Berlin Conference of 1884–5 the Western powers divided up many African lands between them by drawing imaginary borders around various parts of the continent. In some cases they divided indigenous tribal lands; in others the new colonial national boundaries contained African peoples from different tribes with their own belief-systems and languages who collectively did not share an imagined sense of comradeship. The borders of colonial Nigeria established in 1914 circumscribed the lands of peoples who belonged variously to the Yoruba, Hausa, Kanuri and Igbo tribes. In making and imposing such borders, many Western powers reorganised African political space. These borders were not ones that indigenous colonised peoples would have recognised. So in calling for national liberation from colonialism, many anti-colonial nationalisms were working with a map of the world drawn by the colonisers.

The appropriation of these imposed constructions of the nation by anti-colonial independence movements certainly was an expedient and enormously effective manoeuvre in their various struggles for freedom. But they also created several problems. In the settler colonies, for example, colonial settlement had proceeded by denying the legitimacy of 'Aboriginal peoples' claims to the land. The colonisation of Australia was underwritten by the assumption that this South Pacific land mass was *terra nullius*, meaning that it belonged to no-one. As Alice Brittan describes, '[t]he judgement that Australia was *terra nullius* meant not only that the British could claim legal sovereignty over the entire continent, effectively declaring the Crown as the new and undisputed owner, but also that they did not need to negotiate any formal treaties with the Aborigines. Why would one make a deal with people who never held title to the land in the first place?' ('Australasia' in *The Routledge Companion to Postcolonial Studies*, ed. John McLeod, Routledge, 2007, p. 73). As the Australian settlers began to agitate for self-determination in the late nineteenth century and create their own myths of the Australian nation, the assumption of *terra nullius* was not necessarily revoked. As Bob Hodge and Vijay Mishra argue, the new 'national myth' of Australia remained silent on the dispossession of the Aborigines and 'accommodate[d] this major threat to national legitimacy only by not mentioning the matter' (*Dark Side of the Dream: Australian Literature and the Postcolonial Mind*, Allen and Unwin, 1991, p. xiii). For these reasons, settler nationalisms were perhaps not too remote from colonialist discourses, in that the interests of indigenous inhabitants of places such as Australia, New Zealand and Canada were not taken into account in constructions of the nation. Indeed, the assumption that Australia was *terra nullius* was revoked only as recently as 1992 as a consequence of the 'Mabo Case' when the High Court of Australia recognised that Aboriginal peoples had the legal right of 'native title' to the land.

In those colonies where indigenous peoples organised themselves into anti-colonial nationalist movements, in Africa, South Asia and elsewhere, differences of tribe, region and caste were suspended but not surpassed, while gender hierarchies complicated the establishment of 'deep, horizontal comradeship' which gathered different individuals together on an equal footing. Such fault lines and problems suggest that Amilcar Cabral's counterpointing of national liberation against imperialist domination simplifies a more complex situation in more than one historical and cultural context; indeed, and as we shall consider in Chapter 4, even the most militant anti-colonial nationalisms might not be as remote as we might think from the coercive structures of domination they aim to vanquish.

None of this should distract us from the fact of the effectiveness and success of anti-colonial nationalisms across the world, as well as the contribution to postcolonial thought that nationalist-minded intellectuals made in conceptualising transformative modes of resistance (which is the theme of the rest of this chapter). But we do need to keep in mind that imagining a sense of simultaneous national identity for, or amidst, the often heterogeneous groups of people in the colonies has always had to face several challenges. How, then, did writers and intellectuals in the post-war period set about forging national consciousness during this busy period of decolonisation? There are only two (influential) responses we have time to look at in the remainder of this chapter: the first is Negritude, while the second emerges from Frantz Fanon's work on national consciousness and national culture.

Negritude

Although not strictly a national formation, Negritude is useful to explore at this juncture as it was a particularly powerful mode of dissidence used to forge 'deep, horizontal comradeship' between colonised peoples. We might say that it was national*ist* in its design, if not distinctly national in its reach. And it importantly influenced the development of thinking about nationalism and nationalist consciousness which could occasionally contend with some of Negritude's assumptions.

Negritude has been influential in Africa, the Caribbean and America as a mode which enables oppressed peoples to imagine themselves as a particular and united collective. Today it is most often associated with the work of two Francophone writers and statesmen, Aimé Césaire and Léopold Senghor, although they were not its only exponents. As we shall see, Negritude worked with many of the central tenets of the 'myth of the nation'. One of its aims was to unite peoples living in different places through a sense of shared ancestry and common origin, and it retained a distinctly pan-national and indeed pan-continental set of aims. Its significance as an important means of mounting anti-colonial resistance in the twentieth century should not be underestimated, even if it is today less sympathetically regarded than it once was.

Aimé Césaire was born in the French Caribbean colony of Martinique. He came to Paris in the 1930s to study, where he met fellow-student Léopold Senghor, from the French African colony of Senegal. Despite their very different backgrounds, Césaire and Senghor found themselves commonly identified in France as *nègres*, a derogatory insult that approximates to the racist term 'nigger' in English. Outraged at the colonialist and Orientalist attitudes held by the French towards their colonised subjects, and energised by the heady intellectual and artistic environment of Paris, Césaire and Senghor fought back at derogatory views of black peoples in their writing by presenting the condition of being black as profoundly valuable. Whereas colonial discourses frequently represented black peoples as primitive and degenerate, having no culture of any worth, the Negritude writers wrote in praise of the laudable qualities of black peoples and cultures.

Colonial discourses are almost always racist discourses. They frequently evoke blackness as the visible sign of the colonised's degeneracy, and make skin colour the ultimate sign of 'racial' difference. In the nineteenth century, throughout Europe it was commonly believed that the world's population existed as a hierarchy of 'races' based upon skin colour, with white Europeans deemed the most civilised and black Africans as the most savage. According to Robert J. C. Young, 'it was through the category of race that colonialism itself was theoretically focussed, represented and justified' (*Colonial Desire: Hybridity in Theory, Culture and Race*, Routledge, 1995, p. 180). The legacy of this negative sense of blackness is still apparent in the English language today. Think of how many expressions there are in which 'black' is used pejoratively, as in 'black market', 'black balled', or 'black sheep' (the writer Benjamin Zephaniah plays soberly with these resonances in his poem 'White Magic' from the collection *Propa Propaganda*, Bloodaxe, 1996). Negritude was an attempt to rescue and reverse blackness from its definition always in negative terms. Blackness was reconstructed as something positive and valuable, behind which black peoples throughout the world could unite as one body.

At the heart of Negritude was the celebration of blackness, but this was about much more than the colour of skin. 'Blackness' as it was addressed by the Negritude writers enveloped a whole way of life grounded in perceived unique African qualities. For Senghor, Negritude was a project that attempted to return a sense of dignity and value to black peoples and their cultures. Whereas colonial discourses had dismissed African cultures as 'backwards' and 'primitive', in his prose and poetry Senghor celebrated their sophistication and special qualities. Black Africans, he argued, simply had a different relationship with the world than Europeans did, and this influenced how they apprehended reality and represented it in their art. African art was just as aesthetically beautiful as the most treasured works from Europe – it was unjust of the West to consider African culture as 'primitive'.

In pursuing these arguments, Senghor made claims about the specific qualities to be found in all people of black African descent, whether they lived in Africa or had (been) moved elsewhere. For example, in 1962 he argued that Europeans studied reality from the coolly detached vantage of clinical scientific observation. However, black Africans had a more intuitive relationship with the world:

> The African is as it were shut up in his black skin. He lives in primordial night. He does not begin by distinguishing himself from the object [of study], the tree or stone, the man or animal or social event. He does not keep it at a distance. He does not analyse it. Once he has come under its influence, he takes it like a blind man, still living, into his hands. He does not fix or kill it. He turns it over in his supple hands, he fingers it, he *feels* it. The African is one of the worms created on the Third Day ... a pure sensory field. (Léopold Senghor, *Prose and Poetry*, ed. and trans. John Reed and Clive Wake, Oxford University Press, 1965, pp. 29–30)

These intuitive qualities manifested themselves in things like 'emotional warmth' and a 'natural' sense of rhythm. '[W]hen I am watching a game of football', wrote Senghor, 'I take part in the game with my whole body. When I listen to jazz or to an African song, I have to make a violent effort of self-control (because I am a civilised man) to keep myself from singing and dancing' (p. 31). In this sentence, 'civilisation' stands for Senghor's Western education which has impoverished his existence, divided himself from himself, and made himself suppress his instinctual responses because they are not deemed to be acceptable behaviour in France.

Senghor urged all those of black African descent to realign themselves with these special, unique qualities, to embrace their 'characteristics of the African soul' with pride and dignity. As he put it in 1956, 'the spirit of African civilisation animates, consciously or unconsciously, the best Negro artists of to-day, both in Africa and America' (p. 76). Like these artists, all black peoples were compelled to restore their dignity 'by animating this world, here and now, with the values that come to us from our [African] past' (p. 78). Hence, as he defined it, Negritude

> is the awareness, defence and development of African cultural values. Negritude is a myth, I agree. And I agree that there are false myths, myths which breed division and hatred. Negritude as a true myth is the opposite of these. It is the awareness by a particular social group of people of its own situation in the world, and the expression of it by means of the concrete image. (p. 97)

True myths, shared values, the identification of a collective 'particular social group' – in these ideas we can discern how Senghor images a community in a fashion which recalls the construction of the nation and its people. Even though he argued fervently that Negritude was more than skin deep, drawing its resources from the cultural treasures of 'Mother Africa', the concrete image which clinched a sense of unity was ultimately the racialising notion of blackness itself.

Césaire's notion of Negritude was a little different to Senghor's. Because of his birth in Martinique, Césaire grew up at a distance from Africa, both physically and imaginatively. On the one hand he was descended from the African slaves that had been brought to the Caribbean to work, but on the other hand he had never lived in Africa and could not know it like Senghor. His Africa was learned second-hand from books and friends, 'an Africa of the heart' as one critic has described it (A. James Arnold, *Modernism and Negritude*, Harvard, 1981, p. 29). The recovery of an African past as a source of values and renewal was more problematic for black people in the Caribbean. Consequently, Césaire's version of Negritude was based much less on the perceived instinctual or essential differences between whites and blacks. He understood Negritude primarily as something to be measured 'with the compass of suffering'. This meant that black people were united more by their shared *experience* of oppression than by their essential qualities as 'Negroes'. That said, it is also fair to argue that Césaire's work is ambivalent towards the issue of the essential differences between white and black people and is marked by a tension between perceiving Negritude as grounded in instincts or in historical experiences.

Césaire's version of Negritude is best exemplified by his influential poem *Cahier d'un retour au pays natal* (*Notebook of a Return to My Native Land*), published in 1939 and revised several times in the proceeding decade. In what follows we will use the English translation by Mireille Rosello and Annie Pritchard (Bloodaxe, 1995).

Combining Caribbean history with African myth and French Surrealism, *Notebook of a Return to My Native Land* was inspired by Césaire's anticipation of, and reflections on, his return from France to Martinique in the late 1930s. A long, complex and inspiring poem, it is not easy to summarise. The 'native land' of the title is both Martinique and Africa, as Césaire muses upon the connections and disjunctions between these different yet historically linked locations. He reveals the investment that Martinique's black population has in African culture, but does *not* advocate a simple return to Africa (emotionally, culturally, physically) as a salve to colonialism's ills. The narrator speaks out with memorable force against the sorry condition of Martinique's black peoples, subservient to the 'whip's corolla' of colonial order; he chastises blacks (and himself) for accepting too readily the white condemnation of blackness; but he also celebrates black people's perceived valuable aspects that have lain inert during their confinement by colonialism. He urges the black population of Martinique to unite as one and realise themselves specifically as a people within the Caribbean, with their own histories and predicaments. In forging a sense of collective identity they can join the fight with other oppressed peoples around the world against their subjugation. This sense of solidarity through suffering is captured in these famous lines:

> As there are hyena-men and panther-men, I shall be a Jew-man
> a kaffir-man
> a Hindu-from-Calcutta-man
> a man from-Harlem-who-does-not-vote (p. 85)

Oppressed peoples discover their unity in the simultaneity of their suffering, rather than with recourse to a common ancestral past (African or otherwise), although that past also remains a resource for the present. Only when this solidarity is struck can their imprisonment by white Europeans be challenged. Césaire's engagement with Negritude demonstrates the different pathways down which it developed, away from some of the more overtly 'racial' models of anti-colonial dissidence.

It is too quickly forgotten these days that Senghor and Césaire were passionate humanists, and that the long-term aim of Negritude was the emancipation of the entire human race, and not just black peoples, from its subjugation to colonial thought. To be sure, in the short term Negritude offered a way of uniting oppressed black peoples and defying their representation in colonial discourses through the reappropriation of colonialist models of 'race'. But both writers saw as the ultimate goal of Negritude the emancipation of *all* peoples from the sorry condition of colonialism. Although Senghor claimed that European and African cultures were fundamentally different, his ultimate aim was a dynamic synthesis of all cultures that would one day exist outside of the invidious power relations of colonialism. Césaire too wrote with the purpose of promoting universal emancipation.

STOP and THINK

Constructions of Negritude have several potential sticking points that we need to consider in order to assess their strengths and weaknesses. Let us think critically about four:

1. *Negritude inverts the terms of colonial discourses*. It was a familiar trope of colonial discourses that black peoples were mysteriously 'closer to nature' than white Europeans – hence their tendency towards 'savagery'. The Negritude writers countered this view by accepting but *celebrating* their 'elemental' nature, as evidenced by Senghor's comments on intuition and rhythm quoted previously. However, his association of black peoples with 'primordial night' is problematic in that Senghor seems to accept the colonial stereotype of blackness and work with it *inversely*, rather than reject it as arbitrary and specious. For many critics, Negritude did not sufficiently *question* the negative associations of blackness, choosing instead to redeploy them as positives. Negritude is weakened as a transformative revolutionary force because it continues to traffic in colonial stereotypes, not least in the association between 'race' and skin colour. If colonial discourses make skin colour the ultimate mark of the racial degeneracy of the other, then how revolutionary is it to make blackness into the concrete sign of cultural difference and political resistance?

2. *Negritude upholds separatist binary oppositions*. Negritude used the binary distinctions between white and black, African and European, common to many colonial discourses. Although Senghor and Césaire wanted universal synthesis between all people, their philosophies can lead to separatism by dangerously endorsing the racialising conclusion that an individual's destiny is mystically connected to their colour.

3. *Negritude is nostalgic for a mythic African past*. Negritude often posited a 'golden age' of pre-colonial Africa from which black peoples had been separated by colonialism, and to which they must return. This was, to a degree, one of the

great strengths of Negritude, in that it posited a denial of and an affront to colonial representations of African history and culture. Senghor argued for a return to an African spirit, while for Césaire 'return' meant the importance for Caribbean blacks to forge a connection with their ancestral home of Africa. However, less productively, these 'returns' sometimes depended upon the construction of a mythic precolonial African past before the time of colonialism which was free from the ills of the present. But as demonstrated in novels such as *Things Fall Apart* (Heinemann, 1958), by the Nigerian writer Chinua Achebe, such a 'golden age' of perfection never really existed.

4. *Negritude has very little to say about gender differences and inequalities*. In his celebration of African women, Senghor argued that their primary roles were 'the source of the lifeforce and guardian of the house, that is to say, the depository of the clan's past and the guarantor of its future' (*Prose and Poetry*, p. 44). For this reason, 'the African woman does not need to be liberated. She has been free for many thousands of years' (p. 45). But many black women have challenged this view and fought to free themselves from this view of them as primarily domestic, filial people, content with 'keeping house'. As some critics have argued, if Negritude makes a myth of Africa's past, it is very much a *male* myth. It united black peoples around a *masculinist* representation of blackness and cared little for the internal unequal relations of gender.

A word of caution. It is one thing to assess, and perhaps dismiss, a previous mode of anti-colonial resistance because it does not fit current critical attitudes. As a consequence of some of the problems raised above, Negritude is today much less popular than it was. In recent years it has lost popularity and credibility because it is considered to have accepted too uncritically many of the terms of colonial discourses, reversing them rather than challenging them. But any anxieties we might have over the design of such modes should not distract us entirely from remaining sensitive to their historical impact. To express this point proverbially: we do not always want to throw out the historical baby with the conceptual bathwater. To my mind, Negritude achieved much as a political and cultural agent of change, for all of its apparent shortcomings. It provided a means of inspiration in forging unity among oppressed peoples, and offered a different way of conceiving of African history and culture which refused colonial representations. Do you think its conceptual weaknesses should override any approval of its revolutionary agency?

Frantz Fanon, national culture and national consciousness

As we noted in Chapter 1, Frantz Fanon has become a hugely important figure in the field of postcolonialism and is central to any discussion of the theorising of anti-colonial resistance. As we observed previously, in 1953 he was appointed as head of the Blida-Joinville Hospital in Algeria at a time when the Algerians' struggle against France for national independence was mounting. Deeply affected by his experiences of racism in North Africa during the war, and politicised by his work with Algerian patients who suffered mental torment as a consequence of their subjugation to a colonial power, Fanon eventually resigned his post to fight alongside the Algerians for independence and became a leading figure in their struggle. Hated in France, he survived numerous attempts on his life during the 1950s before falling ill with leukaemia. During his illness he worked on his important book *The Wretched of the Earth* (trans. Constance Farrington, Penguin Classics, [1961] 1967), moving first to Russia and then eventually to America, where he died in December 1961. His body was shipped to Algeria and buried on the Algerian battlefield.

Fanon's writings cover a range of areas and have been influential in a number of fields, such as psychiatry, philosophy, politics and cultural studies. In postcolonial studies, his work has been significant as providing a way of conceptualising the construction of identity under colonialism (something we touched upon briefly in Chapter 1), and as a way of configuring the relationship between nation, nationalism, national consciousness and national culture in an anti-colonial context. As regards the latter, his rendering of the role of the 'native intellectual' – writer, thinker, philosopher – in the struggle for national independence is particularly important.

Fanon's exploration of many issues to do with the nation forms part of *The Wretched of the Earth*, and we shall look first at a chapter entitled 'On National Culture' (pp. 166–99 of the aforementioned Penguin Classics translation). Originally it was a statement made at the Second Congress of Black Artists and Writers in Rome in 1959, where Fanon stressed the urgent responsibility of writers and intellectuals to forge new forms of national culture as part of the contribution to the development of the people's national consciousness. National consciousness was something other than unthinking nationalist fervour – it was a particular and important concept in his writing which is bound up with national culture. In 'On National Culture' he described things thus: 'If culture is the expression of national consciousness, I will not hesitate to affirm that ... it is the national consciousness which is the most elaborate form of culture' (pp. 198–9). If national consciousness was 'the all-embracing crystallisation of the innermost hopes of the whole people' (p. 119), then national culture was the aesthetic expression of such hopes.

Fanon's work dealt closely with the nature and dynamism of national consciousness, which was something rather distinctly different to racial consciousness advocated by Negritude. It rejected the call for nostalgic celebrations of a mythic African past and advocated a more dynamic and vacillating relationship between the past and the present. Fanon understood the objectives of Negritude and recognised its urge uncritically to champion indigenous cultures in defiance of colonialist discourses. If Negritude was ultimately a 'turn backwards' (p. 175), it was still a necessary and painful step towards emancipation. But because Fanon's ideas were influenced more by Marxist notions of revolution, his theorising of the resistance to colonialism ultimately refused an uncritical notion of an African past, the universal and unhistorical idea of the 'Negro', and the pan-national collective aspirations of Negritude. Instead, national culture and national consciousness were historical, dynamic things, fashioned by the people under particular conditions and circumstances.

Taking as his focus the operations of colonialism in a specifically

African context, 'On National Culture' begins with Fanon's important critique of Negritude and the native intellectual. The term 'native intellectual' refers to the writers and thinkers of the colonised nation who have often been educated under the auspices of the colonising power. Consequently, the Western-educated native intellectual is in danger of identifying more with the middle-class bourgeoisie of the *colonising* nation than with the *indigenous* masses. This complicates the role which the native intellectual plays in contributing to the people's anti-colonial nationalist struggle. According to Fanon, like the Negritude writers the native intellectual at first refuses the view that colonised peoples had no meaningful culture prior to the arrival of the colonisers. Hence, '[t]he past is given back its value' (p. 170) by the native intellectual who comes to cherish all that colonialism dismisses as evidence of barbarism. However, Fanon is dissatisfied with the pan-national focus of this initial retort to colonialism. He notes how native intellectuals have, in the past, attempted to cherish a *generalised* pan-African culture in their resistance to colonial ways of seeing. But this tendency 'to speak more of African culture than of national culture will tend to lead them up a blind alley' (p. 172). This is because the historical circumstances of African peoples in different parts of the globe cannot be so readily unified. To create an abstract notion of a pan-African culture is to ignore the different conditions of African peoples in a variety of locations, such as in America or the Caribbean. Negritude might promise unity, but it is a unity based in false premises, he asserts. African and African-descended peoples face different challenges in a variety of locations at any one moment in time:

> Negro-ism therefore finds its first limitation in the phenomena which take account of the formation of the historical character of men. Negro and African-Negro culture broke up into different entities because the men who wished to incarnate these cultures realised that every culture is first and foremost national, and that the problems which kept Richard Wright or Langston Hughes [in America] on the alert were fundamentally different from those which might confront Léopold Senghor [in Senegal] or Jomo Kenyatta [in Kenya]. (p. 174)

'Every culture is first and foremost national': in this statement Fanon clearly routes the production of a revolutionary culture through the primary unit of the nation, as it seems to enable the native intellectual to address the *specific* historical circumstances and challenges of one *particular* colonised location.

The construction of a specifically national consciousness (we need always to distinguish this term from national*ism* per se) is dependent in part on important cultural activities. National consciousness and national culture are inseparable from each other; anti-colonial resistance requires them both if it is to be truly revolutionary. Intellectuals have a vital role to play in contributing to the struggle, as Fanon indicates in describing their formulation of a distinctly national culture as moving through three distinct phases.

In the *first phase*, the native intellectual attempts what Fanon calls 'unqualified assimilation' (p. 179). This means that he or she is inspired by and attempts to copy the dominant trends in the literature of the colonising power. In so doing the cultural traditions of the colonised nation are ignored as the native intellectual aspires to mimic and reproduce the cultural fashions of the colonising power. The native intellectual becomes damagingly estranged from the indigenous masses, identifying more with the colonising power rather than with those suffering the effects of colonialism.

In the *second phase*, the native intellectual grows dissatisfied with copying the coloniser and instead becomes immersed in the cultural history of the people. In this phase he or she 'turns backwards' and recalls all things indigenous. Fanon calls this the literature of 'just-before-the-battle' (p. 179) when the native intellectual begins to reflect on the past of the people. However, he or she still stands apart from the mass of the people and maintains 'exterior relations' (p. 179) with them only. In lauding their cultural traditions uncritically, the native intellectual becomes too concerned with cherishing and speaking for the past and ignores the people's struggles in the present. The native intellectual is in danger of fiddling while the country burns. Indigenous cultural traditions are venerated as if the very fact of their existence is enough to challenge the derogation of the colonised. But, as Fanon memorably points out, '[y]ou will never make colonialism blush for shame by spreading out little-known cultural treasures under its eyes' (pp. 179–80). Glorifying the cultural achievements of the past is not enough. Rather, a new way of mobilising inherited culture is required, one that puts it *actively* to work rather than *passively* on display. This involves the native intellectual connecting better with the people and being drawn into closer proximity to their condition and endeavours.

This brings us to the *third phase*, or 'fighting phase' (p. 179), in which the native intellectual becomes directly involved in the people's struggle against colonialism. In this phase, he or she becomes conscious of his or her previous estrangement from the people and realises that '[i]t is not enough to try to get back to the people in that past out of which they have already emerged' (p. 182). Rather than cherishing inert cultural traditions, a more *dynamic* relationship is forged between the cultural resources of the past and the struggle against colonialism in the present. It is in this dynamic encounter that a revolutionary national culture is made, and it is the native intellectual's responsibility to help make it. Traditional culture is mobilised as part of the people's fight against oppression and, consequently, *is transformed in the process*. If the native intellectual wishes to stay in step with the people and be meaningfully involved in the struggle, he or she must participate in the active reinterpretation of traditional cultural resources in the present with the aim of opening up the possibility of a new future. Fanon gives the example of oral storytellers who transform their work in order to participate in the forging of a national consciousness:

> The oral tradition – stories, epics and songs of the people – which formerly were filed away as set pieces are now beginning to change. The storytellers who used to relate inert episodes now bring them alive and introduce into them modifications which are increasingly fundamental. There is a tendency to bring conflicts up to date and to modernise the kinds of struggle which the stories evoke, together with the names of heroes and types of weapons. (p. 193)

It is worth dwelling upon the way in which Fanon configures the relationship between the native intellectual and the people. The native intellectual has *to learn from the people* to modify, reinterpret and reform traditional culture at the service of forging a new national consciousness in which the people's struggle is the bedrock. The creative act cannot be solitary; the native intellectual cannot be a remote figure, displaced from the people. New, unusual forms of artistic expression emerge in this phase that both contribute and bear witness to the dynamism of the people and their gathering for change. In acting as a kind of conduit for the forging of revolutionary culture, the native intellectual is no longer a rarified individual whose intellectual life seems remote from ordinary folk, but part of a wider transformative movement.

We can see, then, that Fanon emphasises national culture as a vital, unstable matter that is always being made and re-made. He calls for a radical 'break-up of the old strata of culture, a shattering which becomes increasingly fundamental' (p. 88). He concludes by underlining the central role culture has to play in creating the conditions for a national consciousness that can overcome colonialism and lay the foundations for a newly, and truly, independent nation. The struggle against colonialism 'in its development and in its internal progression sends culture along different paths and traces out entirely new ones for it' (p. 197). It is the responsibility of the native intellectual to pursue these paths to the future and hence participate in the burgeoning national culture, rather than retrace the steps back to an ossified and inert past which takes him or her away from the dynamism of the people's struggle.

Crucial to Fanon's articulation of national culture, then, is his sense of culture as dynamic and responsive to historical circumstances. There can be no return to an idealised notion of culture, as risked by Negritude; nor do the nation's masses take their cue from Western-educated native intellectuals or succumb to a 'top down' system of elite intellectual authority. Rather, native intellectuals are schooled by the people and must take the struggle as their guide in forging national consciousness and culture. The result will be *unique to the moment of production* rather than a repetition of pre-existing cultural forms, and one which helps unite the intellectuals and the masses.

Fanon's representation of the native intellectual falls somewhere between a descriptive and prescriptive account: it is a vision of what he regards as happening in the decolonising world, as well as what needs to happen. His rendering of this figure is an important attempt to keep co-ordinated the activities of the people and the endeavours of the native intellectual, and as such it tacitly acknowledges that it is by no means an easy affair. Because of their education and status as intellectuals, schooled in part by their encounter with colonising culture, native intellectuals inevitably stand in a particular relationship with the people. When we turn soon to consider Ngugi's *A Grain of Wheat*, we will think about the ways in which the native intellectual as writer can both broker the national consciousness and culture of the people but also stand in a critical relation to them too; and this should help us think about the challenges involved in co-ordinating the native intellectual and the people. But before we get there, we need also to think next about how Fanon remained troubled by the tensions which persisted between Western-educated natives and the people, especially in the realms of political leadership and government.

In his essay 'The Pitfalls of National Consciousness' (also in *The Wretched of the Earth*, pp. 119–65), Fanon warns of the dangers ahead for colonised nations if those who come to occupy positions of power in the nation betray the people in the interests of the privileged few. His argument for the construction of a national consciousness that reflects the will of the people applies both *before* and *after* independence – indeed, the success of the newly independent nation relies upon the maintenance of national con- sciousness once colonialism has formerly ended. The achievement of self-determination through the people's struggle is a first step, not a conclusive victory; the fledgling nation must conduct itself in the best interests of the people if all are to remain permanently free not just from colonial government, but also from colonial systems of authority and colonialist discourses. A nationalist victory against colonialism means little if it does not secure the future of national consciousness and transform the nation once independence has been realised. Little is achieved if the old seats of colonial government are simply occupied by a new indigenous elite.

Fanon warns that the newly independent nation can be placed in jeopardy by the activities of what he terms the educated national middle class whose self-interests conflict with those of the people, and who prefer to align themselves with Western interests rather than act on behalf of the people. In his view:

> In an under-developed country an authentic national middle class ought to consider as its bounden duty to betray the calling fate has

marked out for it, and to put itself to school with the people: in other words to put at the people's disposal the intellectual and technical capital that it has snatched when going through the colonial universities. But unhappily we shall see that very often the national middle class does not follow this heroic, positive, fruitful and just path; rather, it disappears with its soul set at peace into the shocking ways – shocking because anti-national – of a traditional bourgeoisie, of a bourgeoisie which is stupidly, contemptibly, cynically bourgeois. (pp. 120–1)

Here, Fanon is engaging with the issue of *neo-colonialism*: the perpetuation of a nation's subservience to the interests of Europe, supported by an indigenous elite, after colonialism has formally ended. He outlines how the newly independent nation may be administered by an indigenous middle class that uses its privileged education and position cheerfully to replicate the colonial administration of the nation for its own financial profit. This class is 'neo-colonial' in that it continues to exploit the people in a way not dissimilar to the colonialists. It is a situation where, in Fanon's words, 'the national bourgeoisie steps into the shoes of the formal European settlement' (p. 122). The new administration does little to transform the nation economically. It does not set up new industries, or tend to the needs and condition of the people, or redistribute wealth. It does not govern in the interests of the people. Instead it keeps the new nation economically linked to the interests of the old colonial Western powers by allowing foreign companies to secure lucrative contracts in the new nation, by continuing to send profits, goods and materials abroad rather than focus on improving the material existence of the people, by fashioning the new nation into a tourist destination for wealthy Westerners whose ability to spend retains their power over native life. The national middle class profit from these manoeuvres but this wealth never reaches the people, who remain powerless and in poverty. A nation that remains economically dependent on the West, and that treats its people in this way, cannot call itself truly free from the mechanisms and interests of colonialism. (We might want to recall here the point made in Chapter 1 that colonial settlement is only one mode of imperialism, and the West's imperial ambitions can continue after colonialism has finished.)

With some venom, Fanon condemns those he sees as betraying the people's struggle: 'because it lives to itself and cuts itself off from the people, undermined by its hereditary incapacity to think in terms of all the problems of the nation as seen from the point of view of the whole nation, the national middle class will have nothing better to do than to take on the role of manager for Western enterprise, and it will in practice set up its country as the brothel of Europe' (p. 123). Fanon warns that the achievement of independence is not an end but a beginning, one that brings fresh challenges for the fledgling nation. A consciousness grounded in the collective revolutionary energies of the people must continue to set the terms of the nation's conduct after the nation gains the right to self-determination. The nation must not be hijacked by an indigenous middle class which acts like the previous colonial regime and does little to further the interests and conditions of the people. As with the construction of national consciousness, intellectuals and writers have an important role to play in maintaining this vigilance after power has been seized.

Nationalist discourses, national culture

Without wishing to conflate theories of Negritude and Fanon's work on national culture, national consciousness and its pitfalls, it is fair to say that each makes available to colonised peoples several important resources in their struggle against colonialism. We might recap these as follows:

- They assert the rights of colonised peoples to make their own *self-definitions*, rather than be defined by the colonisers.
- They offer the means by which divergent peoples within a colonised nation can co-ordinate *solidarity* across cultural, educational and class differences.
- They *value* the cultural inheritance and current endeavours of colonised people in defiance of colonial discourses, and can use them for revolutionary purposes.
- They offer the means to identify and build *alternative* histories, cultural traditions and knowledges which conflict with colonialist representations.

- With particular reference to Fanon, the advocacy of national consciousness via the forging of national culture looks forward to a future for the newly independent nation which is *meaningfully* free of neo-colonial Western influence, materially and culturally.

In his work on role of the native intellectual and of national culture in the forging of national consciousness, Fanon provides us with a way of thinking about how cultural activities, such as literary creativity, are bound up with the wider political struggles of decolonisation. In a number of erstwhile colonies during and just after the various moments of decolonisation in the history of Empire, writers clearly conceived of their role in wider national terms (some deliberately so, having read Fanon) and thought about the ways in which their work might contribute to decolonising the mind. As the Nigerian writer Chinua Achebe famously remarked in his 1964 lecture 'The Novelist as Teacher' (in *Hopes and Impediments: Selected Essays 1965–87*, Heinemann, 1988, pp. 27–31), '[h]ere then is an adequate revolution for me to espouse – to help my society regain its belief in itself and put away the complexes of the years of denigration and self-denigration' (p. 30). Postcolonial writing could indeed be revolutionary: culturally, psychologically and consequently in political terms too.

C. L. Innes has provided an overview of postcolonial writers' contribution to the moulding of national consciousness in her essay ' "Forging the Conscience of Their Race": Nationalist Writers' (in *New National and Post-Colonial Literatures: An Introduction*, ed. Bruce King, Clarendon Press, 1996, pp. 120–39), and it is useful to review her argument not least to get the measure of the longstanding relationship between postcolonial writing, the nation and national consciousness. Innes looks at the work of writers such as W. B. Yeats in Ireland; Senghor, Achebe and Wole Soyinka in Africa; and Joseph Furphy in Australia. She discovers a set of similar concerns in each, generated no doubt by the fact that different groups of pro-national writers 'were caught up in a similar dialectic, wherein the metropolitan imperial power categorises all "other" groups in opposition to its own self-image' (p. 122). Innes notes several characteristics in much nationalist writing which used

European languages and literary forms (although she demonstrates at length the important differences which also exist between the work of this diverse body of writers), which we might summarise as follows.

First, argues Innes, nationalist writers asserted 'the existence of a culture which was the antithesis of the colonial one' (p. 123). This often meant celebrating the derogatory characteristics assigned to them in colonial discourses. Second, they emphasised the relationship between the people and the land in order to underline the illegitimate intrusion of the colonisers, asserting a 'unity between people and place' (p. 124). Third, there was a tendency in some nationalist writing to gender representations of colonial domination and nationalist resistance. Several nationalist texts featured plots which involved the conflicts of fathers and sons, through which is figured the patriarchal authority of coloniser and resistances to it. This went hand in hand with the feminisation of the nation as a motherland (a problematic issue we will be addressing at length in the next chapter).

Innes's observations reveal the extent of the overlap between nationalist representations made in more overtly political discourses which we have looked at in this chapter and the central concerns of much literary discourse in a variety of locations particularly during times of transition from colonial subservience to political independence. We are going to conclude this chapter by looking at how we might read closely just one literary text as constructing and exploring national consciousness, by using the concepts discovered in this chapter to inform our reading practices and priorities. In addition, this will help anticipate our examination of the postcolonial critique of the nation, and the insoluble *problems* of nation and nationalist representations, which are the subject of the next chapter.

Constructing national consciousness: Ngugi's *A Grain of Wheat*

Ngugi wa Thiong'o's novel *A Grain of Wheat* (1967) concerns the achievement of Kenyan independence ('Uhuru') on 12 December 1963. It explores several issues that have been raised in this chapter: how a writer contributes to the forging of national consciousness by engaging with the people's struggle; the process of forging national symbols as well as its pitfalls; the challenge of independence; the danger of neo-colonialism.

Ngugi wa Thiong'o was born in Kamarithu, Kenya, in 1938. He studied at Makerere University College in Uganda in the early 1960s, and at the University of Leeds, UK, between 1964 and 1967 during which time he wrote *A Grain of Wheat*. He returned to Kenya to work in the Literature Department at the University of Nairobi. On 31 December 1977 he was arrested and detained without charge by the Kenyan police until 12 December 1978. On his release he was not allowed to continue in his academic post, and in 1982 he left Kenya to enter a self-imposed exile (his next visit to Kenya would not be until 2004).

A Grain of Wheat is set during the four days leading up to Uhuru. Its central characters are members of the peasant community of Thabai Ridge, and through their memories Ngugi examines how the struggle for independence impacted on the ordinary lives of the people. Much of the novel occurs in flashback, and bears witness to the 'Mau Mau' rebellion against colonial rule. On 20 October 1952 a State of Emergency was declared in colonised Kenya and several leading members in the push for independence were arrested. As a consequence, many peasants left their homes and took to the hills where they waged a guerrilla war against the British. In Ngugi's novel we hear about the leading figures in the independence movement, such as Jomo Kenyatta, but only indirectly and as part of the wider memories of the central characters. This shows us that Ngugi's prime focus is on ordinary people, not their leaders.

So, Ngugi is following Fanon's lead in making the people the subject of his novel, and the fortunes of the Thabai community can be read as a mirror of the fledgling nation as a whole. As Ngugi writes in his essay 'Moving the Centre', the very choice of writing a novel in the 1960s that examined the lives of the people was part of a wider struggle 'to name the world for ourselves' (in *Moving the Centre*, James Currey, 1993 p. 3). His narrative constitutes a vital attempt to give voice to the people's evolving collective identity and history, and thus join the task of forging national consciousness. The novel's unnamed narrator specifically uses a 'collective' voice in the novel, often using such phrases as '[l]earned men will, no doubt, dig into the troubled times which we in Kenya underwent' (*A Grain of Wheat*, p. 131), and he locates himself as belonging to the people of Thabai in his comment that '[i]n our village and despite the drizzling rain, men and women and children, it seemed, had emptied themselves into the streets' (p. 203). In the following phrase the narrator characteristically speaks *for* the people and *to* the people: 'Most of us from Thabai first saw him at the New Rung'ei Market the day the heavy rain fell. You remember the Wednesday, just before Independence? Wind blew and the rain hit the ground at an angle' (p. 178). In terms of Fanon's work on national culture, the narrative voice of the text contributes to the construction of a national consciousness in its desire to articulate the people's hopes, activities and experiences on *their* terms.

This sense of forging a narrative of the people is borne out by the novel's representation of the Thabai villagers. *A Grain of Wheat* gathers the stories of a series of interrelated characters, none of which is granted the position of its primary hero or heroine (as we shall see, the very issue of heroic status is an important one in the novel). This is not simply a novel lauding an elite band of charismatic leaders. Ngugi's characters each have their own chequered past which we learn about through a series of flashbacks and memories. One of them, Kihika, has been killed by the time of Uhuru. Kihika is remembered as one of the heroes of the anti-colonial movement and had fought as a freedom fighter in the hills. He was betrayed to the colonial forces and subsequently murdered. Another key figure is Mugo. For much of the novel Mugo is believed to have sheltered Kihika while he was on the run. He is celebrated for this and for defending a female villager, Wambuku, from being beaten while digging a trench for the authorities, for which he is sent to a detention camp. He returns to Thabai a hero, but few suspect that he betrayed Kihika and caused his death.

Also sent to a detention camp was Gikonyo, a carpenter and husband of Mumbi, Kihika's sister. Initially a strong supporter of the anti-colonial struggle, Gikonyo freed himself from detention by confessing his oath of allegiance to the 'Movement'. His return to Thabai is marred by his discovery that Mumbi has borne a child to Karanja, his childhood rival and the colonialists' puppet Chief of

Thabai during the State of Emergency. Karanja betrayed those fighting for independence, and is wrongly believed by many to be responsible for Kihika's death. Jealous of Gikonyo's marriage to Mumbi, during the Emergency Karanja attempted to use his office to seduce Mumbi, who steadfastly refused his advances and remained committed to her absent husband. Only when she learned from Karanja that Gikonyo had been freed did she lower her defences, which Karanja ruthlessly exploited.

In many ways a formally complex and innovative novel, *A Grain of Wheat* still clearly promotes the unities of space and time that Benedict Anderson identifies as crucial to the imagining of the nation. It focuses on a specific location common to all the characters, Thabai village, and in the characters' memories we gain a sense of what each was doing during the same period of time.

The novel raises all kinds of issues relevant to the myth of the nation and the coming of independence; we shall touch only upon a few. Let us consider first Kihika, the freedom fighter. In some respects, Kihika has similarities with Fanon's figure of the native intellectual. His resistance to colonial authorities exemplifies Fanon's call for a *dynamic* use of past learning for present struggle. Kihika makes use both of ancestral learning and his colonial education to oppose colonial authority and forge national consciousness. We meet him early in the novel when Mugo remembers attending a rally in Rung'ei Market at which Kihika spoke. Kihika narrates to the crowd the story of the colonisation of the land by the British and early resistance to it, and calls for those at the rally to answer 'the call of a nation in turmoil' (p. 15). In mustering opposition he uses the resources of a Biblical quotation as well as an old proverb: '"Watch ye and pray", Kihika said, calling on his audience to remember the great Swahili proverb: *Kikulacho Kimo nguoni mwako*' (p. 15). The incident is typical of how Kihika inspires people by drawing upon *both* ancestral learning and the knowledge gained from his colonial schooling, and it aligns his resistance with Fanon's third 'fighting phase' of anti-colonial dissidence.

Let's consider this in more detail. As a boy Kihika attended a Church of Scotland school where he received a Christian education and became obsessed with the story of Moses and the children of

Israel. Kihika's knowledge of the Bible is used to resist the colonial teaching to which he has been exposed, by being reframed within indigenous knowledges and needs. The Bible was one of the chief resources that Christian missions used to condemn indigenous African religious practices and was often cited to legitimate the presence of the British in Africa, spreading Christian enlighten-ment in 'heathen' lands. Yet Kihika finds inspiration in the Biblical story of Moses which provides him with a way of rationalising and justifying Kenyan resistance. In effect he transforms a tool of the oppressors into the weapon of the oppressed. His sense of and support of his 'people' as revolutionary is derived from a mixture of Biblical education and ancestral knowledge. This interlacing of different kinds of knowledges gained from ancestral and colonial sources has affinities with Fanon's claim that the native intellectual should reinterpret, reform and modify cultural resources if they further a sense of the people's national unity and revolutionary consciousness.

Kihika preaches the importance of collective action rather than individual endeavour in his advocacy of anti-colonial resistance. Yet, problematically, his support for the movement does give him the aura of an extraordinary figure who soon acquires mythic status among the villagers. Throughout the novel there remains a tension between individual talent and collective action that is never fully resolved. This is an important tension for our purposes, not least because it invites us to think about the possible weaknesses in Fanon's rendering of the native intellectual as always serving the people, as well as wonder if there is a degree of idealism in his argument that intellectuals, elites and the masses can become synchronised and unified through a common nationalist cause. Ngugi certainly recognises the necessity for figures around which collective action can be instigated and organised, but remains suspicious of the cult of personality that is often created in their wake, and the problems this can cause. So he carefully problematises our view of Kihika by referring to his 'immense arrogance' (p. 89) and his egotistical 'visions of himself [as] a saint, leading Kenyan people to freedom and power' (p. 83). There is a sense that the valuing of an extraordinary individual detracts from the attention to the important ordinary and daily acts of courage by the people. To sum up this point, we might note how Ngugi's role as a 'native intellectual' – rather than as a national*ist* – involves not just the *advocacy* but also the *critique* of nationalist politics. In so doing, his work perhaps exposes an issue which Fanon had not thought about at great length: the extent to which the pursuit of national culture *might come to question rather than simply resource* the pursuit of nationalist political endeavours by its advocates.

Ngugi also uses Mugo to question the iconic, extraordinary status afforded to some individuals in the freedom struggle by pointing out the disjuncture between heroic myth-making and the truths that myths may conceal. In the absence of the murdered Kihika, Mugo becomes the village's celebrated war hero and inherits some of the aura that surrounded the man he betrayed. He is invited by members of the Movement to lead a rally in Thabai on the eve of independence day that will honour the sacrifices of those who died fighting the British. He also learns that Karanja will be wrongly accused at the rally of being responsible for Kihika's death, with chilling consequences. For much of the novel Mugo lives under unbearable pressure, wracked with feelings of guilt and made all the more uncomfortable by the praise he receives from those around him. The women of the village often sing songs about his bravery when he passes by. His confession at the rally of the betrayal of Kihika travesties these myths. It is an act which bears witness to Ngugi's ambiguous attitude towards individual actions in the novel. In his fatal public confession Mugo proves himself to be both a villain and a hero; not everyone would admit to a crime that secures their execution.

The occasion of Mugo's confession also questions the nature of the moment of independence. Uhuru is on the one hand an occasion for national joy and celebration, but on the other it is also a disquieting day of judgement. How should the people reckon with those who committed crimes against the nation during the struggle? Who is in a position to judge? In *A Grain of Wheat* it is difficult to separate easily the heroes from the villains as virtually every character could be accused of committing a potentially compromising act during the colonial period. The alternatives are set out early in the novel during a discussion concerning Kihika's death. One of the freedom fighters, Koina, suggests that perhaps they should 'forget the whole thing' (p. 97). His colleague, General R., takes the opposite view by arguing that '[t]raitors and collaborators must not escape revolutionary justice' (p. 27). It is an argument which Mugo's execution does not resolve either way. Through Mugo's fate, Ngugi raises questions about the conduct of the new nation after independence and the difficult challenges it faces: what to remember, what to forget, how to deal with the past and its legacies, how to move forward peaceably in the light of a bloody struggle.

The disquieting aspects of independence also emerge in Ngugi's depiction of those who are assuming the vacated seats of power in newly independent Kenya. In so doing he echoes Fanon's warning about the neo-colonial exploitation of the people by a native bourgeoisie. As Kenya approaches Uhuru many of the British settlers and administrators prepare to leave the country for good. One settler, Richard Burton, puts his farm up for sale. Gikonyo and five others decide they want to buy it. Gikonyo makes the trip to Nairobi to see if his local MP can help him secure a government loan to buy the farm. Gikonyo is made to wait with several others at the MP's office. When the MP eventually arrives late we are told that he 'greeted all the people like a father or a headmaster his children' (p. 62). The MP promises Gikonyo that he is confident he can secure the necessary loan soon. But Gikonyo's trust in the MP is betrayed. Later in the novel Gikonyo discovers that Burton's farm has been bought, and 'the new landowner was their own MP' (p. 169). The implication is that the possessions of the colonialists are passing into the hands of a new indigenous ruling class and not to the people of the Movement. Ngugi suggests that even on the day of independence the people's struggle is threatened with betrayal by a new ruling elite that has little concern for the people and which rules by familiar means:

> General R. recalled Lt Koina's recent misgivings. Koina talked of seeing the ghosts of the colonial past still haunting Independent Kenya. And it was true that those now marching in the streets of Nairobi were not the soldiers of the Kenya Land and Freedom Army but of the King's African Rifles, the ... colonial forces. (p. 220)

In one sense, the occasion of independence itself stands on trial at the end of the novel. Will Uhuru bring new opportunities for the inhabitants of Thabai? How will an independent Kenya differ from its days as a British colony? Who is in charge now? In this passage Ngugi holds a mirror to the nation and is not pleased with the conditions it reflects. This moment should also make visible the extent to which, remembering Fanon, many such representations of independence can be absolutely at the service of a critical national consciousness but not unthinkingly or crudely national*ist*. In other words, Ngugi's care in forging and maintaining national con-sciousness requires that he exposes and challenges the bourgeois hijacking of nationalism in the interests of an illiberal elite. The national consciousness of the people is *not* necessarily the same as the nationalism of the middle-class native elite. It is important to make these kinds of careful distinctions when we regard cultural representations of the nation in postcolonial contexts.

It might seem, then, that Ngugi takes a sombre view of newly independent Kenya, the tenor of which recalls Fanon's misgivings in 'The Pitfalls of National Consciousness'. But there is hope too for a better future for the nation, and this is figured through the relationship between Mumbi and Gikonyo. In order to make this reading we need to recall Innes's point about the *gendering* of the nation in some nationalist representations, and notice that Mumbi is presented as an allegorical mother-figure of the Kenyan nation. Her name recalls the celebrated mother of the Gikuyu, one of the main tribes of Kenya. The fact that she becomes a mother during the State of Emergency is also significant, especially when we remember that her brother Kihika often described Kenya as 'our mother' (p. 89). While in detention, Gikonyo's dreams of freedom are focused upon his desire to return to Mumbi. His fantasy of the Movement's defeat of the British becomes intertwined with his being reunited with Mumbi: 'His reunion with Mumbi would see the birth of a new Kenya' (p. 105). In *A Grain of Wheat*, Mumbi is clearly represented as a mother-figure of the nation central to the revolutionary vocabulary of Kihika and the people's struggle.

The reunion with Mumbi is not the glorious affair about which Gikonyo has dreamt, because he discovers that Mumbi has borne a child to Karanja. Gikonyo imagines that she has been having an affair during the time of his detention (the reality is of course very different) and his subsequent treatment of her eventually makes her leave him. But in the last chapter a potential reunion is hinted at, one which might be read as a nationalist representation. As Gikonyo lies in hospital with a broken arm he is visited by Mumbi. The atmosphere between them is strained, but Gikonyo surprises Mumbi by asking for the first time about her child, who is ill. If Mumbi is the mother of the nation and linked to a tribal past, then it follows that her child perhaps symbolises the fledgling, emerging, newly independent Kenya. The child was born as a result of the union between Mumbi and the collaborator Karanja, suggesting that the new Kenya inherits both the people's struggle against colonialism and their complicity with it. Significantly, the child is sick. The new Kenya is not free from the ills of the old, it seems, and those Kenyans who have survived the struggle must find ways of dealing with their painful past. Mumbi's response to Gikonyo's suggestion of their reconciliation suggests at a wider level how difficult and lengthy this process may be:

> People try to rub out things, but they cannot. Things are not so easy. What has passed between us is too much to be passed over in a sentence. We need to talk, to open our hearts to one another, examine them, and then together plan the future we want. (p. 247)

The happy future of the nation remains to be secured. Mumbi's comments emphasise the need for further collective action in her stress on 'planning together' that furthers the process of healing. This is not a quick forgetting of the past favoured by Lt. Koina nor the ugly one-sided mob-rule of General R. that took Mugo's life so swiftly after his confession. The novel's final image, a carving of a woman big with child, emphasises how Ngugi concludes by stressing the hopes for and possibility of rebirth, growth and redemption.

In our examination of *A Grain of Wheat* we have witnessed the fundamental importance of the idea of the nation as central to postcolonial cultural production during decolonisation, and discovered how an attention to issues of nation, nationalism and national consciousness can illuminate our reading of a text. However, Ngugi's use of Mumbi as a maternal icon of the nation is a questionable manoeuvre; also, his use of the English language and the metropolitan form of the novel as the means to create a distinctly national representation also require comment and critique. These things gesture to a wider series of problems concerning representations of the nation which have been pursued since the time of Fanon, Ngugi and others. These will be the subject of our next chapter.

Selected reading

Achebe, Chinua, 'The Novelist as Teacher' in *Hopes and Impediments: Selected Essays 1965–87* (Heinemann, 1988), pp. 27–31.
   A landmark essay, still extremely useful, in which Achebe discusses the importance of literature in the cultural regeneration of colonised peoples.

Anderson, Benedict, *Imagined Communities: Reflections on the Origins and Spread of Nationalism*, second edition (Verso, 1991).
   A highly influential book which has become the touchstone in much postcolonial criticism concerned with nationalist representations.

Arnold, A. James, *Modernism and Negritude* (Harvard, 1981).
   A wide-ranging, clear and sophisticated study of the origins and influence of Negritude aesthetics.

Boehmer, Elleke, *Colonial and Postcolonial Literature*, second edition (Oxford University Press, 2005).
   Chapter 3, 'The Stirrings of New Nationalism', offers a critical and illuminating literary history of nationalism and postcolonial writing.

Eagleton, Terry, Fredric Jameson and Edward W. Said, *Nationalism, Colonialism and Literature* (University of Minnesota Press, 1990).
   Includes an important essay by each critic and an excellent introduction by Seamus Deane.

Fanon, Frantz, *The Wretched of the Earth*, trans. Constance Farrington (Penguin, 1967 [1961]).
   Collecting together several of Fanon's salient essays, this is recommended reading for any study of nationalist representations, Negritude and anti-colonial resistance.

Gellner, Ernest, *Nations and Nationalism* (Blackwell, 1983).
   A useful, if conservative study of the Western origins of the ideas of nation and nationalism.

Gordon, Lewis, T. Denean Sharpley-Whiting and Renée T. White (eds), *Fanon: A Critical Reader* (Blackwell, 1996).
   A sophisticated and up-to-date collection of critical essays about Fanon which trace the enduring influence of his work. For the more advanced reader.

Hardt, Michael and Antonio Negri, *Empire* (Harvard University Press, 2000).

Although sometimes challenging to read, the early chapters offer a productive account of the emergence of the nation with modernity and its complicity with European colonialism.

Hawley, John C. (ed.), *Writing the Nation: Self and Country in the Post-Colonial Imagination* (Editions Rodopi, 1996).

A lively collection of essays which explores nationalist representations across a range of postcolonial literary texts.

Hutchinson, John and Anthony D. Smith (eds), *Nationalism* (Oxford University Press, 1994).

An excellent anthology of some of the most influential writing on nationalism in a variety of contexts.

Innes, C. L., '"Forging the Conscience of Their Race": Nationalist Writers' in Bruce King (ed.), *New National and Post-Colonial Literatures: An Introduction* (Clarendon Press, 1996), pp. 120–39.

An excellent and highly informative comparative study of nationalist representations in postcolonial literatures, highly recommended for new readers in the field.

Lazarus, Neil, *Nationalism and Cultural Practice in the Postcolonial World* (Cambridge University Press, 1999).

A strong defence of the revolutionary power of anti-colonial nationalism in the wake of recent postcolonial theory (see the next chapter of *Beginning Postcolonialism*). Also includes a first-rate chapter on Fanon.

Renan, Ernest, 'What is a Nation?', trans. Martin Thom in Homi K. Bhabha, (ed.) *Nation and Narration* (Routledge, 1990), pp. 8–22.

An influential statement on the idea of the nation, first delivered in 1882.

Trivedi, Harish, Meenakshi Mukherjee, Vijayasree Chaganti and T. Vijay Kumar (eds), *The Nation Across the World: Postcolonial Literary Representations* (Oxford University Press, 2007).

A collection of essays which explores the themes of nation, nationalism and the imagination in writing from postcolonial, European, US and Latin American contexts.

Young, Robert J. C., *Postcolonialism: An Historical Introduction* (Blackwell, 2001).

This book contains some excellent, long chapters on the emergence of anti-colonial nationalist movements across the colonised world and the key intellectuals and leaders who contributed to the formation of revolutionary national consciousness.

4

The nation in question

The disenchantment with nationalism

Simon Gikandi has argued in his book *Maps of Englishness: Writing Identity in the Culture of Colonialism* (Columbia University Press, 1996) that 'nationalism cannot seriously be considered to be the alternative to imperialism that it was once thought to be' (p. 7). Although debatable, this comment none the less bears witness to the fact that in the years since the busy period of decolonisation there has emerged a disenchantment with the ideas of nation and nationalism. This is in many ways a consequence of the historical experience of decolonisation when several national liberation movements, particularly in Africa, parts of the Caribbean and South Asia, confronted a series of often insoluble problems once formal independence was achieved. As Bruce King argues,

> [w]here the end of the Second World War brought a demand for national political independence to the forefront as a solution to the problems of the colonies, this was soon found to be an unrealistic hope as many new nations became divided by civil war and micro-nationalisms ... or failed to develop economically or to offer social justice to those outside the government and its supporters. (*West Indian Literature*, second edition, Macmillan, 1995, p. 3)

Coupled with these historical experiences is the theoretical critique of nationalism voiced by several influential thinkers. Paul Gilroy has raised concerns about the divisive and prejudicial 'camp mentalities constituted by appeals to "race", nation, and ethnic difference, by the lore of blood, bodies and fantasies of absolute cultural identity' (*Between Camps: Race, Identity and Nationalism at the End of the Colour Line*, Allen Lane/The Penguin Press, 2000, p. 83). Michael Hardt and Antonio Negri have described the imagining of a national people as a creating a potential 'straight-jacket of ... identity and homogeneity' (*Empire*, Harvard University Press, 2000) for the multitude and claim that as soon as a once-colonised nation achieves sovereignty and becomes a state in its own right, 'its progressive functions all but vanish' (p. 109). These are just two examples of a well-established antipathy within postcolonial studies held by some towards the ideas of nation and nationalism, much to the chagrin of many materialist postcolonial critics for whom the critique of such ideas is profoundly problematic.

Prompted by such critiques and debates, this chapter concerns the divisions within the nation which threaten the realisation of its progressive, anti-colonial ideals. We shall consider how nationalist representations might contribute to the continued *oppression* of some groups within the national population who have *not* experienced liberation in the period of formal independence. From their points of view, 'national liberation' seems almost a contradictory term. Do myths of the nation unify all of the people living within the nation's territorial boundaries, or can they stimulate division and conflict? We will be looking in this chapter primarily at the relationship between the imagined community of the nation and its internal divisions, and exploring in particular how the contradictions of nationalism impact upon both reading and writing nationalist representations, with specific reference to Chinua Achebe's novel *Anthills of the Savannah* (1987).

In the previous chapter we noted how many advocates of nationalism often faced two problems: the complicity of national liberation movements in Western myth-making, and the complications caused by the fact that many occupants of colonial lands did not possess a sense of (to use Benedict Anderson's phrase) 'deep, horizontal comradeship' prior to the advent of colonial government. The production of a unified imaginary community can be both nationalism's greatest strength and its ultimate weakness. Although the myth of the nation might function as a valuable resource in uniting a people in opposition to colonialism, it often does so by choosing to ignore the diversity of those individuals it seeks to homogenise – created out of gender, racial, religious and cultural differences, as we shall explore below. Many once-colonised nations have struggled with the internal differences that threaten the production of national unity, especially after formal independence. As we shall see, this does not simply reflect a political failure on the part of the newly independent nations, but perhaps reveals a problem *inherent* in the concept of the nation itself. These historical changes have impacted upon the ways in which the nation is theorised, and we shall be looking at some of these in a specifically postcolonial context. As Etienne Balibar puts it in his essay 'Racism and Nationalism', many decolonised nations have undergone the painful experience of 'seeing nationalisms of liberation turned into nationalisms of domination' (in Etienne Balibar and Immanuel Wallerstein, *Race, Nation, Class: Ambiguous Identities*, Verso, 1991, p. 46).

However, we do not want to begin this chapter by simply accepting Gikandi's view that nations and nationalisms are today old-fashioned ideas discredited by failure. It is true to say that for many commentators the idea of the nation is rapidly becoming challenged. In a world of instant mass communications, multinational capitalism and global travel, the ideas of nation, nationalism and national identity seem increasingly problematic in an increasingly international and globalised world (as we will consider in Chapter 8). A new world order is emerging, perhaps, where the primacy of the nation-state as the central mode of sovereignty and power is being threatened by a more nebulous, web-like and cellular arrangement which cuts across and beyond purely national interests, fuelled by 'the mobile, recombinant, opportunistic, and de-nationalised workings of many global corporations' (Arjun Appadurai, *Fear of Small Numbers: An Essay on the Geography of Anger*, Duke University Press, 2006, p. 27). That said, let us entertain the view that critics of the myth of the nation can often disregard too quickly some of the valuable dissident resources it makes available. Ultimately, by examining nationalist represent-ations and their problems across this chapter and the last, I am inviting you to make up your own minds about the myth of the nation and the pursuit of nationalism as productive things.

So, let us work through some of the salient criticisms which have been made about both the form and the content of anti-colonial nationalist representations.

Nationalism: a derivative discourse?

Paul Gilroy raises a number of salient issues for us when he asks why much of the opposition to racism and colonialism, such as nationalism, 'has so often been content to build its alternative conceptions of the world from the simple inversions of the dismal powers that confront us rather than altogether different conceptions guided by another political morality?' (*After Empire: Melancholia or Convivial Culture?*, Routledge, 2004, p. 61). Gilroy invites us to ponder if forms of dissidence derived from Western modernity can really be suited to the task of transforming an unequal, prejudicial world. As we noted previously, the nation is first and foremost a Western idea, one which emerged at a certain moment in Western history due to specific economic circumstances. How enabling is it, ultimately, as a tool for anti-colonial nationalist movements that are attempting to challenge their subservience to Western views of the world?

This is a matter which has preoccupied Partha Chatterjee in his influential book *Nationalist Thought and the Colonial World* (Zed, 1986). Chatterjee reminds us that the origins of the nation in the West have much to do with the pursuit of a set of human ideals often identified as the European 'Enlightenment'. From this vantage, European forms of nationalism are 'part of the same historical process which saw the rise of industrialism and democracy' and 'nationalism represents the attempt to actualise in political terms the universal urge for liberty and progress' (p. 2). However, this 'liberal' view of the nation repeatedly comes up against a dilemma: how can nationalism *also* facilitate illiberal movements and regimes which created internecine violence, political crises and civil war? Chatterjee points out that there is a conflict right at the heart of nationalism which he calls the 'liberal dilemma': nationalism may *promise* liberty and universal suffrage, but is *complicit* in un-democratic forms of government and domination. The sense of the Western nations as representing the very best in human progress and civilisation, firmly committed to a project of modernisation, becomes all too quickly a way of legitimating colonial expansion in moral terms. That is to say, colonialism can be justified with recourse to nationalism as a liberal, morally just, crusade to conquer the perceived ignorance and savagery of others.

The 'liberal dilemma' of nationalism becomes particularly problematic in colonial contexts. In using nationalism, many anti-colonial movements attempted to *appropriate* the liberal aspects of Western nationalism which promised the moral and political rights of liberty and political self-determination for the people. But as Chatterjee argues, they could not avoid also perpetuating nationalism's 'illiberal' and colonial aspects too:

> Nationalism sought to demonstrate the falsity of the colonial claim that the backward peoples were culturally incapable of ruling themselves in the conditions of the modern world. Nationalism denied the alleged inferiority of the colonised people; it also asserted that a backward nation could 'modernise' itself while retaining its cultural identity. It thus produced a discourse in which, even as it challenged the colonial claim to political domination, it also accepted the very intellectual premises of 'modernity' on which colonial domination was based. (p. 30)

Chatterjee argues that anti-colonial nationalisms inevitably have to use one of the chief tools of the colonists, and this makes them culpable in continuing to traffic in colonial ideas (a matter of concern for critics such as Paul Gilroy, as we noted a moment ago). Not only have many once-colonised nations derived their national borders from the map-making of the colonial powers, the nation *as a concept* is also derived from European colonial thinking.

However, the critique of the nation and nationalism on the grounds that they are derivative of Western colonial discourses raises some important objections. Neil Lazarus is one of several postcolonial scholars who do not accept the argument that '[t]he moment of decolonisation corresponds in all instances to a mere restructuring of "Western" hegemony' (*Nationalism and Cultural Practice in the Postcolonial World*, Cambridge University Press, 1999, p. 123). We might ask, therefore, to what extent do anti-colonial nationalisms significantly differ from Western nationalisms? Do they *perpetuate* problematic colonial assumptions about the necessity to 'modernise' seemingly 'backward' communities? Do colonial and anti-colonial nationalisms regard the colonised nation in the same way? The answers to these questions will differ from nation to nation, but to dismiss the ideas of nation and nationalism on the grounds that they have Western colonial origins seems premature, not least because it denies the fact that old ideas can be put to new purposes. As Lazarus argues in his essay 'National Consciousness and the Specificity of (Post) Colonial Intellectualism' (in *Colonial Discourse/Postcolonial Theory*, ed. Barker, Hulme and Iversen, 1994, pp. 197–220), 'we should be willing to concede that "the people" could or would not have spoken the language of nationalism without transforming it at least to some degree into a discourse capable of expressing their own aspirations' (p. 217).

This is indeed something that Chatterjee explores in relation to anti-colonial nationalism in India, although he claims that the innovations he finds in an Indian context are by no means confined to this location. Echoing perhaps Fanon's three stages of the creation of national consciousness and national culture (which we explored in Chapter 3), Chatterjee's narrative of Indian nationalism in *Nationalist Thought and the Colonial World* also focuses on three important phases in which nationalism is derived from Western thought – but is *transformed* as it is turned to new anti-colonial purposes. In the first phase, the **moment of departure**, anti-colonial nationalist movements emerge which *accept* that modern European culture 'possesses attributes which make the European culturally equipped for power and progress, while such attributes are lacking in "traditional" cultures of the East, thus dooming these countries to poverty and subjection' (*Nationalist Thought and the Colonial World*, p.50). In addition, although European culture may be technologically advanced, the cultures of the East are posited as possessing a heightened 'spiritual' aspect. Anti-colonial nationalism in the first phase aims to marry the technological greatness of the West with the spiritual greatness of the East. Importantly, this aim is pursued chiefly by members of the colonised elites, in whose refined intellects such a plan has been hatched. Fanon had argued that the colonised belonging to the Western-educated, economically elite classes must put themselves 'to school with the people' in an attempt to close the gap between the elite and the masses and co-ordinate their different positions within a shared plan. But Chatterjee argues that historically, and at least in an Indian context, something different happened. The elite attempted to mobilise the masses in their nationalist aims, but also made sure that the masses *remained distant* from the trappings of power and continually subject to the whims and rule of the colonised elite.

This is the second phase, the **moment of manoeuvre**. Often this involves seeming to embrace popular, 'anti-modern' ways as a means of upbraiding the modernising violence of the colonial nation; yet, ultimately such manoeuvres enable anti-colonial nationalist movements to move closer to establishing and administering 'modern' institutions in the colonised nation. The elite appropriates the forms and functions of popular or folk culture, *not* in order to discover alternative, indigenous forms of knowledge that refute Western 'modernity', but as a way of gaining mass support for the elite's attempts to take over control of 'modern' forms of technological, political and economic power from the colonisers. Chatterjee cites the work of Mahatma Gandhi as an example of this 'manoeuvre'.

In the third phase, the **moment of arrival**, the ambitions of the second phase are realised and nationalist thought in the colonial world emerges as a unified, coherent and rational discourse. The nationalist elite claim that their 'modern' attitudes are coterminous with 'popular consciousness' and enjoy the support of the people, deemed to be a unified and singular entity sharing the same political aims. But that co-ordination of the elite with the masses masks an unequal, neo-colonial power relation of the kind which Fanon warned against in 'The Pitfalls of National Consciousness'.

STOP and THINK

Chatterjee's argument raises two main areas of debate which we can bring into focus in a different context by revisiting our exploration of *A Grain of Wheat* conducted in the previous chapter.

First, does the appropriation of nationalism by the colonised eliminate sufficiently its colonial attitudes? Do the various manoeuvres of anti-colonial nationalisms ever dissolve the illiberal tendencies of Western nationalism? As we saw, in Ngugi's novel there are characters (such as General R.) keen to distinguish between those who can and cannot belong to the newly independent nation.

Second, how do the relations between the colonised elite and the masses problematise anti-colonial nationalisms? How 'popular' can they be? Can they claim to represent faithfully the aims, objectives and attitudes of the masses or does anti-colonial nationalism coerce the masses into following an elite project? Who benefits the most from 'national liberation', and what are these benefits? For example, in *A Grain of Wheat* the MP who buys the farm that Gikonyo wanted does not seem to be supporting the initiatives of the poorer people of the region.

As always, we must remember that the answers to such questions may differ according to national context, and it is dangerous to presuppose that all anti-colonial nationalisms, and the problems they encounter and create, are the same. But sometimes it is useful to pose general questions as a means of beginning your explorations of anti-colonial nationalist representations, just as Chatterjee's work on Indian nationalism enabled us to better understand some of the issues at stake in Ngugi's novel of Kenya.

Nationalism, representation and the elite

Chatterjee's attention to the problematic relations between nationalist elites and the masses requires further attention, not least because this impacts upon the ways in which the nation is represented. Interrogations of anti-colonial nationalisms on the grounds of their alleged elitism make two important points. First, following Fanon, anti-colonial nationalism can result in the replacement of a Western, colonial ruling class with a Western-educated, 'indigenous' ruling class who seem to speak on behalf of the people but function to keep the people disempowered. Second, representations of nationalist struggle tend to celebrate the inspirational activities of *individual members of the elite* and do not recognise the role played by less privileged individuals or groups in resisting colonial rule.

This latter issue has been one of the key areas of concern for a number of scholars known collectively as the *Subaltern Studies* group. Influenced variously by the writings of Karl Marx, Antonio Gramsci and Michel Foucault, these critics have explored the ways in which representations of Indian nationalism either ignore the contributions made to anti-colonial struggles by the masses, or explain their activities in such a way that the particular and local forms of 'subaltern consciousness' are not represented adequately. As Ranajit Guha explains in his essay 'On Some Aspects of the Historiography of Colonial India' (in *Selected Subaltern Studies*, ed. Ranajit Guha and Gayatri Chakravorty Spivak, Oxford University Press, 1988), the term 'subaltern' (borrowed from the work of Gramsci) is used to signify the many different peoples who did not comprise the colonial elite. These might include 'the lesser rural gentry, impoverished landlords, rich peasants and upper-middle-class peasants' (p. 44), although members of the subaltern classes could work either for or against the interests of the elite depending on the situation. Guha's essay calls attention to the ways that contemporary representations of Indian anti-colonial nationalism tend to place the subaltern classes as subject to the whims of the elite. Hence, Indian nationalism often reads as 'primarily an idealist venture in which the indigenous elite led the people from sub-jugation to freedom ... The history of Indian nationalism is thus written up as a sort of spiritual biography of the Indian elite' (p. 38). Guha renders these representations suspect on the grounds that they are locked inside a certain way of thinking about Indian nationalism that privileges elite consciousness over subaltern con-sciousness. The activities, efforts and decisions made by members of the subaltern classes are rarely regarded; and when they are, Guha argues that little attention is paid to the specific forms and functions of their insurgency. Nor is the conflictual relationship between elite and subaltern groups explored. As Guha puts it elsewhere in *Selected Subaltern Studies*, the rebellious subaltern too often 'is excluded as the conscious subject of his own history' (p. 77).

Guha's argument raises a particularly important question: how can we recover 'subaltern consciousness' when it is either ignored in historical representations or rendered in such a way as to ignore its specificity? This has proved an insoluble issue which we shall be returning to in more detail when we consider Gayatri Chakravorty Spivak's important essay 'Can the Subaltern Speak?' in Chapter 6. But it is clear in the present context that nationalist representations, in Guha's view, can actually support elitism and fail to bear witness to the (often different) activities and arguments of the people.

Nationalism, 'race' and ethnicity

In her book *The Politics of Home: Postcolonial Relocations and Twentieth-Century Fiction* (Cambridge University Press, 1996), Rosemary Marangoly George makes the succinct and highly useful remark that 'nationalism leads to the interpretation of diverse phenomenon through one glossary, thus erasing specificities, setting norms and limits, lopping of tangentials' (p. 14). It is here that the 'illiberal' aspects of nationalism most starkly appear. Historically, particularly divisive criteria have been used in some countries with a history of colonialism as ways of manufacturing national unity – criteria based upon ideas of racial, ethnic or religious exclusivity. While this has rewarded some with the trappings of power, others have found themselves restricted from positions of authority and condemned as second-class citizens.

Let us consider the ways in which 'race' and ethnicity have been used to set the 'norms and limits' of the nation's imagined community. The first thing to note is that these terms do *not* mean the same thing, although they have some similarities. Taking 'race' first, it is important to realise that all constructions of racial difference are based upon human invention and not biological fact. There exist no objective criteria by which human beings can be neatly grouped into separate 'races', each fundamentally different from the other. Racial differences are best thought of as *political constructions* which serve the interests of certain groups of people. Theories of racial difference are often highly selective in choosing certain biological 'facts' in making distinctions. Skin colour has predominantly been the primary sign of racial difference and a frequent target of racialising discourses, often taken as evidence of some form of 'natural' difference between, say, white and black Africans. We tend not to think of people with different eye colours as fundamentally different, yet this is just as much a biological 'fact' as skin colour. So, we might agree with Paul Gilroy when he writes that '"race" refers primarily to an impersonal, discursive arrangement, the brutal result of the raciological ordering of the world, not its cause' (*After Empire*, p. 42).

In short, we are proposing that our perceptions of racial difference are constructed socially and discursively for particular political purposes, and are, of course, open to contestation and change. 'Race' as a category is the result of this social and historical process which we can call *racialisation*. Racism is the ideology that upholds the discrimination against certain people on the grounds of perceived racial difference and claims these constructions of racial identity are true or natural. Thus, throughout this book we will join Paul Gilroy in placing 'race' within quotation marks as a way of continually emphasising its existence as a *historical construct* and not a biological given.

Both 'race' and ethnicity are concepts used to posit a common bond or identity between individuals. But whereas 'race' tends to prioritise physiological features as evidence of similarity between individuals, the parameters of 'ethnicity' tend to be more wide. As Floya Anthias and Nira Yuval-Davis helpfully explain:

> Ethnic groups involve the positing of boundaries in relation to who can and cannot belong according to certain parameters which are extremely heterogeneous, ranging from the credentials of birth to being born in the right place, conforming to cultural or other symbolic practices, language, and very centrally behaving in sexually appropriate ways. (Anthias and Yuval-Davis, *Racialised Boundaries: Race, Nation, Gender, Colour and Class and the Anti-racist Struggle*, Routledge, 1992, p. 4)

Ethnicity tends to involve a variety of social practices, rituals and traditions in identifying different collective groups. Although 'race' and ethnicity are *not* synonymous, both can be used as the grounds for discrimination. Members of particular ethnic groups or 'races' might find themselves disqualified from certain positions of power.

However, without wishing at all to diminish the potential divisiveness of these constructions, ethnic and racial identities can also be used by marginalised peoples as valuable resources (think, for example, of the work of the Negritude writers we considered in the previous chapter). In particular, an individual's ethnicity can provide an invaluable sense of belonging to a particular group in the present, and also to a tradition or inheritance of cultural and historical treasures. The potential uses of ethnicity and racial difference are variable over time and space, and need not always be divisive.

In the context of nationalism, 'race' and ethnicity have been used to further certain illiberal aims. Etienne Balibar's essay 'Racism and Nationalism' (cited earlier) explores the ways in which nationalism can be complicit with racism by privileging one racialised group above another as the nation's most legitimate or 'true' people. The perception of 'race' can function as a primary strategy in constructing myths of national unity and in deciding who may or may not belong to the rightful people. As part of his argument Balibar makes a useful distinction between *external* and *internal* racism (see pp. 38–40). *External racism* is a form of xenophobia, when groups of people who are located outside the borders of the nation are discriminated against on the grounds of their 'race'. *Internal racism* is directed at those who live within the nation but are not deemed to belong to the imagined community of the national people due to their perceived 'race'. Internal racism can result in its most extreme and violent form in the *extermination* of racialised individuals (as in the destruction of Aboriginal communities in the South Pacific in the nineteenth century, for example) or the *oppression* of racialised groups who are awarded a low position in the social hierarchy (we might think about indigenous or 'First Nations' peoples in Canada as evidence of this point). In these terms, perceptions of 'race' can structure the nation's 'norms and limits'.

One of the effects of racist ideologies is to produce a sense of national identity gained through the exclusion and denigration of others, as Balibar points out:

> racism always tends to operate in an inverted fashion ... the racial-cultural identity of 'true nationals' remains invisible, but it can be inferred (and is ensured) *a contrario* by the alleged, quasi-hallucinatory visibility of 'false nationals': the Jews, 'wogs', immigrants, 'Pakis', natives, Blacks. (p. 60)

This leads Balibar to posit that nationalism always has a *reciprocal* relation with racism (although the nature of that relation can take many different forms): where one is found, the other is never far away. Therefore, in using nationalism, it is claimed that decolonising peoples are in danger of perpetuating a concept which tends to support divisive processes of racialisation. It is no surprise to Balibar that in the process of decolonisation, illiberal racist tendencies have been 'reproduced, expanded and re-activated' (p. 43).

So, if nationalism is derived from the West, then attempts to construct a unifying myth of the nation can exacerbate existing conflicts between groups in some once-colonised nations or between different 'races' or ethnicities. Let us consider one example of this, post-independence Nigeria. Inheriting its borders from British colonialism, Nigeria is an intersection of many different African peoples. Its population consists of peoples from a variety of ethnic groups, such as Hausa, Fulani, Yoruba, Igbo, Kanuri, Tiv and Ijaw (which are all also internally multifarious). In addition to the many different beliefs held by these peoples, a large percentage of Nigerians are Muslims or Christians. Manufacturing a sense of national unity between them within the territorial borders inherited from colonialism has proven a difficult task, and has led to bloody conflict in recent years. In 1966, a few short years after formal independence had been achieved, there were two military coups. The first was led by Igbo army officers in the north, the second by members of the Hausa people. The result was bloodshed and enforced migrations; many Igbos in the north fled to the eastern region of the country in fear for their lives. In 1967 the eastern region declared itself the republic of Biafra, and civil war ensued until 1970 when the Biafran forces surrendered. One million people were killed during the war. Two more military coups followed, in 1975 and 1976. An elected government ruled Nigeria between 1979 and 1983, but then military rule returned. Civil government returned in 1999, but doubts have been raised about the fairness of the elections held in 1999, 2003 and 2007.

STOP and THINK

There is not enough room to deal with the complexity of recent Nigerian history here. But even this thumbnail sketch of Nigeria's fortunes gives some sense of the internal divisions and struggles between groups who feel that their interests are being threatened by others. Manufacturing a sense of unity in this context has become too often a bloody affair with one ethnicity seeking to become the ruling group, or attempting to secede from the nation entirely as in the case of Biafra.

These experiences also enable us to consider the fact that, for some peoples, the imagined community of the nation need not be the primary mode of collectivity: forms of group-identity based on ethnicity can be deemed far more important. We are led to ponder the following question: how productive is the myth of the nation in the decolonised world? It may well have provided a valuable resource in organising anti-colonial resistance movements during colonial rule, but is it as valuable after the colonial period where conditions are different? National borders were, after all, often invented during colonialism. How much sense does it make to use them in a changed and changing world? Why does the nation have to be the primary vehicle of collectivity for once-colonised peoples?

Nationalism, gender and sexuality

In our discussion of Ngugi's *A Grain of Wheat*, we considered the character of Mumbi as an iconic mother-figure of the newly independent Kenya. The metaphorical association between woman, mother and nation is familiar to many nationalist discourses where the nation has frequently been depicted iconically as a female. Robert J. C. Young notes that many anti-colonial nationalist movements often reinvigorated age-old representations of women that perpetuated problematic and objectifying gendered images. 'In the twentieth century', he explains, 'the increasing assertion of national cultural identity became more of a problem for feminists, since the affirmation of an indigenous cultural identity against the imposed culture of

the colonizer tended to involve the reinvocation of more traditional forms drawn from the very social structures against which
they were struggling; for example, the identification of women
with *Bharat Mata*, Mother India, or the good Hindu wife, the
sati' (*Postcolonialism: An Historical Introduction*, Blackwell, 2001,
p. 379). As Young's comments underline, nationalism is very
frequently a *gendered* discourse; it traffics in representations of
men and women which serve to reinforce patriarchal inequalities
between them. Nationalist representations have been in danger
of perpetuating disempowering representations of women in
once-colonised countries.

Several feminist critics have therefore pointed out a tendency
towards *male chauvinism* in many forms of nationalism. In using
women as icons of the nation, nationalist representations reinforce
images of the passive female who depends upon active males to
defend her honour. They also assert the chief agents of
decolonisation as men; thus the process of national liberation is
constructed as an exclusively male endeavour which ignores the
contributions made by millions of women to countless independence struggles around the globe. Many anti-colonial nationalisms
have represented the nation in gendered terms. This has had
important implications for women's relationships with the nation in
many different contexts. As Carol Boyce Davies puts it in her book
Black Women, Writing and Identity (Routledge, 1994), 'nationalism
thus far seems to exist primarily as a male activity with women
distinctly left out or peripheralised in the various national
constructs. Thus the feminine was deployed at the symbolic level, as
in "Mother Africa" or "Mother India"' (p. 12).

Additionally, gendered representations of the nation also
intersect with issues of sexuality and thus re-enact some of the
manoeuvres of Orientalism. As the editors of *Nationalisms and
Sexualities* (ed. Andrew Parker et al., Routledge, 1992) remind us,
representations of the nation as a mother threatened by foreign
aggression often appear specifically in terms of *sexual* violation:
'how deeply ingrained has been the depiction of the homeland as a
female body whose violation by foreigners requires its citizens and
allies to rush to her defence' (p.6).

The extent to which nationalism often traffics in patriarchal representations of women, and the way in which female agency in anti-colonial struggles has been frequently ignored in nationalist representations, have led some to reject nationalism on the grounds that it has done little to challenge female subordination to patriarchal norms in many once-colonised countries. Historically, it seems, men and women experience national liberation differently: women do not reap equal benefits from decolonisation for reasons of gender inequality. Women's contributions to the nationalist struggle are too quickly forgotten after independence is achieved and do not appear in nationalist representations. The editors of *Nationalisms and Sexualities* point out that women have effected the overthrow of colonial power in many times and places but have found the decolonised nation is hardly interested in female liberation: 'In anti-colonial struggles ... feminist programmes have been sacrificed to the cause of national liberation and, in the aftermath of independence, women have been reconsigned to their formerly "domestic" roles' (*Nationalisms and Sexualities*, p. 7). According to these views, the construction of a national people has tended to privilege men as the active agents in national liberation and the chief beneficiaries of political and economic power gained through the nationalist struggle.

The feminist critique of nationalism has been helpfully summarised by Floya Anthias and Nira Yuval-Davis in their introduction to *Woman-Nation-State* (ed. Anthias and Yuval-Davis, Macmillan, 1989), a collection of essays that explores the relationship between women, the nation and state policy in a variety of locations which include Australia, South Africa and Uganda. Of course, any summary always runs the risk of ignoring historical specificity. None the less, it is worth quoting here insofar as it equips us with a useful series of contexts which we can apply in our readings of nationalist representations. Furthermore, it also indicates how gender and sexual issues often become inseparably bound up with ethnicity. We have separated above the issues of ethnicity and gender/sexuality for the purposes of clarity, but we must note that nationalist representations often bind ethnicity, gender and sexuality in complex ways.

According to Anthias and Yuval-Davis, there are 'five major

(although not exclusive) ways' in which women historically have been positioned within nationalist discourses (p. 7):

1. As biological reproducers of members of ethnic collectivities
2. As reproducers of the boundaries of ethnic/national groups
3. As participating centrally in the ideological reproduction of the collectivity and as transmitters of its culture
4. As signifiers of ethnic/national differences – as a focus and symbol in ideological discourses used in the construction, reproduction and transformation of ethnic categories
5. As participants in national, economic, political and military struggles.

Let us briefly take each of these categories:

1. First, as *biological reproducers of members of ethnic collectivities*, women are encouraged by the state to believe that it is their duty to produce children to replenish the numbers of those who 'rightfully' belong to the nation for reasons of ethnicity. Women who are not deemed to belong to the 'proper' ethnic group can find themselves subject to forced sterilisation.
2. As *reproducers of the boundaries of ethnic groups*, women are charged with ensuring that the act of reproduction does not threaten group identity at a symbolic level. To take one example, in some cases it is taboo for women to have sex with men of a different ethnic group or social class. Such borders must not be crossed. Hence the act of biological reproduction is organised in such a way as to support social reproduction.
3. As *transmitters of culture*, women are deemed to be the primary educators of children and responsible for introducing them to the heritage and traditions of the nation's culture. Women's role as reproducers is at once biological and cultural.
4. As *signifiers of ethnic/national differences*, women are used as icons, such as mother-figures of the nation which we explored earlier. These iconic representations offer no means by which women's manifold experiences of and contributions to anti-colonial nationalism can become the subject of nationalist representations.

5. Finally, we are reminded that women are *participants in national, economic, political and military struggles*, contrary to many nationalist representations which depict women 'in a supportive and nurturing relation to men' (p. 10).

This last point is especially important. In making their list, Anthias and Yuval-Davis point out that nationalist discourses attempt to position women in particular ways which serve patriarchal, sexual and ethnic interests. But we must not let these representations distract us from the fact that women actively contributed to nationalist struggles and, after decolonisation, have resisted the operations of forms of patriarchy.

The nation and its margins

One of the most influential and challenging interventions in the debate concerning nationalist representations is Homi K. Bhabha's essay 'DissemiNation: Time, Narrative and the Margins of the Modern Nation'. Bhabha's essay first appeared in a collection of essays *Nation and Narration* (ed. Homi K. Bhabha, Routledge, 1990) and is reprinted in *The Location of Culture* (Routledge, 1994), pp. 139–70 – we shall use the latter in our discussion. Bhabha's essay reveals nationalist representations as highly unstable and fragile constructions which cannot ever produce the unity they promise. This is because, in Bhabha's argument, they become split by similar kinds of ambivalence to those that threaten the coherence of colonial discourses. In making this argument, the essay might make us think about the worrying *similarities* between colonial discourses and nationalist representations.

As we have seen, it is the aim of nationalist discourses to create community out of difference, to convert the 'many' into 'one'. In so doing, Bhabha argues, they engage with two contradictory modes of representation, which he calls the *pedagogic* and the *performative*, each possessing its own relationship with time (or 'temporality'). Nationalist discourses are split by a disruptive 'double narrative movement' (*The Location of Culture*, p. 145). On the one hand, nationalism is a 'pedagogical' discourse. It claims a fixed origin for the nation and asserts a sense of a *continuous* history which links the nation's people in the present to previous generations of national subjects. It is pedagogical because it warrants the authority, legitimacy and primacy of the nation as the central political and social unit which collects the population into a 'people'. The people are the *object* of pedagogical discourse; they are the body which nationalism constructs and upon which it acts. Pedagogical narratives are shaped by a 'continuist, accumulative temporality' (p. 145) which gives the impression of the steady, linear movement of time from past to present to future – as in the narrative of the nation's history, for example, the 'story of the tribe' which offers a genealogical account of the people's common fortunes.

But on the other hand, Bhabha argues that nationalist discourses are *simultaneously* 'performative'. This term refers to the ways in which nationalist icons and popular signs (all those representations which help fix its 'norms and limits') must be *continually rehearsed* by the people in order to keep secure the sense of 'deep, horizontal comradeship'. A national culture must be *endlessly* performed; the arbitrary range of symbols which it uses to forge unity require *repeated* inscription as the stuff of national significance. 'The scraps, patches and rags of daily life must be repeatedly turned into the signs of a coherent national culture' writes Bhabha (p. 145). In these terms, the people are also the *subjects* of nationalist discourses, actively involved in the (re)production of its signs and traditions: they must repeatedly tell their history, perform the nation's rituals, celebrate its great figures and commemorate its anniversaries. Hence, nationalist discourses in their performative aspects function under a *different* temporality, the 'repetitious' and 'recursive' (p. 145).

As a consequence of this 'double' narrative movement, the nation is split by what Bhabha terms the 'conceptual ambivalence' (p. 146) at the heart of its discursive strategies. The nation is always being pulled between two incompatible opposites: the nation as a fixed originary essence (continuist and pedagogic), and the nation as socially manufactured and devoid of a fixed origin (repetitive and performative). Between these two positions, out of this 'disjunctive temporality' (p. 148), a sense of the nation's homogeneous 'people' begins to fragment. The pedagogical representation of the people as 'object' constructs an idealised image of unity and coherence in the past. But because of the necessity for the performance of the nation's signs by the people as 'subject', the pedagogical ideal of the homogeneous people can never be realised. This is because the performative necessity of nationalist representations opens an opportunity for all those who reside within its borders but who are placed on the margins of its imagined 'norms and limits' – such as women, migrants, the working class, the peasantry, those of a different 'race' or ethnicity – perhaps to *intervene* in the signifying process and *challenge* the dominant representations with narratives of their own. A plural population can never be converted into a singular people because plurality and difference can never be entirely banished:

> We are [hence] confronted with the nation split within itself, articulating the heterogeneity of its population. The barred Nation *It/Self*, alienated from its eternal self-generation, becomes a liminal signifying space that is *internally* marked by the discourse of minorities, the heterogeneous histories of contending peoples, antagonistic authorities and tense locations of cultural difference. (p. 148)

So, the necessity for perpetual regeneration of the nation via the performance of its signs cannot help but expose it to the interventions of those which are placed on the margins of its 'norms and limits'. It is through the performative aspects of nationalist discourses that difference returns from *within* to challenge the homogeneous nation with its unified people and myths of origin, as the marginalised people of the population are exposed to the production of the nation's representation of itself to itself. In other words, the performative can corrupt rather than guarantee the operations of the pedagogical. Bhabha fixes upon these counter-narratives of the nation which 'disturb those ideological manoeuvres through which "imagined communities" are given essentialist identities' (p. 149). Nationalist discourses require essence, origin, unity and coherence, and need to *forget* the presence and the narratives of certain peoples within its imaginary boundaries in order to function. But the ideal of coherence remains forever out of reach due to the disjunctive temporality – continuist *and* repetitive – which splits the nation. Counter-narratives interrupt the nation's smooth self-generation at the performative level, revealing *different* experiences, histories and representations which nationalist discourses depend on excluding. Hence, 'the national memory is always the site of the hybridity of histories and the displacement of narratives' (p. 169). It cannot be singular, pure, homogeneous, common to all. The deep, horizontal comradeship it beckons can never be fully achieved.

Bhabha's argument is compelling not least because it represents the nation in its more illiberal guises, while also revealing that its propensity to marginalise certain peoples can never fully realise itself. Nationalist discourses are frustrated in their aims due to the necessity of the performative which renders the nation ambivalent. For those considered marginal to the nation's 'proper' people, this is, perhaps, a valuable and positive argument to pursue. As in his work on colonialist discourses, Bhabha represents nationalist discourses as fragile, split and contradictory, rather than benevolent and inclusive.

Yet problems remain within his essay. First, it is not entirely clear where the agency for counter-narratives exists. Does the agency for resistance derive from the acts of representation by those from the nation's margins, or is it found mystically within nationalism itself? Is it consciously pursued by determined individuals or endemic to all forms of the discourse of the nation, a mystical product of representation rather than effected by willed resistance? If imagining the nation and its people is eternally and internally split, then why have illiberal nationalist discourses been so powerful? Just as Bhabha's critique of 'the discourse of colonialism' fails to account for its continued political authority, so too does his critique of nationalism leave a similar question unanswered. Second, although Bhabha is more culturally specific here than in his work on the ambivalence of colonial discourse, there is still a tendency to universalise his model of the ambivalence of nationalist representations despite the fact that he claims to be making 'no general theory' (p. 170).

Ultimately, Bhabha's essay asserts that there can never be any one, coherent, common narrative through which a nation and its people can be adequately captured. The nation remains a site of heterogeneity and difference. Narratives which claim otherwise can do so only through the marginalisation of certain groups, yet even this claim will be undone by the disjunctive temporalities which they cannot help but create. In Bhabha's work, nationalist discourses are *ultimately* illiberal and must *always* be challenged.

STOP and THINK

In examining the problems with nationalist representations in this chapter so far, we might be tempted to dismiss the ideas of nation and nationalism on the grounds that, ultimately, they cannot ever be free from marginalising, illiberal tendencies. But should nationalism be so readily dismissed?

Benita Parry's work invites us to think flexibly about this. In her book *Postcolonial Studies: A Materialist Critique* (Routledge, 2004), Parry reminds us of the efficacy and value of national discourses in the decolonised world. In looking again at the Negritude writers and the work of Frantz Fanon, often criticised today for accepting too readily colonial forms of knowledge, she argues that 'it is surely necessary to refrain from a sanctimonious reproof of modes of writing resistance which do not conform to contemporary theoretical rules about discursive radicalism' (p. 43). Although Parry acknowledges the ways in which much anti-colonial nationalist writing in North and West Africa during the 1950s and 1960s repeated some of the prescriptive tendencies and chauvinism of nationalism, to dismiss this writing today as ideologically corrupt avoids thinking about nationalist representations in their historical contexts. This manifold archive of anti-colonial writing may well have had its ideological limitations, such as the essentialising of 'blackness' by the Negritude writers. Yet in claiming agency and authority for black subjects, these writers released important 'revolutionary energies' and contributed much to anti-colonial resistance in 'valorising the cultures denigrated by colonialism' (p. 43).

In your view, should the conceptual failings of nationalism as revealed by Bhabha and others detract from its productivity as a revolutionary anti-colonial strategy of resistance? To what extent would you condemn nationalism because it ultimately failed, in Parry's terms, 'to contest the conventions of that system of knowledge it supposedly challenges' (p. 37)?

English in the colonies: a national language?

So far we have examined some of the conceptual problems of nationalist representations. Let us turn next to problems of specific language-use, and address the thorny debates about the role of English as a national language in once-colonised countries.

In many parts of the British Empire, English was the primary language of government and administration, and was used in the education of colonised subjects (we will be exploring this latter issue in detail in the next chapter). After independence, many colonial nations inherited economic, governmental and educational institutions, several of which were often administered in English. The English language is a part of this colonial 'inheritance'. Its existence as the language of colonial power has complicated its status as the language of the independent nation, and there are conflicting attitudes towards English as the national language of once-colonised countries. Can it ever function as the national language of the nation after colonialism? The answer to this question varies from location to location; but let us consider just a couple of brief examples.

English in the settler nations

The English language is one of several European languages (like French, Spanish, Portuguese and Dutch) which has become a national language in once-colonised countries. Yet many writers and critics in the settler nations have been keen to differentiate their usage of English from its standard form, which evolved in Britain. There is a sense that the terms of reference and conceptual vocabulary of English, as well as the cultural values it carried, are not easily suited to describing the experiences of a different place. The Australian poet Judith Wright remarked in 1965 that the European settler was faced with a problem on arrival in Australia, as their sense of European 'tradition' and 'inheritance' soon began to weaken: 'the older culture which had given [the settler's] life a meaning beyond the personal, by linking him with the past, began to lose its power over him. It had authority still, but his real share in it dribbled away; for the true function of an art and a culture is to interpret us to ourselves, and to relate us to the country and the society in which we live' (*Preoccupations in Australian Poetry*, Oxford University Press, 1965, p. xviii). In other words, the English language as it had been previously used was not capable of bearing witness to the particular sights, sounds and experiences of this new, Australian environment. For Wright, European-descended Australian writers were faced with a question: what kind of relationship were they to have with a language they had inherited but was not readily suited to the task of 'making Australia into our real spiritual home' (*Preoccupations*, p. xviii)?

Managing the relationship with English in the settler colonies has remained a problematic issue. One solution to Wright's question has been the *reworking* of English under its new conditions, forcing it to change from its standard version into something new and more suited to the new surroundings. Bill Ashcroft has theorised this process in his essay 'Constitutive Graphonomy: A Post-Colonial Theory of Literary Writing' (in *After Europe: Critical Theory and Post-Colonial Writing*, ed. Stephen Slemon and Helen Tiffin, Dangaroo, 1989, pp. 58–73). Ashcroft explores how all language utterances (let's call them 'texts' for short) are produced and received in specific contexts and emerge from unique situations. Meaning depends upon the *moment* of textual production and the *place* where texts are produced. Each limits and determines the range of meanings available to a text. So, when English is used in a once-colonised location, the specifics of the site of textual production will necessarily force its meanings to *change*. The new forms of 'English' which result are deliberately proclaimed to be *distant* from the received norm, and offer a means for English speakers in the settler colonies to conceive of their difference through their language:

> But even in the most monoglossic settler cultures the sub-cultural distancing which generates the evolution of variant language shows that the linguistic cultures encompassed by the term 'English' are vastly heterogeneous. Most importantly, post-colonial literatures provide ... a writing which actually *installs* distance and absence in the interstices of the text. (p. 61)

Although the new differentiated 'english' can be recognised by standard English speakers – it has a degree of sameness that enables comprehension outside of its specific site of enunciation – it may contain elements that remain distant to the standard English reader and defy their powers of comprehension.

Ashcroft's ideas are central to *The Empire Writes Back: Theory and Practice in Post-Colonial Literatures*, second edition (ed. Bill Ashcroft, Gareth Griffiths and Helen Tiffin, Routledge, 2002), which we discussed in Chapter 1, and many of the criticisms of that book apply to his essay. Although admirable in its attempt to address the specific *situatedness* of all language usage, the argument becomes rather detached from the specifics of place and is rather generalising, both in terms of postcolonial 'english' usage and standard English. None the less, it does provide us with a useful model for explaining how English is adapted in new contexts, a process that has been crucial to the construction of images of national and cultural identity in the settler colonies.

However, English-language representations of the nation in the settler colonies are problematised by the presence of native or Aboriginal peoples descended from communities which existed before Europeans arrived. What status is afforded to the languages of native and Aboriginal peoples? What relationship do these people have with English? Do national representations include these peoples too? More often than not, native and Aboriginal peoples have had a conflictual relationship with the English language. In the preface to Jeanne Perrault and Sylvia Vance's edited collection *Writing the Circle: Native Women of Western Canada* (University of Oklahoma Press, 1993), Emma LaRocque shows how Aboriginal voices have been silenced in Canada due to the primacy of English, particularly in its written forms. Native languages, frequently oral rather than written, have been marginalised or dismissed in educational and other institutions along with the cultural values and traditions to which they testify. In addition, native peoples who have written in English have found it difficult to be heard, or have even had their critical representations of Canada dismissed as 'parochial'. LaRocque describes specifically the relationship between the 'Native woman writer' and the English language with these memorable words which are worth quoting at length:

> To a Native woman, English is like an ideological onion whose stinging layers of racism and sexism must be peeled away before it can be fully enjoyed ... Native readers and writers do not look at English

words the same way as non-Natives may, for we have certain
associations with a host of them. It is difficult to accept the following
terms as neutral: savage, primitive, pagan, medicine man, shaman,
warrior, squaw, redskin, hostile, civilisation, developed, progress, the
national interest, bitter, angry, happy hunting grounds, brave, buck,
redman, chief, tribe, or even Indian. These are just a few of the string
of epithets that have been pejoratively used to *specifically* indicate the
ranking of Indian peoples as inferior to Europeans, thus to perpetuate
their dehumanisation. (p. xx)

LaRocque forcefully asks us to question the extent to which English
functions as a national language in settler countries facilitating a
'deep, horizontal comradeship' for all. In her view, native peoples
have been left out of conventional representations of Canada.
Ashcroft's argument that English is changed into 'english' through
its use in new environs may be true, but the newly created 'english'
may remain a mode of *internal colonialism* for native peoples, whose
language, representation and values are dismissed as parochial to
the nation defined largely in the white settlers' terms. However, this
does *not* lead LaRocque to dismiss or reject English, due to the fact
of its establishment for better or worse in Canada. English does not
solely belong to those of European descent. 'To read, speak and
write in English is the birthright of contemporary Native peoples',
she argues. 'I have sought to master this language so that it would no
longer master me' (p. xxvi).

'Third World' Englishes: elite discourses or nation language?

India's languages are various, including Hindi, Urdu, English,
Punjabi and Bengali, to name a few. Yet there has developed an
exciting body of Indian literature in English, produced by such
figures as R. K. Narayan, Nayantara Sahgal, Anita Desai, Salman
Rushdie and Amitav Ghosh. Can we read this literature as a national
literature? The dangers of doing so are pointed out by the Marxist
critic Aijaz Ahmad in his book *In Theory: Classes, Nations,
Literatures* (Verso, 1992). Ahmad is contemptuous of the ways in
which Indian literature in English is often read as a national
literature particularly in Western universities, despite the fact that it
is produced in the main by an English-speaking minority drawn
from the more wealthy cosmopolitan classes. Ahmad complains that

this creates a situation where 'only the literary document produced in English is a *national* document; all else is regional, hence minor and forgettable, so that English emerges in this imagination not as *one* of the Indian languages, which undoubtedly it is, but as *the* language of national integration and bourgeois civility' (p. 75). This state of affairs is unacceptable to Ahmad. There are a multitude of different languages in India with their own narratives, opinions and values, but these remain marginalised if only English texts are deemed to be constitutive of the 'norms and limits' of Indian national culture. Ahmad claims that the continuing predominance of English in India at administrative and cultural levels is best described as 'neo-colonial', in that it continues to exclude many millions of Indians who are not literate in English. In his view the English language continues to serve the interests of the educated elite and not the people as a whole.

Forceful as it is, Ahmad's argument seems rigidly mechanical. He can offer no account of how English might have been changed by its use in a new context (as Ashcroft does in his essay). Nor does he think about how writers from the 'privileged elite' might use English in subversive ways. As Dohra Ahmad has explained, '[i]f colonialism and its assorted intellectual paraphernalia used English to enforce a deep-seated racial hierarchy, new versions of that same language ... disassembled that hierarchy' (*Rotten English: A Literary Anthology*, W. W. Norton and Company, 2007, p. 21). The assumption that the continued use of English is inevitably neo-colonial seems highly reductive, given Dohra Ahmad's argument. While one might understand Aijaz Ahmad's desire to challenge the continued primacy of a colonial-derived language as national and elite, his argument entirely blocks him from valuing the achievements of Indian writers in English who are dismissed for the language they use without Ahmad bothering to think about how they might be using it and to what ends.

Ngugi wa Thiong'o has also come to adopt a hostile attitude to English. In 1980 he stopped writing in English and now writes in his native tongue, Gikuyu. In his book *Decolonising the Mind: The Politics of Language in African Literature* (James Currey, 1981), Ngugi gives his reasons for rejecting English. As a child Gikuyu was the language spoken in Ngugi's home and by the workers in the fields. His early schooling was also conducted in Gikuyu, but when the State of Emergency was declared in 1952, Gikuyu was replaced at school by English. Children found speaking Gikuyu in school were punished and the language was suppressed. For Ngugi the silencing of Gikuyu was a violent and destructive act of colonialism. To dismiss a language is to dismiss a whole culture:

> Culture embodies those moral, ethical and aesthetic values, the set of spiritual eyeglasses, through which [a people] come to view themselves and their place in the universe. Values are the basis of a people's identity, their sense of particularity as members of the human race. All this is carried by language. Language as culture is the collective memory bank of a people's experience in history. (pp. 14–15)

Ngugi reasons that if he continues to write in English, he remains split off from the 'memory bank' of his community, a split caused by colonialism which he wishes to heal. To write in English is to deal in the values of the oppressor, to see the world through colonial lenses and not through inherited 'spiritual eyeglasses'. Therefore Ngugi declares his determination to 'restore the Kenyan child to his environment' (p. 28) by writing in his mother tongue. He calls on other African writers to renounce English so that, through the use of indigenous language, they might 'reconnect themselves to the revolutionary traditions of an organised peasantry and working class in Africa in their struggle to defeat imperialism' (p. 29). In these terms English *interrupts* the creation of a national con-sciousness after independence, and its continuing use must be opposed.

Of course, Ngugi's relationship with English is different to those of European descent in the settler colonies. He cannot make the same kind of claims which Judith Wright made about English. Still, there is more than a touch of nostalgia in Ngugi's argument, as if he is keen to recover an idealised community experienced in childhood relatively unravished by the effects of colonialism. Can things be so easily reversed? Also, the representation of language here tends to be rather homogenising and tidy. Nevertheless, his stinging attack on English as a major weapon of colonialism asks us to question once again the extent to which English can be freed from the colonial values it supported and articulated.

These rejections of English have by no means proven popular, as the vast body of postcolonial literature in English testifies. Some postcolonial writers have challenged the idea that some languages are not appropriate to certain places. Chinua Achebe offers a different view to Ngugi when he declares that English is an African rather than a foreign language because it is used daily throughout the continent: 'A language spoken by Africans on African soil, a language in which Africans write, justifies itself' ('Thoughts on the African Novel' in *Hopes and Impediments: Selected Essays 1965–87*, Heinemann, 1988, p. 62). In tackling the issue of English we must never forget to take into account the *specific linguistic conditions* of different locations. In the Caribbean for example, English cannot be so easily censured. Along with other European languages such as French and Spanish, English became one of the dominant languages in the region during the colonial period. Indigenous languages perished with the indigenous peoples, while the languages of the African slaves shipped across the Atlantic to work on the plantations were discouraged by the colonial authorities. Today, English remains one of the predominant languages of education and power. In contrast to the situation Ngugi describes in Kenya, it is difficult to recover an 'indigenous' language in the Caribbean to which one 'belongs' when the native languages have been destroyed and the most frequently spoken languages were brought from overseas.

English remains widely spoken in parts of the Caribbean, but its form has been radically changed by its users. Edward Kamau Brathwaite explores these changes in his work on 'nation language'. This is a term used in his influential lecture *History of the Voice* (New Beacon Books, 1984), which is an exploration of the innovative uses of English in Caribbean poetry. Brathwaite celebrates Anglophone Caribbean poets who are attempting to articulate their unique historical and cultural situation through their deployment of 'nation language'. Brathwaite shows how various poets are inflecting the English language with different kinds of rhythms, sounds, syntax and forms of expression which can be traced to African speech patterns. This is 'nation language', and one of its main functions is the articulation of an appropriate register, or 'voice' in which Caribbean experiences can be fully represented. Standard English is transformed in 'nation language' due to the different syncopations and patterns of spoken English in the Caribbean. Indeed, 'nation language' is the language of the people – crucially, it is *not* an elite language – who are finding different ways of giving voice to their experiences which refuse the inherited European models and break out of their confines. These everyday voices become the inspiration for new ways of using English literary and linguistic forms in poetry.

In their turn, the 'nation language' poets of the Caribbean perform a vital social function in their work which Brathwaite explains as follows: 'for the needs of the kind of emerging society that I am defending – for the people who have to recite "The boy/stood on/the burn/ing deck" for so long, who are unable to express the power of the hurricane in the way that they write their words – at last, our poets, today, are recognising that it is essential that they use the resources which have always been there, but which have been denied to them' (p. 42). Through 'nation language', poets find their unique 'voice' that is particular and appropriate to the Caribbean; and not solely derived from, nor obedient to, its European sources.

Brathwaite's essay is a wonderful exercise in claiming artistic dignity and aesthetic sophistication for a use of English which might be seen by some as sub-standard or bastardised. However, his term 'nation language' is more figurative than literal and can be a little misleading. Primarily, it is a concept used to describe language-use in poetry from many Caribbean nations; 'nation language' is not really specific to any one of these nations in particular. It does not advocate a *strict* sense of Caribbean collectivity: the variety of 'nation language' poetry celebrates innovation and heterogeneity. There are no definitive 'norms and limits' set for the use of English. Paradoxically, 'nation language' does not constitute a rigorous nationalist discourse although Brathwaite does demonstrate how poets can stimulate a sense of a unique, valuable culture particular to the region and enable Caribbeans to reconsider their alleged inferior position in relation to European culture. This is an approach to English which contrasts with Ngugi's dismissal.

However, granted that 'nation language' is a fairly elastic term, we are left with little sense of how language-use might differ from place to place, and why. Also, Brathwaite's focus is exclusively on African-descended Caribbeans and thus cannot claim to represent all the peoples in the Caribbean, who may have Indian or European ancestry (or more than one). Although he writes equally enthusiastically about male and female poets, the issue of gender difference is not broached. 'Nation language' is not free from some of the problems with more methodical nationalist representations which we explored earlier. None the less, Brathwaite's *History of the Voice* invites us to think that the concept of nation may continue to perform vital cultural and political work in certain contexts, despite the many theoretical shortcomings which we have been exploring.

STOP and THINK

When you pursue the forms and functions of English in different locations, ask yourself the following questions: how was English introduced to this particular region? What functions (administrative, educational, cultural) did it serve? Who spoke it and how did they learn it? What role does English play there today? Is it a common or minority language? Is it a popular language or the language of the privileged? English as a nation(al) language is never free from problems in all once-colonised countries. We must not assume that postcolonial literary texts in English offer us representative or typical illustrations of the nation as a whole.

The nation in question: Chinua Achebe's *Anthills of the Savannah*

Let us conclude by considering *Anthills of the Savannah* by Chinua Achebe. Achebe was born in 1930 in Ogidi, Nigeria. He was educated at University College, Ibadan and received a BA from London University in 1953. His first novel, *Things Fall Apart* (1958) is often hailed as one of the founding texts of postcolonial literature. *Anthills of the Savannah* was written at a time of growing disenchantment with the revolutionary ideals of anti-colonial nationalism. It is a complex, thought-provoking text, and we will approach it in the light of the issues we have raised in this chapter.

Anthills of the Savannah is Achebe's sober examination of the fortunes of West African nations such as Nigeria since formal independence was achieved. Set in the fictional country of Kangan, the novel's plot depicts the mixed fortunes of the military government and its eventual defeat in a *coup d'état*. Many of its central characters are well-educated members from the upper reaches of Kangan society, each involved with the government at various levels. The male figures – Sam, Christopher Oriko and Ikem Osodi – have known each other from childhood, and each has spent time being educated in Britain. Sam received military training at Sandhurst and, as the novel opens, has assumed control of Kangan after a military coup. Re-naming himself 'His Excellency' and firmly ensconced in the Presidential Palace in Bassa, he has suffered humiliation in a recent referendum in which he hoped to establish himself as president for life. One province in the north-west, Abazon, failed to support him, thus making us question the extent to which the Kangan people share a 'deep, horizontal comradeship'. Throughout the novel Abazon is reported to be suffering a severe drought, and it is hinted that His Excellency has played a part in reducing the water supply to the region as retribution for its lack of support.

His Excellency's cabinet includes Chris as the Minister of Information. Previously, Chris had been editor of the *National Gazette*. This role is now filled by Ikem, an Abazonian by birth and an aspiring poet. Then there is Beatrice Okoh, who works as a Senior Assistant Secretary for the government's Finance Department. Like the others, Beatrice has known Sam from their younger days, and is having a relationship with Chris.

His Excellency is keen to control the flow of information circulating both inside Kangan and to the world at large, and appoints Chris partly to ensure that only those representations supportive of his government are published. However Ikem, as the editor of the *National Gazette*, holds such control in contempt and has been less than sympathetic to the government in some of his editorials. When Ikem meets with a delegation of Abazonians who visit the Presidential Palace to petition His Excellency to visit the region to see the damage wrought by the drought, His Excellency uses this as an excuse to deal with the unruly editor. Ikem is declared an anti-government agitator and dismissed from his post for allegedly helping organise the Abazonians' petition. Undaunted, Ikem gives a lecture at the University of Bassa in which he condemns the government's actions and urges the students to begin mending the corruption that has damaged Kangan. Almost immediately he is arrested and shot in police custody. His death is officially reported as the result of Ikem's foolish attempt to wrestle a gun from a guard.

Appalled at this cover-up of his friend's murder, Chris arranges to meet with members of the international press and tells them the truth, putting him on a collision course with His Excellency. Soon Chris is a wanted man. Ikem's and Chris's supporters decide that Chris should leave Bassa and head for the safety of Abazon. At the edge of the Abazon province, the bus on which he is travelling incognito stops beside a group celebrating the news of His Excellency's downfall in a coup. During the revelry a drunken police officer begins to drag a young girl away, with sinister intentions. When Chris confronts him he is shot dead.

These events do not constitute the whole story, and the novel does not end there. The fortunes of the elite, male characters are placed among other voices and stories, particularly those of women. A crucial figure is Beatrice. Like the others she received a Western-style education in Kangan as a girl and later completed a degree in English at a London university. As a child she suffers the strict discipline of her patriarchal father, and this sensitises her to inequalities of gender. 'That every woman wants a man to complete her is a piece of male chauvinist bullshit I had completely rejected before I knew there was anything like Women's Lib', she remarks. 'You often hear our people say: But that's something you picked up in England. Absolute rubbish! There was enough male chauvinism in my father's house to last me seven reincarnations!' (p. 88).

Through the character of Beatrice, Achebe draws attention to the chauvinism of the powerful male characters and points out that their fortunes do not constitute an adequate representation of the nation's history. This is a point which Beatrice explicitly makes to Chris: 'Well, you fellows, all three of you, are incredibly conceited.

The story of this country, as far as you are concerned, is the story of the three of you' (p. 66). This 'conceited' story could be described in Ranajit Guha's terms as an 'elite historiography' in which 'subaltern' voices remain silenced. Although focusing in the main on the Kangan elite, Achebe is keen to point out that their story can never provide the complete narrative of the nation. Beatrice is one of several characters who disturb the elite male characters' autonomy over the narrative of Kangan's fortunes and enable issues such as gender difference to be raised.

Chauvinism appears at several parts of the text. In an early scene, His Excellency displays chauvinism by inviting Beatrice to a drinks party in order to provide the 'woman's angle' (p. 80) on Kangan for an American journalist. Chris is not free from chauvinism either; prior to the party he hints obliquely that Beatrice should keep all her 'options open' when dealing with His Excellency. The sexual connotations of this suggestion anger Beatrice, and she makes her feelings known to Chris after the party. She also criticises Ikem's radical political views on the grounds that he can imagine 'no clear role for women' (p. 91).

Gender relations are further complicated by other factors. Beatrice's well-educated background and social privilege are underlined in her dealings with her maid Agatha, to whom she talks in 'pidgin' English. As Dennis Walder explains, 'it is important to distinguish between pidgins, which have small vocabularies, restricted structures, lack expressive potential and are usually not a first language, and *creoles*, which are distinct varieties of English spoken as their mother tongue by "native speakers"' (*Post-Colonial Literatures in English*, Blackwell, 1998, p. 47). Beatrice must adopt a different language in order to communicate with her maid. This begs the questions: How representative is Beatrice of women like Agatha? How do differences in women's economic status affect female collectivity? It is difficult to assert a 'deep, horizontal comradeship' among the Kangan women when their potential sisterhood is complicated by 'vertical' social differences.

Another important character in a similar position to Agatha is the market woman Elewa, Ikem's lover, who bears a child after Ikem's death. Like Agatha, Elewa speaks the same form of pidgin English. The Western-educated characters certainly know this language – Chris speaks pidgin on his travels to Abazon – but do not use it when they speak with each other. These different uses of English bear witness to gender and class positions which are not elite, and their presence raises important questions. First, the reader is asked to question the kind of relationship that the ruling, Western-educated characters have with those from other classes. Are their world-views similar if they speak different languages? The differences in register suggest that the English-speaking elite might not be in step with the masses. Second, it raises issues about national languages. Can the nation's language be the received English which is used in government and by the educated elite, but not necessarily at large? These differences of language reveal the difficulties concerning imagining communities through a shared language, while pointing out the distance between the elite and the masses in Kangan.

Thus, *Anthills of the Savannah* gathers a variety of voices from different members of the nation without attempting to homogenise them into one collective voice. This is reflected in the novel's structure, which switches between the first-person narratives of Chris, Ikem and Beatrice, as well as third-person narration. The story is passed from one voice to the other, and in so doing the strengths and limits of each character's views are underscored. We are also made aware of those voices that the novel does *not* gather, but still acknowledges. In his lecture to the students, Ikem points out that those keen to fight the government in the name of a workers' or peasants' revolution should look around the lecture theatre and notice the absence of people from both groups. In a similar fashion, *Anthills of the Savannah* calls attention to the fact that its narrative of the nation cannot depict the nation's people as a whole, just as His Excellency's attempt to represent the nation as its leader is undermined by the unruly province of Abazon. There are always other voices missing. The novel's view, like that of its characters, must be selective and limited.

In these terms, *Anthills of the Savannah* offers an important critique of the nation after independence. On the one hand it suggests in a West African context that the fortunes of the nation have been damaged by a chauvinistic educated elite separated from the bulk of the people by education, class, power and privilege. But the nation as an ideal is not completely rejected. Achebe considers if solutions exist to the nation's ills which do not fall back on familiar nationalist representations. Is it possible to build a nation where all voices count, not just those of the English-speaking privileged males? Can relationships be built between different peoples which do not smother difference, nor set 'norms and limits' which result in marginalisation? Will the nation ever be free of illiberal tendencies?

These issues are raised in the novel's important final chapter, which depicts the naming of Elewa's baby daughter. Whereas the opening chapter of the novel depicted the machinations of His Excellency's male cabinet, the closing chapter is female-centred with Beatrice and Elewa playing important roles. Invited to the ceremony are many characters from outside the elite who have featured in the novel, and whose gathering constitutes an image of a diverse yet interrelated community. This heterogeneous congregation suggests an *alternative* image of nationhood in Kangan which challenges the exclusivity of His Excellency's elite chauvinist cabinet.

Borrowing some terms from Homi Bhabha, we could describe the naming ceremony as a moment when the performative interrupts the pedagogical. The baby-naming ceremony has solemn and fixed protocols, yet in the final scene at Beatrice's flat a different kind of ceremony is performed. Although it takes place on the seventh market day, as tradition dictates, other rules are broken. A male should perform the naming, but instead Beatrice decides to 'improvise a ritual' (p. 222) and conduct the naming herself. The name that is chose, Amaechina ('The-remnant-shall-return'), is a boy's name, but Elewa dismisses this incongruity: 'Girl fit answer am also' (p. 222). The naming of Amaechina depicts a *reconfiguration* of conventional gender roles so that the mapping of the future can be the result of the efforts of both men and women. As the daughter of the subversive writer Ikem and the market girl Elewa, Amaechina is perhaps symbolic of a new egalitarian life for the nation that repudiates the chauvinism and exclusivity of the Western-educated elite. As Elewa's uncle puts it, Kangan has been a troubled nation since independence 'because those who make plans make plans for themselves only and their families' (p. 228). But Amaechina is 'the daughter of all of us' (p. 228): she is a symbol of diversity in collectivity.

In Ikem's writings, His Excellency had been compared to an angry sun whose 'crimson torches fire the furnaces of heaven and the roaring holocaust of your vengeance fills the skies' (p. 30). Significantly, Beatrice is also linked to the sun through the comparisons made between her and the goddess Idemili:

> In the beginning Power rampaged through our world, naked. So the Almighty, looking at his creation through the round undying eye of the Sun, saw and pondered and finally decided to send his daughter, Idemili, to bear witness to the moral nature of authority by wrapping around Power's rude waist a loincloth of peace and modesty. (p. 102)

Idemili ascends to earth in a pillar of water which quenches the famished earth. The myth recalls the situation in Abazon, where the drought-stricken region is suffering under His Excellency's rule. Later in the novel, when Chris and Beatrice make love, Chris calls her a priestess or goddess. By the final chapter, Beatrice has been constructed via the myth of Idemili almost as a new goddess of hope, who has questioned the moral authority of the Kangan elite to govern the nation and introduced peace and modesty into the novel. Although she is an elite character, she challenges and subverts its primacy. She survives the destructive days of His Excellency's government and heralds a new age in the final chapter as she presides over a new form of naming ceremony – just like the anthills of the savannah in Ikem's Hymn to the Sun, 'surviving to tell the new grass of the savannah about last year's brush fires' (p. 31). In these terms, *Anthills of the Savannah* depicts the destructive activities of the Western-educated elite and urges a new kind of nation-building which includes those often left out of conventional nationalist representations. Yet the *idea* of the nation is not rejected outright.

STOP and THINK

In using Beatrice as a means of articulating new hopes and possibilities for Kangan, Achebe perhaps remains guilty of using women primarily as redemptive, mythic icons of the nation. Is Beatrice's role in the novel significantly different to that of Mumbi in Ngugi's *A Grain of Wheat*? In her reading of

Achebe's novel in her book *Stories of Women: Gender and Narrative in the Postcolonial Nation* (Manchester University Press, 2005), Elleke Boehmer persuasively argues that 'the way in which Achebe privileges woman continues to bear familiar markings for gender ... this to a certain extent compromises his reimagined hope' (pp. 60–1). Do you agree? Is Achebe's representation of women free from the charges made by Anthias and Yuval-Davis concerning women in chauvinistic nationalist representations? Does *Anthills of the Savannah* successfully resist the problems in nationalist representations which we have explored in this chapter, despite its best intentions?

Selected reading

Ahmad, Aijaz, *In Theory: Classes, Nations, Literatures* (Verso, 1992).
Offers at times a fierce defence of nationalism in the light of recent innovations in postcolonial theory.

Ashcroft, W. D., 'Constitutive Graphonomy: A Post-Colonial Theory of Writing' in Stephen Slemon and Helen Tiffin (eds), *After Europe* (Dangaroo, 1989), pp. 58–73.
A theoretically ambitious and influential (if problematic) attempt to account for different language uses that can be deemed 'postcolonial'.

Bhabha, Homi K. (ed.), *Nation and Narration* (Routledge, 1990).
Required reading for 'the nation in question'. Has several essays which critique nationalist representations in colonial, postcolonial and other contexts, as well as an earlier version of Bhabha's 'DissemiNation: Time, Narrative and the Margins of the Modern Nation' (in Homi K. Bhabha, *The Location of Culture*, Routledge, 1994).

Chatterjee, Partha, *Nationalist Thought and the Colonial World: A Derivative Discourse?* (Zed, 1986).
Has an excellent overview of critiques of nationalism in relation to colonialism in the opening chapter.

Gikandi, Simon, *Maps of Englishness: Writing Identity in the Culture of Colonialism* (Columbia University Press, 1996).
The opening chapter to this challenging text maps out the disenchantment with nationalism in the latter decades of the twentieth century.

Gilroy, Paul, *Between Camps: Race, Identity and Nationalism at the End of the Colour Line* (Allen Lane/The Penguin Press, 2000).

This book is one of the most penetrating and challenging critiques of the ideas of nation and nationalism to date, in which Gilroy explores the illiberal and linked operations of nationalism, racism and other perceived forms of prejudicial identification. Its dense and demanding written style makes it a challenging read at times, but the intellectual rewards are worth it.

Hardt, Michael and Antonio Negri, *Empire* (Harvard University Press, 2000).

Ostensibly a book about globalisation and the new world order, it contains a succinct if demanding discussion of the perceived unhappy fortunes of anti-colonial nationalism once independence is achieved (see pp. 105–9, 'Subaltern Nationalism').

Jayawardena, Kumari, *Feminism and Nationalism in the Third World* (Zed, 1986).

For the more advanced reader, this text examines the troubled fortunes of women's movements in relation to forms of Asian nationalism.

Lazarus, Neil, 'National Consciousness and the Specificity of (Post) Colonial Intellectualism' in Barker, Hulme and Iversen (eds), *Colonial Discourse/Postcolonial Theory* (Manchester University Press, 1994, pp. 197–220).

An essay which seeks to account for the 'continuing indispensability of national consciousness to the decolonising project' (p. 198).

Lazarus, Neil, *Nationalism and Cultural Practice in the Postcolonial World* (Cambridge University Press, 1999).

This is a complex and forceful materialist response to the denigration of the ideas of nation and nationalism in postcolonial studies. Highly recommended.

Murray, Stuart (ed.), *Not on any Map: Essays on Postcoloniality and Cultural Nationalism* (Exeter University Press, 1997).

Ngugi wa Thiong'o, *Decolonising the Mind: The Politics of Language in African Literature* (James Currey, 1981).

Chapter 1, 'The Language of African Literature', contains Ngugi's argument concerning his decision to no longer write in English.

Parker, Andrew, Mary Russo, Doris Sommer and Patricia Yaeger (eds), *Nationalisms and Sexualities* (Routledge, 1992).

Includes several useful essays which critique nationalist representations for their questionable gender and sexual politics.

Parry, Benita, *Postcolonial Studies: A Materialist Critique* (Routledge, 2004).

This book includes several essays which defend the significance and revolutionary impact of anti-colonial nationalism against the scepticism of much postcolonial theory.

Young, Robert J. C. Young, *Postcolonialism: An Historical Introduction* (Blackwell, 2001).

This book includes some long and detailed chapters on the fortunes of revolutionary anti-colonial nationalisms across the once-colonised world, highlighting the different forms and trajectories they took.

Yuval-Davis, Nira and Floya Anthias (eds), *Woman-Nation-State* (MacMillan, 1989).

Includes a variety of essays which deal with the problematic relations of women and nationalism in several contexts, as well as an excellent theoretical introduction.

5

Re-reading and re-writing English literature

Interrogating the text

Writing about her experience of the study of English literature in India, Meenakshi Mukherjee has defended postcolonialism as an emancipatory concept on the grounds that 'it makes us interrogate many aspects of the study of literature that we were made to take for granted, enabling us ... to re-interpret some of the old canonical texts from Europe from the perspective of our specific historical and geographical location' (*Interrogating Post-Colonialism: Theory, Text and Context*, eds Harish Trivedi and Meenakshi Mukherjee, Indian Institute of Advanced Study, 1996, pp. 3–4). The re-interpretation of 'classic' English literary works has become an important area of postcolonialism and has impacted upon all kinds of literary debates, in particular the ongoing disputes about which texts can be considered as possessing 'literary value' and the criteria we use to measure it.

This chapter will introduce these issues by taking as points of orientation two interrelated themes: the *re-reading* of literary 'classics' in the light of postcolonial scholarship and experience, and the *re-writing* of received literary texts by postcolonial writers. In so doing we shall be looking at two novels: Charlotte Brontë's *Jane Eyre* (1847), and Jean Rhys's *Wide Sargasso Sea* (1966) which engages with Brontë's text.

Colonialism and the teaching of English literature

Mukherjee's phrase 'old canonical texts' refers to the 'canon' of English literature: the writers and their work which are believed to be of particular, rare value for reasons of aesthetic beauty and moral sense. I shall be using the term 'classic' to refer to this kind of text. The inverted commas will be kept to signal that it is a matter for debate whether or not texts are *inherently* valuable or worthy; for some, the status of 'classic' is ultimately awarded by readers. Hence, the literary value of a text is open to disagreement and change.

Many postcolonial writers and critics were taught the 'classics' of English literature in once-colonised locations, where English literature has been an important subject on the curriculum. For example, the Antiguan writer Jamaica Kincaid recalls studying 'the Brontës, Hardy, Shakespeare, Milton, Keats ... They were read to us while we sat under a tree' (in *Caribbean Women Writers*, ed. Selwyn Cudjoe, Calaloux, 1990). The teaching of English literature in the colonies has been understood by some critics as one of the many ways in which Western colonial powers such as Britain asserted their cultural and moral superiority while at the same time devaluing indigenous cultural products. The image of Jamaica Kincaid sitting under her tree in Antigua encountering a series of texts that ostensibly concern British locations, culture and history is a striking example of the ways in which many of those in the colonies were asked to perceive of Western nations as places where the very best in art and learning were produced, the lasting value of which could survive in locations far removed from the texts' point of origin. However, the *responses* to English literature by people in similar positions to Kincaid are particularly interesting and varied, and we shall be considering their character in this chapter.

Education is arguably a crucial ideological apparatus of the state by which certain values are asserted as the best or most true. Colonialism uses educational institutions to augment the perceived legitimacy and propriety of itself, as well as providing the means by which colonial power can be maintained. This is the argument of Gauri Viswanathan's book *Masks of Conquest: Literary Study and British Rule in India* (Faber, 1989). Viswanathan's study concerns the emergence of English literature as a subject in educational establishments in India during the early nineteenth century specifically to serve colonial interests. Many administrators were keen to build an English-speaking Indian workforce that would help carry out the work of the colonial authorities. Lord Macaulay, president of the Council on Education in India, put it thus in his now infamous 'Minute on Indian Education' of 1835:

> It is impossible for us, with our limited means, to attempt to educate the body of the people. We must at present do our best to form a class who may be interpreters between us and the millions whom we govern; a class of persons, Indian in blood and colour, but English in taste, in opinions, in morals, and in intellect. To that class we may leave it to refine the vernacular dialects of the country, to enrich those dialects with terms of science borrowed from Western nomenclature, and to render them by degrees fit vehicles for conveying knowledge to the great mass of the population. (Reprinted in *The Post-Colonial Studies Reader*, second edition, p. 375)

Macaulay's pronouncement rests upon several assumptions. Knowledge is deemed the enriching possession of the 'scientific' West and must be taught to those in India, but the process is not reciprocal. An Orientalist hierarchy is asserted between a knowledgeable, civilised West and an ignorant, savage East. Thus, the education of Indians is part of a civilising process that involves a certain *moral* improvement – it is not just a process that will heighten intellect and opinion. The education of Indians for the purposes of consolidating power is legitimised by appearing morally just and improving.

This was also the concern of many evangelicals in India at the time who were keen that Indians converted to Christianity. However, it became clear during the early nineteenth century that many Indians objected to the denigration of their own religions by missionaries and the teaching of Biblical scripture in schools. Viswanathan argues that evangelicals coped with this problem by trying to promote Christian morality indirectly through the teaching of English literature. Rather than studying issues such as grammar or diction, English literary texts were presented in profoundly moral terms, with students invited to consider how texts conveyed 'truths' at once universal and timeless, yet entirely correspondent with Christian morality. 'The importance of English literature for this process could not be exaggerated', argues Viswanathan; 'as the source of moral values for correct behaviour and action, it represented a convenient replacement for direct religious instruction' (*Masks of Conquest*, p. 93). The study of English literature became the study of models of moral worth to the extent that English literature seemed first and foremost *about* morality. This weaving together of morality with a specifically *English* literature had important ideological consequences. Literature implied that moral behaviour and English behaviour were synonymous, so that the English literary text functioned 'as a surrogate Englishman in his highest and most perfect state' (p. 20). In reading English literature in moral terms, then, Indian students were being exposed to a code of values deemed Christian and universal, yet also specifically identified with the colonising nation.

So, in an Indian context Viswanathan reveals that the teaching of English literature in the colonies was complicit with the maintenance of colonial power. And although it is never wise to generalise, it is fair to say that writers from other colonised locations have often pointed out this relationship. For many in countries with a history of colonialism, English literary texts have become considered *not* as timeless works of art remote from history but as complicit in the colonising enterprise itself. So, when Meenakshi Mukherjee argues that postcolonialism 'makes us interrogate many aspects of the study of literature that we were made to take for granted', we understand that the ability to read literary texts in ways *different* to those which have been laid down, can contribute to resisting the assumptions of colonial discourses which may still circulate today.

It is important to realise this 'interrogation' can take several forms. On the one hand it can lead to the questioning of the value of specific literary texts based upon their perceived ideological moorings. In 1975 Chinua Achebe controversially denounced Joseph Conrad's *Heart of Darkness* (1899) on the grounds that it proved how Conrad was a thoroughgoing racist (see Chinua Achebe, 'An Image of Africa: Racism in Conrad's *Heart of Darkness*' in *Hopes and Impediments: Selected Essays, 1965–87*, Heinemann, 1988, pp. 1–13). Achebe objected to Conrad's derogatory and dehumanising representation of Africa and Africans, and pointed out that it remained one of the most commonly taught books in English departments in American universities as part of the canon of 'great' literature. In continuing to teach this novel as 'great', Conrad's alleged late-Victorian racism was being perpetuated in the present day as this supposedly racist text was falsely presented to students as of exceptional literary value. This approach to 'classic' literature has created all kinds of challenges for critics, and is behind one of the reasons why some people have responded with anger and hostility to postcolonial reading practices. It has been difficult for some to accept that, as Nicholas Harrison has put it, 'a "beautiful" piece of writing may be shot through with delusions and brutality' (*Postcolonial Criticism: History, Theory and the Work of Fiction, Polity*, 2003, p. 2).

But Achebe's dismissal of this 'classic' text is not definitive. Although many object to the 'classics' either because they proffer colonialist views of the world or because they first encountered them as part of a colonial education, several writers have emphasised that the relationship between literary 'classics' and themselves has also been a *productive* one. Writers have *put literary 'classics' to new uses* for which they were scarcely originally intended, and have turned to them as sources of inspiration. Achebe himself has written movingly about his early encounters with William Shakespeare's plays. As a child he remembers coming across an old copy of *A Midsummer Night's Dream* 'in an advanced stage of falling apart. I think it must have been a prose adaptation, simplified and illustrated. I don't remember if I made anything of it. Except the title. I couldn't get over the strange beauty of it. ... It was a magic phrase – an incantation that conjured up scenes and landscapes of an alien, happy and unattainable land' (*Hopes and Impediments*, pp. 23–4). Achebe's subsequent career as a writer, as someone engaged by and involved in the craft of storytelling, is indebted to many sources and forms of inspiration, including the cultural products of the colonising power. As Achebe knows, not all such texts are inevitably colonialist.

Consider too Shakespeare's *The Tempest*, which is set on an unnamed magical island and frequently depicts the magician Prospero in command of his unruly subjects Ariel and (especially) Caliban. As John Thieme explains in his extremely insightful book on postcolonial rewritings – or 'con-texts' as he calls them – 'Prospero and Caliban have become synonymous with the figures of colonizer and colonized for many postcolonial writers and theorists' (*Postcolonial Con-Texts: Writing Back to the Canon*, Continuum, 2001, p. 127). Some postcolonial writers, such as George Lamming and Aimé Césaire from the Caribbean, have conceived of Prospero and Caliban as 'archetypes of the colonizer and the colonized, placing particular emphasis on the psychological consequences of colonialism and Caliban's response to the imposition of Prospero's language' (p. 129), and have appropriated the play to give voice to issues of colonial dominance and postcolonial dissidence (for example, have a look at Lamming's use of Prospero and Caliban in his book of essays *The Pleasures of Exile*, Michael Joseph, 1960). This is *not* the same as claiming that Shakespeare wrote a play about colonialism; although there has been much debate about the extent to which the play takes colonialism as its subject, as in Peter Hulme's excellent book *Colonial Encounters: Europe and the Native Caribbean 1492–1797*, (Routledge, 1986). Rather, we need to consider how the received literary 'classics' can become *resources* for those writing to articulate postcolonial positions who use them as *points of departure*. Many writers enter into a *productive critical dialogue* with literary 'classics'. Thieme's concept of the 'con-text' captures precisely the complexity of the intertextual relationships that I am trying to convey here. As he discovered in his study of postcolonial con-texts, the influence of the 'classic' text 'could seldom be seen as simply adversarial – or, at the opposite extreme, complicitious' (*Postcolonial Con-Texts*, p. 2). Rather than repudiate 'classic' texts, such texts need to be understood as making possible 'counter-discourses that write back to the canon in a multiplicity of ways' (p. 3); they are not merely oppositional or aggressively combative. So while many writers and intellectuals reveal how a 'classic' can be culpable with colonialism, they also make available new ways of dealing with the 'classics' which make new meanings possible. Very few writers take the easy option of merely dismissing 'classic' texts because they seem complicit in colonialist ways of seeing. We shall explore this 'productive critical dialogue' further at the end of the chapter when considering Jean Rhys's *Wide Sargasso Sea*.

Colonial contexts

Let us concentrate first on looking at how literary 'classics' have been re-read. Postcolonial literary criticism has affinities with other kinds of study in recent years concerned with reading literary texts in relation to their historical, social and cultural contexts, rather than as timeless expressions of universally acknowledged moral values. 'Context' refers to something more dynamic and less unified than 'historical background'; it is used to suggest the many dominant issues, debates and knowledges in circulation at the time a text was written, the various and competing ways in which people conceived of their reality in the past. All societies labour under certain assumptions about how the world is ordered. As we have seen previously, colonialism operates in part *discursively* by asserting knowledge about such things as 'race', gender, differences in culture and nation, and so on. Colonialist representations will tend to support a view of the world which justifies the continuing legitimacy of colonialism (although counter-representations can often be discerned too).

Reading a text in relation to its contexts involves doing two things simultaneously: first, identifying how such contexts are made present or absent in a text, and second, exploring how the text itself may *intervene* in the debates of its day and applaud or resist dominant views of the world. We must not forget that literary texts are always *mediations*: they do not passively reflect the world but actively interrogate it, take up various positions in relation to prevailing views, resist or critique dominant ways of seeing. As Nicholas Harrison counsels, we need to remain cognisant of 'the full complexity of the dialogue, so to speak, between a fictional text and the experiences, discourses and debates it brings into play' (*Postcolonial Criticism*, p. 3). To read a text in its historical, social and cultural contexts is to attend to the ways it *dynamically* and *dialogically* deals with the issues it raises. And in a colonial context, it is also perhaps to refute the dominant way of teaching literature as expressing lasting moral truths contradictorily deemed at once timeless yet specifically characteristic of the colonising nation.

For many postcolonial critics, reading an established 'classic' of literature written at the time of colonialism often involves exploring its relationship with many of the issues and assumptions that were fundamental to colonial discourses. In Chapter 2 we thought about how Kipling's 'The Overland Mail' could be read in relation to theories of colonial discourses. The reasons for this were reasonably straightforward: Kipling lived in India as a young man and his poem is set in colonial India, so it would seem appropriate to read the poem in the manner we explored. However, postcolonial re-readings of literary works have in some instances focused upon texts that might seem hardly to deal with colonialism. Just because a literary text is *not* set in a colonial location, nor makes colonialism the predominant theme to be explored, it does not follow that such texts are free from the realities of the British Empire. In recent years, several literary 'classics' have been re-read to reveal, sometimes controversially, a hitherto unseen investment in colonialism.

STOP and THINK

How many 'classic' works of literature can you think of in which the existence and influence of Britain's relationship with colonial lands overseas plays a part? What role do the colonies, or characters from the colonies, play in these texts? To what extent do these texts support or problematise some of the assumptions in colonial discourses which we have met in previous chapters? For example, you might like to consider the importance of the colony of Virginia in Daniel Defoe's *Moll Flanders* (1722) or Australia in Charles Dickens's *Great Expectations* (1861).

Reading literature 'contrapuntally'

Two 'classic' English novels that have been re-read in their colonial contexts are Jane Austen's *Mansfield Park* (1814) and – as we will explore at some length – Charlotte Brontë's *Jane Eyre* (1847). *Mansfield Park*'s relations with colonial contexts have been discussed at some length by Edward W. Said in his book *Culture and Imperialism* (Vintage, 1993). As part of his lucid and convincing argument that Western culture cannot be understood without recognising its fundamental investment in imperialism, Said explores the relations between Austen's *Mansfield Park* and Britain's colonisation of the Caribbean island of Antigua. Said provocatively argues that the Antiguan material in the novel is not marginal but central to the novel's meaning, and the connections between the locations of Mansfield Park and Antigua are vital.

Mansfield Park is the property of Sir Thomas and Lady Bertram. As Said argues, Sir Thomas's economic interests in the Caribbean provide the material wealth upon which the comfortable middle-class lifestyle of Mansfield Park depends. The seemingly domestic interior world of this English country house cannot exist independent from the world outside, no matter how remote it might seem from the plantations of Antigua. Indeed, the inseparability of the world 'inside' and 'outside' the house is reflected in other ways. Throughout much of the novel Sir Thomas is absent from Mansfield Park, tending to some problems that have arisen on his plantation in Antigua. In his absence, the younger characters at Mansfield Park become unruly. On his return, Sir Thomas instantly puts a stop to their disorderly conduct and re-establishes decorum. Said suggests that Sir Thomas's ability to set his house in order on his return is reflective of his role as a colonial landlord:

> There is nothing in *Mansfield Park* that would contradict us, however, were we to assume that Sir Thomas does exactly the same things – on a larger scale – in his Antigua 'plantations'. Whatever was wrong there … Sir Thomas was able to fix, thereby maintaining his control over his colonial domain. More clearly than anywhere else in her fiction, Austen here synchronises domestic with international authority, making it plain that the values associated with such higher things as ordination, law, and propriety must be grounded firmly in actual rule over and possession of territory. She sees clearly that to hold and rule Mansfield Park is to hold and rule an imperial estate in close, not to say inevitable association with it. What assures the domestic tranquillity and attractive harmony of one is the productivity and regulated discipline of the other. (*Culture and Imperialism*, p. 104)

The parallels Said detects between these locations supports his argument that the borders between inside and outside, domestic and international, England and Empire are permeable. The interior world of Mansfield Park is not static or enclosed, but dynamic and dependent upon being resourced from the outside. Fanny's shift in status from her poor Portsmouth beginnings to becoming part of the wealthy Bertram family at Mansfield Park helps secure its future, just as Sir Thomas's movements between England and Antigua safeguard its economic health. Indeed, Said believes Fanny's journey corresponds at a small-scale level to Sir Thomas's transatlantic ventures: both bring resources from the outside into Mansfield Park, upon which subsequent security depends.

There are three consequences of re-reading *Mansfield Park* in its colonial contexts. First, such a reading bears witness to what Said calls the *worldliness* of culture. This term reminds us that literary texts emerge from and have complex engagements with the historical, social and political conditions of their time, among which colonialism is fundamental in the nineteenth century. Second, this approach both exemplifies and encourages *contrapuntal readings* of literary texts. Said defines a contrapuntal reading as one which remains simultaneously aware 'both of the metropolitan history that is narrated and of those other histories against which (and together with which) the dominating discourse acts' (p. 59). For example, in order to read *Mansfield Park* contrapuntally we must recognise that the dominant world-view offered by the novel is grounded in various presumptions. The novel bears witness to the existence of the slave plantations in Antigua but assumes that there is nothing very objectionable in this fact. Reading *Mansfield Park* contrapuntally not only involves spotting moments when the colonies are represented; it is also to bring to the novel a knowledge of the history of the Caribbean which the novel is not necessarily writing about but upon which it ultimately depends. The history which helps to shape *Mansfield Park* is not just limited to the social changes occurring in Britain at the beginning of the nineteenth century, but is also the history of colonisation and its resistance (one wonders why Sir Thomas's Antiguan estate is in such disarray in the first place). Ultimately, contrapuntal readings 'must take account of both processes, that of imperialism and that of resistance to it' (p. 79).

The third point concerns literary value. Reading texts contrapuntally, Said argues, often reminds the critic of the continuing value of the literary work being studied. *Mansfield Park* may have 'affiliations with a sordid history' of slavery (p. 114) but in Said's view there is no need to devalue the novel as a consequence. The brilliance of Austen's work depends upon the complex and subtle ways she configures the relations between Mansfield Park and Antigua. A lesser work 'wears its historical affiliation more plainly; its worldliness is simple and direct, the way a jingoistic ditty ... connects directly to the situation and constituency that coined it' (p. 116).

STOP and THINK

Said's comments about literary value are questionable. Why shouldn't a text's affiliations with a 'sordid history' prompt us to question how and why we value that particular text? And why is a subtle and complex text more valuable than one that is 'simple and direct'? From one position it could be argued that Said's line of thought inevitably takes him to the brink of asking large questions about literary evaluation, yet at the last moment he shrinks from the consequences of his own argument by defending rather too adamantly the unshakeable value of the many literary 'classics' he cites.

Yet, an alternative response might suggest that Said is trying to read the literary 'classics' with more subtlety than someone like Chinua Achebe, whose critique of Conrad's *Heart of Darkness* led it to be condemned because it did not pass a certain ideological test. Said's reinstatement in *Culture and Imperialism* of the value of *Mansfield Park* suggests that literary value need not be entirely dependent upon a text's ideological moorings. In so doing, Said perhaps keeps open a debate on literary value which Achebe's reading of Conrad forecloses.

We shall be returning to the problematic area of literary value in our exploration of *Jane Eyre*. But it is worth giving some thought throughout this chapter to whether, in your view, re-reading texts in their colonial contexts alters how you value them, and why. How might postcolonialism be altering the way you value literary and other cultural texts? And how do you feel about that?

Re-reading Charlotte Brontë's Jane Eyre

Let us now turn to reading a literary 'classic' in the light of some of the ideas we have gathered so far. In what follows we aim to emphasise some of the purposes, methods and the difficult questions raised by reading Charlotte Brontë's *Jane Eyre* in relation to its colonial contexts. We shall be using the Penguin Classics (1985) edition of the novel edited by Q. D. Leavis.

Jane Eyre follows the life of a young girl from her childhood into the first years of adulthood. At the beginning of the novel Jane is a lonely orphan living miserably at Gateshead Hall in the company of her Aunt Reed and three cousins. The subject of much cruelty and little love from the Reeds, she is sent away to the strict regime of Lowood school where, after some initial unpleasantness instigated by the puritanical Mr Brocklehurst, she enjoys a more supportive environment and begins to flourish. She eventually works as a teacher in the school, and as an eighteen-year-old is employed as a governess to a young French child, Adèle, at Thornfield Hall.

At Thornfield she meets Edward Rochester, the wealthy owner of the Hall, and the pair gradually fall in love. Thornfield is a place both of happiness and disquiet for Jane. She enjoys her role as a governess but struggles to control her strong feelings for Rochester. She settles into the house and makes good relationships with many of the staff, but is occasionally disturbed at night by a strange laughter coming from the room above hers. Several mysterious incidents also occur; in one, Jane is forced to pull a sleeping Rochester from his chamber, which inexplicably has been set on fire.

Eventually Rochester and Jane confess their feelings of love for each other and agree to marry. During the night before the wedding, Jane wakes to see reflected in her mirror a strange dark figure ripping her wedding veil in two. The next day, the wedding service is interrupted by John Mason, previously a guest at Thornfield, who claims to Jane's horror that her marriage cannot take place as Rochester already has a wife. Rochester is forced to admit that he is indeed married, to Mr Mason's sister, Bertha. Bertha is the figure that Jane saw the previous night, whom Rochester has kept locked up in the room above Jane's. Rochester explains that his marriage to Bertha was the result of his father's financial dealings. His father had intended that the Rochester family fortune should pass to the eldest son, Rowland. In order to provide an income for his second son, Edward, he secured Edward's marriage to Bertha, the daughter of a planter and merchant living in Jamaica. Bertha's mother was a Jamaican Creole (a term which Brontë uses to signify 'racially mixed' parentage) believed to be dead, but after the marriage Rochester learned that she was locked in a lunatic asylum. Once married, Bertha also sinks swiftly into lunacy. Rochester decides to quit Jamaica and return to Thornfield with his wife, whom he has since kept secretly imprisoned in the attic.

Appalled and upset at these revelations, Jane leaves Thornfield secretly soon after the failed wedding. After wandering lonely, desolate and hungry, she is taken in by a parson, St John Rivers, and his two sisters, Diana and Mary, at Moor House. Calling herself Jane Elliott, she recuperates and soon takes charge of the local village school. By chance, St John Rivers discovers her true identity and reveals that she is the cousin of himself, Diana and Mary. In a further twist, Jane learns that she is to inherit the fortune of £20,000 from her uncle John Eyre, a wine merchant from Madeira (a Portuguese-governed island off the Moroccan coast). Jane shares this inheritance equally between the cousins and then faces another challenge: an offer of marriage from St John Rivers. St John is keen to travel to India to work as a missionary; he has been teaching Jane Hindustani, and wishes her to accompany him. Jane turns down the offer and decides instead to return to Thornfield to be reunited with her beloved Rochester. She finds only ruins. Soon after Jane's departure from Thornfield Hall, Bertha had escaped her confines and set the house ablaze. The fire claimed her life and left Rochester blind and missing a hand – but also a widower. Jane finds Rochester and is lovingly reunited with him, and as she famously announces in the last chapter, 'Reader, I married him' (p. 474). The novel ends with the news that Rochester has regained some sight, that the now-wealthy Diana and Mary have both happily married, and with the image of St John braving the dangers of India as he pursues his pioneering missionary work, although Jane anticipates that she will soon learn of his death abroad.

Such a scant summary of *Jane Eyre* does little justice to the intricate twists and turns of Brontë's narrative, but it should be noticeable even in a brief account like this the extent to which colonialism and colonial locations are crucial to the events of the novel. Two particular colonial scenarios are conjured: via the Masons we are exposed to the plantation-owning community in Jamaica, while St John Rivers connects the novel with British missionary work in India. In addition, elements from colonial locations also emerge in the novel *figuratively*; that is, they supply Jane with a series of images and metaphors which she uses to articulate her own position on several occasions. The economic relationships between the novel's characters are particularly vital to the plot. Edward Rochester's first marriage to Jamaican-born Bertha gains him a fortune of £30,000 which makes possible his affluent lifestyle at Thornfield. And as Susan Meyer reminds us in her excellent essay '"Indian Ink": Colonialism and the Figurative Strategy of *Jane Eyre*', Jane's inheritance of £20,000 also has a colonial source:

> It comes from her uncle in Madeira, who is an agent for a Jamaican wine manufacturer, Bertha's brother. The location of Jane's uncle John [Eyre] in Madeira, off Morocco, on the West African coast, where Richard Mason stops on his way home from England, also indirectly suggests, through Mason's itinerary, the triangular route of the British slave traders, and suggests that John Eyre's wealth is implicated in the slave trade. (Susan Meyer, *Imperialism at Home: Race and Victorian Women's Fiction*, Cornell, 1996, p. 93)

Put bluntly, without the money made from colonialism, Rochester could not enjoy the luxuries of Thornfield Hall, nor could Jane secure a life with Rochester and facilitate the happy and respectable marriages of her cousins Diana and Mary, who were otherwise destined to live as humble governesses for wealthy families in the south-east of England. So, as Judie Newman puts it, at the end of the novel 'Jane and Rochester settle down to a happy married life on the proceeds of the Empire' (*The Ballistic Bard: Postcolonial Fictions*, Edward Arnold, 1995, p. 14).

Yet despite the novel's use of the economics of colonialism, re-readings of *Jane Eyre* in its colonial contexts have emerged only in recent years. One of the most important is Gayatri Chakravorty Spivak's ground-breaking if cryptic essay 'Three Women's Texts and A Critique of Imperialism', first published in 1985 (in *'Race'*,

Writing and Difference, ed. Henry Louis Gates Jr., University of Chicago Press, pp. 262–80). This essay is especially important as it reveals how *Jane Eyre* is implicated in colonialism not just in terms of economic wealth, but *at the level of narrative and representation.* Spivak has markedly revised this essay for her book *A Critique of Postcolonial Reason: Toward a History of the Vanishing Present* (Harvard University Press, 1999), but in what follows we will stick with the 1985 version, mainly because it has been an influential essay in discussions of postcolonial re-writings but also because much of the material in the later version is less specific to the detail of *Jane Eyre*.

In order to explore this claim, we first need to place Spivak's essay in its own context. 'Three Women's Texts and A Critique of Imperialism' is ostensibly a response to Anglo-American feminist literary criticism of the late 1970s, in which *Jane Eyre* had become a celebrated or 'cult' text. Sandra M. Gilbert and Susan Gubar in their ground-breaking book *The Madwoman in the Attic: The Woman Writer and the Nineteenth-Century Literary Imagination* (Yale University Press, 1979) celebrate Jane as a proto-feminist heroine who struggles successfully to achieve female self-determination in an otherwise patriarchal and oppressive world. Spivak suggests that celebratory readings of the novel as politically subversive are flawed in their lack of attention to the fact that 'imperialism, understood as England's social mission, was a crucial part of the cultural representation of England to the English' ('Three Women's Texts and A Critique of Imperialism', p. 262). Jane's journey from subservience to female self-determination, economic security and marriage on her terms could not occur without the oppression of Bertha Mason, Rochester's Creole wife from Jamaica. Spivak points out that Gilbert and Gubar read Bertha always *in relation* to Jane, never as an individual self in her own right. In their words, Bertha is Jane's 'truest and darkest double: she is the angry aspect of the orphan child, the ferocious secret self that Jane has been trying to repress ever since her days at Gateshead' (*Madwoman in the Attic*, p. 360). Thus conceived, Bertha's lunacy represents the anger that Jane represses in order to be deemed an acceptable woman in a patriarchal world. This reading of Bertha purely in relation to Jane's self leaves out the colonial context of

Bertha's imprisonment and fails to examine some of the assumptions concerning Bertha's lunacy and her representation in terms of 'race'.

For example, consider the moment when Rochester takes Jane to see Bertha just after the wedding has been disrupted by Mr Mason. Jane describes seeing a figure 'whether beast or human being, one could not at first sight tell' (*Jane Eyre*, p. 321). Bertha's ambiguous bestiality, her wild and violent nature dovetail with her 'mixed' Creole lineage and Jamaican birthplace. This slippage repeats a frequent assumption in colonial discourses that those born of parents not from the same 'race' are degenerate beings, perhaps not fully human, closer to animals. Bertha is robbed of human selfhood; she has no voice in the novel other than the demoniac laughter and the discomforting noises that Jane reports. Her animalistic character disqualifies her from the journey of human self-determination for which Jane is celebrated by Anglo–American feminist critics.

Bertha's half-human Creole 'savagery' leaves its mark most memorably in the novel when she sets fire to Thornfield Hall and jumps to her death in an apparent act of suicide, rather than allow Rochester to save her from the burning building. But note that this act is of fundamental consequence to the plot: Bertha is the major impediment to Jane's process of movement from the position of misbegotten orphan to one of legitimacy, fortune and especially marriage. Jane can only clinch this position as a consequence of Bertha's death in the blaze. By attending to the ways in which Bertha is derogatively characterised, and the fact that her suicide acts as a crucial cog in the 'structural motors' ('Three Women's Texts', p. 263) of the narrative, Spivak reveals how Jane's journey towards legitimacy, fulfilment and agency cannot occur without the persistent subservience of Bertha Mason to the requirements of the plot. Bertha is always connected to Jane as an 'other'; she never achieves any self of her own. Jane's journey to self-fulfilment and her happy marriage are achieved at the cost of Bertha's human selfhood and, ultimately, her life. As Spivak memorably puts it, Bertha 'must play out her role, act out the transformation of her "self" into that fictive Other, set fire to the house and kill herself, so that Jane Eyre can become the feminist individualist heroine of British fiction' (p. 270). In the later version of this essay, Spivak attends to the intended disruptiveness of her postcolonial reading of *Jane Eyre*, specifically the intervention she is trying to make in metropolitan or 'First World' readings of the novel. Spivak wants to *bring to crisis* the celebration of Jane as a proto-feminist individualist. As she claims, in her postcolonial approach to the novel and celebratory readings of it, 'the effort is to wrench oneself away from the mesmerising focus of the "subject-constitution" of the female individualist' (*A Critique of Postcolonial Reason*, p. 117) in order to recognise the colonialist axiomatics which this focus ultimately ignores and hence tacitly endorses.

Spivak's reading of *Jane Eyre* underlines the novel's investment in colonial realities and thus complicates the ease with which it might be read as a politically subversive feminist text. According to Spivak, a reading which does not take colonialism into account 'reproduces the axioms of imperialism' ('Three Women's Texts', p. 262). By reading Bertha Mason *metaphorically* as the repressed side of Jane's psyche, at most an expression of the 'secret self' of the main character, Gilbert and Gubar stand accused of this charge. Spivak's reading of the novel returns it to its colonial contexts, and ultimately urges new disruptive strategies of reading which take colonialism into account when approaching not only this novel, but nineteenth-century literature in general.

One (perhaps unintentional) result of Spivak's essay is the impression that *Jane Eyre* is entirely complicit with many of the assumptions in colonial discourses. An examination of other passages in the novel might seem to support this reading, although as we shall see later it is not the only conclusion that can be made. The first passage is taken from Rochester's narrative of his marriage to Bertha which occurs in Chapter 27. Rochester is describing a 'fiery West Indian night' (*Jane Eyre*, p. 335) during which he contemplated committing suicide rather than having to endure the future with his lunatic wife:

> Being unable to sleep in bed, I got up and opened the window. The air was like sulphur-streams – I could find no refreshment anywhere. Mosquitoes came buzzing in and hummed sullenly round the room; the sea, which I could hear from thence, rumbled dull like an earthquake – black clouds were casting up over it; the moon was setting in the waves, broad and red, like a hot cannon-ball – she threw

her last bloody glance over a world quivering with the ferment of tempest. I was physically influenced by the atmosphere and scene, and my ears were filled with the curses the maniac [Bertha] still shrieked out. (p. 335)

This passage seems to perpetuate many colonial assumptions. Rochester's terms of reference depict Jamaica as a satanic and apocalyptic location. The references to the 'sulphur-streams' of air, the ominous noise of the sea, and the 'hot cannon-ball' of the moon give the impression of Jamaica as a hell-on-earth. His senses are assaulted and disturbed: he sees a blood-red landscape under black clouds; he hears rumblings like an earthquake and the screams of his wife from another room of the house; the intense heat denies him sleep or comfort. It is as if the very demoniac nature of the landscape gets into the being of those unfortunate enough to live there, as Rochester admits. The crazed world outside is responsible for driving Rochester wild, and his decision to shoot himself shows how much his mind has been deranged by the stormy environment. Consequently, the tumultuous conditions of Jamaica seem to have affected Bertha, who similarly displays fiery, tempestuous and turbulent behaviour. Bertha represents what Rochester could become – indeed, perhaps *has* become – by staying in Jamaica: lunatic and useless, at the mercy of demoniac forces that will turn his life into a living hell.

What saves him from madness and suicide? The answer is particularly revealing. As Rochester describes it, a wind 'fresh from Europe' (p. 335) breaks the storm and offers relief from the crazed conditions of the night. By the morning he, like the weather, has had a change of heart; and the landscape too has also changed:

The sweet wind from Europe was still whispering in the refreshed leaves, and the Atlantic was thundering in glorious liberty; my heart, dried up and scorched for a long time, swelled to the tone, and filled with living blood – my being longed for renewal – my soul thirsted for a pure draught. I saw hope revive – and felt regeneration possible. From a flowery arch at the bottom of my garden I gazed over the sea – bluer than the sky: the old world was beyond; clear prospects opened. (p. 336)

This passage depicts a different Jamaica, one of growth and beauty, as suggested by the references to the clear blue sea, the refreshed leaves, the flowery arch where Rochester looks again at the world. Note that although this passage acknowledges the beauty of the landscape, one that contrasts sharply with the bleak mosquito-infested environment of the night before, 'regeneration' has been produced by the 'sweet' wind from Europe that 'whispers' in the leaves, as opposed to the fiery 'West Indian night' when it seemed the world was in the midst of an earthquake. This series of contrasts – sulphurous/sweet, rumble/whisper, thirst/refreshment – also connects with other contrasts between the scenes such as the black fiery night and the blue regenerative morning.

In comparing these two scenes we notice how Brontë constructs her fictional world in terms of what we might term *manichean* oppositions. This is a term popularised by Abdul JanMohamed in his book *Manichean Aesthetics: The Politics of Literature in Colonial Africa* (University of Massachusetts Press, 1983), which we can borrow for our example. 'Manichean aesthetics' refers to a system of representations which conceives of the world in terms of opposed categories, from which comes a chain of associations. Reality is constructed as a series of polarities which derive from the opposition posited between light and darkness, and good and evil. This provides a structure of both meaning and morality. So, in a system of manichean aesthetics, all that is light is orderly, tractable, rational, angelic and ultimately good; whereas all that is dark is degenerate, chaotic, transgressive, lunatic, satanic and hence evil. In *Jane Eyre*, the blue light of the morning reveals that the 'old world beyond' has magically broken through the tempestuous night of the new world and saved Rochester's life from self-destruction. The relationship between Jamaica and Europe is both contrasting and unequal, the latter having more power than the former despite the spectacular apocalyptic storm of the night before.

These passages would suggest that *Jane Eyre* can be read as reproducing some of the assumptions of colonial discourses. The representation of Bertha and Jamaica, as well as the economic relations of the novel, bear witness to the relationship between *Jane Eyre* and the contexts of colonialism. They remind us that the canonical 'classical' works of English literature did not emerge, and do not exist, remote from history, culture and politics.

STOP and THINK

There remains a problem in re-reading literary 'classics' as colonial discourses. Are we to conclude that Charlotte Brontë is somehow a colonialist in the light of our reading so far? If so, what purpose does this conclusion serve? If, as Patrick Brantlinger points out, in British literature of the mid-nine-teenth century there was an 'easy confidence that rarely saw anything problematic' about imperialism (*Rule of Darkness*, Cornell, 1988, p. 29), should we be surprised that aspects of Brontë's work conform to colonialist views? It might be mistaken to think of Brontë as a typically British colonialist in her outlook, not least because she was the daughter of a Cornish mother and an Irish-born Church of England clergyman (who, incidentally, changed the Irish family name 'Brunty' to the more Germanic-sounding 'Brontë' with its famous umlaut).

To return to an issue we raised earlier: does the novel's investment in colonialism threaten its status as a work of artistic value? Should *Jane Eyre* be stripped of its status as a 'classic'? These have proven difficult questions to answer, and it is worth spending some time thinking about the answers you would give, and why.

Jane Eyre: a postcolonial text?

In the light of Spivak's essay, several critics have pursued relations between *Jane Eyre* and its colonial contexts, but have been more speculative as to the extent to which the novel is complicit with nineteenth-century British colonialism. To re-read *Jane Eyre* as merely reflective of the assumptions of colonial discourse only takes us so far. Re-reading literary 'classics' in relation to their colonial contexts is perhaps not particularly productive if all we do is label and dismiss those texts once and for all as ideologically corrupt or 'colonialist'. We are in danger of imposing upon the literature from the past the concerns of the present, and in one sense we cannot claim to be reading historically at all. Said would describe this critical response as a 'rhetoric of blame' (*Culture and Imperialism*, p. 115) used by some critics to denounce retrospectively literary works which seem to support a colonial view of the world. We need to keep remaining alert to the complexity of the dialogue which texts can conduct with their historical and political contexts, as well as understand the ways in which our readings of the 'classics' can prioritise their dissident rather than colonialist elements.

Furthermore, it is not perhaps wise to assume that the manichean view of the world articulated by Edward Rochester in his descriptions of Jamaica is also the view of Charlotte Brontë. Few, I suspect, would assume that Shakespeare was anti-Scottish after watching a performance of *Macbeth*. But perhaps most importantly, this kind of labelling fails to consider conceiving of texts as potentially *questioning* colonial views. Indeed, for some critics, the point of re-reading these texts is not just to show how they confirm dominant perspectives, but how they might be read as *challenging* these views.

In these terms, 'classic' texts are re-read to uncover emergent, counter-colonialist positions that they may, perhaps unwittingly, make available to the reader. In so doing, by identifying how colonialism was brought to *crisis* in the literature from the past, this critical enterprise lends support to the continued challenge to colonialism in the present by underlining the ways in which colonialism has been subverted. Many literary texts can be re-read to discover the hitherto hidden history of *resistance* to colonialism that they also articulate, often inadvertently. Although this approach also involves reading a past text in the light of present concerns, as all readings unavoidably do, perhaps this reading strategy enables a more dynamic and potentially resourceful relationship between literature from the past and present concerns. In re-reading the 'classic' text readers can *put that text to work*, rather than either placing it on a pedestal or tossing it to one side as a consequence of whether or not it is deemed free from ideological taint. Furthermore, an attention to the counter-colonial properties of the literary 'classic' might also enable a way of challenging the kind of generalising view of literary history that Brantlinger risks in the description of mid-nineteenth-century literature we encountered a moment ago.

In *Jane Eyre*, we can find the possibility of subversion in, perhaps surprisingly, Bertha Mason. As we have seen, Bertha is described as degenerate, half-animal; a figure whose behaviour both reflects and seems created by the tempestuous, chaotic and fiery environs of the West Indies. How can this figure be subversive? Bertha's incendiary character is of particular importance when we recall that Brontë was writing *Jane Eyre* in the 1840s. Many of the slaves working on the plantations in Jamaica were originally Africans who had been captured, shipped in appalling conditions across the Atlantic Ocean and sold to the plantation owners. (This horrific journey, often referred to as the 'Middle Passage', has been an important subject in postcolonial literature from the Caribbean.) Britain abolished the slave trade in 1807 but it still permitted the use of slaves as hard labour on the plantations. Full slave emancipation in the British Caribbean possessions was achieved between 1834 and 1838, the period which Susan Meyer argues roughly corresponds to Jane's time at Thornfield Hall and her eventual marriage to Rochester. During the 1830s, resistance by the slaves to their conditions was widespread. In western Jamaica between December 1831 and early 1832 there occurred what historians call the 'Baptist War', when over 60,000 slaves rose against the British. Fires were started which served as beacons to let other slaves know that an uprising had begun, and the burning of the plantations was an important part of the slaves' resistance (see Peter Fryer, *Black People in the British Empire: An Introduction*, Pluto, 1988, pp. 92–7). It could be argued that Bertha's attempt to set fire to Rochester's chamber while he is asleep, and her eventual razing of Thornfield Hall to the ground, recall the fiery resistant activities of slaves in Jamaica.

Susan Meyer argues that '[t]he story of Bertha, however finally unsympathetic to her as a human being, nonetheless does make an indictment of British imperialism in the West Indies and the stained wealth that came from its oppressive rule' (*Imperialism at Home*, p. 71). Although the novel never allows Bertha to tell her own story (rather than have it narrated by Rochester), it does bear witness to resistance to colonial rule occurring at the time. Firdous Azim reads Bertha's unruly temperament as evidence of the ultimate failure of colonialism to control those from whom it commanded obedience. As she persuasively puts it, '[t]he figure of Bertha Mason is significant, as she represents the failure of the pedagogical, colonising enterprise. Recalcitrant and uneducatable, she escapes the dominating and hegemonising imperialist and educational processes' (*The Colonial Rise of the Novel*, Routledge, 1993, p. 183). Following Said's model, Bertha's unruly presence can be read *contrapuntally* as resistant to the rule of those who deem her less than fully human, and paradigmatic of the plantation slaves who rose against the oppressive rule of the Jamaican slave owners.

Bertha also might be seen to resist the authoritative eye of our narrator, Jane Eyre. Let us briefly recall the dehumanising description of Bertha that interested Spivak:

> In the deep shade, at the farther end of the room, a figure ran backwards and forwards. What it was, whether beast or human, one could not, at first sight tell: it grovelled, seemingly, on all fours; it snatched and growled like some strange wild animal: but it was covered with clothing, and a quantity of dark, grizzled hair, wild as a mane, hid its head and face. (*Jane Eyre*, p. 321)

This is a remarkable moment in the novel. Prior to this passage the reader has been teased by the enigmatic noises and strange figures that disrupt Jane's nights. The revelation of Bertha promises to solve the mystery by allowing Jane to look upon that which has been hitherto concealed. But notice how, in a series of vague phrases, Jane struggles to render what she sees. Bertha is not clearly visible to Jane's eye; she remains in shade, *seeming* to grovel, looking like *some* strange animal. Her head and face remain hidden from view. We could read this passage as evidence of the extent to which colonial discourses (if we take the passage as an example of such) often disqualify the colonised subject from being adequately represented. But from another position we might notice how the presence of Bertha *problematises* Jane's position as an omniscient narrator. Jane's authority as a narrator is challenged as Bertha will not be readily captured within Jane's narrative. She is beyond easy rendering in language. Is Bertha's hiding of her face and head a purposeful act, an attempt to escape representation?

If Bertha exists to make possible Jane's proto-feminist journey from orphanhood to money and marriage, perhaps in this crucial passage she threatens to bring Jane's fictional world to crisis by threatening to escape containment within its descriptive confines. In this imprecise description the omniscient narrative of the nineteenth-century realist novel is pushed to its limits by the presence of an unruly colonised subject who threatens to escape that which sentences her. Maybe at this moment *Jane Eyre* is more a postcolonial than a colonial text.

STOP and THINK

As we noted above, *Jane Eyre* connects with colonialism in at least two locations: Jamaica and India. Think about how India is represented in the text. At one point, at the climax to Chapter 24, Jane compares herself to Indian Hindu women who ascend their husbands' funeral pyres and perform the act of *sati*, or widow burning. How would you read this passage? What is at stake in Jane's appropriation of this position?

Also, how might the final chapter of the novel, including details of St John Rivers's life in India as a missionary, influence the extent to which this novel supports or critiques British colonialism?

Postcolonial re-writings: Jean Rhys, *Wide Sargasso Sea*

Earlier we noted that many writers have entered into a productive critical dialogue with literary 'classics', where the 'classic' text is interrogated but also can function as an important imaginative resource. Let us conclude this chapter by exploring how Jean Rhys re-writes *Jane Eyre* in her novel *Wide Sargasso Sea* (1966). We shall use the Penguin Classics (1997) edition of the novel, edited and introduced by Angela Smith.

Jean Rhys was born in the Caribbean island of Dominica in 1890 and moved to Britain as a sixteen-year-old, where she endured a difficult and at times controversial life. Her Welsh father had come to the island as a young man while her mother's family had been based there throughout the nineteenth century and had once owned slaves. Rhys had a significant relationship with the Caribbean and Britain, yet her sense of belonging to both was complicated by the circumstances of her birth. As a descendent of the white slave-owning class, her relations with black Caribbeans descended from slavery could not be unaffected by the historical circumstances of the region, and as a Dominican-born white woman she could not consider herself first and foremost British. As Helen Carr summarises, 'Rhys was a colonial in terms of her history, even though she can be considered a postcolonial in her attitude to the Empire and in her employment of many postcolonial strategies' (*Jean Rhys*, Northcote House, 1996, p. 18).

Perhaps because of her Caribbean background, Rhys became preoccupied with Brontë's Bertha Mason with whom in some respects she occupied a similar position. Bertha's father is Jonas Mason, a planter and merchant, and thus a member of the colonising community in Jamaica. Both Bertha's mother and Rhys's mother were Creoles; both Bertha and Rhys left the Caribbean for England as young women. We might describe *Wide Sargasso Sea* as a novel in which Rhys takes as her point of inspiration the figure of Bertha Mason and places her centre-stage, allowing her the possibility to achieve selfhood and granting her the opportunity of telling things from her point of view (although, as we shall see, there are problems in making this statement). This is not done for the purposes of 'completing' *Jane Eyre*, adding the story that is missing from the novel like a missing piece from a jigsaw. Instead, the relationship between the two novels is much more dynamic and dialogic, enabling an *interrogation* of the agency of the 'classic' text to fix meaning. Furthermore, the extent to which *Wide Sargasso Sea* can be (or should be) read squarely in terms of *Jane Eyre* is also open to debate. As we shall, Rhys's novel both *engages with* and *refuses Jane Eyre* as an authoritative source. We can regard this refusal as part of the postcolonial strategies which Carr claims for Rhys's writing.

Wide Sargasso Sea proceeds through three parts. The first is narrated by Antoinette Cosway, who records her childhood with her widowed mother Annette in a large house, Coulibri, in Jamaica just after the Emancipation Act which formally ended slavery. She remembers her childhood as a time of both beauty and danger. With the power of the plantation-owning class in decline, the relationship between the black and white communities becomes increasingly tense. Antoinette's mother marries Mr Mason, who attempts to reinvest Coulibri with some of its previous grandeur and authority.

But Coulibri is set on fire and Antoinette's brother Pierre is killed. The incident drives Annette to distraction, and Antoinette is sent away to a convent school during which time her mother dies. Later, as a seventeen-year-old she is visited by her stepfather Mr Mason who invites her to live with him in Jamaica.

In Part 2 the narrative shifts unexpectedly to an un-named male character, who, it quickly transpires, has married Antoinette. The couple are on their honeymoon at Granbois. Although this figure is never named, the reader familiar with *Jane Eyre* might assume that this character is analogous to Brontë's Rochester. At first it seems their relationship is benign, but it soon becomes fraught with tension. The un-named narrator takes to calling his wife 'Bertha', a name to which she objects. Antoinette's husband is uncomfortable with the island and its inhabitants, especially his wife's black servant Christophine. Eventually he is contacted by one Daniel Cosway who claims to be Antoinette's half-brother. He informs the narrator about the madness of the Cosway family and links Christophine to the practice of obeah (or voodoo). Choosing to believe Daniel, the narrator convinces himself that he has been tricked into marriage, and his relationship with Antoinette deteriorates. Antoinette interrupts the narrative and tells briefly of how she pleads with Christophine to give her a potion that will make her husband love her again. Instead, her husband has a sexual encounter with a black servant, Amélie, and decides to return to England with the wealth he has inherited through his marriage. Antoinette will come too, although under duress.

The third part of the novel is set in England, in a large house. The opening paragraphs are narrated by Grace Poole but the rest is delivered by Antoinette. She contrasts her memories of Caribbean life with the grey surroundings of her attic cell, and tells of her wanderings through the house at night. In a remarkable climax to the novel she dreams of setting the house on fire and jumping from the rooftop. On waking she resolves 'what I have to do' (*Wide Sargasso Sea*, p. 124). She takes a candle and the keys from the slumbering Grace Poole and leaves the room. The novel ends with Antoinette walking with the candle along a dark passage.

There are two elements of the text on which we shall particularly focus: the novel's curious narrative structure and the importance of naming. As might be clear from our summary, one of the novel's complexities concerns narrative voice. The text has two major first-person narrators, Antoinette and her husband, as well as other contributors such as Grace Poole and Daniel Cosway. This beckons questions concerning the overall control of the narrative in *Wide Sargasso Sea*. Antoinette's representation of events comes into competition with her husband's. On several occasions in the text our attention is drawn to the incompatibility of each other's vista, as they both compete for the control of meaning. For example, at one point in the husband's narrative he argues with Antoinette about the appearance and manner of Christophine:

> 'Her coffee is delicious [I said] but her language is horrible and she might hold her dress up. It must get very dirty, yards of it trailing on the floor.'
>
> 'When they don't hold their dress up it's for respect' said Antoinette. 'Or for feast days or going to Mass.'
>
> 'And is this feast day?'
>
> 'She wanted it to be a feast day.'
>
> 'Whatever the reason it is not a clean habit.'
>
> 'It is. You don't understand at all. They don't care about getting a dress dirty because it shows it isn't the only dress they have.' (*Wide Sargasso Sea*, pp. 52–3)

In this exchange, Antoinette's husband lacks knowledge of local custom. His interpretation of events is not allowed to stand unchallenged. The incident is in stark contrast to Rochester's position in *Jane Eyre*, where his version of life in the Caribbean is the only one the reader has, while Bertha is reduced to shrieks and unintelligible noises. In the quotation above the husband is confronted with his own ignorance of cultural specificity. But he refuses to learn and dismisses Antoinette's view ('Whatever the reason it is not a clean habit'). In this clash of perspectives we can trace a contest of power which is simultaneously colonial and patriarchal. In this exchange we might also find figured the relationship between *Jane Eyre* and *Wide Sargasso Sea*, with the latter *answering back* and critically challenging the views of Caribbean people and places in the former.

Antoinette's husband wishes to be the arbiter rather than the recipient of knowledge, and he aims to assert his control over his wife by contesting her views. This is reflected in the novel's structure by the fact that (apart from one hiatus) he is the narrator of their married life in the Caribbean which constitutes Part 2. In marrying Antoinette, he also lays claim to the authority over her *representation*. Antoinette's debasement takes place entirely within his first-person narrative. He chooses to believe Daniel Cosway's slander that 'there is madness in that family' (p. 59) and that she has had intimate relations with her cousin Sandi, preferring these allegations to Antoinette's version of her family history. By the end of Part 2 he has *made for himself* his own version of events in which he believes that his father and eldest brother have married him off to Antoinette so as to be rid of him, situating her as the focal point for his anger:

> They bought me, *me* with your paltry money. You helped them do it. You deceived me, betrayed me, and you'll do worse if you get the chance ... (*That girl she look you straight in the eye and talk sweet talk – and it's lies she tell you. Lies. Her mother was so. They say she worse than her mother.*) (p. 110)

In this quotation the un-named narrator's interior monologue slips into the voice of Daniel Cosway. The italicised sentences are a quotation of a speech made by Daniel to Antoinette's husband earlier in the novel. It is these *masculine* voices which attempt to define and confine Antoinette, (re)constructing her character and passing judgement on her behaviour. Hence, Rhys exposes the ways in which colonial discourses create their own images of alterity rather than reflect an existent reality, while undercutting this process by highlighting the extent to which the husband's knowledge is based on the flimsiest of evidence. This passage also exposes the complicity between colonialism and patriarchy which we will pursue in Chapter 6.

Significantly, Antoinette's husband makes a drawing which anticipates both her fate and that of Bertha Mason in *Jane Eyre*:

> I drew a house surrounded by trees. A large house. I divided the third floor into rooms and in one room I drew a standing woman – a child's scribble, a dot for a head, a larger one for the body, a triangle for a skirt, slanting lines for arms and feet. But it was an English house. (pp. 105–6)

This quotation is crucial on two counts. First, it represents the extent to which Antoinette's husband lays claim to the power of representing her on his own terms. She becomes what he makes her. Second, the 'child's scribble' of Antoinette as a crude line drawing hardly approximates to the complex character we have met in the first section of *Wide Sargasso Sea* and reminds us that, both in this novel and in *Jane Eyre*, Antoinette and Bertha are *not* the crude definitions given by their husbands. No matter how much others try to define Antoinette's identity, we know she is not what her husband represents in his narrative. His power of representation is not secure, not complete in this text.

In these terms, Antoinette is both *confined by* and *escapes* her representation by other characters in *Wide Sargasso Sea*. This is reflected in the novel's structure. Her husband may relate the longest section of the narrative, reflecting his desire to control meaning, but Antoinette's voice interrupts his at the novel's central point in Part 2. She is also the novel's first and last narrator, making her husband's narratives contained inside hers. Neither character is fully in control. Meaning and definition are continually contested in this narrative, and it is difficult to fix meaning in the ways that Antoinette's husband would like. Significantly, unruly voices are *always* deemed threatening to authority in the novel. Antoinette's husband fears that if he stays in the Caribbean 'I'd be gossiped about, sung about (but they make up songs about everything, everybody. You should hear the one about the Governor's wife)' (p. 105). According to Grace Poole, there are complaints about the gossip concerning Antoinette in the attic: '*There were hints about the woman he brought back to England with him. Next day Mrs Eff wanted to see me and she complained about the gossip. I don't allow gossip*' (p. 115). Rhys draws attention to the presence of unruly voices of people in subservient positions which challenge and unnerve those in positions of power. In so doing the novel explores the ways by which those made subject to others can resist the attempts by authority figures to fix meaning and establish their voices as the dominant and controlling ones. This contest, I would argue, is epitomised in the relationship between Antoinette and her husband.

Attending to how some characters attempt to fix meaning while others resist being fixed through voicing their own perspectives helps us consider the important intertextual relationship between *Jane Eyre* and *Wide Sargasso Sea*. As we have seen, Rhys's novel does much more than 'fill in' the gaps missing in Brontë's work. Yet in tethering *Wide Sargasso Sea* to *Jane Eyre*, Rhys might be in danger of constructing an unequal power relationship between the two by positioning *Jane Eyre* as an authoritative source-text from which the meanings of Rhys's novel are derived. In making *Jane Eyre* the point of authoritative reference, it could be argued that *Wide Sargasso Sea* remains dependent upon Brontë's novel in a way that mirrors Antoinette's subservience to her husband's design. Indeed, one might go so far as to say that the dependent relationship between two texts echoes the colonial relationship between Britain and its Caribbean colonies, with Rhys's novel 'governed' by the dictates of *Jane Eyre*.

However, *Wide Sargasso Sea* complicates its relationship with *Jane Eyre* in several ways which make it difficult to draw these conclusions. To take but two: first, consider how *Wide Sargasso Sea* is set during the 1830s and 1840s, specifically *after* much of the action of *Jane Eyre* takes place. Yet, if the novel is meant to be the life of Bertha Mason *before* her transportation to England as the first Mrs Rochester then this cannot be right: the action must have occurred much earlier in time. This oddity has led the novel to be called a 'post-dated prequel' of *Jane Eyre*. The temporal anomaly makes *Wide Sargasso Sea* seem to pre-date *Jane Eyre*, and position Rhys's novel as that which anticipates the action of Brontë's text (as opposed to the other way round). As Judie Newman succinctly puts it, '[b]y commandeering *Jane Eyre* has *her* sequel, therefore, Rhys enjoins future readers to envisage Victorian Britain as dependent upon her colonies, just as Brontë's heroine depends upon a colonial inheritance to gain her own independence' (*The Ballistic Bard*, p. 15). So, in complicating the potentially dependent relationship between the texts, Rhys attempts to resist her novel being fully contained by Brontë's. Indeed, Antoinette's challenge to the narrative authority of her husband reflects the novel's relationship as a whole with *Jane Eyre*. *Wide Sargasso Sea* stands in a similar relationship to *Jane Eyre*, engaging with Brontë's novel in order to challenge its meaning by criticising its representations. This activity of 'putting meaning on the move' is an important postcolonial strategy which motivates the re-writing of 'classic' texts. *Wide Sargasso Sea* is in part engendered by *Jane Eyre*, but its meanings are not fully determined by it. Instead, Rhys's novel turns to challenge the meanings made available in Brontë's work by entering into critical dialogue with it.

Which leads us, finally, to the naming of characters in *Wide Sargasso Sea*. Names are often central to our sense of identity. Note how Antoinette's name is constantly changing in the novel as her family circumstances alter (some critics refer to her as Bertha Antoinette Cosway Mason Rochester!). Such a long convoluted name calls attention to the extent to which Antoinette's identity is always being defined in relation both *to* men and *by* men. To what extent is Antoinette ever really free of others' definitions of her identity and in control of herself? In addition, why is her husband never named as Rochester?

It is tempting perhaps to fix 'Bertha Antoinette Cosway Mason Rochester' as simply 'Bertha' and her husband as 'Rochester', but in so doing we perhaps re-enact something not too dissimilar from Antoinette's husband's 'child's scribble' of a woman in a house in England: we trap these characters inside representations made by somebody else which only *approximate* to the individuals we have met. If we identify Brontë's novel as the source of meaning which can explain and resolve the ambiguities of naming in Rhys's text, we perhaps do what Rhys does not do: we as readers construct that hierarchical relationship in which *Wide Sargasso Sea* is contained and determined by *Jane Eyre*. We no longer think of Antoinette and her husband as fictional creations of Rhys independent from semantic determination by another text.

Through the complications surrounding naming, Rhys reminds us that *we as readers always have an active role to play* in the creation and questioning of meaning. *Wide Sargasso Sea* demands that we think carefully about our attempts to fix meaning and resolve ambiguity, to discover one authoritative voice among the clamour of many voices. It invites us to consider that such attempts might not be too remote from colonial and patriarchal impulses to fix representations of others whose voices are consequently silenced. Ultimately, the extent to which *Wide Sargasso Sea* confirms or resists the authority of *Jane Eyre* is the responsibility of the reader, who may or may not choose to treat *Jane Eyre* as an authoritative source and settle the nature of the relationship between the two. Rhys may well deploy postcolonial narrative strategies, as Helen Carr claimed; but we need to think also about our agency and responsibility as readers if we are not to erase the subversive potential of *Wide Sargasso Sea*.

'Re-writing': possibilities and problems

In the light of our discussion, let us recap what can be involved in the 're-writing' of a literary 'classic':

- A re-writing does much more than merely 'fill in' the gaps perceived in the source-text. Rather, it enters into a *productive critical dialogue* with the source text.
- A re-writing takes the source-text as a point of inspiration and departure, but its meanings are not fully determined by it.
- A re-writing often exists to *resist* or *challenge* colonialist representations of colonised peoples and cultures perceived in the source-text and popular readings of it. In this way we might consider a re-writing of a 'classic' text as 'postcolonial'.
- A re-writing often implicates the reader as an *active agent* in determining the meanings made possible by the dialogue between the source-text and its re-writing.

But for some, re-writings of literary 'classics' are not without their problems which must also be faced when exploring the interface between the source-text and the re-writing.

First, a re-writing often imagines the reader will be familiar with the source-text it utilises, and thus is addressed first and foremost to an educated reader versed in the literary works of the colonising culture. For some this makes re-writings directed at a small privileged and educated elite. Those of us who have not had access to the source-text will be in a relatively deficient position. Second, a re-writing will always remain tethered in some degree to its antecedent. This problematises the extent to which postcolonial re-writings of literary 'classics' can ever be really independent of colonial culture. The re-writing will always invest value in the source-text as a point of reference, no matter how much it is challenged as a consequence. For this reason, some critics believe that re-writings can never fully challenge the authority of the 'classic' text; indeed, re-writings continue to invest literary 'classics' with value by making them a point of reference for postcolonial texts.

STOP and THINK

In this chapter we have looked at *Jane Eyre* as containing both colonial *and* postcolonial moments, and it is worth concluding by thinking about the tethering of *Wide Sargasso Sea* to *Jane Eyre*. Can Rhys's text fully eradicate its dependence on Brontë's work? In reading *Wide Sargasso Sea* as a postcolonial text we must also recognise the possible perpetuation of a colonial relationship between the source-text and its re-writing. If *Jane Eyre* is not simply a colonial text, then *Wide Sargasso Sea* is perhaps not readily regarded as postcolonial. As we are discovering in this book as a whole, these categories are by no means mutually exclusive or absolute.

Selected reading

Azim, Firdous, *The Colonial Rise of the Novel* (Routledge, 1993).
    An excellent study of nineteenth-century fiction in its colonial contexts.
Brantlinger, Patrick, *Rule of Darkness: British Literature and Imperialism 1830–1914* (Cornell University Press, 1988).
    A wide-ranging examination of mostly nineteenth-century English literature which plots changing attitudes to colonialism and their manifestation in the writing of the period. The chapter on Conrad's *Heart of Darkness* is especially useful.
Carr, Helen, *Jean Rhys* (Northcote House, 1996).
    A short and compelling study of Jean Rhys which accounts for Rhys's particular kinds of modernist, feminist and postcolonial writing. Chapter 2, 'Feminist and Postcolonial Approaches to Jean Rhys', is particularly useful.
Childs, Peter (ed.), *Post-Colonial Theory and English Literature: A Reader* (Edinburgh University Press, 1999).
    A useful collection of salient essays which deal in the main with the re-

reading of the 'classics', including Shakespeare's *The Tempest*, Daniel Defoe's *Robinson Crusoe* (1719), Brontë's *Jane Eyre*, Conrad's *Heart of Darkness* and James Joyce's *Ulysses* (1922).

Hulme, Peter, *Colonial Encounters: Europe and the Native Caribbean 1492–1797* (Routledge, 1986).

Includes a long, scholarly study of Shakespeare's *The Tempest* in its colonial contexts, highly recommended.

James, Selma, *The Ladies and the Mammies: Jane Austen and Jean Rhys* (Falling Wall Press, 1983).

Meyer, Susan, '"Indian Ink": Colonialism and the Figurative Strategy in *Jane Eyre*' in *Imperialism at Home: Race and Victorian Women's Fiction* (Cornell, 1996).

In my view the best essay on *Jane Eyre* and its colonial contexts, and a good example of 'contrapuntal' reading. Witty, erudite and highly persuasive. Reprinted in Peter Childs's collection cited above.

Newman, Judie, *The Ballistic Bard: Postcolonial Fictions* (Edward Arnold, 1995).

A stimulating, lively and challenging text which looks at several different postcolonial re-writings of 'classic' texts and offers a series of imaginative readings. The first chapter, 'I Walked with a Zombie', is a wonderful reading of the intertextual relationship between *Jane Eyre* and *Wide Sargasso Sea*. The introduction is also highly recommended.

Said, Edward W., *Culture and Imperialism* (Vintage, 1993).

A major work in postcolonialism in which Said traces the relations between Western culture and Western imperialism in a variety of genres and looks at the work of Conrad, Austen, Yeats and others. The second half of the book deals with the resistance to Western culture and imperialism by colonised peoples.

Spivak, Gayatri Chakravorty, 'Three Women's Texts and A Critique of Imperialism' in Henry Louis Gates, Jr. (ed.), *'Race', Writing and Difference* (University of Chicago Press, 1985), pp. 262–80.

This is Spivak's influential reading of *Jane Eyre, Wide Sargasso Sea* and Mary Shelley's *Frankenstein*, and required reading when thinking about re-reading and re-writing 'classic' texts. This essay features moments of some difficulty and can be hard to follow in places, so proceed through it slowly. A substantially revised version of this essay can be found in Spivak's challenging work *A Critique of Postcolonial Reason: Toward a History of the Vanishing Present* (Harvard University Press, 1999), pp. 112–48.

Thieme, John, *Postcolonial Con-Texts: Writing Back to the Canon* (Continuum, 2001).

This is a very useful book which explores the re-writing of 'classic' canonical texts by a wealth of postcolonial writers. Thieme's notion of the 'con-text' is very helpful indeed in conceptualising the postcolonial purposes of the writing he discusses.

Viswanathan, Gauri, *Masks of Conquest: Literary Study and British Rule in India* (Faber, 1989).

A prolonged and detailed study of the teaching of English in India, which has proven highly influential for postcolonial critics and writers.

Zonana, Joyce, 'The Sultan and the Slave: Feminist Orientalism and the Structure of *Jane Eyre*', *Signs: Journal for Women in Culture and Society*, 18 (3), 1993, pp. 592–617.

An examination of Brontë's problematic use of Orientalism for her own feminist purposes. (Reprinted in Peter Childs's collection cited above).

6

Postcolonialism and feminism

Some definitions

Postcolonial feminist criticism is extensive and variable. Its analyses range across representations of women in once-colonised countries and in Western locations. Some critics have concentrated on the constructions of gender difference during the colonial period, in both colonial and anti-colonial discourses; while others have concerned themselves with the representations of women in postcolonial discourses, with particular reference to the work of women writers. At the level of theory, postcolonial feminist critics have raised a number of conceptual, methodological and political problems involved in the study of representations of gender, some of which we will be looking at in detail in this chapter. These problems are at once specific to feminist concerns, such as the possibility of finding an international cross-cultural sisterhood between 'First World' and 'Third World' women, as well as more general problems concerning who has the right to speak for whom, and the relationship between the critic and their object of analysis. Indeed, it would be fair to say that some of the most ground-breaking, thought-provoking and challenging work within post-colonialism has emerged out of debates concerning representations of gender difference in postcolonial contexts.

That said, some critics remain unhappy with the relatively marginal position that matters of gender are assigned in postcolonialism. Elleke Boehmer has argued that '[i]n mainstream postcolonial studies, gender is still conventionally treated in a tokenistic way, or as a subsidiary to the category of race' (*Stories of Women: Gender and Narrative in the Postcolonial Nation*, Manchester University Press, 2005, p. 7). With this point in mind, it is worth noting that the title of this chapter is not intended to imply that feminism is somehow anterior to postcolonialism when speaking of 'feminism *and* postcolonialism'. The two concepts are firmly hinged. Yet, the title also recognises that postcolonialism and feminism are sometimes seen to share tense relations with each other, and this chapter is concerned with the unfolding of these tensions. As we shall presently explore, feminists working out of different locations have also questioned the extent to which Western, or 'First World' feminism is equipped to deal with the problems encountered by women in once-colonised countries or those living in Western societies with ancestral connections to these countries (such as migrants and their descendants). So, by using these terms 'postcolonialism' and 'feminism' in conjunction I hope to maintain, on the one hand, a sense of the potential tensions between postcolonial and feminist critical practices, while, on the other, suggest their rapport.

A note on terminology is needed before we look at some of these debates, particularly concerning how to define 'feminism' and 'patriarchy'. As we would expect, it is as challenging to define 'feminism' as it is to define 'postcolonialism'. The variable range of work which can be called 'feminist' makes it difficult to summarise feminism in a sentence. But we need a place to start if we are to use it. June Hannam has suggested that we might understand 'feminism' to mean

> a set of ideas that recognize in an explicit way that women are subordinate to men and seek to address imbalances of power between the sexes. Central to feminism is the view that women's condition is socially constructed, and therefore open to change. At its heart is the belief that women's voices should be heard – that they should represent themselves, put forward their own view of the world and achieve autonomy in their lives. (*Feminism*, Pearson Longman, 2006, pp. 3–4)

There are some key issues raised by Hannam which immediately find their resonance in postcolonial studies: matters of subordination, power, the social construction of lived experiences, an investment in change, concerns about representation and self-representation. As we shall see, this last matter (representing women) has become a particular preoccupation for postcolonial critics in a feminist frame. In a cultural context, we might ask how the act of reading can contribute to the goals of feminism. In their introduction to *The Feminist Reader: Essays in Gender and the Politics of Literary Criticism* (ed. Belsey and Moore, Macmillan, 1989), Catherine Belsey and Jane Moore argue that a feminist reader is 'enlisted in the process of changing the gender relations which prevail in our society, and she regards the practice of reading as one of the sites in the struggle for change' (p. 1). They suggest that a feminist reader might ask of a text questions such as 'how [it] represents women, what it says about gender relations, how it defines sexual difference' (p. 1). In addition, those texts which do not mention women at all are interesting for this very reason. So, as we can see from these two quotations, the possible standpoints of postcolonial and feminist critics might at first sight not appear to be too far apart.

In talking of 'imbalances of power' and the 'struggle for change', we can understand that feminist reading practices are involved in the contestation of patriarchal authority. The term 'patriarchy' refers to those systems – political, material and imaginative – which invest power in men and marginalise women. Like colonialism, patriarchy manifests itself in both concrete ways (such as denying women a vote) and at the level of the imagination. It asserts certain representational systems which create an order of the world presented to individuals as 'normal' or 'true'. Also like colonialism, patriarchy exists in the midst of resistances to its authority. Furthermore, as a singular term, 'patriarchy' can be misleading. As much feminist criticism has shown, there are many different forms of patriarchy, each with its own specific effects: indeed, this latter point is particularly important in postcolonial feminist criticism. So, feminism and postcolonialism share the mutual goal of challenging forms of oppression.

Two further terms require comment before we proceed: 'First World' feminism and 'Third World' women. These terms relate to a system of ways of mapping the global relationships of the world's nations which emerged after the Second World War. The 'First

World' referred to the rich, predominantly Western nations in Europe, America and Australasia; the 'Second World' denoted the Soviet Union and its communist allies; while the 'Third World' consisted in the main of the former colonies such as countries in Africa and South Asia which were economically under-developed and dependent upon the wealthy nations for their economic fortunes. This mapping of the world has remained influential, for better or worse, in a variety of discourses. In terms of postcolonialism and feminism, the phrase 'First World' feminism is an unhappy generalisation which glosses over the variety of feminisms, and the debates within and between them, in Europe and America. As with 'race' I think it is worthwhile keeping the quotation marks to remind us continually that it is *not* a transparent term. Yet the naming of a 'First World' feminism has proved a productive means of acknowledging and questioning the limits of feminist scholarship in the West, particularly its relations with 'Third World' women. Of course, this latter phrase is also problematic because it similarly conflates the experiences and representations of a diverse body of people often in once-colonised countries, as we will be discovering presently, yet it too has acted at times as an enabling conceptual category. So, although such phrases will be used in this chapter, they remain provisional *categories of convenience* rather than factual denotations of fixed and stable groups.

In what follows, we will begin by locating the various kinds of patriarchal authority to which women from countries with a history of colonialism may be subjected, and address the concept of 'double colonisation'. Then we will look at postcolonial critiques of 'First World' feminism in thinking about the problems and possibilities when using 'First World' feminism in postcolonial contexts. This will involve examining some important and challenging essays by Gayatri Chakravorty Spivak. Finally, we shall apply some of the ideas and concepts introduced in this chapter when reading Sally Morgan's autobiographical text, *My Place* (Virago, 1988).

The 'double colonisation' of women

Kirsten Holst Petersen and Anna Rutherford have used the phrase 'a double colonisation' to refer to the ways in which women have *simultaneously* experienced the oppression of colonialism and patriarchy. In the 'Foreword' to their edited collection *A Double Colonisation: Colonial and Post-Colonial Women's Writing* (Dangaroo, 1986), Petersen and Rutherford argue that colonialism celebrates male achievement in a series of male-oriented myths such as 'mateship, the mounties, explorers, freedom fighters, bush-rangers, missionaries' (p. 9), while women are subject to representation in colonial discourses in ways which collude with patriarchal values. Thus the phrase 'a double colonisation' refers to the fact that women are twice colonised – by *colonialist* realities and representations, and by *patriarchal* ones too. Much postcolonial feminist criticism has attended to the representations of women created by 'double colonisation', and questioned the extent to which both postcolonial and feminist discourses offer the means to challenge these representations.

Let's consider this 'double colonisation' in more detail, because it affects women from *both* the colonised and colonising cultures in various ways. In her book *Imperial Fictions: Europe's Myths of Orient* (Pandora, rev. 1994) Rana Kabbani looks at the production of the Eastern female as a figure of licentiousness, and Western heterosexual male desire, in travel writing and paintings of the 'Oriental' woman and the harem. Kabbani shows how the depiction of Eastern women in the eighteenth and nineteenth centuries objectified them as exotic creatures who epitomised and promised the assumed excessive delights of the Orient. She shows how in reading these representations we must be aware of the mutually supportive processes of colonialism and patriarchy which produce Eastern women in eroticised terms. In addition, as Vron Ware explains in her book *Beyond the Pale: White Women, Racism and History* (Verso, 1992), colonial representations in the Victorian period tended to traffic in iconic representations of white women as epitomising the West's perceived higher moral and civil standards. Thus, as she explains, 'one of the recurring themes in the history of colonial repression is the way in which the threat of real or imagined violence towards white women became a symbol of the most dangerous form of insubordination' (p. 38). You may like to consider E. M. Forster's novel *A Passage to India* (1924) in the light of this statement, particularly the expatriate British community's reaction to the alleged rape of the newly arrived Adela Quested by Dr Aziz. So patriarchal values in colonial discourses impacted upon both *colonised* and *colonising* women, albeit in different ways.

Of course, this does *not* mean that colonised and colonising women were placed in the same position through their 'double colonisation'. Rana Kabbani makes reference to Victorian Western colonial travellers who also depicted the Orient in patriarchal terms. She argues that these women were 'token travellers only, who were forced by various pressures to articulate the values of patriarchy' (*Imperial Fictions*, p. 7). Kabbani draws our attention to the presence and complicity of Western women in the colonising mission, and the ways in which they were also subject to the patriarchal imperatives of colonial discourses. Although Kabbani sees Western women as complicit with colonial discourses, in *Imperial Eyes: Travel Writing and Transculturation* (Routledge, 1992) Mary Louise Pratt has explored the extent to which some Western women represented the colonies in different ways. In her criticism of Mary Kingsley's *Travels in West Africa* (1897), Pratt demonstrates that Kingsley's work distances itself from some of the masculinist tropes and narrative set-pieces prevalent in men's writing about Africa during the period through the use of 'irony or inversion' (*Imperial Eyes*, p. 213). Yet, Kingsley's 'feminised' narrative cannot escape complicity with colonialism and in its turn constructs a different form of mastery over Africa entirely in keeping with colonialist values. As Pratt's work shows, Western women's relationship with the dual workings of colonialism and patriarchy is often particularly complicated as members of the 'civilised' colonising nation, yet disempowered under a Western patriarchal rubric (you might also like to recall here Sara Mills's work on women's travel writing which we looked at in Chapter 2).

For colonised women in many 'Third World' colonies, Western patriarchal values had profound effects on indigenous gender roles. In her essay 'White Woman Listen! Black Feminism and the Boundaries of Sisterhood' (in Centre for Contemporary Cultural

Studies, *The Empire Strikes Back: Race and Racism in 70s Britain*, Hutchinson, 1982, pp. 212–35), Hazel Carby argues that in many colonised countries British colonialism interrupted indigenous familial and community structures and imposed its own models instead. 'Colonialism attempted to destroy kinship patterns that were not modelled on nuclear family structures, disrupting, in the process, female organisations that were based upon kinship systems which allowed more power and autonomy to women than those of the colonising nation' (p. 224). This had a significant impact on gender roles in indigenous communities, whose established traditions, customs and social systems were irreparably broken, sometimes to the detriment of women. Carby's argument suggests that indigenous gender roles could be more equitable than the sexist and chauvinist gender stereotypes and social roles brought from the colonising culture.

However, we might also take a more critical view of indigenous gender roles, not least because many feminist postcolonial writers have explored the oppression of women *within* native communities. Colonialism can *add* other kinds of patriarchal systems to an already unequal situation; it is not always the sole or primary source of patriarchy. For example, in her novel *The Joys of Motherhood* (Heinemann, 1979) Buchi Emecheta depicts the life of Nnu Ego, an Igbo woman from the village of Ibuza in Nigeria. Her father, Agbadi, chooses to marry her to Amatokwu, who duly pays her 'bride price' and sends Agbadi an additional six kegs of palm wine when he finds that Nnu Ego's virginity is intact. However, when Nnu Ego does not become pregnant she is seen to be 'failing' by Amatokwu in her primary task as a woman to provide male children for her husband. Her inability to conceive causes her much personal distress. Soon she learns from Amatokwu that she must leave their house and move to a hut kept for older wives because a younger wife has been found for him by his father, who is desperate to preserve the male line. When Nnu Ego complains to him that she misses their former intimacy, his answer leaves her in no doubt as to her value:

> 'What do you want me to do?' Amatokwu asked. 'I am a busy man. I have no time to waste my precious male seed on a woman who is infertile. I have to raise children for my line. If you really want to know, you don't appeal to me any more. You are so dry and jumpy.

When a man comes to a woman he wants to be cooled, not scratched
by a nervy female who is all bones.' (p. 32)

This moment demonstrates how Nnu Ego is significant to
Amatokwu only as a means by which the male line of the family can
be preserved. His demands concerning how a woman should act
clinically reveal that male power is in the ascendancy in this Igbo
community. As an object of exchange between men and the
guarantor of the survival of their hereditary line, her identity and
social role are male-constructed and she suffers if she does not
comply. After the birth of Amatokwu's younger wife's child, Nnu
Ego privately takes to suckling the child at her breast when it cries.
But Amatokwu discovers this and beats her for daring to perform
the task of a mother when she has failed to fulfil this role. He then
'returns' her to her father Agbadi, who says that he does not blame
him for beating Nnu Ego and acknowledges that she has brought
shame on the family. Eventually another husband is found for her in
Lagos.

Nnu Ego's plight is culturally and historically specific, but
women in other countries with a history of colonialism would
recognise her subservience to indigenous forces of compulsion.
Gender inequalities exist in both the indigenous and the colonial
culture: both often simultaneously oppress women during
colonialism and in its wake. Thus, as Susheila Nasta puts it in her
introduction to *Motherlands: Black Women's Writing from Africa, the
Caribbean and South Asia* (Women's Press, 1991), '[t]he postcolonial woman writer is not only involved in making herself heard,
in changing the architecture of male-centred ideologies and
languages, or in discovering new forms and language to express her
experience, she has also to subvert and demythologise indigenous
male writings and traditions which seek to label her' (p. xv).

This beckons an important general question: do *postcolonial*
representations perpetuate or question patriarchal values? Or can
they be complicit in oppressing women? Petersen and Rutherford
argue that a male ethos 'has persisted in the colonial and postcolonial world' (*A Double Colonisation*, p. 9). They crucially point
out that both colonialism *and* resistances to it can be seen as male-
centred. This complicates the extent to which they offer freedom to
women.

For example, Ketu H. Katrak has argued in 'Indian Nationalism, Gandhian "Satyagraha," and the Engendering of National Narratives' (in *Nationalisms and Sexualities*, ed. Andrew Parker et al., Routledge, 1992) that Mahatma Gandhi's resistance to British colonial rule in India during the 1920s and 1930s used specifically gendered representations for the purposes of Indian nationalism but ultimately did little to free Indian women from their patriarchal subordination to men. According to Katrak, Gandhi appropriated images of passive women to promote his campaign of 'passive resistance' to British colonial rule. Both men and women were encouraged to adopt a passivity exclusively associated with femininity, although *only* for the purposes of breaking colonial authority and *not* patriarchal authority:

> Gandhi's involvement of women in his 'satyagraha' (literally, truth-force) movement – part of his political strategy for national liberation – did not intend to confuse men's and women's roles; in particular, Gandhi did not challenge patriarchal traditions that oppressed women within the home. Furthermore, his specific representations of women and female sexuality, and his symbolising from Hindu mythology of selected female figures who embodied a nationalist spirit promoted ... a 'traditional' ideology wherein female sexuality was legitimately embodied only in marriage, wifehood, domesticity – all forms of controlling women's bodies. (pp. 395–6)

Katrak's critique invites us to consider at a more general level the extent to which resistances to colonialism bear the traces of unequal gender relationships. (It is worth reminding ourselves here of the chauvinism in many nationalist representations, which we explored in Chapter 4).

A similar charge has been levelled at forms of postcolonial theory which have emerged in the wake of Said's *Orientalism*. Said's book may have pointed to the importance of gender in the discourse of the Orient, but it has been up to others such as Anne McClintock and Sara Mills to pursue this issue in depth. Homi K. Bhabha's work on the ambivalence of colonial discourses explores the relationship between a 'colonising subject' and a 'colonised subject' in highly abstract terms without reference to how the specifics of gender might complicate his model. Do colonial discourses interact with colonised men and women in the same way? As we considered,

Bhabha's concepts of 'ambivalence' and 'mimicry' do not always prove useful in answering this question.

Elleke Boehmer has pointed out that since the 1980s 'male-authored postcolonial theory, however well-intentioned, has ... remained relatively untouched by any serious consideration of gender' (*Stories of Women*, p. 7). Like other feminist critics, Boehmer reminds us that postcolonial thought must remain sensitive to issues of gender difference if postcolonialism is going significantly to challenge male dominance. Otherwise, post-colonialism will, like colonialism, be a male centred and ultimately patriarchal discourse in which women's voices are marginalised and silenced.

STOP and THINK

If postcolonialism is involved in the necessity of, in Ngugi's famous phrase, 'decolonising the mind', we must ask ourselves: who decolonises? And for whom? It is easy to speak of decolonisation as an abstract process, the wheels of which are kept turning by the various forms of postcolonial critique. But the feminist critiques of postcolonialism demand that we consider exactly *who* undertakes this task, *whose* interests decolonisation serves, and *who* the main beneficiaries are. Do women have substantially more freedom after colonialism, or do they remain subservient to forms of patriarchal power and familiar gendered representations? Do postcolonial repre-sentations sustain these unequal gender differences or offer the means to challenge them? Is postcolonialism a male-centred field?

Postcolonial critiques of 'First World' feminism

In this section, we shall consider the extent to which Western feminist discourses are able to address the double colonisation of women living in once-colonised societies and in Western locations. As we shall see, Western or 'First World' feminism has come in for much criticism from postcolonial critics due to the lack of attention paid to the problems suffered by women with links to countries with a history of colonialism. John Thieme has explained that 'Western feminist writers and theorists have frequently seen parallels between their struggles and those of post-colonial women and have particularly identified with women who suffer a "double colonisation". Nevertheless, simple conflation of the two groups as victims of oppression is reductive and many Asian and African women have disputed the relevance of Western perspectives to their situation, particularly when they ignore material realities' (*Post-Colonial Studies: The Essential Glossary*, Arnold, 2003, p. 102). In opening up these disputes and debates, we can also think about issues such as female agency, the articulation of women's voices, and the relationship between feminist critics and their subject matter, as well as recognise the creative dialogues that are enabled by the encounters between 'First World' feminism and women from once-colonised countries. We shall attend to three important issues: Feminism and 'race', the limits of 'First World' feminism, and the problems in thinking about 'Third World' women.

Feminism and 'race'

How do differences in women's 'racial' identity impact upon feminism? In the early 1980s several critics explored the difficulties black women faced in working with popular feminist discourses. To what extent was feminism sensitive to their double colonisation?

Helen Carby explores these issues in an early and influential essay 'White Woman Listen! Black Feminism and the Boundaries of Sisterhood' (cited previously). In identifying and discussing the condition of 'Western feminism' in the 1970s, Carby explains that black and Asian women are barely made visible within its discourses. And when they *are* addressed, their representation remains highly problematic. Western feminism is criticised for the Orientalist way it represents the social practices of other 'races' as backwards and barbarous, from which black and Asian women need rescuing by their Western sisters. In so doing it fails to take into consideration the particular needs of these women, or consider different cultural practices *on their own terms*. The different meanings made by black and Asian women in their narratives (which Carby calls 'herstories' as opposed to 'histories') remain unheard. Carby gives the example of Western feminist horror about the arranged marriages of Asian women. In advocating an end to arranged marriages for Asian women because they are deemed oppressive, Western feminists do not consider Asian women's views and assume instead that their 'enlightened' outlook is the most progressive and liberating:

> The 'feminist' version of this ideology presents Asian women as being in need of liberation, not in terms of their own herstory and needs, but *into* the 'progressive' social mores and customs of the metropolitan West. The actual struggles that Asian women are involved in are ignored in favour of applying theories from the point of view of a more 'advanced', more 'progressive' outside observer. (p. 216)

In Carby's view, Western feminism frequently suffers from an ethnocentric bias in presuming that the solutions which white Western women have advocated in combating their oppression are equally applicable to all. As a consequence, issues of 'race' have been neglected, which has hindered feminists from thinking about the ways in which racism and patriarchy interact. In addition, white women have failed to see themselves as the potential oppressors of black and Asian women, even when adopting benevolent positions towards them.

As Laura Donaldson helpfully summarises, 'a predominantly white middle-class feminism exhibits not an overt racism that conjures active dominance and enforced segregation but a more subtle "white solipsism" that passively colluded with a racist culture' (*Decolonising Feminisms: Race, Gender and Empire-Building*, Routledge, 1993, p. 1). How can this be changed? Hazel Carby argues that the answer is *not* simply grafting black and Asian women into the current models of Western feminist analysis, nor situating black women as the new 'objects' of research. Rather, Carby asks us to recognise the ways in which white women have oppressed black and Asian women in the past, and explore how Western feminism excludes black and Asian women in the present. White women must listen and learn from black and Asian women, and be willing to transform their prevailing attitudes so that their use of the collective pronoun 'we' (as in 'we women') is no longer imperious.

Learning the limits of 'First World' feminism

In urging white and Western women to listen to black and Asian women, Hazel Carby made an important intervention in feminist discourse. But her essay raises persisting questions: who is able to speak *for* or *about* 'Third World' women? Can Western women ever adequately deal with the experiences of others? Or do only 'Third World' women occupy this position? How can 'Third World' women intervene in 'First World' feminist debates? These questions have been recurrent preoccupations in the deconstructive criticism of Gayatri Chakravorty Spivak, which we will look at closely in what follows.

In Chapter 5 we considered Spivak's critique of Gilbert and Gubar's *The Madwoman in the Attic* as ignoring the colonial contexts of *Jane Eyre* when celebrating Jane as a proto-feminist heroine. The essay raises important theoretical questions: to what extent is the work of Western, or 'First World', feminists useful in addressing 'Third World' concerns? Might 'First World' feminism suffer from its own complicity with some of the assumptions of colonial discourses? Spivak's work offers some of the most insightful and challenging explorations of these questions which have impacted upon many areas of post-colonialism. She sees her task as a deconstructive one, where conceptual categories such as 'First World' and 'Third World' are brought to crisis by exposing their limits, shortcomings and blind-spots.

Before reading Spivak's work, a word of caution is required. Spivak's writing can, at first, seem sophisticated to the point of impenetrability. She works closely with the insights of post-structuralist thinkers such as Jacques Derrida and Michel Foucault, and her own writing displays much of the slipperiness with language associated with their deconstructive texts. This is not merely for appearance's sake. Spivak's attention to detail, the range of her scholarship and her remarkable ability to expose the limitations in various forms of knowledge are enabled by her semantically compact prose style. Yet, inevitably, this is at the cost of a certain clarity and accessibility, especially for the beginner, and she cannot escape the charge that she sometimes presumes her readers will be as theoretically expert as herself. Stephen Morton (one of the best commentators on Spivak's work) explains that 'Spivak's essays and books carefully link disparate histories, places and methodologies in ways that often refuse to adhere to the systematic conventions of western critical thought. Such a refusal to be systematic is ... a conscious rhetorical strategy calculated to engage the implied reader in the critical interrogation of how we make sense of literary, social and economic texts in the aftermath of colonialism' (*Gayatri Chakravorty Spivak*, Routledge, 2003, p. 6). So, in what follows, I by no means claim to relay her ideas in embryo, as each of her essays is difficult to reduce systematically to a central or key idea, such is their richness. Rather, I wish to extrapolate from them certain ideas relevant for our purposes at the moment. Hopefully this will function as a useful means of orienting your own reading of Spivak's work. And don't be discouraged if you struggle at first. Spivak's writings reward patient, repeated readings and continually yield new ideas, directions and problems.

In her chapter 'French Feminism in an International Frame' in *In Other Worlds: Essays in Cultural Politics* (Routledge, 1987), Spivak problematises the relationship between 'Third World' women and their representation via 'First World' scholarship. The essay begins with Spivak recording her surprise on meeting a young Sudanese woman in the Faculty of Sociology at a Saudi Arabian university who claimed to have written 'a structural functionalist dissertation on female circumcision in the Sudan' (p. 134). Although Spivak is a little disconcerted that the Sudanese woman uses the term 'female circumcision' rather than 'clitoridectomy' (the removal of the clitoris is not commensurate with the removal of the foreskin in male circumcision), she is particularly surprised by the 'structural functionalist' approach taken. Structural functionalism claims to be disinterested in its subject matter and to applaud all systems which operate successfully. But, asks Spivak, could this young Sudanese woman ever take a 'disinterested' approach to clitoridectomy? Does she mean to applaud the practice of clitoridectomy? Spivak is doubtful. The example raises two fundamentally important methodological questions. First, what is the relationship between the investigator, their methodology, and the object they study – can the researcher ever be 'disinterested'? Something must motivate and limit research. Second, are concepts drawn primarily from Western scholarship suitable to contexts which are culturally divergent?

In pursuing these questions, Spivak reflects on her own Western education as an upper-class woman from Calcutta who studied French avant-garde philosophy in America. In examining her own training in 'International Feminism' (which she describes as the aggregation of feminist thinking from England, France, West Germany, Italy and Latin America), she records how as a younger woman she laboured under a particular assumption when applying International Feminism to 'Third World' women. 'When one attempted to think of so-called Third World women in a broader scope', she remarks, 'one found oneself caught, as my Sudanese colleague was caught and held by Structural Functionalism, in a web of information retrieval inspired at best by: What can I do *for* them?' (pp. 134–5). Spivak is pointing out here the problematic assumption that systems of knowledge can be generally applicable around the globe. Furthermore, the position of the critic is also raised as a problem. The younger Spivak believed that she could complete meaningful work *on behalf* of oppressed women. Her privileged situation as a well-educated woman made her feel empowered, that she was in a position to help less privileged women. This was an error. Spivak suggests that her younger self should have been asking self-critical questions such as: is my approach best suited to reading and writing about 'Third World' women? How might engaging with 'Third World' women reveal the limits of my approach? What can *they* do for *me*?

So, Spivak is demanding that the relationship between the critic and her research must be more *interactive*; she must be willing to explore how divergent cultural contexts may reveal hitherto unseen problems in her approach. Or, as she sardonically puts it, '[t]he academic feminist must learn to learn from them, to speak to them, to suspect that their access to the political and sexual scene is not merely to be *corrected* by our superior theory and enlightened compassion' (p. 135). Note too how Spivak complicates the idea of a 'First World' feminist. As an Indian working in America skilled in European philosophy, and like the Sudanese woman using structural functionalism in Saudi Arabia, the younger Spivak is complicit with 'First World' feminism in her intellectual approach to 'Third World' women.

Spivak proceeds to provide a detailed example of the problems involved when a 'First World' feminist attempts to deal sympathetically with 'Third World' women, by looking at French feminist Julia Kristeva's work on Chinese women. Spivak argues that a 'First World' feminist is often mistaken in considering that her gender authorises her to speak for 'Third World' women. She must 'learn to stop feeling privileged *as a woman*' (p. 136). (I shall note only in passing the problematic assumption here that the 'First World' feminist is female.) In indulging in this erroneous privilege, Kristeva's attempts to offer a feminist account of women in Chinese culture fails to engage dynamically with the specifics of her subject matter. Instead, she indulges in a 'wishful use of history' (p. 138) where her own ethnocentric speculations into Chinese culture masquerade as historical fact. Chinese culture becomes *appropriated* in order to serve Kristeva's particular feminist ends, and her priorities remain firmly self-centred. Ultimately, argues Spivak, Kristeva is less interested in Chinese women per se as she is concerned with how the exploration of a 'Third World' culture allows her to raise questions about the 'First World'. In taking a voyeuristic detour through women in Chinese culture, Kristeva's terminus is in reality a self-centred critique of Western philosophy. Questions are raised such as 'who then are we (not), how are we (not)' (p. 137), with the 'we' relating exclusively to 'First World' feminists. We might want to consider here the uncomfortable resemblances which Spivak exposes between Kristeva's work and the project of Orientalism.

So, using a phrase at the end of Spivak's essay, we can describe the appropriation of 'Third World' women to serve the self-centred ends of 'First World' feminists as a compelling example of 'the inbuilt colonialism of First World feminism toward the Third' (p. 153). In attempting to discover what 'they can do *for* them', Kristeva, the Sudanese woman and the younger Spivak stand accused of this charge. Feminists must learn to speak *to* women and not *for* women; they must be willing to *learn the limits* of their methodologies through an encounter with women in different contexts, rather than assimilate differences within a grander design.

It is important to notice that Spivak's argument avoids the charge of *ethnocentrism* by refusing the logic that, for example, only Indian women can speak for other Indian women. Spivak has consistently advocated that critics must always look to the specifics of their own positions and recognise the political, cultural and institutional contexts in which they work. The space from which we speak is always on the move, criss-crossed by the conflicting and shifting discourses of things like our social class, education, gender, sexuality and ethnicity. It is very different to assume that the critic can ever speak 'on behalf' of anybody, because the position of both the critic and their 'object' is never securely fixed.

'Third World' women

As we noted earlier, 'First World' feminism and 'Third World' women are inadequate phrases which traffic in untenable generalisations and ring-fence internally various voices. Yet, as Spivak's work shows, their *strategic* deployment can be supported insofar as it enables critics to point out how even the most benevolent and supportive attempts on the part of some feminists to engage with different groups of women are not always empowering. However, other critics can be less sensitive to the inadequacies of the term, and there always remains the danger that some feminists will use the term 'Third World' women not as a useful *figure of speech*, but as a clearly defined empirical group.

Chandra Talpade Mohanty warns against precisely this in her important essay 'Under Western Eyes: Feminist Scholarship and Colonial Discourses' (in *Colonial Discourse and Post-Colonial Theory*, ed. Williams and Chrisman, pp. 196–220). In this essay Mohanty exposes the production of a singular category of 'Third World' women in Western feminism which damagingly creates the 'discursive homogenisation and systematisation of the oppression of women in the third world' (p. 198). She recognises that Western feminism's attention to 'Third World' women is valuable and laudable, not least in its attempts to forge international links between different women. Yet the means by which this scholarship has proceeded remain problematic. For a variety of reasons, 'Third World' nations remain subservient to the West, at the levels of economic wealth, scientific development and technological resources. Mohanty argues that Western feminism cannot escape implication in these global economic and political frameworks and must be careful not to replicate unequal power relations between the 'First World' and 'Third World'. Yet Western feminism is in danger of doing this in its analysis of 'Third World' women.

Mohanty discovers worrying analytical presuppositions in 'First World' analyses of 'Third World' women. First, it is presumed that all women exist as a 'coherent group with identical interests and desires, regardless of class, ethnic or racial location' (p. 199). This coherency is established by assuming that all women in divergent contexts are first and foremost *victims* of different kinds of oppression: male violence, the structure of the family, economic structures and so on. Although an attention to context might appear sensitive to difference, context always remains secondary to the universal assumption of victimage. 'Women are taken as a unified "powerless" group prior to the historical and political analysis in question. Thus, it is then merely a matter of specifying the context *after the fact*' (p. 202). Furthermore, if women are eternally cast as victims then men are posited as perpetual victimisers. There is little attempt to consider the different types of social relations *between* women created by social and ethnic differences (although Mohanty doesn't mention it, we might add sexuality here too).

The second presumption concerns the ways by which 'universal womanhood' is proved. Mohanty deals with three different methods of such proof. The first, the 'arithmetic method', presumes that certain forms of oppression are universal if they circumscribe large numbers of women. Mohanty uses the veiling of Muslim women as an example of the 'arithmetic method'. It is assumed that because Muslim women in places such as Saudi Arabia, Iran, Pakistan, India and Egypt wear the veil, they all suffer from the same form of oppression. Yet, is the symbolic significance of the veil in each of these locations necessarily the same? Might there be political circumstances where women *choose* to wear the veil, as an important act of political empowerment for themselves? The second methodology concerns the point Spivak made in her critique of international feminism, namely the assumption that concepts (such as patriarchy, reproduction, the family etc.) are often used 'without their specification in local cultural and historical contexts' (p. 209). There may well be a sexual division of labour in families living in America and India, but is it tantamount to the same thing in different locations? Mohanty asks: 'how is it possible to refer to "the" sexual division of labour when the *content* of this division changes radically from one environment to the next, and from one historical juncture to another?' (p. 210).

Lastly, Mohanty makes the rather complicated assertion that some critics 'confuse the use of gender as a superordinate category of organising analysis with the universalistic proof and instantiation of this category' (p. 211). By this she means that there is an important difference between the ways we construct patterns or systems of representations, and the empirical, lived order of societies – for convenience's sake we might simplify this as a difference between imagined order and lived experience. All systems of representations need patterns to work; they posit fundamental differences which function as a centre of reference for all other differences in the system. For example, the fundamental opposition of nature/culture underpins other patternings like wild/domestic or biology/technology. These are the convenient aesthetic distinctions *we make* to conceptualise the world. Mohanty argues that some critics mistakenly go searching for empirical proof of these patterns in lived experience. They try to squeeze societies into preconceived frames or patterns of reference, rather than consider that their imaginary models of order might be inappropriate. Thus, in a feminist context, although it might be strategically and politically productive to imagine sometimes a difference between 'First World' and 'Third World' women, it is a mistake to believe that these categories exist securely at the level of lived experience and can be empirically 'proved' through field work. The lived experiences of women in countries with a history of colonialism cannot be easily fitted into the homogenising, imaginary category of 'Third World' women.

So, by conceiving of 'the average third-world woman' (p. 199), Western feminists construct a template for female identity in the 'Third World' based on a series of questionable conceptual and methodological manoeuvres, with scant regard for context. This is tantamount to a colonial act, in the imposition of a homogeneous identity on 'Third World' women without regard to the historical and cultural differences which inevitably exceed this category. Furthermore, the assimilation of 'Third World' women *within*

Western feminist discourse suggests that *Western* feminism remains the primary means by which patriarchy, sexism and chauvinism are challenged. As objects of Western feminist analysis, 'Third World' women are robbed of their agency.

STOP and THINK

Mohanty's problematisation of the category of 'Third World' women accomplishes much, but her essay creates some problems of its own.

First, is a 'First World' feminist critique of women in 'Third World' locations possible? Mohanty gives an example of one by looking briefly at Maria Mies's book *The Lace Makers of Narsapur: Indian Housewives Produce for the World Market* (Zed, 1982). By attending closely to the economic and ideological specifics of an Indian lace-making industry in terms of its female workers, Mohanty argues that Mies successfully produces a 'careful, politically focused' study ('Under Western Eyes', p. 207). However, Mies deals with the power relations of the lace-making industry through a series of familiar approaches and concepts derived from Western materialism. Is Mies's approach *conceptually* different? Mohanty does not say.

The example of Mies's study partly answers a second problem: how does Mohanty avoid asserting an ethnocentric feminism in her privileging of exploring context? It seems that Mohanty accepts that 'First World' women *can* write constructively about 'Third World' contexts. Also, Mohanty advocates the forging of 'strategic coalitions' (p. 211) between different groups of women at apposite moments when contesting the many forms of oppression, although she does not explore this at any length.

However, one serious problem remains. How do critics working in one context gain access to the cultural, historical and social specificities of another context? If the Western analyses of 'Third World' contexts always run the risk of misrepresentation by approaching them through a series of concepts or methodologies which are ill-equipped to bear witness to the specifics of other times and places (as Spivak also exposed in her reading of Kristeva's approach to Chinese women), then how can 'First World' feminists ever write about 'Third World' women without imposing their own conceptual systems? Mohanty's repeated stress on context is in danger of making context seem rather transparent and easily seized, unproblematically rendered by those critics who do some appropriate research. But is cultural difference so easily accessible? Is it always available to those approaching from other contexts? It is all very well arguing that we must read texts in their appropriate contexts, but *how* do we read context in the first place?

Can the subaltern speak?

It should be clear from the ideas we have explored so far that the category of 'Third World' women is an *effect of discourse* rather than an existent, identifiable reality. It does not approximate to any stable, collective body. Similarly the singular 'Third World' woman is an ideological construct wholly produced within 'First World' intellectual debates, and *not* an individual subject. As we have considered, the concepts and methodological approaches used to bear witness to 'Third World' experiences may be inappropriate to the task and result in generalisation, falsification and conjecture. But this leaves a problem: how *does* one bear witness to the agency of those women throughout history who today are inadequately represented as 'Third World' women?

This is an issue which Spivak has explored in one of her most challenging and intellectually rich essays, 'Can the Subaltern Speak?' (reprinted with abridgements in *Colonial Discourse and Post-Colonial Theory*, ed. Williams and Chrisman, pp. 66–111). This essay, published in 1988, is a complex critique of the representation of human subjectivity in a variety of contexts, but with particular reference to the work of the *Subaltern Studies* scholars (which we encountered in Chapter 4). It has become one of the most influential and notorious essays in postcolonialism, and Spivak has been asked on many occasions about the ideas it raises. She has also returned again to several of its key ideas later in her career, as in her book *A Critique of Postcolonial Reason: Toward a History of the Vanishing Present* (Harvard University Press, 1999; see pp. 269–79 in particular); but when beginning postcolonialism it is very useful to deal first with the essay in its initial form. The abridged version in Williams and Chrisman's collection remains an excellent place to start, and we'll use it when exploring Spivak's ideas below.

As we might recall, the *Subaltern Studies* scholars were interested in the representation of 'the subaltern' in colonialist texts, with subalterns defined as those who did not comprise the colonial elite – such as the lesser rural gentry, impoverished landlords, rich peasants and upper-middle-class peasants. As a way of mounting her critique of the scholars' assumptions concerning how we might access the experiences and consciousness of the subaltern in colonialist texts, Spivak begins by turning first to the work of poststructuralist thinkers such as Michel Foucault and Gilles Deleuze who have challenged the notion that human individuals are 'sovereign subjects' with autonomous agency over their consciousness (summed up in the Cartesian dictum 'I think therefore I am'). As poststructuralism would have it, human consciousness is constructed *discursively*. Our subjectivity and consciousness are constituted by the shifting discourses of power which endlessly 'speak through' us, situating us here and there in particular positions and relations. In these terms we are not the authors of ourselves. We do not simply construct our own identities but have them written for us; the subject cannot be wholly 'sovereign' over the construction of selfhood. Instead, the subject is 'de-centred' in that its consciousness is always being constructed from positions outside of itself. It follows then, that the individual is *not* the point of origin for consciousness, and human consciousness is *not* a transparent representation of the self but an effect of discourse. Spivak argues that, surprisingly for these figures, when Foucault and Deleuze talk about oppressed groups such as the working class they fall back into precisely these uncritical notions of the 'sovereign subject' by restoring to them a full 'centred' consciousness – or to use her terms, they are guilty of 'a clandestine restoration of subjective essentialism' ('Can the Subaltern Speak?', p. 74). In addition, they also assume that the writing of intellectuals such as themselves can serve as a transparent medium through which the voices of the oppressed can be represented. The intellectual is cast as a reliable mediator for the voices of the oppressed, a mouthpiece through which the oppressed can be retrieved and clearly speak.

Spivak is concerned that these two theoretical failings also problematise the study of colonised subjects as in the work of Ranajit Guha and other *Subaltern Studies* scholars. As we have already noticed, these critics read documents recording subaltern insurgency produced by colonial authorities in order to retrieve from them the hitherto absent perspectives of the oppressed subalterns. Spivak is entirely sympathetic to the aims of the scholars and supportive of their politics. But she urges that critics must always beware of attempting to retrieve a 'subaltern consciousness' from texts, as this will merely replicate the two problems in the work of Foucault and Deleuze: perceiving of the subaltern as a 'sovereign subject' in control of his or her own consciousness, and assuming that the intellectual is a transparent medium through which subaltern consciousness can be made present. Representations of subaltern insurgency must *not* be trusted as reliable expressions of a sovereign subaltern consciousness; like 'Third World' women, 'subaltern consciousness' is fiction, an effect of discourse. To retrieve the unruly voice of a 'subaltern subject' from the colonial archives is to risk complicity in an essentialist, specifically Western model of centred subjectivity in which 'concrete experience' is (mistakenly) preserved. Therefore, all forms of representation which claim to identify and articulate subaltern consciousness are conceptually compromised and actually complicit in the very colonialist discursive dynamics they seek to challenge. It is not possible to retrieve and encounter subaltern consciousness in this way, the argument goes, because the theoretical methods we use when we try to do this are incommensurate with subaltern consciousness, which will always remain beyond the boundaries of the discourses we use to articulate them.

To put this point inelegantly: we cannot encounter the subaltern *on their own terms* but are fated instead to render their consciousness with recourse to dominant models. In that act of giving visibility and voice to the subaltern, ironically the subaltern actually disappears and is silenced. These problems are further compounded by the issue of gender, because representations of subaltern insurgency tend to prioritise men. 'As object of colonialist historiography and as subject of insurgency, the ideological construction of gender keeps the male dominant. If, in the context of colonial production, the subaltern has no history and cannot speak, the subaltern as female is even more deeply in shadow' (pp. 82–3). Note here how the subaltern as female is not properly represented within the context of colonialism *and* resistance to it, 'colonial production' *and* 'insurgency'. Both authority and the resistance to it are gendered in worrying ways. This famous quotation raises further questions: can oppressed women's voices ever be recovered from the archive? Can the subaltern as female, confined in the shadows of colonial history and representation, ever be heard to speak? The answer, it seems, is no, so long as intellectuals go searching for an originary, sovereign and concrete female consciousness which can be discovered and readily represented with recourse to questionable assumptions about subjectivity. Rather than hunting for the 'lost voices' of women in the historical archives in an act of retrieval, intellectuals should be aware that this kind of work will continue to keep the subaltern as female entirely muted.

Let us think carefully about this argument, in order to avoid some common misconceptions about 'Can the Subaltern Speak?' which have arisen in the wake of its publication. As Robert J. C. Young puts it in his reading of the essay, the problem which Spivak identifies is 'not that the women cannot speak as such, that no records of the subject-consciousness of women exit, but that she is assigned no position of enunciation [and therefore] everyone else speaks for her, so that she is rewritten continuously as the object of patriarchy or of imperialism' (*White Mythologies: Writing History and the West*, Routledge, 1990, p. 164). The subaltern as female is always being written with recourse to a form of representation which is incapable of bearing adequate witness to her subject-position. Spivak gives examples of these silenced subaltern women by looking at the documentation of *sati*, or widow sacrifice, in colonial India. Ultimately, she suggests, it is better to acknowledge that the subaltern as female exists as the unrepresentable in discourse, a shadowy figure on its margins. Any attempt to retrieve her voice will disfigure her speech. So, she concludes, intellectuals must instead critique those discourses which claim to rescue the 'authentic' voices of the subaltern as female from their mute condition, and address their complicity in the production of subalterneity. Simply inserting subaltern women into representation is a cosmetic exercise as long as the *system* of representation endorses discredited models of essential, centred subjectivity. As Spivak memorably concludes, '[t]here is no virtue in global laundry lists with "woman" as a pious item' (p. 104).

To summarise: in 'Can the Subaltern Speak?' Spivak complicates the extent to which women's voices can be easily retrieved and restored to history. As Stephen Morton clarifies, this is because subaltern consciousness and resistance are 'always already filtered through dominant systems of political representation' (*Gayatri Chakravorty Spivak*, p. 66). Rather than making the subaltern as female seem to speak, intellectuals must *bring to crisis* the representational systems which rendered her mute in the first place, challenging the very forms of knowledge that are complicit in her silencing.

By rendering the subaltern as female as a discursive construct and not a 'sovereign subject', Spivak's essay potentially derails the work of critics like the *Subaltern Studies* scholars. Their attention to subaltern insurgency is part of an important political project which opposes the false images of Indian history constructed in elite historiography. But after reading 'Can the Subaltern Speak?', critics might be discouraged from pursuing subalterns if their voices are forever lost inside colonial discourses. Why bother? Spivak seeks to get round this *impasse* in another piece from *In Other Worlds*, 'Subaltern Studies: Deconstructing Historiography' (also available in *The Spivak Reader*, ed. Donna Landry and Gerald MacLean, Routledge, 1996). In exploring how the subaltern scholars attempt to retrieve subaltern consciousness from history, Spivak argues in her typically verbose fashion that their work can be described as '*strategic* use of positivist essentialism in a scrupulously visible political interest' (*In Other Worlds*, p. 205). By this, she suggests that although it is theoretically improper to assume the existence of a sovereign or essential subaltern consciousness, it is none the less important to continue to use the concept of an essential subject as part of a wider political project. In other words, in trying to change things we sometimes have to use ideas or tools which we know are problematic. Spivak's influential notion of *strategic essentialism* involves us actively choosing to use a concept which we know is flawed, often as a way of challenging the very system which has fashioned that concept in the first place. However, she does open herself up to the charge of having things both ways by dismissing on theoretical grounds the subaltern subject while supporting elsewhere those projects which still subscribe to notions of essential subjectivity.

Not least because of the abstruse and highly theoretical tenor of her essay, Spivak's ideas have not been entirely welcomed by some postcolonial scholars. Benita Parry has objected to ways in which Spivak brings to crisis the representation of native or colonised resistance and has objected to her 'deliberate deafness to the native voice' (*Postcolonial Studies: A Materialist Critique*, Routledge, 2004, p. 23), arguing that she 'severely restricts (eliminates?) the space in which the colonized can be written back into history' (p. 23). In his book *Postcolonial Theory: Contexts, Practices, Politics* (Verso, 1997), Bart Moore-Gilbert makes the important point that 'the more the subaltern is seen as a "theoretical" fiction . . . the more the suffering and exploitation of the subaltern becomes a theoretical fiction, too' (p. 102). In other words, by regarding the subaltern as an effect of discourse and not as an actual individual, Spivak treats material realities as purely textual or theoretical phenomena. (Note too that exactly the same might be said of positing 'Third World' women as an entirely discursive category.) Moore-Gilbert has also suggested that one major implication of 'Can the Subaltern Speak?' is the way it leaves the non-subaltern critic in an impossible position, unable to do anything positive on behalf or in support of the subaltern as female. '[T]he non-subaltern must either maximally respect the Other's radical alterity, thus leaving the status quo intact, or attempt the impossible feat of "opening up" to the Other without in any way "assimilating" that Other to his/her own subject-position, perspectives or identity' (p. 102).

Spivak has reflected on the ideas raised in 'Can the Subaltern Speak?' and the responses they provoked, in an interview printed as

'Subaltern Talk' in *The Spivak Reader* (ed. by Donna Landry and Gerald MacLean, 1996, Routledge, pp. 287–308). An important point she makes concerns the use of the term 'speak' in the title of her essay, which she claims has been misunderstood. In discussing the silence of the subaltern as female, she suggests that she was not using the term literally to suggest that such women never *actually* talked. Rather, she wanted to consider the inability of their words to enable *transactions* between speakers and listeners. Their muteness is created by the fact that even when women uttered words, they were still interpreted through conceptual and methodological procedures which were unable to understand their interventions with accuracy. It is not so much that subaltern women did not speak, but rather that others *did not know how to listen*, how to enter into a transaction between speaker and listener. The subaltern cannot speak because their words cannot be properly interpreted. Hence, the silence of the female as subaltern is the result of a failure of *interpretation* and not a failure of articulation. Furthermore, as Stephen Morton describes, 'Spivak's conclusion that the subaltern cannot speak is often taken out of context to mean that subaltern women have no political agency because they cannot be represented. ... The crucial point, however, is that these disempowered women receive their political and discursive identities within historically determinate systems of political and economic representation' (*Gayatri Chakravorty Spivak*, p. 67). It is not the act of 'speaking' that is at issue, but the *system* of representation in which such speaking is (not properly) 'heard'.

For all of their brilliance and gravity, Spivak's conclusions can leave the critic feeling rather hamstrung. What is the point in trying to engage with oppressed voices if these voices are eternally doomed to perish due to the methods and concepts we use? If voicing resistance to colonialism is just as conceptually suspect as colonial discourses themselves, are we fated forever to be locked inside a discursive imperium, always serving not sundering colonialist relations of power?

Consider this interesting moment in Spivak's *A Critique of Postcolonial Reason* when she recounts a series of visits to a famous pink stone palace in Jaipur as part of her research into the subaltern figure of the Rani of Simur (for more on the significance of this figure in Spivak's work, see Stephen Morton, *Gayatri Chakravory Spivak*, pp. 60–1). On Spivak's first visit, while search-ing for the palace she came across some 'shy hardy women' who 'gathered leaves and vegetation from the hillside to feed their goats' (p. 242):

> They were the rural subaltern, the real constituency of feminism, accepting their lot as their norm, quite different from the urban female sub-proletarian in crisis and resistance. If I wanted to touch their everyday without the epistemic transcoding of anthropological field work, the effort would be a much greater undoing, indeed, of life's goals, than the effort to catch the Rani in vain, in history. (p. 242)

On the one hand, there is enormous value in this passage where Spivak points to one such constituency of 'Third World' women (which she provocatively declares as 'real') that may not register on the radar of 'First World' feminism or have access to its languages, politics and insights – and which does not display a conventional political consciousness of the day-to-day 'norm' as an experience of subjugation. Who would dare speak for these women, or presume to articulate their 'lot' within systems of thinking and speaking that transcode their subjectivities into objects of knowledge and concern? What do we begin to do to them if we spoke of them in terms of 'Third World' women's resistance or as an exploited underclass of global capitalism? Yet on the other hand, while Spivak can expose how 'speaking about' can quickly morph into *speaking for* and hence *silencing* the subaltern, she seems to offer hardly any resources at all for dynamically 'undoing' the old colonialist ways and opening new modes of engagement or discursive strategies which might take us beyond such an *impasse*. Has Spivak's sophisticated learning and heady postcolonial critique actually made it harder for her to 'touch' the 'everyday' here? Must we always end up standing at the limit with broken tools in our hands? The image of Spivak silently watching these women work in Jaipur as she cogitates about the gulf between herself and these women, unsure of how all their lives might touch without immense effort on her part, might well be taken as a figure for the limits of postcolonial theory itself.

'Going a piece of the way': creative dialogues in postcolonial feminism

After reading Spivak and Mohanty, we might be left doubting if 'First World' feminism can be used purposefully in 'Third World' contexts at all, and be tempted to dismiss it as a contemporary form of colonial discourse that silences the subaltern as female. But other ways of thinking about the relationship between 'First World' feminism and 'Third World' women are available, and they turn on thinking about the ways in which the experiences of women from different locations and cultures can indeed 'touch' and cohere in exciting and novel ways. As we have seen, the work of Spivak and Mohanty demanded that we must be vigilant in using certain kinds of approach to subaltern and 'Third World' texts. But, taking a different view, the dismissal of 'First World' feminism at a stroke because of these problems might risk losing its resources which *can* contribute to feminist critique, as well as deny the possibilities for the coalitions between 'First World' and 'Third World' feminists that Mohanty advocates. Spivak herself would never wish to dismiss entirely 'First World' feminism on these grounds. Maybe other kinds of relationships might be built, more equitable, vigilant and transformative for all involved.

The possibility of building such new, vigilant and transformative relations between women *across* 'First' and 'Third World' feminism is evidenced by a book of literary critical essays edited by Susheila Nasta titled *Motherlands: Black Women's Writing from Africa, the Caribbean and South Asia* (Women's Press, 1991). In her introduction, Nasta argues that a 'creative dialogue' (p. xvi) is possible where 'First World' and 'Third World' voices both contribute to and learn from each other. This is not at all a convenient compromise between positions – far from it. Rather, Nasta argues that the insights of 'First World' feminism can illuminate postcolonial texts which, in their turn, enable women readers in the 'First World' to 're-evaluate the cultural assumptions which inform their own readings' (p. xvii). The relationship is mobile, dialogic and *mutually* transformative. Nasta's argument is borne out by the essays in the collection written by a variety of scholars, many of whom have links to once-colonised countries and work in British and American universities. The critics' explorations of representations of motherhood in a variety of post-colonial texts emerge from the intersections between 'First World' and 'Third World' work on this subject and others, and are in part facilitated by many of the critics' own relations with both 'First World' and 'Third World' locations. Thus, Jane Bryce-Okunlola uses the work of a diverse body of thinkers which include Micere Mugo, Julia Kristeva, Carole Boyce Davies, Alice Walker, Sandra Gilbert and Susan Gubar in her reading of the novels of Flora Nwapa, Rebeka Njau and Bessie Head. As these essays demonstrate, 'First World' and 'Third World' voices need not always construct antago-nistic relationships with each other. New ways of negotiating between and listening to voices dialogically can be achieved.

The creative writers studied in *Motherlands* all use various forms of English in their work, and Nasta acknowledges how as a 'father tongue' English remains a problematic language for these women in that it houses both colonial and patriarchal values. None the less, language is also 'both source and womb of creativity, a means of giving birth to new stories, new myths, of telling the stories of women that have been previously silenced' (p. xiii). Language is both disabling and enabling. Although many of the women writers studied in *Motherlands* could not be described as subaltern in the strict sense used by Guha, Spivak and others, Nasta's words none the less act as a corrective to the potential denial of agency for women's speech in 'Can the Subaltern Speak?' Nasta reminds us that we must attend to the ways in which women from once-colonised countries are transforming English to enable *new* kinds of representation through which they *can* speak. Similarly, critical approaches are being negotiated which bear better witness to the specificities of this speech. In attending to the ways in which our critical practices render the subaltern as female unable to speak, Spivak's work perhaps comes too close on occasions to denying women the *possibility* of changing the dominant modes of inter-pretations, an agency which the essays in *Motherlands* variously demonstrate with memorable verve. In showing how a 'creative dialogue' is possible, *Motherlands* makes an important contribution to the debates concerning postcolonialism and feminism while also calling readers' attention specifically to the agency and voices of black women from Africa, the Caribbean and South Asia.

In terms of postcolonial theory, a similar 'creative dialogue' can be discovered. For all of their attention to the problematics of Western concepts and methodologies, we must remember that the work of Mohanty, Spivak and others is facilitated by their own non-systemic and creative dialogues between Western theory and postcolonial contexts. A good example is Spivak herself. In recent years she has translated the fiction of the Bengali writer Mahasweta Devi (see *Imaginary Maps: Three Stories by Mahasweta Devi*, trans. Gayatri Chakravorty Spivak, Routledge, 1995). Her commentaries on Mahasweta's work, and the challenges it poses for the translator, have intervened in a wealth of academic debates about post-coloniality, nationalism, the subaltern, ethics and ecology. Spivak admits that these interventions are born out of a 'habit of mind' which 'may draw a reader to Marx, to Mahasweta, and to Derrida, in different ways' (*The Spivak Reader*, p. 274). The directions and tensions engendered by this eclectic group of thinkers bear witness to the valuable possibilities enabled by bringing diverse materials into dialogue with each other and revealing new directions and limits, as Spivak's body of often brilliant work aptly evidences.

Carole Boyce Davies makes a valuable point in *Black Women, Writing and Identity* when she uses the phrase 'going a piece of the way with them' to explain her own encounters with Western theory. Davies argues that it is impossible for her to work fully with the various theoretical schools available, such as feminism and Marxism, because they have the potential to marginalise her as a black woman in their methodological assumptions. None the less, existing schools of thought can be engaged in a process of negotiation which yields useful critical tools. Davies proposes 'a kind of *critical relationality* in which various theoretical positions are interrogated for their specific applicability to Black women's experiences' (p. 46). In negotiating with existing schools of thought, black women become active agents in intervening in dominant discourses and producing enabling conceptual frames. Davies stresses that black women must be ever mobile, departing from and returning to different critical positions in a migratory movement. Although some might be concerned about the itinerant aspects of this theory (sometimes it is important to take a 'fixed' position as a critic) her notion of 'going a piece of the way with them' bears witness to the ways in which black women (and, I would argue, other such subaltern figures) have unsettled received ideas and challenge the biases of 'First World' theory and male-centred postcolonialism, as well as transforming each in the process.

Representing women in Sally Morgan's *My Place*

Let us conclude by considering a literary text in 'critical relationality' to some of the ideas we have met in this chapter.

Set in Australia, *My Place* is an autobiographical text which explores the history of Sally Morgan's family in the wider context of Australian history. Sally records her childhood as a time of difficulty. The family are often short of money. Her father, a veteran of the Second World War, suffers from illness and dies while Sally is a young girl. Her mother, Gladys, has a variety of cleaning jobs to make ends meet. Sally spends most of her young life with her brothers and sisters, and her grandmother Daisy. During the course of her youth she begins to realise that she is not always regarded by others in the same way as white children. On pressing her mother about her family background she is told that she is an Indian. However, she learns later that this is a lie, and she is instead descended from Australia's Aborigines. This sets Sally on a determined quest to discover the hitherto hidden branches of her family tree. Her mother and especially her grandmother are frequently reluctant to talk about their pasts, but gradually Sally pieces together a story of her Aboriginal inheritance. This involves her travelling to the places where her mother and grandmother grew up and meeting Aboriginal peoples whom she had no idea existed, as well as tape-recording the voices of other Aboriginal members of her family which she transcribes and includes in her autobiography.

At one level, *My Place* offers a corrective to historical representations of Australian history. As Sally reflects, 'there's almost nothing written from a personal point of view about Aboriginal people. All our history is about the white man. No one knows about what it was like for us. A lot of our history has been lost, people have been too frightened to say anything' (p. 163). The writing of Australian history privileges the white (and the) male. In opposition to this, Sally's narrative calls attention to the experiences of women and records the exploitation of Aboriginal peoples by white settlers, who often broke up Aboriginal families and employed Aboriginal women as domestic servants without paying them a wage. The text evidences what we have called the 'double colonisation' of women on many occasions, as many characters find themselves subservient to colonialist and patriarchal values. It exposes how Aboriginal women could become objects of sexual desire for white men who compelled them to have intercourse and cared little for the devastating effect this could have on them, particularly regarding pregnancy. Throughout the text there is uncertainty as to the identity of Daisy's father, who could be one of several possible white men. In addition, Gladys's narrative records how the children fathered by white men and born to Aboriginal women were taken from their mothers and forced to grow up separately. As a child she was placed in a boarding school and rarely saw her mother, who was in service to a white family in Perth. *My Place* enables a feminist critique of the patriarchal values enshrined in historical representations of Australia, and in the institutions which impacted terribly on many women's lives.

The position of white women is also an issue. On the one hand *My Place* shows how they are subject to the patriarchal authority of white men and have to endure the men's sexual encounters with Aboriginal women. They suffer their own, distinct forms of oppression. Yet they are also complicit in the marginalisation of Aboriginal women due to the ways that colonial discourses position them in relation to Aboriginal peoples. For example, Gladys remembers one incident as a child while staying in Perth with Daisy. The mother of the white family, Alice, comes into the kitchen with her daughter June, who is carrying a beautiful doll with golden hair and blue eyes. Gladys is captivated by the doll as it reminds her of a princess. Alice proceeds to give her a doll of her own, but this one is 'a black topsy doll dressed like a servant. It had a red checked dress on and a white apron, just like Mum's. It had what they used to call a slave cap on its head' (p. 261). Gladys is devastated:

> That's me, I thought, I want to be a princess, not a servant. I was so upset that when Alice placed the black doll in my arms, I couldn't help flinging it onto the floor and screaming, 'I don't want a black doll, I

don't want a black doll'. Alice just laughed and said to my mother,
'Fancy, her not wanting a black doll'. (p. 262)

Alice has internalised a patriarchal set of values which secure a
differential hierarchy between white and Aboriginal women. These
values in their turn help to buttress the colonialist attitudes which
endure in Australian constructions of 'race'. It is crucial to grasp
that, at this moment, both Alice and Gladys remain doubly
colonised in different ways, despite the fact that Alice seems to
occupy a position of authority and privilege. None the less, this
example shows how white women were complicit in constructing
subservient roles and racialised identities for Aboriginal women,
and exposes the difficulties faced by advocating a universal notion
of sisterhood when contesting patriarchal representations of
Australian history.

My Place is also fascinating to consider in terms of the issues
raised by the debates surrounding Spivak's essay 'Can the Subaltern
Speak?' Of course, Spivak's focus is nineteenth-century India and
her essay cannot be freely mapped onto Morgan's text. Yet the
problems of accessing and representing the consciousness of doubly
colonised women otherwise silent in received historical
representations are central in *My Place*, and we might (to borrow
Carole Boyce Davies's phrase) 'go a piece of the way' with some of
the conceptual vocabulary gleaned from our exploration of Spivak's
work when looking at *My Place*.

Of particular interest is Sally Morgan's identification of an
'Aboriginal consciousness'. In the latter stages of the book, Sally
takes a journey with her family to her grandmother's birthplace,
Corunna Downs. After a series of emotional meetings with her
Aboriginal relations, she describes how their tentative search for
family knowledge had 'grown into a spiritual and emotional
pilgrimage. We had an Aboriginal consciousness now, and were
proud of it' (p. 233). What does she mean by 'Aboriginal consciousness' here? What is the relationship between Sally's
'Aboriginal consciousness' and the Aboriginal characters she meets
at Corunna Downs, many of whom speak Aboriginal languages and
communicate with Sally through an interpreter? Are the subject-
positions of these women correspondent? Do they occupy the same
'place'? In constructing an 'Aboriginal consciousness' and laying

claim to it, Sally Morgan could be criticised for fictionalising a form of essentialised, sovereign subjectivity which homogenises all Aboriginal peoples and papers over the important historical and cultural specifics of Sally's position. Her version of 'Aboriginal consciousness', like Spivak's subaltern as female, is perhaps a convenient fiction of her own making. Ultimately, is she imperiously speaking *for* these peoples more than she is speaking *with* them?

However, we might read this novel from a different direction too. Sally's Aboriginality is not easily fixed, and significantly she inherits her Aboriginality from a maternal line. Her father was a white Australian, while her mother Gladys was born to an Aboriginal mother, Daisy, and a white father. To complicate things further, Daisy's Aboriginality is also at issue as she was born to a white father and Aboriginal mother. It is clear that in the text 'Aboriginality' is more than a description of physiological 'race'. It appears that Sally could choose to conceal her Aboriginality and claim a non-Aboriginal identity. Indeed, this was the approach her mother Gladys had taken by telling the children they were Indian and keeping their Aboriginal heritage a secret. So we might argue that Sally's firm decision to embrace and explore an Aboriginal identity is *an important political decision*, despite the problems of her claims to 'Aboriginal consciousness' examined in the previous paragraph.

The importance of this act can be measured in one particularly moving moment at Corunna Downs, when Sally is told by an old Aboriginal woman that her explorations into her past mean a great deal to her community because Sally is so proud to acknowledge and treasure (rather than conceal) her Aboriginal past: 'You don't know what it means that you, with a light skin, want to own us' (pp. 228–9). Figured in this quotation are, first, the differences between the women – Sally cannot ever *know* the meaning of her actions for the Aborigines – which splits a sense of a homogeneous 'Aboriginal consciousness' connecting these women; and second, the vital political significance of Sally's quest which potentially overrides these conceptual problems. We might go so far as to think about Sally's acknowledgement of an 'Aboriginal consciousness' as an exercise in 'strategic essentialism', which enables her to build affiliations with Aboriginal peoples and involve herself in bringing their lives to bear upon Australian history, despite the fact that their experiences will remain out of reach of her knowledge. Read in these terms, *My Place* is both a feminist and a postcolonial text in its contestation of the mutually supportive projects of patriarchy and colonialism.

Selected reading

Alexander, M. Jacqui and Chandra Talpade Mohanty (eds), *Feminist Genealogies, Colonial Legacies, Democratic Futures* (Routledge, 1997).

A wide-ranging collection of essays which examine the challenges for different groups of feminists in an often neo-colonial and patriarchal world.

Boehmer, Elleke, *Stories of Women: Gender and Narrative in the Postcolonial Nation* (Manchester University Press, 2005).

An exciting collection of essays that deal with the representation of women in mainly African and South Asian literature. The introduction is useful when considering the issue of gender in postcolonial studies more widely.

Davies, Carole Boyce, *Black Women, Writing and Identity: Migrations of the Subject* (Routledge, 1994).

A sustained and conceptually sophisticated critique which challenges some orthodox positions in postcolonial theory and negotiates new theoretical frames for reading black women's writing.

Donaldson, Laura E., *Decolonising Feminisms: Race, Gender, and Empire-Building* (Routledge, 1992).

Kabbani, Rana, *Imperial Fictions: Europe's Myths of Orient* (Pandora, rev. 1994).

An excellent critique of the gender politics of Orientalist art and writing.

Lionnet, François, *Postcolonial Representations: Women, Literature, Identity* (Cornell University Press, 1995).

McClintock, Anne, *Imperial Leather: Race, Gender and Sexuality in the Colonial Context* (Routledge, 1995).

An exciting and thought-provoking critique of colonial discourses and their intersections with 'race', gender and sexuality.

Mohanty, Chandra Talpade, 'Under Western Eyes: Feminist Scholarship and Colonial Discourses' in Williams and Chrisman (eds), *Colonial Discourse and Post-Colonial Theory*, (Harvester Wheatsheaf, 1993), pp. 196–220.

Mohanty's influential and important essay is required reading for discussions of postcolonialism and feminism.

Moore-Gilbert, Bart, *Postcolonial Theory: Contexts, Practices, Politics* (Verso, 1997).

Moore-Gilbert's chapter on Spivak is one of the finest to date in rendering and critiquing her influential ideas.

Morton, Stephen, *Gayatri Chakravorty Spivak* (Routledge, 2003).

The best introduction to Spivak available, and highly recommended if you are seeking to get to grips with her ideas.

Nasta, Susheila (ed.), *Motherlands: Black Women's Writing from Africa, the Caribbean and South Asia* (Women's Press, 1991).

An excellent collection of critical essays which exemplifies the manifold voices of postcolonial and feminist criticism.

Petersen, Kirsten Holst and Anna Rutherford (eds), *A Double Colonization: Colonial and Post-Colonial Women's Writing* (Dangaroo, 1986).

A landmark text which features creative and critical writing that addresses the 'double colonisation' of women.

Rajeswari, Sunder Rajan, *Real and Imagined Women: Gender, Culture, and Postcolonialism* (Routledge, 1993).

Spivak, Gayatri Chakravorty, 'Can the Subaltern Speak?', reprinted with abridgements in Williams and Chrisman (eds), *Colonial Discourse and Post-Colonial Theory*, (Harvester Wheatsheaf, 1993), pp. 66–111.

Probably one of the most important essays in postcolonialism, 'Can the Subaltern Speak?' has proved influential in feminist criticism and theories of colonial discourses. A very difficult essay at times, but one which rewards patient reading.

Spivak, Gayatri Chakravorty, *The Spivak Reader*, ed. Donna Landry and Gerald MacLean (Routledge, 1996).

This collection features some of Spivak's most influential and ground-breaking work, and includes highly valuable introductions to her essays.

Spivak, Gayatri Chakravorty, *A Critique of Postcolonial Reason: Toward a History of the Vanishing Present* (Harvard University Press, 1999).

This is Spivak's longest and most difficult book and orchestrates many of the key ideas for which she has come to be known, often revising well-known essays quite heavily at times. You should attempt this once you've become familiar with her key ideas and after you've read some good secondary criticism on Spivak (such as Stephen Morton's book, cited above).

Trinh, T. Minh-ha, *Women, Native, Other: Writing Postcoloniality and Feminism* (Indiana University Press, 1989).

A ground-breaking and challenging study of postcoloniality and feminism which explores the role of writing in contesting dominant patriarchal representations.

7

Diaspora identities

Migration, colonialism and decolonisation

It seems an obvious point that the British Empire was an international affair. Through the work of colonialism countless people voyaged *out* from Britain, often settling around the world in a variety of different places – the Americas, the South Pacific and elsewhere. But significant too were the voyages *in* by colonised peoples from around the world who travelled to the major European empires where many remained for the rest of their lives. Often these voyages took place under duress, as in the instances of plantation owners taking slaves to put to work as servants in their homes, or the use of South Asian women as 'ayahs' by families employed by the East India Company during and after their return to Britain. If the European empires changed life in colonised countries, then Europe too was changed forever by its colonial encounters.

As Sandra Ponzanesi and Daniela Merolla argue, '[m]igrations have always been a part of human civilization from ancient times to our days' (*Migrant Cartographies: New Cultural and Literary Spaces in Post-Colonial Europe*, Lexington Books, 2005, p. 2). Although it is not often acknowledged, the populations of most Western nations have consisted for many centuries of people from many different 'races' and cultures. The advent of European colonialism augmented the voyages in and out of Europe and the peoples who have settled there. The existence of African people in Britain, for example, can be traced back to and indeed before Elizabethan times, as testified by Peter Fryer's books *Staying Power: The History of*

Black People in Britain (Pluto, 1984) and *Black People in the British Empire: An Introduction* (Pluto, 1988). Anna Marie Smith has recorded that '[t]he black population in London numbered between 15,000 and 20,000 in the late eighteenth century – almost 3 per cent of the total population of the city' (*New Right Discourse on Race and Sexuality: Britain 1968–1990*, Cambridge, 1994, p. 134). In the context of the British Empire, there is now a well-established field of study concerning the writings of those colonised peoples who became located in Britain during the colonial period. One example is Ignatius Sancho. Born on a slave-ship and raised in south London, Sancho served as a butler, wrote music, corresponded with many fashionable literary figures and had his portrait painted by none other than Thomas Gainsborough. *The Letters of the Late Ignatius Sancho, An African* were published posthumously in 1782. Another figure is Olaudah Equiano, born in Nigeria and transported to Barbados, later arriving in England at the age of twelve. His book, *The Interesting Narrative of the Life of Olaudah Equiano, or Gustavus Vassa, the African* was published in 1789 and became an important text in the movement to abolish slavery. As a consequence of the postcolonial critique of the relations between culture and imperialism which has effected the retrieval of these texts, such cultural endeavours are now much more well known to students and scholars than they would have been as recently as twenty-five years ago.

In addition, while human migration needs to be recognised as an ancient phenomenon with a long colonial history, decolonisation has had major consequences for the migration of peoples from once-colonised countries to the European metropolitan centres. A wealth of cultural texts has been created as a consequence of twentieth-century migrations and these often take the themes of migration and diaspora as their subject matter. Throughout the twentieth century, but especially since the end of the Second World War, the former colonising nations have experienced the arrival of many peoples from once-colonised countries who have established new homes at the old colonial centres. The reasons for migration have been variable. In Britain, some colonial peoples were specifically recruited by the government to cope with labour shortages, such as the drive after the Second World War to employ

Caribbean peoples in public services like health and transport. Others arrived to study, or to escape political and economic difficulties in their native lands. Some followed family members who migrated before them. As a consequence, today many contemporary European nations can boast a wide variety of diaspora communities that may trace connections to locations such as Australia, Africa, South Asia, the Caribbean, China or Sri Lanka.

For reasons of focus, the bulk of this chapter will deal with examples from the British experience of migration and diaspora in recent decades, but it is hoped that some of the ideas we explore will prove useful to those beginning their studies in a number of diasporic contexts within Europe and perhaps even beyond too. We will think about migration and diaspora primarily in the context of decolonisation in this chapter and think about some of the most influential ways in which postcolonial diasporas have been conceptualised often by focusing on the key issue of identity.

What is a 'diaspora'?

In an important essay, James Clifford has noted that the term 'diaspora' has become 'loose in the world, for reasons having to do with decolonization, increased immigration, global communi- cations, and transport – a whole range of phenomena that encourage multi-locale attachments, dwelling, and travelling within and across nations' ('Diasporas', *Cultural Anthropology*, 9 (3), 1994 pp. 302–38, p. 306). Immediately we can identify some key issues which are linked to this term: migration, new settlement, border crossings, a world in motion rather than in stasis. As Michelle Keown, David Murphy and James Procter explain in a recent edited collection on the subject, '[t]he term once referred specifically to the dispersal of the Jews, but within contemporary cultural analysis the term is now more likely to evoke a plethora of global movements and migrations: Romanian, African, black, Sikh, Irish, Lebanese, Palestinian, "Atlantic" and so on' (*Comparing Postcolonial Diasporas*, Palgrave, 2009, p. 1). Within postcolonialism, then, 'diaspora' has come to signify *generally* the movement and relocation of groups of different kinds of peoples throughout the world.

It is just as important to understand that the terms 'diaspora' and 'diasporic' have come to mean something more than concrete, historical occurrences. As Mark Shackleton explains in his edited collection of recent essays on the subject, 'of even greater significance to postcolonial theory has been the consideration of the epistemological implications of the term – diaspora as theory. Such studies see migrancy in terms of adaptation and construction – adaptation to changes, dislocations and transformations, and the construction of new forms of knowledge and ways of seeing the world' (*Diasporic Literature and Theory – Where Now?*, Cambridge Scholars Publishing, 2008, p. ix). In other words, within postcolonialism 'diaspora' also names a new way of being, an emergent mode of perception and engagement with the world.

Let's begin to probe these ideas which cluster around notions of diaspora in postcolonial contexts. The first thing to do is secure a solid definition of the term. In his excellent book *Global Diasporas: An Introduction* (UCL Press, 1997) Robin Cohen tentatively describes diasporas as communities of people living together in one country who 'acknowledge that "the old country" – a notion often buried deep in language, religion, custom or folklore – always has some claim on their loyalty and emotions' (p. ix). The emphasis on collectivity and community here is very important, as is the sense of living in one country but looking across time and space to another. Vital too is the emotional element of this acknowledgement of another place, that sense of having a cultural and affective relationship with a faraway location. Cohen continues that 'a member's adherence to a diasporic community is demonstrated by an acceptance of an inescapable link with their past migration history and a sense of co-ethnicity with others of a similar background' (p. ix). It is tempting perhaps to think of diaspora peoples as migrant peoples, and indeed many living in diasporas certainly are. However, *generational differences* are important here. Children born to migrant peoples in Britain may lay claim to British citizenship, but their sense of identity and subjectivity borne from living in a diaspora community can be influenced by the 'past migration history' of their parents or grandparents that makes them forge emotional, cultural and imaginative bonds with more than one nation. The emotional and affective link these people might have to a distant location can be powerful and strong – perhaps more so than that of migrants, in some instances – even if they have never lived in or indeed visited the place in question.

This is one reason why it is more accurate to talk about 'diaspora identities' rather than 'migrant identities'; not all of those who live in a diaspora, or share an emotional connection to the 'old country', have experienced migration. This point also should make us aware that diasporas are therefore *composite* communities. As Avtar Brah puts it in *Cartographies of Diaspora: Contesting Identities* (Routledge, 1997), distinct diaspora communities are created out of the 'confluence of narratives' of different journeys from and links to the 'old country' which create the sense of a shared history (p. 183). Yet we must not forget that 'all diasporas are differentiated, heterogeneous, contested spaces, even as they are implicated in the construction of a common "we"' (p. 184). Differences of gender, 'race', class, religion and language (as well as generational differences) make diaspora spaces dynamic and shifting, open to repeated construction and reconstruction, contestation and change.

The experiences of migrancy and living in a diaspora have animated much recent postcolonial literature, criticism and theory, to the extent that postcolonial studies can often appear to prioritise diasporic concerns. Indeed, the slippings between the terms 'diaspora', 'migrant' and 'postcolonial' have been frequent and are not free from problems, as we shall consider. The literature produced by 'diaspora writers' – as have been called Monica Ali, Buchi Emecheta, Fred D'Aguiar, Romesh Gunesekera, Amitav Ghosh, Hanif Kureishi, Jhumpa Lahiri, Bharati Mukherjee, Caryl Phillips, Zadie Smith and Benjamin Zephaniah – has proved immensely popular in Western literary criticism. Similarly, in the work of academics such as Homi K. Bhabha, Avtar Brah, Rey Chow, Paul Gilroy, Stuart Hall and Sudesh Mishra, the new possibilities and problems engendered by the experience of migrancy and diaspora life have been readily explored. These possibilities include creating new and progressive ways of thinking about individual and communal identities and critiquing established schools of critical thought. Such work has often been resourced by critics who turn to issues of migration and diaspora to discover new ways to understand contemporary human existence beyond older, potentially outdated models that stressed the centrality of static ideas of land, belonging, home, nation and the like.

But diaspora communities and diasporic thinking are not free from problems, and these days many people who study diasporic thought and culture are wary of its pitfalls, especially in the wake of the popularity of postcolonial accounts of migration and diaspora in the 1990s which often enthusiastically presented diasporic modes of thinking and multicultural communities as making possible the end of imaginative as well as concrete acts of prejudice and division. As Paul Gilroy has argued, in the wake of events such as the 2001 terrorist attacks on New York and Washington, diasporic peoples have continued to suffer as a consequence of new and remoulded forms of prejudice pedalled in metropolitan countries against those of so-called different 'races', religions and ethnicities, while having their rights of tenure in certain nations questioned at the levels of state and street. Rather than assuming that the settlement of diasporic peoples results in the gradual and inevitable creation of a genuinely equitable and multicultural society where differences are eventually embraced rather than feared, Gilroy notes how in an increasingly uncertain world things like '"race" and its certainties can claim to heal or at least calm the anxieties over identity, which have been precipitated by the insecurities and inequalities of globalization' (*After Empire: Melancholia or Convivial Culture?* Routledge, 2004, p. 60). Diaspora peoples often remain ghettoised and excluded from feeling they belong to the 'new country' and suffer their cultural practices to be mocked and discriminated against. Many diaspora peoples who live in Europe do so in the perpetual face of forms of prejudice that violate their human rights. Nowhere is this more prevalent than in the treatment of asylum seekers, refugees and economic migrants who have found themselves demonised in many Western locations and subject to unsympathetic treatment by state institutions.

Furthermore, diaspora communities can be coercive as well as progressive locations, and in no way should be idealised or glibly celebrated. As Susheila Nasta argues, 'the predominant focus in contemporary postcolonial criticism on the celebratory elements of exile and displacement, the *heroic* potential of migrancy as a metaphor for a "new" form of aesthetic freedom, does have a number of significant limitations which dehistoricize and elide important questions of class, gender and cultural difference' (*Home Truths: Fictions of the South Asian Diaspora in Britain*, Palgrave,

2002, p. 4). As contested communities of confluence, diasporas are not free from their own internal inequalities of power and divisive prejudices. If postcolonial studies has often thought enthusiastically about diasporic matters in terms of possibility, we should not let this obscure the recurring issue which so many postcolonial writers deal with more and more these days: namely, that the concrete experience of living 'out of place' can often seem like a perpetual tryst with pain on a number of fronts.

In this chapter we will explore such possibilities and problems with specific attention to the theme of identity, a key preoccupation of diaspora theory. In so doing we will meet and define a range of conceptual terms, such as 'hybridity', 'borders', 'new ethnicities' and 'cultural diversity', that have often been pursued with enthusiasm in postcolonial studies. We will think critically about these conceptual tools and use them to help us read Beryl Gilroy's novel of diaspora identities, *Boy-Sandwich* (1989).

'Of, and not of, this place': home and displacement

Let's proceed by looking at a memorable moment in V. S. Naipaul's memoir 'Prologue to an Autobiography' (in *Finding the Centre: Two Narratives*, Penguin, 1984). Now living in Britain, Naipaul grew up in the Caribbean island of Trinidad and came from a family descended from Indian migrants to the Caribbean. He records an incident which occurred in the summer of 1932, when Indian indentured labourers were promised the passage back to India from Trinidad by the government once their contracts had expired. This had also happened in the previous year, when the *S. S. Ganges* collected a number of Indian labourers in Trinidad and sailed for India. The ship returned to Trinidad in 1932, collected more immigrant Indians and set off for Calcutta again:

> Seven weeks later the *Ganges* reached Calcutta. And there, to the terror of the passengers, the *Ganges* was stormed by hundreds of derelicts, previously repatriated, who wanted now to be taken back to the other place. India for these people had been a dream of home, a dream of continuity after the illusion of Trinidad. All the India they had found was the area around the Calcutta docks.
>
> Our own past was, like our idea of India, a dream. (p. 53)

Note how often the word 'dream' is repeated, as well as the reference to 'illusion'. Naipaul points out that migration alters how migrants think about their *home* and *host* countries. It has far-reaching, irreversible *imaginative* consequences as well as material ones. The Trinidad which many Indians had expected had been something of an illusion, far from the reality of the environment which they had found and which had not lived up to its promises. When viewed from India, it seemed a place of opportunity and promise, but the experience of the miserable working conditions meant it did not live up to the myth. But note too how, due to migrancy, India *also* had changed into something illusory, a dream: an imaginative location overseas, a home elsewhere, remembered as a salve to the ills of Trinidadian life. When viewed from the poverty of Trinidad, India can seem to the migrants a refuge from their miserable conditions, a fiction of a happy homeland where the ills of the present may be relinquished. Yet, their voyage home reveals this view of India similarly to be more imaginary than true, as the return does not alleviate their hardships. The migrant's illusion of home does not square with the experience of going home, to the extent that 'home' seems to exist above and beyond either Trinidad or India, perpetually out of reach for the migrants. The indentured labourers have in Trinidad constructed a different, imaginary India which is *discontinuous* with the real location. It exists primarily in the mind, and no act of actual, physical return can facilitate it. Where do these migrant figures now belong, if both India and Trinidad have become more illusory than homely? Are such peoples forever going to be 'at sea', both literally and emotionally, bound to be restlessly on the move and devoid of a fixed or stable locus of belonging?

Naipaul's example helps us begin to understand how migration often results in the *idea* of the home country becoming split from the *experience* of returning home, and the challenges of belonging which this inevitably creates. As Avtar Brah states, '"home" is a mythic place of desire in the diasporic imagination. In this sense it is a place of no-return, even if it is possible to visit the geographical territory that is seen as the place of "origin"' (*Cartographies of Diaspora*, p. 192). Naipaul uses this episode to convey his own dreamlike view of India as a home, as somebody born in Trinidad into an Indian family; and thus, strictly speaking, *not* an Indian migrant. For him, India is also an illusory place from which he is fractured in both time and space, but which retains an emotional influence over his life. His example invites us to think about migrancy as constructing certain ways of seeing that impact upon *both migrants and their descendants* in a number of ways (although the response of different generations is not always the same).

Hence, we need quickly to understand that migrancy has effects which last long after the act of migrating has finished, and which impact on how people think and feel. As Russell King, John Connell and Paul White argue in the preface to their edited collection *Writing Across Worlds: Literature and Migration* (Routledge, 1995), '[f]or some groups, migration is not a mere interval between fixed points of departure and arrival, but a mode of being in the world – "migrancy"' (p. xv). In talking of migrancy, then, we are looking at the problems and new possibilities that result from a particular mode of existence. These things are both matters of knowledge (epistemology) and of being (ontology). For many postcolonial thinkers, migrancy and diaspora describe *perpetual* conditions that release *new forms of knowledge and being*. These words describe more than a finite journey or a particular locale of residence.

For migrant and diasporic peoples in particular, 'home' is a particularly complex idea which impacts in central ways on their existence. The concept of 'home' often performs an important function in our lives. It can act as a valuable means of orientation by giving us a fixed, reliable sense of our place in the world. It is meant to tell us where we originated from and apparently where we legitimately belong. As an *idea* it stands for shelter, stability, security and comfort (although actual experiences of home may well fail to deliver these promises). To be 'at home' is to occupy a location where we are welcome, where we can be with people we may regard very much like ourselves, where we are not at sea but have found safe harbour. But what happens to the *idea* of 'home' for those on the move who live far from the lands of their or their ancestors' birth?

In considering these matters, let us turn to Salman Rushdie's landmark essay 'Imaginary Homelands' (in *Imaginary Homelands: Essays and Criticism 1981–1991*, Granta, 1991, pp. 9–21). Rushdie was born in 1947 in Bombay, where he spent his childhood. He moved to England as a young man to attend Rugby School and later

Cambridge University, and he eventually settled in London. In his essay Rushdie reflects upon the process of writing his novel *Midnight's Children* (1981) which is set in India and Pakistan, while living in north London. Significant sections of the novel concern the Bombay of Rushdie's youth which he recalls from afar, in a different country and at a later moment in time. Rushdie reveals that one of the reasons which motivated his writing of the novel was an attempt to restore the world of his childhood home, distant in both time and space, to the present; indeed, he notes that on the wall of his London study was a black and white photograph of his childhood home in Bombay. But it proved an impossible task to 'return home' via the process of writing. In a sense, we all leave home at one time or another in our lives and may feel a sense of loss for doing so; but, as Rushdie argues 'the writer who is out-of-country and even out-of-language may experience this loss *in an intensified form*. It is made more concrete for him by the physical fact of discontinuity, of his present being in a different place from his past, of his being "elsewhere"' (p. 12 – emphasis added).

This disjunction between past and present, between here and there, makes 'home' seem far-removed in time and space, available for return only through an act of the imagination. But as we have been considering, it is not possible simply to go back, either physically or imaginatively. Speaking of Indian migrants, Rushdie writes that 'our physical alienation from India almost inevitably means that we will not be capable of reclaiming precisely the thing that was lost; that we will, in short, create fictions, not actual cities or villages, but invisible ones, imaginary homelands, Indias of the mind' (p. 10). In this formulation, home becomes an especially unstable and unpredictable mental construct built from the incomplete odds and ends of memory that survive from the past. It exists in a fractured, discontinuous relationship with the present, forever just out of reach and impossible to restore. Rushdie remarks that when thinking back to his Bombay childhood, he could recall only fragmentary, partial memories, often of small, mundane occurrences. In a useful turn of phrase, he records that his reflections were made 'in broken mirrors, some of whose fragments have been irretrievably lost' (p. 11).

So, if we take Rushdie's comments as applicable to other acts of migration (not just Indian), we can argue that the migrant occupies a *displaced* position, dislocated from a past homeland that can only ever be imperfectly imagined but not fully grounded in their present location or residence. Migrants envision their existence in terms of fragments and fissures, full of gaps and breaches. The transformations wrought by the experience of migrancy make impossible the recovery of a plenitudinous sense of home.

If imagining home beckons only fragmentation, discontinuity and displacement for the migrant, can new homes be secured in the host country? In migrating from one country to another, migrants inevitably become involved in the process of setting up home in a new land. This can also add to the ways in which the concept of home is disturbed. Migrants tend to arrive in new places with baggage; both in the physical sense of possessions or belongings, but also the less tangible matter of beliefs, traditions, customs, behaviours and values. This can have consequences for the ways in which others may or may not make migrants feel 'at home' on arrival in a new place. In Chapters 3 and 4 we looked in detail at the ways in which nationalist discourses attempt to construct 'deep, horizontal comradeship' by setting 'norms and limits' for the nation's people. Although migrants may pass through the *political* borders of nations, crossing their frontiers and gaining entrance to new places, such 'norms and limits' can be used to exclude migrants from being accommodated inside the *imaginative* borders of the nation. The dominant discourses of 'race', ethnicity and gender may function to exclude them from being recognised as part of the nation's people. Migrants may well live in new places, but they can be deemed not to belong there and disqualified from thinking of the new land as their home. Instead, their home is seen to exist elsewhere, back across the border. How easy is it to make a new place into your home, if you are perpetually told that you don't belong and if your right to call a new place 'home' is aggressively challenged?

For these reasons and others, many diasporic writers have been keen to point out that home can no longer be relied upon as a stable and stabilising concept. To be a migrant, or to live in a diasporic location, is to live without or beyond old notions of being 'at home' or securely 'in place'. It is to embrace movement, motion and fragmentariness as key forms of existence and being, instead of stability, rootedness and wholeness. For migrants and their descendants, no single location can act as a secure home; instead, the multiple experiences, contacts and cultural affiliations which such people nurture mean that their sense of identity and belonging may be eternally split across two or more locations. So some have argued that they live 'in-between' locations and feel permanently displaced from each one. This has led to a rethinking of concepts such as home, belonging and rootedness as exclusionary and troublesome rather than benign, and ill-equipped to bear witness to the new realities of the contemporary world.

Consider the example of the writer Caryl Phillips, who was born in St Kitts in the Caribbean and arrived in England as a baby. Phillips left England as a young man and travelled extensively, and he now spends a large amount of time in the United States. He has written of his sense of connection to Africa (the location of many of his ancestors), the Caribbean (where he was born), Britain (where he grew up and was educated) and the US (where he works as a Professor). In the introduction to his book of essays *A New World Order* (Secker and Warburg, 2001) he remembers variously visiting Sub-Saharan Africa, his first trip to the United States, arriving at St Kitts airport, and going to the cinema one afternoon in Leeds. Each vignette ends with the words, 'I recognise the place, I feel at home here, but I don't belong. I am of, and not of, this place' (p. 4). Notice that there is no smooth continuum here between notions of place, home, belonging and identity. Rather, the words jar against each other as Phillips tries to find a new rhetoric of identity – one which can only be hinted at in the sobering and contradictory phrase 'of, and not of'. Later in his book he writes of the difficulties of living out of place and being excluded, calling it the 'high anxiety' (p. 308) of belonging. Phillips's choice of vocabulary should leave us in little doubt as to the difficult emotional consequences of living, and feeling, displaced. But note too how the attempt to bear witness to the predicament of diasporic belonging seems to bankrupt conventional vocabularies and requires *a new rhetoric of belonging* that takes us beyond the problems of the old one.

Whereas Rushdie migrated to Britain as a schoolboy, Phillips arrived as a small child with no significant subsequent recall of his birth in the Caribbean. The affinities between their different senses of displacement and vexed belonging should alert us to the overlap that exists between the predicament of those who can remember a place overseas and those who cannot, as well as enable us to turn next to making some distinctions. Naipaul's use of the incident of the *S. S. Ganges* also demonstrated an affinity between two generations: Indian migrants to Trinidad like the sailors and 'Indian-born' Trinidadians like himself. Yet, the descendants of migrants are not always in the same position. Consider for a moment the photograph of Rushdie's childhood home hanging on his wall. At the beginning of 'Imaginary Homelands' Rushdie recalls re-visiting the house in Bombay after many years in Britain and being amazed at how different it looked, both to the photograph on his wall and to his memory. The visit affords Rushdie the opportunity to indulge a childhood memory, even as it underlines the fact this return does *not* eliminate feelings of displacement. Standing outside, he prefers not to announce himself to the new owners as he 'didn't want to see how they'd ruined the interior' (p. 9). We can borrow this remark to suggest that migrants in positions similar to Rushdie with their childhood memories of a distant place, have a certain degree of 'interior knowledge' no matter how fragmentary and fissured it may be. But to the children of migrants, the 'interior knowledge' of a distant place is unavailable. Thus, their reflections about these places in terms of 'home' are often differently constructed.

These often *generational* differences are not absolute. Migrants can share both similarities and differences with their descendants, and the relationship between generations can be complex and overlapping, rather than forming a neat contrast. To get a sense of this, let us turn to an essay called 'The Rainbow Sign' by Hanif Kureishi, a writer born in Britain with a Bombay-born father and English mother (the essay is collected in his book *Dreaming and Scheming: Reflections on Writing and Politics*, Faber, 2002, pp. 25–56). This essay records Kureishi's experiences as a boy growing up in London, a visit to Pakistan as a young man, and some comparisons between life in both locations. As a child, Kureishi admits to having 'no idea of what the subcontinent was like or how my numerous uncles, aunts and cousins lived there' (p. 25). His relationship with South Asia is obviously different to his father's.

Yet at school he was mistakenly identified as an Indian by his teachers, one of whom placed pictures of Indian peasants in mud huts before his class in order to show the other children Kureishi's 'home'. 'I wondered: did my uncles ride on camels? Surely not in their suits? Did my cousins, so like me in other ways, squat down in the sand like little Mowglis, half-naked and eating with their fingers?' (p. 25). The reference here to the figure of Mowgli from Rudyard Kipling's *The Jungle Book* (1894) suggests how Kureishi's identity was similarly fictionalised by others as an outsider who belonged to a land overseas, despite the fact that Kureishi was born, like his mother, in Britain. He was not readily permitted to 'belong' to Britain like his classmates. This is an example of the ways in which the descendants of migrants can suffer similar experiences to their parents or grandparents.

On a visit to his relations in Karachi as a young adult, Kureishi also found it difficult to think of this place in terms of 'home'. He admits to 'a little identity crisis' (p. 33). His uncles' anti-British remarks make him feel uncomfortable and strangely patriotic towards Britain, feelings he had not previously experienced. Although he does not try to indulge in feeling 'Pakistani', as this would be a dubious act of sentimentality, his identity crisis is outlined when an acquaintance declares to him: 'we are Pakistanis, but you, you will always be a Paki – emphasising the slang derogatory name the English used against Pakistanis, and therefore the fact that I couldn't rightfully lay claim to either place' (p. 34).

Living 'in-between': from *roots* to *routes*

Kureishi's articulation of his identity crisis is both an index of the pain of feeling devoid of secure roots, and also something we might use as a pivotal moment when thinking about the creative necessities of migrancy and diaspora. On the one hand, and without wishing to ignore generational differences, his comment quoted above indicates the perilous intermediate position that *both* migrants and their children are deemed to occupy: living 'in-between' different nations, 'of, and not of' each place, feeling neither here nor there, unable to indulge in sentiments of belonging to either location, defined by others often in unflattering ways. Kureishi feels devoid of the 'rightful' claims to belong. But on the other hand, and more productively perhaps, this moment shows that the conventional ways we use to think about ideas such as 'belonging' can no longer work in a diasporic context. As Phillips's essay also implied, we need new ways of thinking about identity which free figures like Kureishi from such unhappy, awkward, inaccurate definition.

As we have considered, conventional ideas of 'home' and 'belonging' often depend upon clearly defined, static notions of being 'in place', firmly rooted in a community or a particular geographical location. We might think of the discourses of nationalism, ethnicity or 'race' as examples of models of belonging which attempt to root the individual within a clearly defined and homogenised group. But these models or 'narratives' of belonging no longer seem suited to a world where the experience and legacy of migration are altering the ways in which individuals think of their relation to place, and how they might 'lay claim' to lands that are difficult to think of in terms of 'home' or 'belonging'. Instead, new models of identity are emerging which depend upon reconsidering the mobile and perilous 'in-between' position of someone like Kureishi as a site of excitement, new possibilities and even privilege.

Let us approach these new models of identity by returning for a moment to Salman Rushdie's essay 'Imaginary Homelands'. In registering his displacement from the Bombay home of his childhood, Rushdie does not dwell nostalgically upon this loss, although he registers loss in his remarks. Instead, he makes a virtue from necessity and argues that the displaced position of the migrant is an entirely valuable one. In learning to reflect reality in 'broken mirrors', the migrant comes to treasure a *partial, plural* view of the world because it reveals *all* representations of the world are incomplete. 'Meaning is a shaky edifice we build out of scraps, dogmas, childhood injuries, newspaper articles, chance remarks, old films, small victories, people hated, people loved; perhaps it is because our sense of what is the case is constructed from such inadequate materials that we defend it so fiercely, even to the death' ('Imaginary Homelands', p.12). The migrant seems in a better position than others to realise that all systems of knowledge, all views of the world, are never totalising, whole or pure, but incomplete, muddled and hybrid. To live as a migrant may well evoke the pain of loss and of not being firmly rooted in a secure place; but it is also to live in a world of immense possibility with the realisation that new knowledges and ways of seeing can be constructed out of myriad combinations of the 'scraps' which Rushdie describes – knowledges which challenge the authority of older ideas of rootedness and fixity. Similarly, Kureishi's identity crisis in Pakistan is both a source of pain and possibility, in that it opens up the chance to explore alternative modes of belonging. For such reasons does James Clifford declare that '[d]iaspora consciousness lives loss and hope as a defining tension' ('Diasporas', p. 312). The displaced position of the diasporic subject exposes the pain of not belonging but also unleashes the possibility of thinking and doing something new. That 'defining tension' between loss and hope has proven to be remarkably fertile.

In such terms, the tense space of the 'in-between' has become re-thought as a place of immense creativity and possibility, as Kureishi's essay 'The Rainbow Sign' indeed testifies. Kureishi recalls seeing a photograph in his uncle's house in Pakistan of his father as a young boy. This fragment from the past, like the photograph in Rushdie's study, becomes a valuable 'scrap' which he can use when stitching together new ways of thinking about his identity and his place in the world. He cannot ever think of his uncle's house as his 'home', but it is a vital treasure-house of manifold possibilities. Kureishi describes it as 'a house full of stories, of Bombay, Delhi, China; of feuds, wrestling matches, adulteries, windows broken with hands, card games, impossible loves, and magic spells. Stories to help me see my place in the world and give me a sense of the past which could go into making a life in the present and the future' ('The Rainbow Sign', p. 52). Notice here how Kureishi must become actively involved in *forging new narratives* which will accommodate his position more adequately than older, totalising (or 'holistic') narratives. To borrow some terms from Paul Gilroy's book *The Black Atlantic* (Verso, 1993), he does not have secure *roots* which fix him in a place, in a nation or an ethnic group; rather he must continually plot for himself itinerant cultural *routes* which take him, imaginatively as well as physically, to many places and into contact with many different peoples. This forges a shifting and mobile relationship between past, present and future, one that does not presume an even, continuous passage through time but which reconstellates these different moments. Kureishi's family history in South Asia may appear to him as just stories, the fragments of lives and experiences very removed from his own; yet they are vital resources which he can use to orient his way into the future. They can commingle in new, unexpected and exciting ways with his love of popular music and radical black culture that he pursued as a youth in the late 1960s, combining in novel ways to make a new hybrid multicultural tapestry out of disparate source materials. Like the Bombay-born Rushdie, but not identical to him of course, Kureishi also stands at a liminal position where new forms of vision can be constellated from the scraps and patches of his multicultural, liminal existence. The grounded certainties of *roots* are replaced with the transnational contingencies of *routes*.

Let us pause for a moment and review the ideas we have encountered so far:

- Migrancy constructs modes of existence and ways of seeing that last beyond the actual journey between countries.
- Migrancy can expose the migrant and his or her children to displacement, fragmentation and discontinuity.
- Home is a problematic concept, both in the past and in the present.
- Living 'in-between' can be painful, perilous and marginalising.
- Migrants and their children occupy different positions due to generational differences, but they can have similar experiences of feeling rootless and displaced.
- The dominant narratives of belonging and identity cannot accommodate those who live 'in-between' or are 'of, but not of' a singular location of belonging.
- But new, transnational models of identity and belonging are possible which, in Paul Gilroy's terms, challenge the certainty of *roots* with the contingency of *routes*.

Hybrid identities at the 'in-between'

Several of the issues and ideas raised in Rushdie's and Kureishi's essays have preoccupied postcolonial theories of diasporic identity. In particular, the 'in-between' position of the migrant, and his or her errant, impartial perceptions of the world, 'of, and not of' every place, have been used as the starting point for creating new, dynamic ways of thinking about identity which go beyond older static models, such as national identity and the notion of 'rootedness'. These frequently merge the circumstances of migration with the theoretical ideas and languages of poststructuralism.

One particularly enthusiastic exponent of this line of thought has been Homi K. Bhabha, himself a migrant from Bombay to Britain who now lives in America. Some of the essays collected in his book *The Location of Culture* (Routledge, 1994) advocate new, exciting ways of thinking about identity born from 'the great history of the languages and landscapes of migration and diaspora' (p. 235). Bhabha specifically describes these as new forms of *postcolonial* identity, making a slippage between 'migrant' and 'postcolonial' which is not free from problems. We are going to focus in detail upon the introductory chapter, called 'Locations of Culture' as it contains many ideas about identity which are elaborated at many points in his influential book.

'Locations of Culture' addresses those who live 'border lives' on the margins of different nations, in-between contrary homelands, such as migrants and diasporic peoples. For Bhabha, living at the border, at the edge, requires a new 'art of the present'. This depends upon embracing the contrary logic of the border and using it to rethink the dominant ways we represent things like history, identity and community. Borders are important thresholds, full of contradiction and ambivalence. They both separate and join different places. They are intermediate locations where one contemplates moving beyond a barrier. As Bhabha defines it, the 'beyond' is an in-between site of transition: 'the "beyond" is neither a new horizon, nor a leaving behind of the past ... we find ourselves in the moment of transit where space and time cross to produce complex figures of difference and identity, past and present, inside and outside, inclusion and exclusion' (p. 1). The space of the 'beyond' is often described in terms which emphasise this transitory, 'in-between' sense: such as 'liminal', 'interstitial' or 'hybrid'. Look how, in the quotation just given, the emphasis is placed on *crossing*, or shuttling between seemingly opposed states. For Bhabha, the border is the place where conventional patterns of thought are disturbed and can be disrupted by the possibility of crossing. At the border, past and present, inside and outside no longer remain separated as binary opposites but instead commingle and conflict. From this emerge new, shifting complex forms of representation that deny binary patterning. So, and as we keep noticing in this chapter, Bhabha suggests that *imaginative* border-crossings are as much a consequence of migration as the *physical* crossing of borders.

Bhabha turns the possibility of such imaginative crossings against received notions of identity and subjectivity which precisely depend upon fixed, binary definitions: such as native/foreigner, home/ unhomely, master/slave. These are contested as ideologically suspect and inappropriate; the 'art of the present' requires a habit of mind in which movement and crossing are paramount, and where fixed sedentary ideas are superseded. Bhabha urges that we must 'think beyond narratives of originary and initial subjectivities and ... focus on those moments or processes that are produced in the articulation of cultural differences. These "in-between" spaces provide the terrain of elaborating strategies of selfhood – singular or communal – that initiate new signs of identity' (p. 1). There are three things to notice here. First, like Gayatri Chakravorty Spivak whose work we explored particularly in Chapter 6, Bhabha also opposes the idea of a 'sovereign' or essentialised subject. For Bhabha and Spivak identity is a discursive product. Second, because subjectivity is discursively produced, it is possible for it to be remade and remodelled in new and innovative ways – hence his attention to the processes of 'articulation' and 'elaboration' in the quotation. The border is a place of possibility and agency for new concepts, new narratives, new ideas. Third, the new 'signs' of identity which are possible impact upon both individuals *and* groups. Rethinking identity is not a solipsistic activity but is bound up in a group identity, group formation and group hostilities. So, the imaginative crossings at the 'beyond' offer ways of thinking about communal identity that depart from old ideas, such as the 'deep, horizontal comradeship' of the nation which can fall foul of the binary logic of same/different, inside/outside, citizen/stranger.

A crucial manoeuvre in this line of thought is the refusal to think of cultures as pure or holistic, with received wisdom handed down from generation to generation in a way which preserves knowledge. Instead, culture is regarded as intermingled and manifold, something which migration and diasporas especially facilitate and emphasise. As in his essay 'DissemiNation', Bhabha stresses the importance of *performance* as the means by which new, hybrid identities are negotiated. We saw above how both Rushdie and Kureishi claimed that meaning could be made from the discontinuous scraps and fragmentary remains of their different South Asian inheritances, bringing the resources of the past to bear upon their lives in the present. Bhabha makes a similar point, in an albeit more compact and dense fashion. Standing at the border, the migrant is empowered to intervene *actively* in the transmission of cultural inheritance or 'tradition' (of both the home and host land) rather than *passively* accept its venerable customs and pedagogical wisdom. He or she can question, refashion or mobilise received ideas. The migrant is empowered to act as an agent of change, deploying received knowledge in the present and transforming it as a consequence, just as Kureishi could make the photograph of his father mean something new and important in an unpredictable context. As this example demonstrates, this does *not* mean that received or traditional knowledge becomes dismissed. Rather, inherited knowledge can be reinscribed and given new, unexpected meanings by becoming cross-hatched with cultural resources from other locations and sources, other times and places. Bhabha calls this action 'restaging the past'. From a migratory, minority position, the restaging of the past 'introduces other, incommensurable cultural temporalities into the invention of tradition. This process estranges any access to an originary identity or a "received" tradition' (p. 2).

This quotation has two important consequences. First, the subject becomes produced from the process of *hybridisation*. His or her subjectivity is deemed to be composed from variable sources, different materials, many locations – demolishing forever the idea of subjectivity as stable, single, or 'pure'. The concept of hybridity has proved very important for diaspora peoples, and indeed many others too, as a way of thinking beyond exclusionary, fixed, binary notions of identity based on ideas of rootedness and cultural, racial and national purity. Hybrid identities are never total and complete in themselves, like orderly pathways built from crazy-paving. Instead, they remain perpetually in motion, pursuing errant and unpredictable routes, open to change and reinscription. They are border subjectivities, no longer reliant on fixed notions of home and identity to anchor them to a singular sense of self. Rather, the loss of these fixed ideas has been transformed into a hopeful new paradigm where motion, multiplicity, errancy, unpredictability, hybridity and impurity are gleefully welcomed.

Second, in using the term 'incommensurable cultural temporalities', Bhabha anticipates the next stage in his argument where he traces how an aesthetics of the border impacts upon received binary knowledges. These ideas, exciting and challenging, need contextualising first in terms of Bhabha's influence by the psychoanalytical work of Sigmund Freud and Jacques Lacan. In his Introduction, Bhabha turns to Freud's writings on the *unheimlich*, often translated as the 'unhomely' or 'uncanny'. As Freud uses the term, an uncanny experience can be prompted when something that we have hitherto regarded as imaginary appears before us in reality, or when something that has been previously concealed or forgotten disturbingly returns. In Bhabha's thinking, the disruption of received totalising narratives of individual and group identity made possible at the 'border' can be described as an 'uncanny' moment, where all those forgotten in the construction of, say, national groups return to disturb and haunt such holistic ways of thinking. This uncanny disruption brings with it trauma and anxiety. It serves as a reminder that exclusive, exclusionary systems of meaning are forever haunted by those who are written out and erased. At the limits of conventional knowledge, these figures return as disruptive 'unhomely' presences that cannot be articulated through existing patterns of representation. It is this uncanny presence which Bhabha seizes upon as having the power to disrupt the exclusive binary logic upon which a range of discourses – nationalist, colonialist, patriarchal – depend.

This is where culture plays an important part. Bhabha suggests that literature concerning 'migrants, the colonised or political refugees' (p. 12) could take on the task of unhousing the received ways of thinking about the world and discovering the hybridity, the difference that exists within. However, and importantly, these internal differences are displaced, existing beyond representation. This is why Bhabha calls them 'incommensurable'. This term refers to the existence of something that cannot be measured or described *by the prevailing system of language*. Cultural differences are figured as unrepresented, uncanny presences which bear witness to displaced experiences, histories and lives that cannot be figured with recourse to the sedentary concepts of so-called common sense (home, belonging, etc.). As Bhabha argues, 'As literary creatures and political animals we ought to concern ourselves with the understanding of human action and the social world as a moment when *something is beyond control, but it is not beyond accommodation* ... the critic must attempt to fully realise, and take responsibility for, the unspoken, unrepresented pasts that haunt the historical present' (p. 12). 'Accommodation without control': this is the challenge for new hybrid forms of knowledge, one which the binary discourses of fixed individual and group identity failed. Bhabha gives examples of this new literature by referring, among others, to Toni Morrison's novel *Beloved* (1987), in which the uncanny, ghostly appearance of a young black girl on the outskirts of Cincinnati in 1873 points to the unspoken histories of American slaves. These unspoken alternative histories return to haunt the received history in which they find no voice.

It is worth comparing Bhabha's ideas with those in Spivak's essay, 'Can the Subaltern Speak?' (explored in Chapter 6). Whereas both Spivak's subaltern as female and Bhabha's unhomely presences are beyond conventional modes of representation, Bhabha's use of Freud's sense of the 'uncanny' keeps open the possibility that oppressed voices maintain the propensity to make their (absent) presence felt, to menace the scene of representation. Can the same be said for Spivak's subaltern?

It would be useful to pause here and make a summary. We have been thinking about how Bhabha's attention to the border, the 'beyond', considers the opportunity for new, hybrid forms of knowledge, but does not fix or prescribe them. An element of incommensurability always remains. As Bhabha declares early in the piece with deliberate ambiguity, the boundary is the place 'from which *something begins its presencing*' (p. 5). To secure exactly what this 'something' is, would be to fall back on a logic which demands fixity, limitation, definition. Rather, we must attend to what is incommensurable and unhomely in conventional systems of thought. Suitably, an uncanny, incommensurable presence is eerily registered in the choice of italics which animate the quotation and reveal the possibility of that 'something' half-hidden inside Bhabha's characteristically cryptic sentence.

STOP and THINK

Bhabha's work moves from the crossing of physical borders to imaginative borders, where new ways of thinking about identity, community and knowledge suitable to a changed world can be fashioned. This changed world is specifically named as 'postcolonial'. But we might wish to beware of the generalising tendency in this argument. Bhabha's declaration that the experience of migrants encapsulates the common 'contemporary compulsion to move beyond' (p. 18) seems to position the migrant as a late-twentieth-century universal 'everyman' (the gender is not inappropriate here, I think). Bhabha has been accused of neglecting cultural and historical specificities in his work by abstracting a general theory from particular experiences. As Aijaz Ahmad points out in his essay 'The Politics of Literary Postcoloniality' (in *Race and Class*, 36 (3), 1995, pp. 1–20), the image of the postcolonial subject which results from Bhabha's work 'is remarkably free of gender, class, [and] identifiable political location' (p. 13). This is not always a fair criticism, but the swift movements in Bhabha's work, (between nineteenth-century India to 1980s South Africa, for example) does reveal a globetrotting tendency in his writing that threatens to decontextualise the experiences of different times and places.

Other problems present themselves too. Bhabha is often called a cosmopolitan due to his transnational terms of reference. His work is itself in perpetual motion, facilitated by border crossings and hybrid combinations at the level of ideas. Yet, is this hybrid mixture *definitive* of postcolonialism? Bhabha seems to suggest that it is, such is the ease with which the logic of the 'beyond' is described as 'postcolonial'. As he bluntly puts it in one essay, '[t]he postcolonial perspective resists the attempt at holistic forms of social explanation' (*The Location of Culture*, p. 173). This formulation, however, ignores the perspectives of those in countries with a history of colonialism who have never migrated. Are their perspectives wrong if they do not fit Bhabha's formula? What would happen to Ngugi's arguments (which we encountered in Chapter 4) concerning the need to protect and enrich Gikuyu, if we accept Bhabha's ideas? For a thinker as subtle and exciting as Bhabha, it is perhaps disappointing to come across totalising representations of the 'postcolonial perspective'. As we have seen throughout this book, such moves are perilous.

New ethnicities

Bhabha's work represents one example of how critical thought has attempted to build new forms of postcolonial knowledge that are energised by the experiences, predicaments, losses and hopefulness unleashed by migration. Other key thinkers to do so include Stuart Hall and Paul Gilroy, and it is to their work that we next turn. Let us consider Stuart Hall's essay 'New Ethnicities' (in *Critical Dialogues in Cultural Studies*, ed. David Morley and Kuan-Hsing Chen, Routledge, 1996, pp. 441–9), first published in 1989. This piece also deals with the transformations wrought by migration in similar ways to Bhabha, but it deals specifically with changes made by Britain's black community and less generally about what may or may not qualify as a 'postcolonial' perspective. Whereas Bhabha's writing is situated more within the realm of literary theory and criticism, Hall's work emerges from the fields of sociology and cultural studies, although the work of both figures bears witness to the increasing interdisciplinarity of postcolonialism since the 1980s. As with Bhabha, Hall is keen to conceptualise migrant and diasporic cultures in terms of motion, multiplicity and hybridity.

In 'New Ethnicities' Stuart Hall considers the ways in which members of the black British diaspora have represented themselves in response to the 'common experience of racism and marginalisation in Britain' (p. 441). He identifies two separate yet overlapping phases or moments. In the first, the term 'black' was used as a way of uniting people of different ethnic or racial backgrounds and organising them into communities of resistance. In asserting a common black experience, black Britons created a 'singular and unifying framework based on the building up of identity across ethnic and cultural difference between the different communities' (p. 441). These communities could be from African, Caribbean or South Asian locations, yet they were united through the representation of a common 'black' community. This served two purposes: first, it raised the question of rights of access to representation by black writers and artists, and second, it enabled the stereotypical and derogatory representations of black people at large to be contested by positive images of the black community, often through the coherence of an essentialised black subject who typified black experience in general.

But in the second moment these unifying modes of representation become contested from *within* the black community, as individuals begin to question the existence and purpose of believing in an essential black subject. In its place, the 'extraordinary diversity of subjective positions, social experiences and cultural identities' (p. 443) are asserted and explored. Diasporic black identities are presented instead as multiple and mobile, with their own inner tensions. This 'inevitably entails a weakening or a fading of the notion that "race" or some composite notion of race around the term black will either guarantee the effectivity of any cultural practice or determine in any final sense its aesthetic value' (p. 443). In other words, black artists and writers no longer work *on behalf* of the black community, because that composite community cannot be easily homogenised. Furthermore, the work they produce cannot be celebrated simply because it comes from the diaspora. Instead, more critical and conflictual responses become possible. This creates a challenge for the black community: how can a politics be constructed 'which works with and through difference, which is able to build those forms of solidarity and identification which make common struggle and resistance possible but without suppressing the real heterogeneity of interests and identities' (p. 444).

In his description of the first 'moment' of black representations, Hall shows how diaspora communities have used unifying and homogenising modes of representation in response to some of the less welcome experiences of diaspora. This gives the lie to Bhabha's work on the 'border lives' of migrant individuals who concern themselves with the critique of totalising systems of representation, by showing that this need not be the only kind of response engendered by their 'border' position. Hall's work shows that, for historical and cultural reasons, the construction of a generalised black community and an essentialised black subject has, in one context, served an important political purpose, despite the fact that we might want to question some of the assumptions upon which these representations rest.

Speaking more generally, this point also beckons questions concerning the production of community by diaspora peoples. *How* are they organised, and *who* organises them? In addition, it is tempting to regard Hall's 'two moments' as bearing witness to the responses of different generations in Britain, yet Hall warns against this. These phases of response are 'of the same movement, which constantly overlap and interweave. Both are framed by the same historical conjuncture and both are rooted in the politics of anti-racism and the post-war black experience in Britain' (p. 441). Hall's essay demonstrates that these different responses to the experience of living in a diaspora are *simultaneously* possible. It is not wise to make generalisations about a typical 'migrant perspective' or a 'diaspora experience'.

In speaking of a 'second moment', Hall's work opens up debates concerning the variety of different subject positions within diaspora communities. By focusing on a variety of contemporary cultural representations of black peoples, Hall calls attention to the ways in which the generalising images of a diaspora community or typical subject may not be representative of all those who would consider themselves as living in a diaspora. In addition, attention must be given to the power relations *within* diaspora communities which can often favour certain groups over others. In his discussion of black British cultural studies during the 1980s, Kobena Mercer points out how black lesbian and gay groups helped effect a paradigm shift from the essentialised, generalised notion of a black community to a situation similar to Hall's notion of 'new ethnicities', where 'mobile and flexible frameworks for studying the shifting landscapes of diaspora' became the norm (in *Welcome to the Jungle: New Positions in Black Cultural Studies*, Routledge, 1994, p. 16). These 'new ethnicities' – fluid, contingent, multiple and shifting – can be compared to Bhabha's 'border lives', where the concepts of over-lapping, hybridity, *routed* identity, and shifting subjectivity become enthusiastically promoted as the new 'art of the present' and are seen as 'crucial and vital efforts to answer the "possibility and necessity of creating a new culture": *so that you can live*' (*Welcome to the Jungle*, p. 4).

In concluding this section, it is important to realise that the possibilities engendered by rethinking identity in terms of fluidity and hybridity (*routes* rather than *roots*) have the propensity to alter the ways in which identities are formed for *all* people in one location, not just those who are constructed as 'diaspora communities'. Indeed, *all* oppositional divides between 'native inhabitants' and 'diaspora peoples', 'majority' and 'minority' communities, are threatened with dissolution. Avtar Brah captures this idea in her concept of 'diaspora space' (*Cartographies of Diaspora*, p. 209). A diaspora space is an intersection of borders where all subjects and identities become 'juxtaposed, contested, proclaimed, or disavowed; where the permitted and the prohibited perpetually interrogate, and where the accepted and the transgressive imperceptibly mingle even while these syncretic forms may be disclaimed in the name of purity and tradition' (p. 208). It is important to understand that this space is *not* some kind of postmodern playground of 'anything goes', where all kinds of identities are equally valuable and available as if in a 'multicultural supermarket'. Discourses of power which seek to legitimate certain forms of identity and marginalise others by imposing a logic of binary oppositions remain operable and challenge new forms of identity from emerging. We must not forget the troublesome politics of diaspora identities when promoting their possibilities. None the less, the transformative propensity of a 'diaspora space' remains potent not just for those *within* diaspora communities but those who, in Brah's words, 'are constructed and represented as indigenous' (p. 209). New routes are opened for all.

STOP and THINK

The enthusiastic support for the new forms of fluid, hybrid identity can often mask a number of difficulties with these 'new ethnicities'. First, are fluid hybrid identities always a favourable option? As Hall's attention to the first moment of black British representation evidences, there may be circumstances when the representation of an essentialised diaspora subject or homogeneous diaspora community may serve important purposes: such as offering support and a sense of belonging for migrant peoples, or as a way of uniting people against acts of discrimination. Also, does everybody experience diaspora life in the same fashion? How do differences of class, gender, sexuality, region and age all impact upon diaspora communities?

Cultural diversity, cultural difference and the 'Black Atlantic'

Brah's concept of 'diaspora space' recognised the ways its possibilities are contested by established discourses of power which attempt to organise people into communities of 'us' and 'them'. Indeed, one of the dangers in too-quickly celebrating hybridity as a solution to all problems is that it stops us thinking about the divisive ways in which *reactionary* responses to diasporic cultural practices can operate. Individual and collective identities are things which we fashion for ourselves to a degree; but they are also fashioned by others for us, whether we like it or not. In terms of diaspora identities, the dominant discourses of 'race', nation, ethnicity, class and gender in the West can militate against the possibility of embracing and exploring hybrid forms of identity, by seeking to fix diaspora peoples into certain positions and host communities into others, in such a way that recalls to an extent the stereotypical representation of colonised peoples into discourses such as Orientalism. Throughout this book we have seen how the imaginative legacy of colonialism remains after the colonialism has formally ended in once-colonised countries. But the same is also true of Western colonial nations, where the discursive apparatus of colonialism remains available to members of the host nation as a means by which diaspora peoples can be represented.

As R. Radhakrishnan has pointed out in *Diasporic Meditations: Between Home and Location* (University of Minnesota Press, 1996), critical theories of diaspora identities which celebrate hybridity and difference can be 'completely at odds with the actual experience of difference as undergone by diasporic peoples in their countries of residence' (p. 174). Although *theories* of migrant or diaspora identities emphasise new emergent forms of thinking about identity in terms of fluidity and hybridity, these often clash with dominant ways of representing cultural difference in Western locations that have been inherited from colonial discourses that depend upon constructing borders which are traversed only on special occasions. Phrases like 'cultural diversity', 'pluralism' and 'multiculturalism' are frequently used these days to bear witness to the fact that Western countries in Europe and the Americas have a variety of different diaspora communities whose values, cultural practices or religious beliefs differ from those of the majority. These terms would seem to depict Western nations as locations of tolerance, where all cultural practices are happily accommodated. However, some critics have interrogated representations of 'cultural diversity' as convenient fictions which mask the continuing economic, political and social inequalities experienced by migrants from countries with a history of colonialism, and their descendants. In these terms, multiculturalism is a media mask, little more than a public advertising campaign that promotes glossy images of certain cities or nations as culturally manifold and tolerant but ignores the underlying and continuing inequalities and prejudices that blight the lives of diasporic peoples in these places.

For example, in his essay 'On Cultural Diversity' (in *Whose Cities?*, ed. Mark Fisher and Ursula Owen, Penguin, 1991, pp. 97–106) the British-based Guyanese writer David Dabydeen comments that '[c]ultural diversity can be a cosy term, evolved out of a blend of European post-colonial guilt and enlightenment, to justify tolerance of our presence in the metropolis' (p. 101). He contends that 'a sizeable segment of the British people of a certain generation, those above forty, say, would prefer it if we went away and never came back' (p. 101). Dabydeen uses the image of a beehive when talking about the 'cultural diversity' of a city like London. Although there may be a number of different cultural groups present in one place, each is confined to its own 'cell' with little communication between different groups taking place. White Britons 'don't spend long enough in the West Indian cells to appreciate the syntax, metre, chords, daubs, noises and smells created in these cells' (p. 104), nor do they invite West Indians to *their* cells either. Dabydeen concludes that 1990s London 'is culturally diverse, but there is little cross-fertilisation of cultures taking place' (p. 104). The engagement with 'cultural diversity' becomes purely recreational, like visiting an Indian or Chinese restaurant or spending an afternoon at an annual carnival. Very little happens by way of cultural *exchange*; people cross back to their cells having had a brief, diversionary encounter with 'cultural diversity'. In these terms, uses of 'cultural diversity' can mask the continuing separation of cultures in Western locations into separate cells, rather than encourage border-crossings which make possible cultural exchange, interactive experiences and new kinds of relationships for all.

Homi K. Bhabha deals with this issue in more theoretical terms in his chapter 'The Commitment to Theory' in *The Location of Culture*. He also takes issue with the term 'cultural diversity' as a misleading one which depicts the separate, equitable co-existence of many cultures. In his typical style, Bhabha attacks cultural diversity as giving the false impression that cultures are holistic, separated and static with 'pre-given cultural contents and customs' (*The Location of Culture*, p. 34). Instead, we must recognise the *porous* borders between cultures, the fact that they are always leaking into each other, criss-crossing the supposed barriers. Bhabha uses the phrase 'cultural difference' to advocate this second way of thinking about cultures as hybridised and fluid, where 'cultural interaction emerges only at the significatory boundaries of cultures, where meanings and values are (mis)read or signs are misappropriated' (p. 34). For Bhabha, the subscription to a notion of culture as interactive, constantly recomposed from a wide variety of possible sources becomes an important *political* act. It *matters* how we conceptualise difference. This is why Bhabha is so enthusiastic about using 'the cultural and historical hybridity of the postcolonial world ... as the paradigmatic place of departure' for his theoretical work (p. 21). If the experience of diaspora communities in Western nations may be one of segregation and ghettoisation rather than border-crossings and cultural exchange, then the need to rethink how cultures interrelate becomes even more urgent, in order to demolish the divisive ways of thinking that keep us in place, and displaced, in the first place. The act of reconceptualising identity and culture in diasporic rather than static terms is one way of exposing all people to a new sense of themselves and their communities as indelibly stamped by the migratory and multicultural histories that impact upon us all. (I challenge all readers of *Beginning Postcolonialism* to map their family tree through three or four generations without finding an ancestor who was a migrant from another land, or of a different 'race' or religious faith, or who was adopted, or who married beyond the boundaries of ethnicity or class). Or as Caryl Phillips puts it in different context, '[a] truly multicultural society is one which is composed of multicultural individuals; people who are able to synthesise different worlds in one body and to live comfortably with these different worlds' (*A New World Order*, p. 279). Although Bhabha's thinking would want to emphasise the essential permeability and inner hybridity of these 'worlds', both Bhabha and Phillips demand in their different ways a diasporic overhaul of received notions of selfhood for all people that departs from singularity and purity and embraces difference and hybridity.

Recent history proves that this is easier said than done, as figures like Bhabha, Phillips and others have acknowledged. The problem posed in 'New Ethnicities' by Stuart Hall has remained: how are new communities forged which do *not* homogenise people or ignore the differences between them; communities based on crossings, interactions, partial identifications? Can there be 'solidarity through difference'?

One key response to this question is found in the work of Paul Gilroy, especially in his highly influential concept of the 'Black Atlantic' which he explores in his influential book *The Black Atlantic: Modernity and Double Consciousness* (Verso, 1993). Gilroy's work deals in the main with the ancestors of the African slaves in the Caribbean, the US and Britain, but as Walter Goebel and Saskia Schabio record in their edited collection, Gilroy's key concepts have proved very useful indeed to thinkers working in a *variety* of diasporic contexts who have critically engaged with some of his key concerns 'by specifying the heterogeneity of Black Atlantic experiences, whether national or transnational, by looking beyond the Atlantic to the Indian Ocean and the Indian diaspora ... and by emphasizing exchanges and parallel developments in "black" and "white" cultural networks' (*Beyond the Black Atlantic: Relocating Modernization and Technology*, Routledge, 2006, p. 4).

In the opening chapter, 'The Black Atlantic as a Counterculture of Modernity', Gilroy explores the transnational connections, crossings, tensions and affiliations between black people located and moving between Africa, the Caribbean, America and Britain. Part of his purpose is to oppose ideas such as ethnic or 'racial' particularism and nationalism on the grounds that they are falsifications. In looking at a number of black radical thinkers in Britain and America in the nineteenth and twentieth centuries, Gilroy shows the extent to which their work was bound up with, and contributed to, the development of Western modernity. This makes a nonsense *both* of a sense of the West as ethnically and racially homogeneous, and of ideas concerning an essentialised, common 'black' community separated from Western influence: black people have been at the heart of Western modernity since its inception. Furthermore, black peoples in history have been travellers: brought from Africa to America and the Caribbean on the slave-ships across the 'Middle Passage' of the Atlantic Ocean; migrating to Britain after the 1950s due to the shortage in British labour; throughout the nineteenth and twentieth centuries making journeys between the Americas, Britain and Africa. These crossings created myriad ways of thinking which drew from and contributed to the prevailing ideas in each of these places. For these reasons, Gilroy pits the *transnational* quality of black history and experience against those ideas of community grounded in mistaken ideas of purity or cultural essentialism. He suggests that 'cultural historians could take the Atlantic as one single, complex unit of analysis in their discussions of the modern world and use it to produce an explicitly transnational and intercultural perspective' (p. 15). The prefixes 'trans-' and 'inter-' in this sentence call our attention to Gilroy's attempt to expose all borders as porous, across which ideas move and are changed as a consequence. Like other thinkers, Gilroy is keen to embrace notions of fluidity, motion and crossing when challenging received ideas about home, belonging, roots and 'race'.

In the spirit of the untidy journeys and crossings of the 'Black Atlantic' which disturb the neat borders of ethnicity, 'race' and nation, Gilroy fixes on the image of the ship as a way of symbolising a new form of politics based on a transformed idea of community. The ship symbolises 'a living, micro-cultural, micro-political system in motion' (p. 4) which bears witness both to the history of black oppression (in recalling the slave-ships of the Middle Passage) but also the possibility of putting ideas and cultural practices 'on the move', circulating them across different places in perpetual motion. The ships which criss-crossed the Atlantic Ocean in previous centuries may have been a part of the sordid history of slavery, but they also provided the means by which radical, oppositional ideas could be spread transnationally. For Gilroy, these transnational *routes* provide a better way of thinking about black identities in the present than notions of *roots* and rootedness, which merely recapitulate the absolutist principles common to colonialist, nationalist and racist discourses. In using the ship as a key image for the routes and crossings which define the unsteady and compound character of black cultures, politics and identities, Gilroy exemplifies the diasporic tension between loss and hope of which Clifford speaks, not least in turning a vehicle of the profound losses and traumas of the Middle Passage (and remember too Naipaul's ship-travelling Indian workers) into a figure for the hopefulness and resourcefulness of an entirely new way of conceptualising diasporic life.

However, Gilroy also worries that the eager embracing of 'new ethnicities' which emphasise the constructed, hybrid nature of all identities tends to forget the ways that racism still operates in the present. There is still the necessity for a black politics of resistance. How, then, is one created without falling foul of the problems of the usual ways of thinking about identity we have just considered? Gilroy's answer lies in the ways in which different cultural practices circulate in the black Atlantic between groups in different locations, creating *contingent* transnational forms of community. 'Solidarity through difference' can be built by plotting the ways in which diaspora peoples in any one location draw upon the resources and ideas of other peoples in different times and places in order to contest the continuing agency of colonialist, nationalist or racist discourses at various sites. These mobile, transitory circuits of transnational solidarity help formulate acts of local resistance that are always themselves finite and on the move, recasting and remoulding ideas from elsewhere in new and unexpected ways.

An example of this concerns uses of black popular music. Music is not simply a form of recreation or cultural diversion from the world of politics; as evidenced by the songs of black slaves, music can be the means of 'communicating information, organising consciousness, and testing out or deploying the forms of subjectivity which are required by political agency, whether individual or collective' (p. 36). In his essay 'It Ain't Where You're From, It's Where You're At: the Dialectics of Diaspora Identification' (in *Small Acts: Thoughts on the Politics of Black Cultures*, Serpent's Tail, 1993, pp. 120–45), Gilroy describes the fortunes of the hit song 'I'm So Proud', originally written and performed by the Chicago vocal trio The Impressions. Later it was re-released in Britain by Macka B and Kofi, and titled 'Proud of Mandela'. In a rather breathless sentence which bears superb witness to the untidy, manifold routes of the 'Black Atlantic', Gilroy describes the song as 'produced in Britain by the children of Caribbean and African settlers from the raw materials supplied by black Chicago but filtered through Kingstonian sensibility in order to pay tribute to a black hero whose global significance lies beyond his partial South African citizenship' (*Small Acts*, p. 141). Notice how the plotting of this transnational route *belies* an essentialised sense of cultural identity, and the view that meaning is forever fixed, closed and static.

The continual transformations of 'I'm So Proud' engendered by its reproduction by black peoples in different locations underlines the fact that the black diaspora is discontinuous, historically contingent, locally variable and internally heterodox. Yet, the purpose for reproducing 'I'm So Proud' emphasises the *political* character of the 'Black Atlantic' as a webbed space which makes available important political resources to black peoples for new uses that, in the process, transform the received materials. So, Gilroy proclaims that '[f]ore-grounding the role of music allows us to see England, or perhaps London, as an important political junction point on the web of black Atlantic political culture' (p. 141). Thus, forms of radical culture circulate within and between black diasporas in various locations, promoting a sense of a protean collective culture and set of mutual experiences which forge contingent transnational communities. Yet the notion of a *singular* transnational black community is resisted due to the emphasis on the localised, discontinuous and unpredictable ways in which cultural resources are put to new uses.

We can clarify this idea by concluding with an example of our own, this time from Hanif Kureishi's memoir 'The Rainbow Sign'. Kureishi remembers a 'great moment' as a child when he visited a sweet-shop and saw a television in the backroom showing the 1968 Olympic Games: 'Thommie Smith and John Carlos were raising their fists on the victory rostrum, giving the Black Power salute as the "Star Spangled Banner" played. The white shopkeeper was outraged. He said to me: they shouldn't mix politics and sport' ('The Rainbow Sign', p. 29–30). As a British-born Londoner with one Asian parent, Kureishi is at some remove from the struggle against racism by the Black Power movement in America in the 1960s, to which the gesture refers. But the gesture becomes *routed* transnationally from black American politics to the Mexico Olympics, and onwards via television to the sweet-shop in London into which Kureishi chanced. Conjoined to his avid reading of black American writers such as James Baldwin and Richard Wright, this momentary gesture becomes a valuable political resource for Kureishi in his contest against London's racism, exemplified all too clearly by the outraged white sweet-shop owner. The 'solidarity through difference' forged here is contingent, discontinuous and transnational, bringing together for a moment oppressed peoples in disparate locations. Yet it is of immeasurable value to the young Kureishi's attempt to think beyond the prevailing discourses of power which fix and marginalise his identity, and to construct solidarity with others in different and similar positions to his own.

Moving pictures: Beryl Gilroy's *Boy-Sandwich*

Let us conclude this chapter by looking briefly at Beryl Gilroy's
Boy-Sandwich (Heinemann, 1989) in the light of some of the
concepts we have explored. Beryl Gilroy was born in Berbice,
Guyana in 1924 and moved to Britain in 1951. She worked as a
teacher in both places (indeed, she was London's first black Head
Teacher) and has written books for both children and adults.

Set in London in the 1980s, *Boy-Sandwich* is narrated by
Tyrone Grainger, a British-born black teenager whose parents
and grandparents were born in the Caribbean and migrated to
Britain. Tyrone is on the verge of going to Cambridge to study
but has taken a year out to help look after his grandparents. The
novel opens with his grandparents' eviction from their London
home amidst the taunts of a racist crowd, and their removal to
an old peoples' home called The Birches. Tyrone spends the vast
majority of his time at The Birches listening to his grandparents' stories of 'the Island' (such is the name Gilroy gives their
Caribbean home) and battling with the home's authorities to
make sure they are properly cared for.

On one of the rare occasions when he ventures to other parts of
London, he attends a house-party where his girlfriend Adijah is
working with her brother Dante, a DJ. The party is firebombed by
racists. Twelve black partygoers are murdered, and Adijah is badly
burned. For Tyrone, this incident is another tragedy to add to his
list. A couple of years previously, his brother Goldberg had been
killed in a racist attack when a brick was thrown from a passing
truck. So, when Tyrone comes into an unexpected fortune, he
decides to spend it on moving the three generations of his family
back to the village of Picktown on the Island, a decision applauded
in a local newspaper. But after spending some time away, Tyrone
decides to return to Britain as he feels he cannot be readily
accommodated in a Caribbean environment. The novel ends at an
airport terminal, with Tyrone looking to the future back in London.

At one level, *Boy-Sandwich* paints a sobering picture of black
diaspora experience in London. His family have not been
accommodated and allowed to settle, as witnessed by the fact that
the novel begins with the 'unhousing' of his grandparents. The fire

at the party recalls the New Cross fire of 1981 in which thirteen black Londoners were killed, while Goldberg's tragedy references the everyday, seemingly random acts of violence and abuse which historically have overshadowed diaspora experience in Britain. Tyrone also recalls being stopped as a child by a local policemen on the grounds of his 'race'. He remembers the incident 'left me feeling disembodied and anxious and marked me for years' (p. 48).

Recalling Caryl Phillips's words quoted previously, Gilroy allows us to experience how the British-born Tyrone feels 'of, and not of' his native London. Tyrone's attitudes to London as 'home' are complex. On the one hand, the continuing experience of racial violence makes him identify strongly with the 'old country' of his grandparents' island home. He spends a large part of the novel looking through their old photographs of the Island, and these become an important means by which his sense of an 'imaginary homeland' overseas is constructed, through fragmentary texts and arbitrary relics of a lost world. But on the other hand, the fact that he is British-born complicates matters further. 'I belong', he declares, 'regardless of those who say I don't. Inside me there is an oasis where my identity blooms precariously and my certainties flicker like lights and then die down' (p. 30). The novel explores the ways in which this blooming, precarious identity can be nurtured, but it requires a way of thinking about identity which goes beyond the 'certainties' of fixed notions of roots, belonging and home.

For much of the novel, Tyrone takes refuge in the photographs and stories of his grandparents. These seem to offer him a sense of certainty and rootedness which combats his precarious feelings. Yet he cannot ever have the 'interior knowledge' of his grandparents, whose relationship with this photographic record is different. His almost obsessive pursuit of their past becomes a hindrance to his own 'blooming' identity as he tries to build a fixed self continuous with their memories of the Island's past. This is suggested by the connections between his grandparents' photograph album and the recurring descriptions of his grandmother's bag, in which she hoards various relics and leftovers from her past:

> The bag in protest spills its contents – buttons, peanuts probably years old, letters, postcards, orange peel, folded-up mini plastic bags, combs of all sizes and coins in ancient cloth purses that the market

women of the Island use. In the midst of everything are biscuits, chocolate and clumps of cheese. (p. 28)

There are at least two ways of thinking about this bag. On the one hand, we might describe it in terms of the fragmentary, untidy remains of the 'old country' which signify both the *connection with* and the *displacement from* the Island. Grandma conjures memories of home through these scraps, odds and ends which she refuses to discard. The bag is, then, an important means of orientation for Grandma in London to an imaginary homeland. But from Tyrone's perspective, the bag looks rather different. It remains a point of reference to the Island, to be sure; but without the same kind of 'interior knowledge' which attaches particular emotional associations to these objects, the bag might also look like an arbitrary collection of junk with little meaning for the youthful, British-born Tyrone. This makes us question whether or not the heavy investment in the past which Tyrone makes through his grandparents' memories is his best way of tending his blooming identity.

Later in the novel, a new way of negotiating between past and present is mooted. Tyrone finds in Grandma's bag some gold doubloons. This leads him to root about in his parents' attic for other potential valuable treasures, and by chance he happens across a painting of a group of peasant women and children wearing masks. On taking it for cleaning and valuation, he learns its title is 'The Masks' (which, appropriately enough for a novel concerned with colonised identities, recalls Fanon's *Black Skin, White Masks*) and that it was painted by a Spanish artist who travelled to the Caribbean in the early twentieth century. It attracts an extremely large amount of money at auction. This is the money which Tyrone uses to relocate his family in Picktown.

It is worth pausing at this juncture and tracing the transnational crossings upon which this incident turns. The first crossing is of the Spanish artist from Europe to the Caribbean where 'The Masks' is painted; next, the crossing of Grandma and the picture from the Caribbean to London; its storage in an attic and subsequent sale to an unknown new owner; which in turn finances the Graingers' travels back to Picktown (and Tyrone's journey back to London). Recalling Paul Gilroy's idea of the 'Black Atlantic', we might consider how the continual crossings which surround the painting unexpectedly provide valuable resources which enable Tyrone to rethink his identity in terms of unpredictable *routes* and not sure *roots*. As he puts it, the Spanish artist '[w]hatever he was, cut-throat or priest, black or white, his greed or his sense of beauty now reaches across the decades and touches my life' (p. 97). Tyrone forges a transnational connection to a cultural artefact from a parallel but different history to his own, one that puts him physically on the move but also exposes him to new opportunities to understanding how he can negotiate between the past and the present, the Caribbean and London, without having to settle for either place as the exclusive location of his roots.

In visiting Picktown, Tyrone realises that the villagers regard him as a London-born black man and he finds it hard to identify with their community. The *route* from London to Picktown has not established firm *roots*. Rather, it emphasises Tyrone's necessity to move beyond such forms of identity and create new, more precarious forms for himself. (In addition, the return to the Island is not an unproblematic one for his grandparents and particularly his parents, as Picktown creates for them some insoluble challenges born from their continuing displacement.) Tyrone begins to embrace the possibilities, and not just the problems, of thinking of himself as a London-born black man with affiliations to more than one locale. He confesses that he feels trapped on the Island and desires to recover his 'space' in London. It is a space which is both real and imaginary. In concrete terms, Tyrone has previously shunned London spaces as dangerous and intimidating, preferring the insular environment of The Birches. But now, in Picktown, London is reconsidered as an important space in imaginative terms too, a space where he can understand and nurture his difference. This involves putting the past 'on the move'. Like the selling of the painting, pictures from the past offer the means for routeing but cannot be treated as providing order, certainty and identity for Tyrone's generation. As he comments after the fire at the party, 'there is no picture in the album to compare with those that have been taken of the ruins, of the house that has been razed' (p. 84). The Caribbean past cannot frame the diasporic present of Tyrone's youth. The received narratives of the past do not account for the problems of the present. New narratives need to be forged where past and present, the Caribbean and London, are part of a dynamic, evolving and hybrid sense of identity and multiple belonging.

Hence, the family's past is not wholly rejected as rubbish by Tyrone in the novel. Grandma's bag has led to a valuable source of treasure. It has opened up new transnational routes which take him back to the 'old country' *and beyond*. But neither has the past remained an obsession for Tyrone, as his grandparents' memories of the Island cannot be used to provide the certainties he wishes for at times. Instead, the past has been *put to work* for the present. Past images have been reinvested with value (both financial and symbolic) in order to put them and Tyrone 'on the move', opening the opportunity for him to think about identity beyond old certainties and embrace the precarious possibilities of his life in the here and now. These images must be used dynamically and mixed with other ones, as resources for helping him inhabit a diasporic identity. *Boy-Sandwich* brings to crisis ways of thinking about identity as a 'certainty' with secure roots, an accessible home and a continuous relationship between past and present, by showing that it does not work for migrant and diasporic peoples. It is no coincidence that the text ends at a border location, among the 'fragments of conversation and the inquisitive glances of passers-by' (p. 121) in the terminal of an airport as Tyrone prepares to travel yet another route. That these will be *imaginative* as well as *geographical* passages is suggested by him finding a copy of *Dylan Thomas in America* left 'fortuitously forgotten' on his seat on the plane – a story of another past route which might also prove a resource for Tyrone's future?

Selected reading

Bhabha, Homi K., *The Location of Culture* (Routledge, 1994).
    Bhabha is often seen as the high priest of diaspora theory. Pay particular attention to the introduction and Chapters 8, 9, 11 and 12.
Brah, Avtar, *Cartographies of Diaspora: Contesting Identities* (Routledge, 1997).
    An excellent, theoretically sophisticated account of diaspora communities in Britain.
Bromley, Roger, *Narratives for a New Belonging* (Edinburgh University Press, 2000).

An informed and approachable study of diasporic literatures in Britain and the United States.

Clifford, James, 'Diaspora', *Cultural Anthropology*, 9 (3), 1994, pp. 302–38.
An excellent and detailed essay that gets to grips with meanings and critical deployments of diaspora in intellectual debates, and well worth reading if you want to understand the rise of diaspora thinking in subsequent years.

Cohen, Robin, *Global Diasporas: An Introduction* (UCL Press, 1997).
Perhaps the clearest and best introduction to the different diaspora communities around the globe.

George, Rosemary Marangoly, *The Politics of Home: Postcolonial Relocations and Twentieth-Century Fiction* (Cambridge University Press, 1996).
The introductory chapter on constructions of 'home' is excellent, as is the final chapter, '"Travelling Light": Home and the Immigrant Genre'.

Gilroy, Paul, *The Black Atlantic: Modernity and Double Consciousness* (Verso, 1993).
A ground-breaking and influential work which explores the transnational diaspora aesthetics of black cultures between Africa, America, the Caribbean and Britain.

Gilroy, Paul, *Small Acts: Thoughts on the Politics of Black Cultures* (Serpent's Tail, 1993).
A wonderful collection of essays, often witty and incisive, which build upon some of Gilroy's ideas in *The Black Atlantic*.

Gilroy, Paul, *After Empire: Melancholy or Convivial Culture?* (Routledge, 2004).
This is Gilroy's thought-provoking study of British cultural life in the light of both the nation's changing fortunes and the struggle to secure a multicultural future.

Hall, Stuart, 'New Ethnicities' in David Morley and Kuan-Hsing Chen (eds), *Critical Dialogues in Cultural Studies* (Routledge, 1996), pp. 441–9.
Hall is one of the most insightful writers on diaspora communities in Britain. This is one of his most influential essays.

Keown, Michelle, David Murphy and James Procter (eds), *Comparing Postcolonial Diasporas* (Palgrave, 2009).
A lively collection of essays that explores different examples of world diasporic cultures, spanning Europe, Latin America, Australasia and elsewhere. The introduction is highly recommended.

King, Russell, John Connell and Paul White (eds), *Writing Across Worlds: Literature and Migration* (Routledge, 1995).
An excellent collection of essays which looks at diasporic writings in a variety of contexts. Highly recommended.

McLeod, John, *Postcolonial London: Rewriting the Metropolis* (Routledge, 2004).

A study of the imaginative diasporic transformation of London since the 1950s in the face of enduring problems of racism and prejudice.

Mercer, Kobena, *Welcome to the Jungle: New Positions in Black Cultural Studies* (Routledge, 1994).

An enthusiastic critique of diaspora aesthetics in Britain and America with particular reference to film, video and photography.

Mishra, Sudesh, *Diaspora Criticism* (Edinburgh University Press, 2007).

A complex, critical and stimulating engagement with diasporic frames of thought, although the sophistication of its writing might challenge a beginner at first.

Phillips, Caryl, *A New World Order: Selected Essays* (Secker and Warburg, 2001).

An illuminating collection of essays by one of the world's leading diasporic writers, which often probes the challenges and possibilities created by migration and its consequences.

Ponzanesi, Sandra and Daniela Merolla (eds), *Migrant Cartographies: New Cultural and Literary Spaces in Post-Colonial Europe* (Lexington, 2005).

A busy and exciting collection of essays that moves the discussion of diasporic culture beyond a more familiar British-centred context by considering the myriad European diasporas of the twenty-first century.

Procter, James, *Dwelling Places: Post-War Black British Writing* (Manchester University Press, 2003).

An excellent study of black British writing which includes an extremely useful introduction.

Radhakrishnan, R., *Diasporic Mediations: Between Home and Location* (University of Minnesota Press, 1996).

Rushdie, Salman, *Imaginary Homelands: Essays and Criticism 1981–1991* (Granta, 1991).

Rushdie is one of the foremost writers to reflect upon the impact of migrancy and diaspora experiences upon literary practices. The essays in this collection deal severally with the issues raised by migrancy.

Shackleton, Mark, *Diaspora Literature and Theory – Where Now?* (Cambridge Scholars Publishing, 2008).

A very readable collection of essays which critically probes the dominant ideas of diasporic theory in relation to a range of cultural texts.

Stein, Mark, *Black British Literature: Novels of Transformation* (Ohio State University Press, 2004).

An entertaining and engaging study of recent black British writing in the context of diasporic critical thought.

8

The limits of postcolonialism?

The habit of self-critique

This concluding chapter is designed to allow us to revisit some of the comments we made when defining postcolonialism in Chapter 1, and to think again about the problems and possibilities of the term in the light of some of the ideas we have encountered throughout *Beginning Postcolonialism* while meeting some new ones too. We will have an opportunity, then, to reflect critically upon the beginnings we have made. Ultimately, the purpose of this chapter (if not *Beginning Postcolonialism* as a whole) is to assist you in reaching some conclusions about the extent to which 'postcolonialism' is an enabling term. In so doing, we are entirely keeping with the spirit of postcolonial studies, which has featured a large degree of self-critique since its emergence in the latter years of the twentieth century. As Graham Huggan has argued, '[t]he history of postcolonial studies ... is one of informed self criticism – one in which the value of the term "postcolonial" itself has been continually interrogated, its methodological biases unearthed, the potential applicability of its theories put to the test' (*The Postcolonial Exotic: Marketing the Margins*, Routledge, 2001, p. 230). As you make your own progress with postcolonialism, it will be very important that you develop a habit of mind which constantly challenges and interrogates the vocabularies and assumptions of the different kinds of postcolonial approaches you will meet. Vigilance is essential in a field like ours. A sense of some of the existing self-critiques and interrogation of postcolonialism will gather in what follows below.

Because the spirit of critique runs throughout this chapter, there are no 'Stop and Think' sections. Instead, think of this chapter as a single 'Stop and Think' section and work patiently through the criticisms of postcolonialism, stopping at each turn to reflect upon the complaints being raised. Several of the critiques of post-colonialism below confront postcolonialism at its possible limits – limits of temporality, geography, history, theory and others besides. What are the appropriate limits of postcolonialism? How far can it go, or should it go? Does postcolonialism enable or limit critical thought? Postcolonialism often prides itself in working at and against the limits of received ways of thinking, especially in its more theoretical modes; but the limitations of postcolonialism must also be entertained too, if we are to avoid using it uncritically and without an enabling awareness of its shortcomings and faultlines.

Each matter we encounter in this chapter comes with a series of responses that we might make to it. These responses are offered *not* as definitive ways of solving the problems raised, if indeed they can be solved, although they will convey something of my own position on certain matters. Rather, they offer resources to stimulate your own ways of thinking critically about the pros and cons of each objection. The conclusions you make concerning each, either in agreement or disagreement, ultimately must be your own.

Postcolonial times? The limits of temporality

A famous criticism of postcolonialism, as we have considered many times in this book, concerns its connection to the historical and material world. As we defined the term in Chapter 1, post-colonialism stressed both *continuity* and *change* by recognising the continuing agency of colonial discourses as well as resistances to them. Yet, for some critics the use of the prefix 'post' brings with it too many troubling associations which hinder more supple renderings of the term. In particular, these associations have to do with the particular representation of historical time implied by the 'post' in postcolonial.

In her 1992 essay 'The Angel of Progress: Pitfalls of the Term "Postcolonialism"' (in *Colonial Discourse/Postcolonial Theory*, pp. 253–66), Anne McClintock takes issue with the 'post' in postcolonial on the following grounds. First, although postcolonial theory often challenges binary oppositions, the use of the 'post' represents global history through a binary division: colonial/ postcolonial. Second, by conferring on colonialism 'the prestige of history proper' (p. 255) non-European cultures become historicised with recourse to European chronology. Colonialism becomes the 'determining marker of history' (p. 255); alternative ways of dividing historical epochs or narrating historical time which do *not* privilege colonialism, are ignored. In adding her voice to those who believe that postcolonialism cannot accommodate the multiplicity of histories and experiences it covers, McClintock argues that the term does not allow us to think about how postcolonialism is 'unevenly developed globally' (p. 256). Different countries encounter decolonisation at different times, while others have not experienced it at all. In addition, not all forms of decolonisation are the same. By collapsing these different times into one temporality, 'the postcolonial', we lose the opportunity to think about the historical differences that exist between contrasting locations. Ultimately, the 'post' in postcolonial is too prematurely celebratory, implying an end to all things colonial. Its celebratory emphasis damagingly directs attention away from the continued, neo-colonial operations throughout the globe.

Similar arguments are raised by Ella Shohat in 'Notes on the "Post-Colonial"' (*Social Text*, 31/32, 1992, pp. 99–113). Shohat shares McClintock's misgivings that the term implies the end of colonialism, and worries about the collapse of chronology which this effects. 'When exactly, then, does the "post-colonial" begin? Which region is privileged in such a beginning? What are the relationships between these diverse beginnings?' (p. 103). It is very difficult to 'begin postcolonialism' if we can never be certain when the postcolonial originates. Shohat is also concerned about the inability of postcolonialism to address neo-colonialism. In the late twentieth century, it is argued, Western multinational companies are the new 'colonialists', while America continues the military aggression of certain nations. The global economic relationships between the wealthy Western nations and their poorer neighbours reflect 'colonialism's economic, political, and cultural deformative-traces in the present' (p. 105). Hence:

> The term 'post-colonial', when compared with neo-colonialism, comes equipped with little evocation of contemporary power relations; it lacks a political content which can account for the eighties and nineties-style U.S. militaristic involvements in Granada, Panama, and Kuwait-Iraq, and for the symbiotic links between U.S. political and economic interests and those of local elites. (p. 105)

There are three responses that can be made here. First, let us remember that when we addressed postcolonialism in the introduction to this book, we carefully decided that we would use the term to refer specifically to aesthetic practices: representations, discourses and values. 'Postcolonialism' is not a strict historical marker; it does not exclusively denote an epoch. But much of the confusion surrounding the term comes from its use *simultaneously* to describe, on the one hand, historical, social and economic *material conditions* (Marx's 'base', if you like) and, on the other, historically situated *imaginative* products and practices (Marx's 'superstructure'). To keep this confusion at bay, we reserved 'postcolonialism' to describe the latter of these. Shohat in particular stresses the need for us to be vigilant at all times in defining the term precisely, but 'Notes on the "Post-Colonial"' could be accused of failing to differentiate adequately between 'postcolonial' as a historical marker *and* an aesthetic critical practice. If carefully defined, postcolonialism perhaps can recognise the continuing agency of colonial discourses and relations of power in the contemporary world as we have seen at various points in this text. The problem is not with the term, perhaps, but in its articulation.

That said, in trying to make a distinction between postcolonialism as an imaginative marker rather than a term which describes the world, are we guilty of driving the postcolonial away from its primary historical and cultural contexts? Can such a division ever be cleanly made in the first place? Has postcolonialism *avoided* resolving the challenging relationship it opens between concrete and historical contexts on the one hand and their representation and critique on the other?

New maps (f)or old? The limits of geography

William Walsh divided his 1973 book *Commonwealth Literature* into
six chapters, each dealing with a separate area: India, Africa, the
West Indies, Canada, New Zealand and Australia. According to
some, postcolonial studies today apparently has moved beyond this
selective mapping – very much an 'area studies' model of the field's
remit – and has rejected many of the critical assumptions with
which critics of Commonwealth literature worked, creating instead
a wide-ranging critical vocabulary of its own which draws upon the
work of other disciplines. But for others, that shift between
'Commonwealth' and 'postcolonial' mappings of the field has not
been as pronounced as might be expected, while its critical
assumptions still suffer from the rather generalising and abstract
approach often found in Commonwealth literary studies. There are
two problems we can raise in this context:

- Postcolonialism still accepts uncritically the *geographical
  divisions* of Anglophone Commonwealth literature.
- Postcolonialism does not discriminate adequately between
  different experiences of colonialism.

Let us take first the issue of postcolonialism's geographies. John
Thieme's excellent *The Arnold Anthology of Post-Colonial
Literatures in English* (Edward Arnold, 1996) divides the field
geographically as follows: West Africa, East Africa, Southern Africa,
North Africa, Australia, Canada, the Caribbean, New Zealand and
the South Pacific, South Asia (consisting of Malaysia, Singapore,
the Philippines, Thailand), and 'Trans-Cultural Writing'. Look
how in Thieme's anthology there is a greater sensitivity to the
differences within particular regions (and between them) than is
found in Walsh's 1973 book, as well as the inclusion of something
called 'trans-cultural' literature, which cannot be contained within
tidy national categories. Yet the old map of Commonwealth
literature is still determining to a degree Thieme's subdivisions
twenty-three years later, despite his increased nuance and
sensitivity to difference: note how, for example, Ireland remains
absent from both Walsh's and Thieme's subdivision of the field.

Meanwhile, Gregory Castle's useful collection of essays *Postcolonial Discourses: An Anthology* (Blackwell, 2001) also seems animated by a more familiar 'area studies' way of conceptualising the field – although Ireland does feature – as five of its six sections deal with particular and predominantly Anglophone postcolonial locations: South Asia, Africa, the Caribbean, settler colonies and Ireland.

Such mappings of the field can be regarded from two contrasting perspectives, as cause either for complaint or congratulation. To take the criticisms of this mapping first, we can consider two objections. If the study of Commonwealth literature privileged Britain as a central point of reference for the new literatures in English, then postcolonialism does little to dislodge this privileging when critiquing the cultural endeavours of once-colonised countries. It continues the *collecting and tethering of these literatures to the colonial centre* via the use of the term 'postcolonial literatures' which, for some, performs essentially the same task as the study of Commonwealth literature. Furthermore, the scope of post-colonialism remains limited to a *selective* number of those countries with a history of colonialism, derivative of the key areas of concern in Commonwealth literature. How radical is postcolonialism if it continues to privilege a way of mapping the world which is essentially colonialist and belongs to a previous world order?

There are two ways we might respond to these complaints. First, we might note that postcolonialism *has* expanded in range and focus, and the kinds of privileging found in Walsh's book are long gone. Ireland is a case in point. Several critics have argued in recent years that many of the issues raised in postcolonial studies – such as language, representation, resistance, nationalism, gender, migrancy and diaspora – are central in the study of Ireland, and have suggested that Irish culture is considered squarely within the history of colonialism and resistance to it, and with recourse to postcolonial critical methods. The inclusion of Irish materials in Castle's anthology is one good example of this. Elleke Boehmer has pointed out how late-nineteenth-century Irish nationalists often understood their opposition to the British Empire as coterminous with anti-colonial resistance elsewhere, as in South Africa for example (see the introduction to her book *Empire, The National and the Postcolonial, 1890–1920: Resistance in Interaction*, Oxford

University Press, 2002). In *Culture and Imperialism*, Edward Said argues that the Anglo-Irish writer W. B. Yeats should be read as an 'indisputably great *national* poet who during a period of anti-imperialist resistance articulates the experiences, the aspirations, and the restorative vision of a people suffering under the dominion of an offshore power' (Vintage, 1993, pp. 265–6). He proceeds to read Yeats's poetry in tandem with the work of the likes of the Chilean poet Pablo Neruda and Césaire's Negritude poetry (which we looked at in Chapter 3). In a similar vein, in his book *Anomalous States: Irish Writing and the Post-Colonial Moment* (Lilliput Press, 1993), David Lloyd argues that '[f]or the theory and practice of decolonisation, however, Ireland is, to a sometimes distressing extent, more exemplary than anomalous' (p. 7). Lloyd's own work looks closely at the likes of Seamus Heaney, Samuel Beckett, W. B. Yeats and James Joyce in the various contexts which emerge from Ireland's postcolonial 'moment'. And Simon Featherstone has explored the 'circular traffic' (*Postcolonial Cultures*, Edinburgh University Press, 2005, p. 54) of the Irish diaspora's musical endeavours in post-war London in parallel with Caribbean migration to London and with a nod to Paul Gilroy's model of the 'Black Atlantic'.

In addition, it has occasionally been pointed out that the literatures from the British Isles, such as Wales and Scotland, can be thought of as postcolonial. These countries have suffered the institutional and cultural authority of England which the writing from each has attempted to challenge. As Berthold Schoene has provocatively argued in his essay 'A Passage to Scotland: Scottish Literature and the British Postcolonial Condition' (*Scotlands*, 2 (1), 1995, pp. 107–22) '[a] discussion of Scottish literature in light of current postcolonial theory is bound to lead to interesting results. Here we find not only individual works of postcolonial literature but a whole tradition of postcolonial writing' (p. 110). Meanwhile, Jane Aaron and Chris Williams have argued forcefully that

> the application of questions, hypotheses and concepts drawn from postcolonial thinking to such issues as Welsh culture and politics has the potential to be extremely fruitful. ... Postcoloniality embraces concepts such as ambivalence (the mix of attraction and repulsion that may characterize relationships between imperial power and

colony) and hybridity (the creation of 'transcultural' forms in the
contact zone between the two) that raise many awkward questions for
Wales and the people of Wales. ('Preface' to *Postcolonial Wales*, ed.
Jane Aaron and Chris Williams, University of Wales Press, 2005,
p. xvi)

It might be argued, therefore, that it is not the case that postcolonialism these days works solely with the old map of the
Commonwealth; instead, new contexts and intercultural relations
are being reconsidered in the light of postcolonial concepts and
habits of thought. Deborah L. Madsen's edited collection of essays
Post-Colonial Literatures: Expanding the Canon (Pluto, 1999) is one
such deliberate attempt to go 'beyond the Commonwealth' and
regard the work of (among others) Chicano/a and Hispanic writers
as postcolonial, calling attention to a body of work often neglected
in anthologies of postcolonial writing.

Furthermore, a key development in recent years has been the
expansion of postcolonial studies beyond a distinctly Anglophone
frame to engage with other colonial legacies and contexts –
Francophone, Hispanic, Dutch, Lusophone. This has not meant
simply applying familiar (Anglophone-forged) conceptual tools to
new historical and cultural circumstances, but has often involved
opening up postcolonial studies to transition and transformation as
a consequence of such new developments which are very much 'live'
issues today, and which often involve a distinctly comparative
standpoint that looks across different European examples of
colonialism and its aftermath (see, for example, Nicholas Harrison,
Postcolonial Criticism: History, Theory, and the Work of Fiction,
Polity, 2003, in which British and French materials are counter-
pointed). In their recent edited collection Charles Forsdick and
David Murphy provide a sense of how the field is excitingly
evolving as a consequence of the work of scholars in a variety of
language traditions in their comments about the newly emerging
area of Francophone postcolonial studies: 'Francophone
Postcolonial Studies exists as a challenge to any exclusive definition
of the postcolonial. ... [It] also permits ... comparisons of
situations emerging from different colonial traditions, attenuating
the risks of generalization and ensuring the grounding of
postcolonial reflections in specific situations' (*Francophone*

Postcolonial Studies: A Critical Introduction, Arnold, 2003, p. 13). So it seems that postcolonialism has widened its scope and ceased to privilege the British Commonwealth by looking at other relevant colonial contexts, sometimes quite provocatively. We might argue as a consequence that one of the strengths of postcolonialism is that it has made available a variety of concepts and reading practices that can be productively applied to contexts that go beyond the older, selective areas of concern which preoccupied critics of Commonwealth literature.

That said, from a contrary position, we might regard as a *strength* the fact that the geographical divisions of Commonwealth literature determine mappings of postcolonialism, and be more wary of these attempts to 'expand the canon' or stretch postcolonialism so that it accounts for so many diverse materials. For example, one of the problems of applying postcolonial concepts and reading strategies to a variety of contexts is that postcolonialism maybe becomes detached from its historical and geographical referents: Empire, colonialism, and the once-colonised countries. There is a danger in using terms like 'colonialism' and 'postcolonialism' too sweepingly. Although the experiences of the Irish, Welsh and Scots, and those who suffered from British and French rule, may be cited as examples of colonialism, are these experiences and versions of colonialism necessarily the same? Is it accurate to think of Wales as suffering colonialism, and if it did, was this colonialism significantly the same as the colonisation of Canada or New Caledonia? Problems may arise when worlds like 'colonialism' and 'postcolonialism' become attached to any and every example of international or intercultural conflict at the expense of an attention to the specifics of each case. From one perspective the Irish, Welsh and Scots may appear as colonised peoples, but in other parts of the Empire (such as India, for example) they functioned as agents of colonialism and prospered under colonial rule. Does thinking about an expanded litany of locations as postcolonial actually threaten a respect for historical specificity, rather than secure it? Benita Parry has voiced concern about the blanket application of postcolonial theory across myriad contexts as having 'stimulated studies which by extending "colonisation" as an explanatory notion applicable to all situations of structural domination, are directed at formulating a grand theory valid for each and every discursive system' (*Postcolonial Studies: A Materialist Critique*, Routledge, 2004, p. 33).

These problems of *reference* lead to the second aspect of the proximity between postcolonialism and the study of Commonwealth literature, which concerns the issue of different *experiences* of colonialism. In particular, the continued collecting together of the literature from settler and 'Third World' countries under the umbrella term 'postcolonial' smacks of the lack of attention to history for which critics of Commonwealth literature stand accused. One vocal argument which runs along these lines is given by Ella Shohat in an influential essay, 'Notes on the "Post-Colonial"' (*Social Text*, 31/32, 1992, pp. 99–113):

> Positioning Australia and India, for example, in relation to an imperial center, simply because they were both colonies, equates the relations of the colonised white-settlers to the Europeans at the 'center' with that of the colonised indigenous populations to the Europeans. It also assumes that white settler countries and the emerging Third World nations broke away from the 'center' in the same way. Similarly, white Australians and Aboriginal Australians are placed in the same 'periphery', as though they were co-habitants vis-à-vis the 'center'. The critical differences between the Europe's [*sic*] genocidal oppression of Aboriginals in Australia, indigenous peoples of the Americas and Afro-diasporic communities, *and* Europe's domination of European elites in the colonies are levelled with an easy stroke of the 'post'. (p. 102)

Shohat's accusation that postcolonialism levels the 'critical differences' *within* and *between* nations is a recurring complaint made against postcolonialism. The equation of diverse peoples as postcolonial conveniently forgets that their historical fortunes can be widely different. Seen in this light, 'postcolonialism' becomes a vague, ahistorical, obfuscatory term that merely skates over the historical and political surfaces of various nations and refuses to attend to them in depth. Here we must also add the criticisms of postcolonialism by feminists which we looked at in Chapter 6, particularly the remark that postcolonialism continues to privilege men and gives little attention to the multiple experiences of women.

The generalising tendency of postcolonialism remains, perhaps, its greatest weakness. Shohat's focus on the collapsing together of settler and 'Third World' communities is a common cause of complaint. The thorny issues of the relationships between white settler communities and Aboriginal or First Nations peoples has made it difficult to refer unproblematically to the old dominions of the British Empire in terms of the postcolonial. In his essay 'Postmodernism or Postcolonialism?' (*Landfall*, 155, 1985, pp. 366–80), Simon During has seen fit to split the term 'post-colonialism' in two, using the phrases 'postcolonising' and 'postcolonised': 'The former fits those communities and individuals who profit from and identify themselves as heirs to the work of colonising. The latter fits those who have been dispossessed by that work and who identify with themselves as heirs to a more or less undone culture' (pp. 369–70). Although this is an admirable attempt to bear witness to the political differences and tensions *within* nations, not just between them, During's splitting of 'post-colonialism' reveals just how quickly the term begins to break up under the pressure of historical accuracy. We might wonder, then, if the term 'postcolonialism' could be dispensed with entirely and more accurate concepts discovered.

None the less, we can respond to this issue by noticing how a swift review of criticism in the field suggests that Shohat's fears these days might be much less easy to argue for. Edward Said's *Culture and Imperialism* offers a range of exciting ways to read a variety of cultural texts in relation to each other and to the various forms of anti-colonial resistance around the globe, one which does not seem to sacrifice historical specificity. Simon Featherstone's *Postcolonial Cultures* exemplifies the value of engaging not only with cultural specifics but comparatively across diverse postcolonial phenomena. Elleke Boehmer's *Empire, The National, and the Postcolonial, 1890–1920: Resistance in Interaction* engages with the central position of Ireland in resistance to Empire and the ways in which Irish dissidence resourced and was inspired by activities in other colonised contexts. Each of these three critics demands that we *think comparatively within* postcolonialism, rather than bundle all things postcolonial into the same homogeneous entity. Finally, Robert J. C. Young's *Postcolonialism: An Historical Introduction* (Blackwell, 2001) has attempted to redefine and enhance our sense of the postcolonial by anchoring the concept securely in the long and varied history of resistance to colonialism, often taking us beyond a 'Commonwealth' bias by engaging with Latin American, Chinese, Francophone African and other significant locations (as we consider again, see below). So, the charge that postcolonialism is insufficiently responsive to the historical specifics of colonial contexts and examples of postcolonial resistance and trans-formation seems difficult to defend in the light of recent scholarship in the field.

The problem of 'Western' theory

One of the traditional critiques of postcolonialism is that its theoretical vocabularies and key concerns prioritise allegedly Western modes of thought and highlight the legacy of coloniser–colonised relations above other local concerns. One useful example of this critique can be found in *Interrogating Post-Colonialism: Theory, Text and Context* (ed. Harish Trivedi and Meenakshi Mukherjee, Indian Institute of Advanced Study, 1996). In the opening chapter, 'Interrogating Post-Colonialism' (pp. 3–11), Meenakshi Mukherjee makes the point that the concepts and nomenclature of postcolonialism have been fashioned in Western, especially American, universities and are not always adequate to meet the contemporary needs of countries with a history of colonialism, such as India. The imperatives of postcolonialism are being set elsewhere, particularly by migrant Indian intellectuals who have helped to make postcolonialism the fashion in Western academia by drawing upon the latest advances in literary theory. Think of Bhabha's penchant for Freud and Lacan, or Spivak's indebtedness to deconstruction. According to Mukherjee:

> Several diasporic Indians have been pioneers in the area of post-colonial theory, and the field is now densely populated with academics in American universities who originally came from the ex-colonies. But as of now no major theoretical contribution has come to this discourse from home-based Indian intellectuals. (p.8)

This leads Mukherjee to argue that countries with a history of colonialism are being colonised again, this time by Western theoretical imperatives and the current focus in Western universities upon cultural difference. In terms of literary studies, the colonies provide literary texts as 'raw materials' which are imported by the West to be 'processed' using postcolonial theory, with the resulting intellectual product shipped back to the erstwhile colonies for academic consumption. For example, Indian literatures are read *exclusively* as postcolonial in their representations and politics, as if this is the only frame within which they can be understood. As Arun P. Mukherjee (not to be confused with Meenakshi Mukherjee) similarly puts it in another essay in the collection called 'Interrogating Postcolonialism: Some Uneasy Conjunctures' (pp. 13–20), much literature from India 'cannot be answered within the framing grid provided by postcolonial theory where readers are instructed solely on how to decode the subtle ironies and parodies directed against the departed coloniser. I think I need another theory' (p. 20).

So, because the West always remains the place of power and privilege with Western-based academics dictating the shape and form of postcolonial literary studies, we might argue that there is engendered *an unequal neo-colonial relationship* between academics based inside and outside the Western nations. According to this view, postcolonialism is nothing but a Western practice using Western theories that is performed in 'First World' universities in the main by privileged migrants from the once-colonised nations who have been able to secure lucrative academic posts. Thus defined, the asymmetrical, unequal relationship between the West and the once-colonised countries resembles too closely colonial relationships.

There are two ways of responding to this criticism of postcolonialism. First, Meenakshi Mukherjee and Arun P. Mukherjee do not seem to realise that some of the most popular 'First World' postcolonial theorists expend a great deal of time interrogating exactly the kind of neo-colonial relations they describe. An excellent example is Gayatri Chakravorty Spivak's essay 'How to Read a Culturally Different Book' (collected in both *The Spivak Reader*, pp. 237–66, and *Colonial Discourse / Postcolonial Theory*, pp. 126–50). In this essay, Spivak argues against those literary critics who teach *The Guide* (1980) by Indian novelist R. K. Narayan as, variously, typical of Indian literature in English, or the Indian people as a whole, or postcolonialism in general. In an attempt to stop 'the international readership of Commonwealth literature' (*The Spivak Reader*, p. 241) from imposing its own agenda onto this novel, Spivak explores the character of Rosie/Nalini who is a *devadasi* or temple dancer, on the way to exposing the novel's complicity with patriarchal and neo-colonial values. In so doing she uses the insights of postcolonial theory actually to expose just what would be missed by those who approach it unthinkingly through the 'framing grids' of a certain kind of postcolonialism which assumes that (in this instance) Anglo-Indian novels are 'repositories of postcolonial selves, postcolonial*ism*, even postcolonial resistance' (p. 239). So, it seems that Spivak *is* thinking responsibly and critically about the unequal, neo-colonial relations between postcolonial texts and their Western readerships: her essay is an attempt to expose neo-colonial machinations at the heart of institutionalised approaches to postcolonial writing which bypass knotty questions of history and politics. Indeed, her attempt to challenge prevailing frames of interpretation chimes exactly with Arun P. Mukherjee's suspicion of received norms of reading. One wonders, then, why Mukherjee is so keen to dismiss postcolonial theory as complicit with rather than critical of 'First World' frames of reference when evidence can quickly be found to the contrary, and when such evidence actually seems to resource the very critique which Mukherjee is making.

Indeed, one might argue that Spivak's work has often attempted to bring to crisis exactly the kind of blasé reading of postcolonial cultural endeavours which appropriates them entirely to an elite or 'First World' agenda. In attempting to disrupt via a number of demanding conceptual manoeuvres the ease with which so-called culturally different texts are 'understood' and consumed in the West, Spivak challenges '[o]ur own mania for "third world literature" anthologies, when the teacher or critic often has no sense of the original languages, or of the subject-constitution of the social and gendered agents in question (and when therefore the student cannot sense this as a loss)' (*A Critique of Postcolonial Reason: Toward a History of the Vanishing Present*, Harvard University Press, 1999, p. 164). Arguably, Spivak turns to 'theory' in order to *contest from within* the languages and locations of elite knowledge the very things which seem to bring incommensurate or disruptive cultural phenomena safely within the bounds of 'First World' knowledge. Her work does not necessarily uphold a way of reading postcolonial texts which always prioritises the relationship between coloniser and colonised or which privileges the end of colonialism as the most important theme. Instead, Spivak is often keen to point out what is missed by such approaches to postcolonial writing, and exposes how little is cultural and historical specificity accounted for in more conventional approaches to postcolonial texts as allegories of the nation, or depictions of a colonised condition, and so on.

Let's consider a different but related point by turning to Gareth Griffiths's essay 'Representation and Production: Issues of Control in Post-Colonial Cultures' (*Interrogating Post-Colonialism*, pp. 21–36), which will add another welcome complication. Objecting to the wave of 'anti-theory', Griffiths takes issue with Arun P. Mukherjee's argument that only local and specific frames of reference are the appropriate ones for Indian literature. Griffiths wonders if this line of thinking is questing nostalgically for an area of indigenous Indian culture which has remained untouched by colonialism. He accuses Arun P. Mukherjee and others of asserting a 'politics of recuperation which suggests that the recovery of an unproblematic alternative history [as] a simple and sufficient resistant practice in itself, and one which has no inherent dangers' (p. 22). In other words, in demanding that Indian literature is read with recourse to local and historical specifics and not via the niceties of postcolonial reading practices, such critics posit a version of Indian history and culture which has remained untouched by colonialism. Such a cleavage between that which has been influenced by colonialism and anti-colonial resistance, and that which has not, is too neat and tidy for Griffiths. Where does one draw the dividing line? Rather, such critics need to wake up to the 'necessary, indeed inevitable, "hybridity" resulting from the impact of colonisation on both the colonised and, it needs to be said, the coloniser' (p. 23). 'Hybridity', then, is not just a term bandied about in cool metropolitan theory but actually describes the inevitable and vexed condition of all once-colonised cultures.

Bearing in mind this debate, let us note the existence of an all-too-familiar division which can occur within postcolonialism. On the one side are those who decry postcolonial concepts and modes of analysis as unable to deal with the particular concerns of literature that often exist *outside* the frame of colonialism and resistance to it. On the other side are those who argue that such anterior positions do not exist: 'local' concerns *cannot help but be influenced* by the legacy of colonialism. Each critical position is condemned by the other as 'neo-colonialist'. The anti-theorists are deemed neo-colonial for refusing to learn from the insights of postcolonial theory, while the pro-theorists are seen as Western-oriented, insensitive to historical context and happy to generalise. (For a more complicated and patient description of this kind of division, see Stephen Slemon, 'The Scramble for Post-Colonialism' in *De-Scribing Empire: Post-Colonialism and Textuality*, ed. Chris Tiffin and Alan Lawson, Routledge, 1994, pp. 15–32).

The new 'ghetto' of postcolonialism

Courses in postcolonial literatures, postcolonial theories and postcolonial cultures are increasingly familiar in universities throughout the world these days. But how much impact are they having on curricula at large? Does the existence of such courses represent a triumph for postcolonialism in opening up new fields of enquiry and knowledge, or is their advent part of a containment strategy which pays lip-service to the ideas of postcolonialism while delimiting their impact in a new intellectual 'ghetto'?

Arun P. Mukherjee makes a powerful point in 'Interrogating Postcolonialism: Some Uneasy Conjunctures' when arguing that the Western-constituted field of postcolonialism is little more than a trendy 'grab bag of canonical, predominantly male, writers from Africa, the Caribbean, South Asia, south Pacific, and sometimes Canada' (p. 14). Mukherjee describes the division of labour in the English department where she works in Canada into fields such as 'Shakespeare', 'Renaissance' or 'Romanticism'. Each often focuses squarely upon one nation (Britain) and is confined to a limited period of time. But academics teaching 'Postcolonial Literature' courses are expected to deal with a much wider category of literature which can span the globe and range across the nineteenth and twentieth centuries – an impossible task in a one-semester-length course. For Mukherjee, this state of affairs is another example of neo-colonialism. Courses in 'Postcolonial Literature' are merely fashionable gestures, tacked on to existing degree schemes in university Literature departments to make them seem up-to-date and sensitive to cultural difference. But little thought is given to the academic reasons and intellectual challenges of the field, nor the ways in which it might contest the existing division of academic labour within the department as a whole. Instead, post-colonialism neatly ring-fences a wide body of diverse texts which conveniently can be added to a department's course provision, without disturbing too much the more conventional approaches to canonical English literature.

Once again, a response to this point is given by Gareth Griffiths. It is wrong, he argues, to see the division of labour in some academic departments as the *result* of postcolonialism (See footnote 3 on p. 34 of his essay). Mukherjee's complaint about having to teach the full range of postcolonial literatures on one course in her department tells us more about the department's appointment system and less about postcolonialism, which is precisely attempting to break down some of these divisions. The fault lies not with the *theory* but with the *institution*. This is a fair point, perhaps, but Mukherjee's argument invites us to be suspicious of the current popularity of postcolonialism in English departments, especially in Europe and America. To what extent are the insights of postcolonialism impacting more centrally on degree schemes and undergraduate curricula? Whose interests does it serve to construct new glossy courses in 'Postcolonial Literatures' which enable students to sample a handful of 'different' literary products? What status is assigned to these texts?

This sense of postcolonial literature courses as primarily gestural on the part of institutions is an important one, not least because it exposes how institutions may contain the unruly methodologies and awkward questions asked by postcolonial critics (just what *is* the relationship between modernism and primitivism? etc.) within the *cordon sanitaire* of a singular module in 'world literatures', 'post-colonial cultures' or some such formulation. Such manoeuvres may result in the ossification of a select canon of postcolonial writers who, across many different countries, come to stand in for postcolonial writing as a whole, ultimately depriving teachers and students of the chance of pursuing postcolonial issues and texts across a range of courses and subject areas and over many semesters rather than in just one. As Jopi Nyman's recent survey of twenty postcolonial writing courses in predominantly European and North American universities has uncovered, often the same writers appear again and again across various institutions. Nyman's 'top five' are Chinua Achebe, Salman Rushdie, J. M. Coetzee, Tsitsi Dangarembga and Derek Walcott, with Achebe's work taught on at least 50% of the surveyed courses (see Jopi Nyman, 'A Post-Colonial Canon? An Explorative Study of Post-Colonial Writing in University-level Courses' in *Diasporic Literature and Theory – Where Now?*, ed. Mark Shackleton, Cambridge Scholars Publishing, 2008, pp. 36–56). We considered in Chapter 5 how postcolonial studies has been involved in re-reading the established canon of English literature, and we noticed the challenges to cultural value which these re-readings engender. But if postcolonial studies is being restricted to fashioning its own canons partly as a result of institutional procedures, how far-reaching will be its critical impact on the study of cultural production more generally? And might the new postcolonial canons play into the hands of the commodification of perceived cultural otherness and the increased marketability of postcolonial literature as chic rather than challenging? Might the gestural politics of brief or singular postcolonial studies courses be a sign of anxious neo-colonial containment rather than bold postcolonial transformation?

Postcolonialism, or the logic of capitalist modernity?

Much penetrating criticism of postcolonialism has been voiced by Marxist critics, whose objection to postcolonial theory rests upon the view that its 'culturalist' bias severs the sphere of intellectual and cultural endeavour from the realm of direct action: resistance movements, political dissidence, even armed struggle. Benita Parry decries this tendency in postcolonialism as part of 'a wider shift within social theory itself away from materialist understandings of historical processes and the symbolic order, and towards collapsing the social into the textual' (*Postcolonial Studies: A Materialist Critique*, Routledge, 2004, p. 4). Several influential critics of postcolonialism challenge this perceived critique-collapsing of the social into the textual in postcolonial theory, and they staunchly refuse the primacy of the discursive which is deemed to characterise the writing of thinkers such as Bhabha, Said and Spivak. Rather than view language as a medium which constructs reality, other postcolonial critics argue that reality is actually much more than an 'effect' of language or merely a discursive product. Because post-colonial theory seems to privilege the discursive over the material, it is accused of having little to offer those keen both to critique and intervene in the conflicts of the tangible, historical world. As Terry Eagleton sees it, the prioritising of culture has helped 'depoliticize the question of post-colonialism, and inflate the role of culture within it, in ways which [chime] with the new post-revolutionary climate in the West' (*After Theory*, Allen Lane, 2003, p. 12). Post-colonialism, then, is more reactionary rather than revolutionary, ultimately neo-colonial rather than counter-colonial, and part of a general Western intellectual malaise.

The following moment from Arif Dirlik's oft-quoted essay 'The Postcolonial Aura: Third World Criticism in the Age of Global Capitalism' (*Critical Inquiry*, 20, 1994, pp. 328–56), offers a particularly bracing example of this standpoint. Dirlik objects strongly to the ascendancy of the theoretical paradigms of hybridity, fragmentation and difference in postcolonialism, and suggests that the preferred discursive or culturalist approach to postcolonialism is furthered by an elite band of intellectuals who seem unwilling to offer a critique of ongoing social conflicts partly because they are the lucky beneficiaries of the very global capitalism which has caused so much contemporary strife.

> Within the institutional side of the First World academy, fragmentation of earlier metanarratives appears benign (except to hidebound conservatives) for its promise of more democratic, multicultural, and cosmopolitan epistemologies. In the world outside the academy, however, it shows in murderous ethnic conflict, continued inequalities among societies, classes, and genders, and the absence of oppositional possibilities that, always lacking in coherence, are rendered even more impotent than earlier by the fetishisation of difference, fragmentation, and so on. (p. 347)

According to this line of argument, postcolonial theory has conceded too much ground by questioning oppositional discourses such as nationalism and Marxism *at the very moment* when we need these discourses more than ever to combat conflicts around the world. For Dirlik, postcolonialism promotes a vision of the world which does not acknowledge sufficiently the ongoing foundational impact of capital and modernity on the contemporary world's reality – and because it does not acknowledge this foundational impact it cannot offer any way of critiquing it. Hence, Dirlik angrily asserts that postcolonialism is in effect practised by a select few 'Third World' intellectuals who have taken up 'First World' fashionable theory for their own purposes. From their elite, privileged position as intellectuals, and empowered by their command of the cosmopolitan languages of transnational academic theory, this select few construct the world in their own hybridised self-image by projecting globally 'what are but local experiences' (p. 345). Meanwhile, outside the ivory tower oppressed people continue to kill each other, oblivious to the 'hybridity' of their decentred subjectivities and their mistaken pursuit of discredited metanarratives. Postcolonial intellectuals do not want us to think about the relationship between intellectual debate and economic power because they do not want to be exposed as profiting from global capitalism: 'To put it bluntly, postcoloniality is designed to *avoid* making sense of the current crisis and, in the process, to cover up the origins of postcolonial intellectuals in a global capitalism of which they are not so much victims as beneficiaries' (p. 353). Dirlik's suspicions are raised by the sudden interest in transnationalism and multiculturalism of people working within capitalist industries. A little local knowledge of cultural 'otherness' and difference can go a long way to assisting capitalism's flexibility in establishing itself in different times and places. Dirlik concludes by hoping that the postcolonial intelligentsia 'can generate a thoroughgoing criticism of its own ideology and formulate practices of resistance against the system of which it is a product' (p. 356). For Dirlik, postcolonialism is little more than an elite discourse with nothing to offer political dissidence and critique. It is a symptom of capitalist modernity, not a critique of it.

For some, postcolonialism remains too caught up in abstruse and baffling debates about the minutiae of philosophy and critical theory which are remote from the myriad struggles of the wretched of the earth; for others, the healthy condition of postcolonial literature as a viable academic subject keeps the focus of postcolonialism on a perceived elite form of representation often produced by a (Western-educated) wealthy postcolonial intelligentsia, rather than on less rarified and maybe more transformative forms of dissident cultural endeavour made by (once-)colonised people: music, dance, food, sport, radio. This critical view is captured well by Kwame Anthony Appiah's famous remark first made in 1990: 'Postcoloniality is the condition of what we might ungenerously call a comprador intelligentsia: of a relatively small-scale, Western-style, Western-trained, group of writers and thinkers who mediate the trade in cultural commodities of world capitalism at the periphery' (*In My Father's House: Africa in the Philosophy of Culture*, Oxford University Press, 1992, p. 149). Appiah's words suggest that postcolonial literature, culture and critical studies do not signal a critique or transformation of Western, 'First World' society; instead, award-winning postcolonial novels and books on postcolonial theory are merely more commodities in the global marketplace, which convert cultural difference into safe and palatable packages, change nothing significantly and shore up the unequal global status quo of the twenty-first century.

In challenging postcolonialism in this manner, many have strongly contested the ways in which Marxist modes of critical and political analysis appear to have been jettisoned in postcolonial thought. Class analysis is one example; another would be anti-colonial nationalism, one of the most successful modes of popular resistance in the once-colonised world that is indebted to Marxism. As we have seen in Chapters 3 and 4, the concepts of nation and nationalism have undergone severe critique in postcolonial studies, and for some these notions have become discredited, especially in the light of the unhappy fortunes of nations in the wake of independence. For many Marxist critics of postcolonialism, the critique of nationalism and Marxist modes of political dissidence is totally unacceptable and the worst consequence of the turn to theory and the advocacy of the discursive in postcolonial studies. Hence according to Neil Lazarus, the kind of postcolonial criticism in which Bhabha and others are involved should really be called 'post-Marxist criticism', and he decries 'the strong anti-nationalist and anti-Marxist dispositions of most of the scholars working within postcolonial studies' ('Introducing Postcolonial Studies' in *The Cambridge Companion to Postcolonial Literary Studies*, ed. Neil Lazarus, Cambridge University Press, 2004, pp. 4, 5).

In thinking about the several issues raised above, a number of points might be made. First, Dirlik's argument that thinkers such as Bhabha, Said and Spivak are deliberately breeding obfuscation as a way of concealing their origins in global capitalism seems remarkably ignorant, if not downright contemptuous, of the origins of much postcolonial thought in dissident contexts and the commitments which many postcolonial thinkers have to critiquing the unequal conditions of global contemporaneity, albeit in post-Marxist modes. Dirlik can appear as a peculiar kind of intellectual Luddite, in that he objects to the fact that postcolonialism tries to make sense of the world in new ways and with new vocabularies which he is unwilling to learn, rather than in the familiar lexicon of Marxist critique. His argument that postcolonialists ignore the primacy of capitalism as a primary foundation of reality is not really borne out by the evidence. A great deal of postcolonial thought has absolutely contended with the material realities of the contemporary world derived from capitalism, as we have been seeing (and as work on globalisation most recently evidences), while figures like Gayatri Chakravorty Spivak, Stuart Hall and Paul Gilroy have been debating productively with Marxist modes of thinking for many years as part of their own postcolonial engagements with Marxist and materialist modes of thought. To argue that postcolonialism is simply driven by the interests of capitalism, and is inevitably complicit with it, convinces few commentators who do not detect the kinds of concealment of complicity which Dirlik asserts with an alarming degree of paranoia. In his critique of Dirlik's thought, David Scott notes how postcolonial thinkers encourage 'more *partial* and *situated* determinations' (*Refashioning Futures: Criticism after Postcoloniality*, Princeton University Press, 1999, p. 139) of the role of capital in history, rather than dispense with an attention to capitalism entirely in their work. He also wonders why postcolonialism's alleged indebtedness to capitalist modernity automatically condemns it to toothless complicity: 'It would be an interesting question whether the themes and modalities that animate [postcoloniality's] deployment in critical practices are in some ways dependent upon the material conditions produced in the wake of the rise of a distinctively trans-national or global capitalism. But to acknowledge that a practice has determinate conditions does not *thereby* make it a mere ideological *reflection* of any one of them' (p. 140). Postcolonialism is inevitably fated to inhabit the contemporary milieu of capitalist modernity and use its institutions in order to disseminate its ideas, but does this inevitably condemn it to complicity with global capital?

The notion that complicity leads automatically to rapport or obedience is a contestable one. One lesson we can learn from the history of resistance to Empire is that complicity does not equal collusion. As Gayatri Chakravorty Spivak argues, while one can never be fully outside a structure of power we can attempt to negotiate tactically within such structures and institutions in order to destabilise them, unleash new knowledges within them, buckle their smooth operations and bring them to crisis. Spivak calls this process one of 'negotiation' during an interview from 1990:

> If there is anything I have learnt in and through the last 23 years of teaching, it is that the more vulnerable your position, the more you have to negotiate ... you must intervene even as you inhabit those structures. ... I guess all I mean by negotiation here is that one tries to change from something that one is obliged to inhabit, since one is not working from the outside. In order to keep one's effectiveness, one must also preserve those structures – not cut them down completely. And that, as far as I can understand, is negotiation. You inhabit the structures of violence and violation, here defined by you as Western liberalism. (*The Post-Colonial Critic: Interviews, Strategies, Dialogues*, ed. Sarah Harasym, Routledge, 1990, p. 72)

To be within is not necessarily to be complicit – to inhabit does not condemn one to obedience. Working with Western theory does not necessarily make us support the 'West' or uphold the assumptions of Western theory, as Spivak herself demonstrated in her essay 'Can the Subaltern Speak?' which we looked at in Chapter 6. Reading a novel for a university postcolonial literature course does not automatically doom us to complicity with the ghettoising protocols of some institutions. Maybe because Dirlik's own Marxist critical standpoint is non-negotiable he mistakes inhabitation for collusion and entirely fails to value at least the *aims* of Spivak's critical endeavours. Happily, most subsequent Marxist-led critiques of postcolonialism have been far subtler and more convincing than Dirlik's, and as a consequence their critical arguments have often been much more penetrating and convincing.

Postcolonialism or tricontinentalism? The limits of materialist critique

One of the most important recent Marxist-inspired critiques of postcolonialism is Robert J. C. Young's book *Postcolonialism: An Historical Introduction* (cited above). In contrast to Dirlik, Young's key concern is not to dismiss postcolonialism as the enemy of Marxist thinking but rather to reorient postcolonialism in terms of the Marxist-inspired political movements which challenged colonialism and Empire across the world. Young exposes an alternative narrative of the evolution of postcolonialism which grounds it not only in the fortunes of abstruse critical theory but binds it entirely to the long history of anti-colonial dissidence. This involves Young in two particular tasks: first, he exposes and evaluates the Marxist and nationalist revolutionary thought and action in what he terms the 'tricontinent': Latin America, Africa and Asia. Resistance to colonialism, he reminds us, 'goes back to the beginnings of colonialism itself. Most of those subjected to colonialism resisted from the first moment of European incursions, from the Caribs in the Caribbean, to the Indian Mughal rulers, to the Maoris in New Zealand' (p. 161). Historically, Marxism has provided the most effective means of organising and pursuing resistance, he suggests. The wealth of anti-colonial action could not have happened without the impact of Marxist thought and its various interpretations around the world which made possible Zapata's Mexican rebellion of 1910, the Peruvian Marxist Mariátegui's radical writings, the revolutionary achievements of Che Guevara and Fidel Castro in Cuba and Latin America, resistance in Anglophone and Francophone Africa, the insurgency of women's revolutionary groups, Kwame Nkrumah and

Pan-Africanism, socialism and Gandhi-ism in India, and many other forms of dissidence besides. Second, Young underscores the indebtedness of 'First World' thinkers such as Jacques Derrida and Michel Foucault to the history of Empire and resistance, in order to challenge the opposition between theoretical and material realms which seems to operate in the work of many critics of postcolonial theory. While these two figures seem to have little to say about colonialism and resistance to it in their writing, Young firmly and provocatively connects their intellectual endeavours to the longer history of colonialism and its resistance and effects a powerful and far-reaching reorientation of postcolonialism towards its Marxist and materialist contexts, especially the revolutionary dissident achievements discovered in Latin America, Africa and Asia.

In reconnecting postcolonial theory with the long history of dissidence to which it is indebted, Young's book returns critical attention to a number of intellectuals and radicals – the Ghanaian Kwame Nkrumah, the Trinidadians C. L. R. James and George Padmore, and others – whose work and achievements have been in danger of being entirely forgotten in recent years, especially within the rarified philosophising of much postcolonial theory. Whereas one or two radical figures from the days of the various anti-colonial struggles have been remembered – the most visible example is Frantz Fanon, whose early work has preoccupied Bhabha – many other such figures have not. After reading Young's book, however, it is impossible to endorse the (always questionable) cliché that postcolonialism magically begins in 1978 with the publication of Said's *Orientalism*. While it is true to say that postcolonialism as an *academic practice* was in part engendered by the seismic shift engendered by Said's book, as we have considered above, Young demonstrates how Said and other contemporaneous thinkers stand at the far end of a much longer trajectory of thought and action, indebted to Marxism, and their work needs to be understood historically in these terms.

Throughout *Postcolonialism: An Historical Introduction* Young writes with patience, fairness, even-handedness, clarity and refreshing directness. Yet like all books it is not flawless, and when encountering it for the first time it is useful to keep in mind the view that its 'historical' narrative of postcolonialism is not necessarily authoritative. Two points of contention arising from it are worth mentioning here, partly as a way of encouraging you to encounter this richly rewarding book in a critically fertile manner. Young's intervention in postcolonial debates arguably does not resolve them fully, and indeed opens up some additional problems to consider too.

First, Young's model of the 'tricontinental', inspired by the 1966 conference in Havana of the Organisation of Solidarity of the Peoples of Africa, Asia and Latin America, takes sustained attention away from other locations which have featured diverse and divergent forms of colonial settlement and resistance. Specifically, settler colonies such as Canada, New Zealand and Australia play virtually no part in Young's discussion of postcolonialism – a term which, as he says at one point, he would indeed much prefer to do away with and replace provocatively with '*tricontinentalism*' (p. 57 – italics in the original). On one or two occasions Young addresses the particular circumstances of the settler colonies and is mindful of the particular challenges they create. As he puts it, 'settler societies with indigenous inhabitants as in North, Central and South America, South Africa, Taiwan, Australasia, [are places] whose settlers in historical terms often broach the boundaries between colonizers and colonized, and where settler-based national and cultural identities are under long-standing challenge – for example, by the Maori claim to ethnocracy in New Zealand' (p. 60). Yet Young chooses not to explore in depth the particular challenges and phenomenon of settler nationalism on the one hand, when European-descended peoples agitated for self-rule distinct from European jurisdiction, or the various forms of indigenous resistance to settlement on the other.

Although it is always a little churlish to challenge a book for what it excludes rather than what it includes, it is worth wondering if a history of postcolonialism can really ever be written without greater reference to the particular conditions of the settler colonies. Young's lack of attention to such locations, I would hazard, is because they would trouble his version of postcolonialism's history as *fundamentally* indebted to Marxist forms of revolution and dissidence. On the one hand, the growth of settler nationalism in places such as Canada and Australia was not the product of Marxist-inspired politics nor did it always mount a far-reaching critique of capitalism. On the other hand, Aboriginal or 'First Nations' forms of resistance in such places have often been fuelled by indigenous forms of knowledge which are in many ways incommensurate with Western-derived modes of thought and indeed do not necessarily require such resources (including Marxism) in order to make entirely legitimate claims for territorial freedom and self-governance. The lack of a significant presence of Marxist influence in these contexts possibly explains why they do not show up for long in Young's book, but their absence limits the range of his 'historical' account of postcolonialism, especially as regards indigenous and Aboriginal modalities of resistance. For these reasons, Young's insistently Marxist account of postcolonialism results in some important and perhaps damaging omissions.

The issue of omission leads to the second question we might have about Young's work, and it concerns his perpetual focus on the leaders of revolutionary groups and colonised peoples: Che Guevara, Mahatma Gandhi, Léopold Senghor, Tiémoho Garan Kouyaté, Amilcar Cabral and several others. Young's focus on the political sacrifices and brave radicalism of these and other great figures is vital. Yet, with the possible exception of his focus on women's groups, Young is less skilled at communicating the endeavours and activities of less extraordinary folks in the colonies, whose day-to-day acts of dissidence were part of their difficult experiences and practices of everyday life, and whose unspectacular, often ordinary-looking acts of resistance to colonial rule were every bit as important as the activities and inspiration of their leaders in challenging colonial authority. In seeming to organise his work through the accomplishments of the great figures of anti-colonial dissidence, at times Young comes closer to writing an heroic rather than historical introduction to postcolonialism, one which confects an emotive hagiography of anti-colonial Marxist-influenced radicals. The presence, roles and practices of everyday life of the oppressed 'subaltern' peoples can seem a little muted as a consequence.

The thrust of these two critical questions which I am making here do not necessarily diminish the achievements of Young's book, which are manifold. But they do modestly point to one or two concerns we might have about the accuracy or stability of the term 'historical' in its subtitle, and alert us to the fact that even a book as wide-ranging and impressive as this is still only one kind of intervention in a perpetually contested field. Can postcolonialism be oriented so securely to this tricontinental history? What do we include, and who gets left out, in the various ways we might historicise postcolonialism? And what about postcolonialism's future?

Globalisation and 'postcoloniality': the new imperium?

One evening a few months ago I was sat at home in West Yorkshire, talking on my land-line telephone to my partner who happened to be staying in a hotel in Sydney. During the conversation I sent her some information she needed via a text message from my mobile phone. Within about a second or so of sending the message, I heard her mobile phone bleep in her hotel room: the message had travelled a distance of approximately 10,500 miles and had been received safely before I had time to place my handset back on the table. We also talked about her flight arrangements back to Britain; despite being half a world away, she would be back home within a mere 48 hours.

For those of us who have grown up used to air travel, the internet, mobile phones, digital and satellite technology, the vignette of my phone-call to Australia probably seems hardly worth pausing over, so ordinary will it seem. Yet the realities of today's transport and communication networks that it records would have been unthinkable only a few decades ago, and we might want to reflect for a moment or two on just how far-reaching have been the transformations of technology on so many elements of life. In his work on 'supermodernity', Marc Augé has talked about the remarkable transformations of scale that have occurred as a consequence of technologies that have made the globe appear a much smaller place than it used to:

> We are in an era characterised by changes of scale – of course in the context of space exploration, but also on earth: rapid means of transport have brought any capital within a few hours' travel of any other. And in the privacy of our homes, finally, images of all sorts,

relayed by satellites and caught by the aerials that bristle on the roofs of our remotest hamlets, can give us an instant, sometimes simultaneous vision of an event taking place on the other side of the planet. (*Non-Places: Introduction to an Anthropology of Supermodernity*, trans. John Howe, Verso, 1995, p. 31)

The consequences of living in a world that appears smaller due to the new technologies and practices of contemporary life have been described with recourse to terms like 'postmodernity', 'super-modernity', 'late capitalism', 'capitalist modernity', and others besides. These days the most common name for the condition which Augé describes is globalisation. The emergence of globalisation both as a lived reality and the focus of academic studies has had consequences for the evolution of postcolonialism, not least because several issues which preoccupy postcolonial thinkers seem at the heart of debates about globalisation. These include things like international migration, the perceived decline of the nation-state, globalisation as a form of imperialism, the neo-colonial operations of globalisation, cultural transformation, and the necessity and challenge of resistance in the face of a new form of international power. What does globalisation mean for different cultures around the world? What is it doing to so-called cultural otherness or difference? How might postcolonialism offer us a way of critiquing globalisation? Is postcolonialism up to the job of dealing critically with globalisation, or has it met its historical and intellectual limits in globalisation?

Globalisation names a contemporary world condition charac-terised by the transformation of economic, political and cultural relations on a planetary scale. Key to these transformations is the sense that the nation-state is declining as the most important form of sovereignty around the world and emerging instead are new networks and institutions which operate transnationally, often cutting across the physical borders and political interests of nation-states. These institutions include economic agencies like the International Monetary Fund (IMF) and the World Bank, wealthy transnational corporations (TNCs) such as Microsoft, Coca-Cola and General Motors (whose annual turnover can rival that of some nations), non-governmental organisations (NGOs) such as Oxfam or Greenpeace, and international media outlets (television companies, publishing houses, etc.) through which cultural products circulate across large global audiences. Globalisation emerges as a web-like structure facilitated by instant and often virtual communication networks, where wealth, business contracts, financial transactions and cultural images can be circulated at the click of a mouse or by pressing the return key on your PC – and where the fate of thousands of people can be altered by the decisions of those sat in boardrooms thousands of miles away, maybe speaking a different language or living a much more luxurious life to those whose economic fortunes are in their hands (for an excellent and concise way into thinking about globalisation, see Manfred B. Steger, *Globalisation: A Very Short Introduction*, second edition, Oxford University Press, 2009).

Globalisation scholars have long been interested in the interaction between such global flows and their local impact, and the relationship between the global and local is one which has particular resonance within postcolonialism. A key commentator on globalisation is Arjun Appadurai, whose work offers a number of important ways of engaging with the cultural consequences of globalisation. In an early and influential book, *Modernity at Large: Cultural Dimensions of Globalisation* (University of Minnesota Press, 1996), Appadurai describes the emerging globalised world as constituted by a series of disjunctures which cannot be understood with recourse to older centre–periphery models (such as metropolis–colony, for example) or with older, stable and more predictable notions of production, consumption and migration. Instead, he identifies five dimensions of globalisation that feature the suffix '-scape': ethnoscapes, mediascapes, technoscapes, financescapes and ideoscapes. The use of '-scape' signifies 'the fluid, irregular shapes of these landscapes' that are best thought of as 'perspectival constructs, inflected by the historical, linguistic, and political situatedness of different sorts of actors: nation–states, multinationals, diasporic communities, as well as subnational groupings and movements (whether religious, political or economic), and even face-to-face groups, such as villages, neighbourhoods and families' (p. 33). Note here the emphasis on the essential malleability of these phenomena, endlessly morphing as the global and local interact with one another in complex and unpredictable ways. Appadurai uses 'ethnoscape' to refer to increasingly mobile and fluid groups or communities which inhabit the globe (such as tourists, immigrants, refugees, exiles and guest workers). His term 'technoscape' refers to the new technological networks which integrate different locations and which facilitate global flows of information at high velocities, while 'financescapes' refers to the structure and circulation of global capital around the world. 'Mediascapes' refer 'both to the distribution of the electronic capabilities to produce and disseminate information' (p. 35), primarily image-based, while 'ideoscapes' refers to the circulation of ideas to do with power: freedom, rights, sovereignty, democracy and other such terms.

Appadurai's list of '-scapes' vividly captures the chaotic integration of and interaction between technology, wealth, information, the media, power, people and culture which characterises the globalised world. His work offers a way of thinking about migrant and diasporic peoples beyond the centre-periphery axis of metropolitan motherland-colonial outpost which has informed much thinking about postcolonial diasporas of the first and second generations which we explored in Chapter 7, and opens up new ways to consider the realities and consequences of living 'in-between' that encompass a range of constituencies of peoples. In a later highly readable book, *Fear of Small Numbers: An Essay on the Geography of Anger* (Duke University Press, 2006), Appadurai offers further frameworks for thinking about globalisation. He describes an older world order as a 'vertebrate' world system where individual nations are locked together into an international body where the sovereignty of each nation is paramount. But the '-scapes' and systems of the contemporary world seem more 'cellular' than vertebrate: the term 'cellular' is used to capture a world 'clearly linked up by multiple circuits along which money, news, people, and ideas flow, meet, converge, and disperse again' (p. 25). Contemporary globalisation is an amalgam of the two systems, he argues, requiring some stable forms of organisation and exchange but clearly operating in an unpredictable, mobile and complex fashion. We can discern this situation by thinking for a moment about the contemporary phenomena of asylum-seekers, refugees and economic workers who, on the one hand, are often caught up in the cellular logics of globalisation, moving from place to place in search of employment, or, on the other hand, are fleeing the murderous activities in their native lands and whose attempts to cross national borders are met with unsympathetic and dehumanising agencies of border control, internment and deportation.

For some critics, the operations of globalisation represent a new phase in the pursuit of imperialism, and it is here that postcolonialism becomes especially interested in globalisation. We saw in Chapter 1 that colonialism was only one kind of example of an imperial structure, defined by the activity of different forms of European settlement. We might like to think of globalisation as a form of imperialism by remote control, one which no longer requires colonial settlement but which can obtain power over other locations and peoples – their resources, cultural and social activities, and wealth – precisely with recourse to the new technologies and '-scapes' which characterise the contemporary. Michael Hardt and Antonio Negri have famously articulated this sense of contemporary globalisation as a new imperium, by bluntly describing globalisation as a new 'Empire'. They acknowledge that contemporary globalisation is indebted to colonialism in the communication networks, international relations and histories of migration and settlement which colonialism has bequeathed the present, as well as the international initiatives of the dissenting 'multitude' (*Empire*, Harvard University Press, 2000, p. 43) which opposed colonialism often by opening up channels of international solidarity and inspiration. Yet rather than moving us beyond an imperial world, globalisation creates 'its own relationships of power based on exploitation that are in many respects more brutal than those it destroyed' (p. 43). Under today's Empire, the multitude of people which historically laboured under colonialism and capitalism find themselves ensnared again by a global imperium which subjects them to further exploitation, poverty and hardship. Once-colonised nations increasingly find themselves servicing debts owed to wealthy 'First World' organisations often in the global North which charge high interest on the loans they made available for development projects. Communities of low-paid workers can find themselves quickly redundant when a TNC moves its production to an entirely different part of the world because of cheaper labour costs, or be forced unexpectedly to move thousands of miles around the globe in search of work. Hence, '[t]he end of modern colonialisms, of course, has not really opened an age of unqualified freedom but rather yielded to new forms of rule that operate on a global scale' (p. 134). As Hardt and Negri see it, then, the new world order is characterised by the decline of the sovereignty of the nation–state and the emergence of a new form of international authority which considers it just and right to intervene self-interestedly in conflicts around the world in the guise of being at the service of right and peace (we might want to think here about the US-led invasion of Iraq or the conflicts in Afghanistan as part of a global 'War on Terror'). These acts of intervention service the interests and demands of global capitalism – TNCs, powerful financial concerns and the like, often headquartered in North America and other 'First World' locations – and assist in binding the world more tightly together as a complex market in which more and more commodities can be traded. Meanwhile, the multitude is faced with the challenge of responding to and resisting the new imperial authority of the globalised Empire, while suffering increased economic wretchedness and uncertainty.

It might seem, then, that postcolonialism can play an extremely important part in contesting the new global imperium due to the conceptual tools it has at its disposal. Yet Hardt and Negri cast doubt on the effectiveness of postcolonial thinking to offer any meaningful challenge to the new world order. *Empire* contains a short but stark critique of postcolonialism in which they suggest that key concepts of postcolonialism actually mimic rather than confront the machinations of contemporary globalisation. Although postcolonial theorists tend to prioritise fragmentary subjectivities, evolving forms of becoming and hybrid modes of thought and cultural production, it is claimed that their intellectual strategies 'that appear to be liberatory would not challenge but in fact coincide with and even unwittingly reinforce the new strategies of rule!' (*Empire*, Harvard University Press, 2000, p. 138). This is because global capitalism often mobilises the fragmentary, hybrid, the different and fluid as part of its machinery (as Appadurai's engagement with '-scapes' testified). For Hardt and Negri, then, those postcolonial theorists 'who advocate a politics of difference, fluidity and hybridity in order to challenge the binaries and essentialism of modern sovereignty have been outflanked by the strategies of [Empire's] power' (p. 138) because they have not come up with tools to challenge the globalised present; rather, their theoretical terms of reference are entirely in tune with the interests of global capital. For these reasons, Hardt and Negri argue that postcolonialism is an effective critique of the colonial and decolonising past but *not* the global present: 'postcolonial theory [may be] a very productive tool for rereading history, but it is entirely insufficient for theorizing contemporary global power' (p. 146). Or in other words, postcolonialism offers an effective way of critiquing the world characterised by modern sovereignty, akin to the vertebrate model of international order of which Appadurai spoke. But it offers no effective way of critiquing or challenging the more cellular condition of the new imperial sovereignty of Empire, because its vocabularies and key concepts offer no meaningful alternative to the methods and design of Empire. In this view, then, postcolonialism has been rendered bankrupt by globalisation.

The engagement with globalisation in postcolonial studies has tended to take at least three paths. First, some critics have contested the claims made by the likes of Hardt and Negri, especially their argument that the modern sovereignty epitomised by the nation-state has waned so spectacularly and the hard-won freedoms of once-colonised peoples have been effectively eradicated in a new imperium (see, for example, Benita Parry, *Postcolonial Studies: A Materialist Critique*, Routledge, 2004, pp. 93–103). Second, others have called for and attempted to theorise new democratic forms of politics, dissidence and ethics that are required in a globalised world where cultures are interacting more and more and where the experience of cultural difference – in the media, at work, on the street, on the move – is becoming the norm and not the novelty of everyday life. A new globalised world requires new ways of thinking and acting ethically. How can we live together as part of a global community without necessarily supporting exploitation, and how can we act ethically and responsibly in a world where different peoples have markedly different views on how to live? Some of this work has taken place in the name of 'cosmopolitanism', a term that was previously used pejoratively to bear witness to an elite class of the affluent and internationally mobile but is more and more coming to name an ethical situation in which, as Kwame Anthony Appiah suggests, we acknowledge both our general obligation to others unlike ourselves and recognise the legitimacy of specific people's differences. As Appiah contends, 'there will be times when these two ideals – universal concern and respect for legitimate difference – clash. There's a sense in which cosmopolitanism is the name not of the solution but of the challenge' (*Cosmopolitanism: Ethics in a World of Strangers*, Penguin, 2006, p. xiii). Paul Gilroy has also written about the need for a vernacular form of cosmopolitanism which 'finds civic and ethical value in the process of exposure to otherness. It glorifies in the ordinary virtues and ironies – listening, looking, discretion, friendship – that can be cultivated when mundane encounters with difference become rewarding' (*After Empire: Melancholia or Convivial Culture?* Routledge, 2004, p. 75). In experiencing forms of cultural experience beyond one's immediate purview, it becomes much harder to think in a parochial or unethical fashion about the lives of others. Such ideas have led Gilroy to talk of the need for a new form of planetary consciousness or 'planetary humanism' (*Between Camps: Nations, Cultures and the Allure of Race*, Allen Lane, 2000, p. 356) which grounds a new ethics and politics fit for the present and which takes us beyond the encamped and entrenched politics based on modern concepts of race and nation.

A third postcolonial response to globalisation has focused on the relationships between postcolonial cultural endeavours and the globalised markets in which many postcolonial writers in particular have prospered. It has often been remarked upon that since Salman Rushdie's novel *Midnight's Children* (1981) won that year's Booker Prize for fiction – one of Britain's most prestigious literary awards – at the time of writing the Man Booker Prize (as it is now called) has been won by a postcolonial writer no less than thirteen times in twenty-seven years. This might mean that postcolonial writing is effectively transforming how certain readers understand and inter-act with the world in inducting them into different cultural horizons and experiences. Or it might mean something else entirely: namely, that postcolonial literature has become a brand. Postcolonial litera-ture these days might be culturally visible and popular, but who is reading these texts, and why? As Robert Fraser has pointed out, while the work of the twice-Booker winner J. M. Coetzee seems to attract attention in 'First World' countries and is popular in his native South Africa, 'north of the Zambezi it is hardly known' (*Book History Through Postcolonial Eyes*, Routledge, 2008, p. 186). Is post-colonial literature as it is understood in the West actually read in postcolonial locations? Might this matter? Furthermore, what are 'First World' readers making of the postcolonial texts that have proven so popular and such big money-spinners for certain publishing houses? Is it because they invite readers into worlds which they enjoy reading about simply because they appear exotic, safely sanitised by the conversion of difference into amusing distraction? Are colonialist habits of thoughts really changing?

These kinds of questions have been explored by Graham Huggan in his influential study *The Postcolonial Exotic: Marketing the Margins* (Routledge, 2001), in which he explores the popularity of postcolonial studies and postcolonial cultural texts within the context of global markets, pointing out that cultural difference is often a highly saleable commodity and big business. In perceiving of cultural objects as exotic and commodifying them as such for cheerful global consumption, strategies of marketing effectively neutralise their disruptive potential and seize upon their cultural marginality as a unique selling point. The result is what Huggan calls the postcolonial exotic, where the dissident potential of postcolonial cultures comes into conflict with global markets which seek to turn postcolonial texts into bland, apolitical ciphers of cultural diversity for their own financial gain:

> The postcolonial exotic, I have been suggesting, occupies a site of discursive conflict between a local assemblage of more or less related oppositional practices and a global apparatus of assimilative/commercial codes. More specifically, it marks the intersection between contending regimes of value: one regime – postcolonialism – that posits itself as anti-colonial, and that works towards the dissolution of imperial epistemologies and institutional structures; and another – postcoloniality – that is more closely tied to the global market, and that capitalises both on the widespread circulation of ideas about cultural otherness and on the worldwide trafficking of culturally 'othered' artefacts and goods. (p. 28)

Huggan's point perhaps recalls Hardt and Negri's in a different context: that globalisation profits from the very things which postcolonialism holds dear, namely a regard for cultural specificity and difference. Huggan's sense of market-driven 'postcoloniality', where strangeness sells, might be thought to hold the upper hand today, as 'First World' peoples read exotic Booker-winning paperbacks and visit foreign climes as chaperoned tourists in order to have an exotic experience with scant regard for the peoples, places and cultures at stake. If this is the case, how can the kinds of cosmopolitanism and planetary humanism advocated by Appiah and Gilroy ever obtain? Postcoloniality and exoticism may act as a prophylactic to the kinds of cultural encounters which postcolonialism often demands as an ethical imperative.

Huggan is careful not to give up on postcolonialism, however, and he maintains faith in the agency of postcolonial cultural texts to challenge the new imperium of global markets that characterise postcoloniality. Huggan argues that postcolonial writers might be thought of as having the agency to intervene within the global commodifying endeavours of contemporary capitalism and use their exotic and fashionable status to engender critical, transformative thought by 'manipulat[ing] the exotic to their own ends' (p. 32). In other words, assumptions about the exoticism of other cultures can be manipulated and deployed tactically by postcolonial writers in order to contest the machinations of postcoloniality via a kind of 'strategic exoticism' (p. 32) that is consciously chosen (Huggan's term echoes Spivak's 'strategic essentialism' which we discussed in Chapter 6). Like other critics, Huggan does not presume that complicity always leads to compliance. Indeed, it is perhaps the job of a committed postcolonial scholar to expose how subversive cultures retain their agency and transformative abilities in the midst of residual, dominant and emergent structures of inequality and exploitation. Globalisation presents new challenges to postcolonialism, but evidence suggests that it is beginning to meet those challenges in important ways that continue to resource critical thought.

Where do we go from here?

In the introduction to *Beginning Postcolonialism*, we considered 'postcolonialism' as potentially a vague umbrella term that perhaps lets too much in. Looking back, over the many issues we have raised in this book, it remains doubtful if a coherent sense of post-colonialism in general can be found; nor should we be looking for one. But this is, as I hope we have realised, an immensely fruitful discovery, and we might close by considering it as a key and valuable strength. The range of matters which postcolonialism involves us in is wide, to be sure, and it keeps expanding. But this range should indicate both the far-reaching legacies of colonialism and colonial discourses across the globe, as well as the extent of the transformation of our habits of thought which we, in our different positions, might have to welcome as we move forward from our beginnings in the field. There is much to look forward to.

As I hope this book has underlined, when we use terms like 'postcolonialism', 'the postcolonial', 'postcolonialist' and 'post-coloniality' we are often doing several important things either consciously or by default, depending on our standpoint and critical viewpoint. We are refusing to forget the historical contexts of oppression and resistance which inform the cultural products of colonialism and its aftermath. We are choosing not to sever culture from imperialism, or think that the so-called privileged world of intellectuals, culture and the arts has nothing to do with those whom Fanon called the wretched of the earth. We are committing ourselves to asking challenging questions about the past and the present, often by using forms of knowledge and vocabularies that eschew received modes of wisdom and which we may find hard to understand at the best of times. We are acknowledging that the material and imaginative legacies of colonialism remain with us today and perhaps are being remoulded and refashioned in our contemporary world, in the midst of globalisation and the so-called 'War on Terror'. We are acknowledging that 'First World' cultures are not of universal value. We are declaring that the standpoint from where we read the world is both a privilege and a loss, a vantage and a limit. We are admitting that knowledge is inseparable from power, and that one way to help change the world is to transform the way we come to know the world. We are beginning to make decisions about where we stand in key debates about postcolonialism, and to understand why we hold the views that we do. We are realising that attending to cultural, historical, social, political and geographical differences is paramount to us of course; but so too is thinking *between* and *across* postcolonial contexts.

Throughout this book we have concluded each chapter with a selected reading list, and collectively these lists should give you a wide-ranging set of texts from which you can continue your work in postcolonialism. Listed after the Appendix are some good texts, many of which have been mentioned in the previous selections, for you to open next as you develop your thinking on postcolonialism. Like all reading lists, my choices are inevitably selective and partial. I have divided them into different sections to help you navigate your work as you move on. In one sense you will have already begun these texts by finishing *Beginning Postcolonialism*. I hope your enjoyment and critical understanding of postcolonialism will be all the more satisfying for having done so.

Appendix

'The Overland Mail (foot-service to the hills)' (Rudyard Kipling)

In the name of the Empress of India, make way,
    O Lords of the Jungle, wherever you roam,
The woods are astir at the close of the day –
    We exiles are waiting for letters from Home.
Let the robber retreat – let the tiger turn tail –   5
In the Name of the Empress, the Overland Mail!

With a jingle of bells as the dusk gathers in,
    He turns to the footpath that heads up the hill –
The bags on his back and a cloth round his chin,
    And, tucked in his waistbelt, the Post Office bill: –   10
'Despatched on this date, as received by the rail,
'*Per* runner, two bags of the Overland Mail.'

Is the torrent in spate? He must ford it or swim.
    Has the rain wrecked the road? He must climb by the cliff.
Does the tempest cry halt? What are tempests to him?   15
    The service admits not a 'but' or an 'if'.
While the breath's in his mouth, he must bear without fail,
In the Name of the Empress, the Overland Mail.

From aloe to rose-oak, from rose-oak to fir,
    From level to upland, from upland to crest,   20
From rice-field to rock-ridge, from rock-ridge to spur,
    Fly the soft-sandalled feet, strains the brawny, brown chest.
From rail to ravine – to the peak from the vale –
Up, up through the night goes the Overland Mail.

There's a speck on the hillside, a dot on the road –   25
    A jingle of bells on the footpath below –
There's a scuffle above in the monkey's abode –
    The world is awake and the clouds are aglow.
For the great Sun himself must attend to the hail: –
'In the Name of the Empress, the Overland Mail!'   30

Further reading

General introductions

Ashcroft, Bill, Gareth Griffiths and Helen Tiffin, *The Empire Writes Back: Theory and Practice in Post-Colonial Literatures*, second edition (Routledge, 2002).

An important book when it first appeared in 1989, and now revised in the light of recent developments in the field. Although often subject to criticism, this book remains a touchstone for much work in postcolonial literary studies and is essential reading in the field.

Boehmer, Elleke, *Colonial and Postcolonial Literature: Migrant Metaphors*, second edition (Oxford University Press, 2005).

Still the best critical history of the literatures in the field.

Chew, Shirley and David Richards (eds), *A Concise Companion to Postcolonial Literatures* (Blackwell, 2010).

A clear and approachable collection of essays which introduce some of the key areas of postcolonial studies.

Childs, Peter and Patrick Williams, *An Introduction to Post-Colonial Theory* (Harvester Wheatsheaf, 1997).

An excellent and thorough text, if a little challenging for a beginner, which deals with the theoretical writings of Bhabha, Gilroy, Said, Spivak and others, and which also engages usefully with the problems of postcolonialism. Highly recommended.

Featherstone, Mike, *Postcolonial Cultures* (Edinburgh University Press, 2005).

The best introduction to the emerging field of postcolonial cultural studies, which engages critically with literature, music, dance, sport, film, museums and other cultural forms.

Gandhi, Leela, *Postcolonial Theory: An Introduction* (Edinburgh University Press, 1998).

A reasonably clear introduction, if somewhat disorganised and idiosyncratic. Includes a useful chapter on 'Postcolonial Literatures' in relation to postcolonial theory.

Innes, C. L., *The Cambridge Introduction to Postcolonial Literatures in English* (Cambridge University Press, 2007).

A useful and clear text which reads postcolonial writing in relation to the field's major themes which we have explored in *Beginning Postcolonialism*.

Lazarus, Neil (ed.), *The Cambridge Companion to Postcolonial Literary Studies* (Cambridge University Press, 2004).

A challenging collection of essays, if a little uneven in helpfulness for a beginner, that are often voiced from a sceptical and/or materialist position and which engage with many of the key issues in the field.

Loomba, Ania, *Colonialism/Postcolonialism*, second edition (Routledge, 2005).

A patient and very thorough introduction to postcolonial theory and criticism, particularly noteworthy for its engagement with theories of colonial discourses. Highly recommended.

McLeod, John (ed.), *The Routledge Companion to Postcolonial Studies* (Routledge, 2007).

This edited collection includes very useful introductory essays on the British, French, Spanish and Portuguese empires, diverse postcolonial locations, postcolonial formulations and theoretical models, and key writers and thinkers in the field.

Moore-Gilbert, Bart, *Postcolonial Theory: Contexts, Practices, Politics* (Verso, 1997).

Although this does not claim to be an introductory text, the clarity of its writing and excellence of its criticism makes it a very useful book for those getting to grips with the work of Bhabha, Said and Spivak in particular, and should be an important port-of-call (as well as a place to return to) as you develop your engagement with postcolonial theory and criticism.

Walder, Dennis, *Post-Colonial Literatures in English: History, Language, Theory* (Blackwell, 1998).

An excellently clear introduction, recommended for newcomers to the field. Features sensible chapters on the issues of history, language and theory in postcolonialism, in which Walder reads a variety of literary texts (such as Indo-Anglian fiction and black British poetry) in imaginative and thought-provoking ways.

Young, Robert J. C., *Postcolonialism: A Very Short Introduction* (Oxford University Press, 2003).

A refreshing introduction to postcolonialism that eschews more conventional theoretical approaches and engages with a variety of cultural predicaments and contexts. Short, pithy and very readable.

Reference Books (A–Z format)

Ashcroft, Bill, Gareth Griffiths and Helen Tiffin (eds), *Post-Colonial Studies: The Key Concepts*, second edition (Routledge, 2008).
Contains many useful definitions of the key terms in the field, along with helpful suggestions for further reading.

Poddar, Prem and David Johnson (eds), *A Historical Companion to Postcolonial Literatures in English* (Edinburgh University Press, 2005).
A superb, detailed collection which features short, informative essays on the key historical events, intellectual concepts and primary locations in postcolonial studies. Each essay concludes with a useful bibliography that points readers to key literary and historical texts. An excellent reference work.

Thieme, John, *Post-Colonial Studies: The Essential Glossary* (Arnold, 2003).
An informative work which includes expert entries on many key concepts and influential writers.

Wisker, Gina, *Key Concepts in Postcolonial Literature* (Palgrave, 2007).
A quirky reference guide that approaches key concepts in the field in relation to a range of postcolonial writing.

Anthologies and readers: literature, criticism, theory

Ahmad, Dohra (ed.), *Rotten English: A Literary Anthology* (Norton, 2007).
An illuminating and instructive anthology of (predominantly) postcolonial short fiction and poetry written in vernacular, non-standard forms of English. The final section, called '"A New English": essays on vernacular literature', brings together some excellent reflections on writing non-standard English by such figures as Kamau Brathwaite, Gabriel Okara and Amy Tan.

Ashcroft, Bill, Gareth Griffiths and Helen Tiffin (eds), *The Post-Colonial Studies Reader*, second edition (Routledge, 2005).
A large and wide-ranging volume which collects together a variety of extracts from key critical essays under useful thematic headings and which features good, short introductions to each one. While the use of extracts rather than whole essays or chapters can sometimes be at the cost of sophistication, the clarity and range of the volume as a whole makes it a worthy and much-used resource.

Boehmer, Elleke (ed.), *Empire Writing: An Anthology of Colonial Literature, 1870–1918* (Oxford World's Classics, 1998).

A very interesting and useful collection of writing from and about the colonies from the late nineteenth and early twentieth centuries.

Castle, Gregory (ed.), *Postcolonial Discourses: An Anthology* (Blackwell, 2001).

A very good resource, full of extended extracts from many key writings in the field that are excellently introduced by the editor. The section on Ireland is particularly valuable and an excellent resource for newcomers keen to develop their interest in Ireland and postcolonialism.

Childs, Peter, *Post-Colonial Theory and English Literature: A Reader* (Edinburgh, 1999).

Collects together several important and influential postcolonial critiques of eight literary texts, including work by William Shakespeare, Daniel Defoe, Joseph Conrad and Salman Rushdie.

Desai, Gaurav and Supriya Nair (eds), *Postcolonialisms: An Anthology of Cultural Theory and Criticism* (Rutgers University Press, 2005).

An extensive collection of key writings in the field, divided into nine thematic sections.

Gilbert, Helen (ed.), *Postcolonial Plays: An Anthology* (Routledge, 2001).

A first-class collection of postcolonial dramatic texts from the latter decades of the twentieth century, one which underscores the richness and significance of the theatre in postcolonial locations and contexts (still an under-researched area of the field, one might add).

Gregg, Stephen H. (ed.), *Empire and Identity: An Eighteenth-Century Sourcebook* (Palgrave, 2005).

One of the best collections of writing from the colonial period that exposes the intimate relations between culture and imperialism in the eighteenth century.

Mongia, Padmini (ed.), *Contemporary Postcolonial Theory: A Reader* (Arnold, 1996).

An excellent volume which includes essays not often anthologised elsewhere.

Moore-Gilbert, Bart, Gareth Stanton and Willy Maley (eds), *Postcolonial Criticism* (Longman, 1997).

A useful and wide-ranging anthology of postcolonial criticism which also includes an informative introduction.

Ross, Robert L. (ed.), *Colonial and Postcolonial Fiction in English: An Anthology* (Garland Publishing, 1999).

A fine collection of postcolonial writings, organised around different notions of 'encounter'.

Thieme, John (ed.), *The Arnold Anthology of Post-Colonial Literatures in English* (Arnold, 1996).

A superb and wide-ranging collection of Anglophone postcolonial literature from around the world, sensibly organised and attentive to cultural specifics.

Williams, Patrick and Laura Chrisman (eds), *Colonial Discourse and Post-Colonial Theory: A Reader* (Harvester Wheatsheaf, 1993).

One of the earliest but still among the best postcolonial theory readers available, which brings together many salient writings in the field. Its materials can be challenging at first, but the ultimate rewards of working through this book are many. The editors' introductions to the various sections of this book are also very valuable. Highly recommended.

Postcolonial theory: some key texts

Ahmad, Aijaz, *In Theory: Classes, Nations, Literatures* (Verso, 1992).

A renowned polemical critique of postcolonialism which argues for the continuing significance of Marxism and nationalism as political and analytical weapons in the decolonised world.

Ashcroft, Bill, *Post-Colonial Transformation* (Routledge, 2001).

A solid engagement with the key issues of postcolonialism in relation to a range of cultural texts.

Bhabha, Homi K. (ed.), *Nation and Narration* (Routledge, 1990).

An influential collection of essays which interrogates literature and nationalism from a variety of standpoints.

Bhabha, Homi K., *The Location of Culture* (Routledge, 1994).

This landmark text is one of the core books of postcolonial theory and contains many of Bhabha's influential writings on 'the discourse of colonialism', cultural difference and postcolonialism.

Fanon, Frantz, *Black Skin, White Masks*, trans. Charles Lam Markmann (Pluto, [1952] 1986).

Fanon's ground-breaking critique of the psychological consequences of French colonialism remains an important interrogation of colonised identities. Highly influential in contemporary postcolonial theory, especially the earlier work of Bhabha.

Fanon, Frantz, *The Wretched of the Earth*, trans. Constance Farrington (Penguin [1961] 1967).

Includes Fanon's important discussions of colonial violence, national culture, and the pitfalls of national consciousness.

Gilroy, Paul, *The Black Atlantic: Modernity and Double Consciousness* (Verso, 1993).

Gilroy's influential and ground-breaking text which articulates the unruly transatlantic aesthetics of black peoples as offering innovative new models of post-national culture.

Gilroy, Paul, *After Empire: Melancholia or Convivial Culture?* (Routledge, 2004).

An examination of contemporary British multiculturalism in terms of key ideas regarding cultural difference, cosmopolitanism and in the context of the unhappy consequences of contemporary globalisation, including the remoulding of divisive models of 'race' and nation.

Huggan, Graham, *The Postcolonial Exotic: Marketing the Margins* (Routledge, 2001).

A highly thought-provoking and prominent attempt to consider the commodification of postcolonial endeavours and ideas in a globalised milieu. Also contains some excellent sections on the evolution of postcolonial studies and its key intellectual debates.

Lazarus, Neil, *Nationalism and Cultural Practice in the Postcolonial World* (Cambridge University Press, 1999).

Wide in scope and sophisticated, this book offers a materialist critique of many salient postcolonial ideas, social movements and cultural practices, such as anti-colonial nationalism.

McClintock, Anne, *Imperial Leather: Race, Gender and Sexuality in the Colonial Context* (Routledge, 1995).

An exciting critique of colonial discourses and their intersections with 'race', gender and sexuality predominantly in the nineteenth century.

Parry, Benita, *Postcolonial Studies: A Materialist Critique* (Routledge, 2004).

A rigorous and firm critique of postcolonialism from a materialist standpoint which includes sobering critiques of the work of Bhabha, Spivak, Hardt and Negri, and others.

Pratt, Mary Louise, *Imperial Eyes: Travel Writing and Transculturation*, second edition (Routledge, 2007).

A very popular critique of colonial travel writing which turns on the influential concept of 'transculturation' in the 'contact zones' of the colonies.

Said, Edward W. *Orientalism*, second edition, (Penguin [1978] 1995).

Probably *the* major landmark text for postcolonialism. The second edition contains an important 'Afterword' in which Said addresses the major criticisms of his work and discusses the relationship between Orientalism and postcolonialism.

Said, Edward W., *The World, the Text, and the Critic* (Vintage [1984] 1991).

An important book of essays that attend to literature, politics and the intellectual.

Said, Edward W., *Culture and Imperialism* (Vintage, 1993).

Another major text. Said interrogates the relations between culture and imperialism throughout the world, and critiques forms of anti-colonial resistance.

Spivak, Gayatri Chakravorty, *In Other Worlds: Essays in Cultural Politics* (Routledge, 1987).

Includes a variety of challenging and important essays, such as 'French Feminism in an International Frame' and 'Subaltern Studies: Deconstructing Historiography'.

Spivak, Gayatri Chakravorty, *The Post-Colonial Critic: Interviews, Strategies, Dialogues*, ed. Sarah Harasym (Routledge, 1990).

A book of interviews in which Spivak elaborates on several of her critical positions. An approachable if challenging text, and a good place to begin reading Spivak.

Spivak, Gayatri Chakravorty, *A Critique of Postcolonial Reason: Toward a History of the Vanishing Present* (Harvard University Press, 1999).

A highly complex book which often features some of Spivak's better known essays (such as 'Can the Subaltern Speak?') in a heavily revised form.

Spivak, Gayatri Chakravorty, 'Can the Subaltern Speak?', reprinted with abridgements in Williams and Chrisman (eds), *Colonial Discourse and Post-Colonial Theory* (Harvester Wheatsheaf, 1993), pp. 66–111.

Probably one of the most important essays in postcolonialism: heavy going at first for a beginner perhaps, but well worth the effort. Spend some time getting to grips with the ideas raised in this essay.

Trinh, T. Minh-ha, *Woman, Native, Other: Writing Postcoloniality and Feminism* (Indiana University Press, 1989).

A ground-breaking and challenging study of postcolonialism and feminism which explores the role of writing in contesting dominant patriarchal representations.

Young, Robert J. C., *Postcolonialism: An Historical Introduction* (Blackwell, 2001).

Don't be misled by the subtitle: this is a long, considered and vital materialist intervention in postcolonialism that significantly reorients the field towards the long history of anti-colonial dissidence in the 'tricontinent' of Africa, Asia and Latin America.

Selected collections of essays dealing with postcolonialism

Adam, Ian and Helen Tiffin (eds), *Past the Last Post: Theorising Postcolonialism and Post-Modernism* (Harvester Wheatsheaf, 1991).

Includes several useful essays on the intellectual affiliations of postcolonial theory and its relation to postmodernist aesthetics.

Bery, Ashok and Patricia Murray (eds), *Comparing Postcolonial Literatures: Dislocations* (Macmillan, 2000).

A busy collection of essays that focus on the themes of borders, diasporas, internal exiles and hybridity.

Chambers, Iain and Lidia Curti (eds), *The Post-Colonial Question: Common Skies, Divided Horizons* (Routledge, 1996).

An eclectic and enjoyable collection which includes several stimulating essays by several leading figures in the field.

Forsdick, Charles and David Murphy (eds), *Francophone Postcolonial Studies: A Critical Introduction* (Arnold, 2003).

A landmark text in the evolution of Francophone postcolonial studies which develops and critiques the field from a number of vantages beyond a conventionally Anglophone context.

Goldberg, David Theo and Ato Quayson, *Relocating Postcolonialism* (Blackwell, 2002).

A strong collection of essays which explores the connections between postcolonial studies and a variety of familiar and new contexts, including 'race', memory, pedagogy, the internet and disability.

Keown, Michelle, David Murphy and James Procter (eds), *Comparing Postcolonial Diasporas* (Palgrave, 2009).

A timely collection that considers comparatively diasporic cultures across the globe and challenges the extent to which Anglophone postcolonial and diasporic theories are applicable to divergent and often non-Anglophone cultural experiences.

Madsen, Deborah L. (ed.), *Post-Colonial Literatures: Expanding the Canon* (Pluto, 1999).

A thought-provoking collection which attempts to deal with hitherto neglected literatures as postcolonial.

Rutherford, Anna (ed.), *From Commonwealth to Post-Colonial* (Dangaroo, 1992).

A large and varied collection of essays on postcolonial literatures edited by one of the key figures in the field.

Tiffin, Chris and Alan Lawson, *De-Scribing Empire: Post-Colonialism and Textuality* (Routledge, 1994).

Includes essays concerning the theorising of postcolonialism, and some stimulating readings of various literary texts in the light of theoretical concerns.

Trivedi, Harish and Meenakshi Mukherjee (eds), *Interrogating Post-Colonialism: Theory, Text and Context* (Indian Institute of Advanced Study, 1996).

A collection of short, readable critical essays which deal with postcolonialism from a variety of positions.

Selected Journals

ARIEL: A Review of International English Literature (http://english .ucalgary.ca/engl/ariel).

Published at the University of Calgary, Canada, ARIEL features a high standard of critical essays on a wealth of contemporary and postcolonial literary texts, as well as review articles and book reviews.

Interventions: The International Journal of Postcolonial Studies (www. postcolonialinterventions.com).

Since its emergence in 1999, *Interventions* has firmly established itself as one of the major journals in postcolonial studies and regularly features cutting-edge new scholarship from established and emerging figures in the field. It is edited by Robert J. C. Young, a leading figure in postcolonial studies.

Journal of Commonwealth Literature (http://jcl.sagepub.com)

Established at the University of Leeds, UK, in 1965, and still going strong under the editorship of John Thieme. Publishes lots of literary criticism from around the world as well as an invaluable annual bibliography of Commonwealth literature.

Journal of Postcolonial Writing (www.tandf.co.uk/journals/RJPW)

Formerly called *World Literature Written in English* (*WLWE*), this journal features new scholarship in postcolonial literary studies along with reviews, occasional interviews and creative writing. It is affiliated to the Postcolonial Studies Association (PSA). An excellent resource.

Kunapipi: Journal of Post-Colonial Writing (www.uow.edu.au/arts /kunapipi)

Kunapipi was established by the late Anna Rutherford in Australia in 1979, and its title refers to the Australian Aboriginal myth of the Rainbow Serpent which is a symbol of both regeneration and creativity. It features critical essays alongside creative writing and interviews.

Moving Worlds: A Journal of Transcultural Writings (www.movingworlds .net)

Created by Shirley Chew, *Moving Worlds* publishes critical essays, creative works and book reviews, and often produces special issues on topical postcolonial writers or themes (such as 'New New Zealand',

'Performing Arts and South Asian Literature' and 'Telling Stories, Telling Lives'). Highly recommended.

Postcolonial Studies (www.tandf.co.uk/journals/routledge/13688790.html) Affiliated to the Institute of Postcolonial Studies in Melbourne, Australia, this journal engages with a variety of topical historical, cultural and theoretical contexts.

Wasafiri: The Magazine of International Contemporary Writing (www. wasafiri.org)
Begun in 1984 under the editorship of Susheila Nasta, *Wasafiri* (which means 'travellers' in Kiswahili) features the latest creative endeavours from writers and artists around the world, along with critical essays, interviews and book reviews. A lively and readable publication, it is a leader in its field.

Index